SELLING
BY
OBJECTIVES

W9-AlA-535

SELLING
BY
OBJECTIVES

Tony Alessandra, Ph.D.

Jim Cathcart

Phillip Wexler

Selling by Objectives

All Rights Reserved. Copyright©1998 Anthony Alessandra,
James Cathcart and Phillip Wexler

No part of this book may be reproduced or transmitted in
any form or by any means, graphic, electronic or mechanical,
including photocopying, recording, taping, or by any
information storage or retrieval system, without the
permission in writing from the publisher.

ISBN 0-9625161-2-0

Library of Congress Catalog Card Number: 98-88985

Printed in the United States of America

0 9 8 7 6 5 4 3 2 1

Contents

Preface   ix

Part I   OVERVIEW

ONE

The Philosophy of Non-Manipulative Selling   3

THE FOOT-IN-THE-DOOR IMAGE   ADEQUATE TRAINING
APPROPRIATE TRAINING   NON-MANIPULATIVE SELLING
THE NMS SALES PROCESS   INFORMATION-GATHERING
ENHANCEMENT SKILLS FOR SUCCESSFUL NON-MANIPULATIVE SELLING
SUMMARY

Part II   RELATIONSHIP SKILLS

TWO

Tension Management   19

CATEGORIES OF TENSION   TENSION MANAGEMENT AND RELATIONSHIPS
SUMMARY

THREE

Relationship Strategies   30

BEHAVIORAL STYLES   BEHAVIORAL STYLE IDENTIFICATION
BEHAVIORAL FLEXIBILITY   IN CONCLUSION . . .
SUMMARY

FOUR

The Image of Excellence   57

THE CHARACTERISTICS OF EXCELLENCE   SUMMARY

Part III   PERSONAL SALES MANAGEMENT SKILLS

FIVE

Territory Management   81

PART ONE: TERRITORY ANALYSIS
THE MARKETING PLAN   THE SALES PLAN MODEL   SALES PLANNING
PART TWO: KNOWING WHAT YOUR TIME IS WORTH
ACCOUNT ANALYSIS
PART THREE: TERRITORY OBJECTIVES AND STRATEGIES
TERRITORY OPPORTUNITIES AND PROBLEMS   CONTROL
SUMMARY

SIX

Prospecting   118

REPLENISHING THE SOURCE OF CUSTOMERS   QUALIFYING PROSPECTS
SYSTEMS OF SUCCESS   SUMMARY

SEVEN

Promotional Strategies   139

YOUR PROMOTIONAL STRATEGY   SUMMARY

EIGHT

Preparation for the Sales Call   151

SALES CALL PLANNING GUIDE   SUMMARY

Part IV NON-MANIPULATIVE SELLING SKILLS

NINE

Meeting the Prospect 163

CONTACTING A CUSTOMER   SUMMARY

TEN

Studying Needs 184

ESTABLISHING TRUST   ASSESSMENT OF SITUATION AND GOALS
BE ORGANIZED   SETTING PROBLEM-SOLVING PRIORITIES   SUMMARY

ELEVEN

Proposing Solutions 195

TRUST, AGAIN   THE PROCESS OF PROPOSING SOLUTIONS
THE PRESENTATION   SUMMARY

TWELVE

Confirming the Purchase 213

CONFIRMING VS. CLOSING   MANAGING OBJECTIONS
CONFIRMING THE SALE   SUMMARY

THIRTEEN

Assuring Customer Satisfaction: The Follow-Through Process 231

SERVICING YOUR ACCOUNTS   MAINTAINING CUSTOMER SATISFACTION
EXPANDING YOUR SERVICES   SUMMARY

Part V COMMUNICATION SKILLS

FOURTEEN

The Fine Art of Questioning 243

QUESTIONING STRATEGIES   TYPES OF QUESTIONS
STRATEGIC USES OF QUESTIONS   SUMMARY

FIFTEEN

The Power of Listening   253

LEVELS OF LISTENING   GUIDELINES FOR ACTIVE LISTENING
IRRITATING LISTENING HABITS   SUMMARY

SIXTEEN

Feedback   265

TYPES OF FEEDBACK   EFFECTIVE USES OF FEEDBACK   SUMMARY

SEVENTEEN

Body Language   273

INTERPRETING BODY LANGUAGE GESTURES   TRAIT OR STATE?
YOUR USE OF BODY LANGUAGE   SUMMARY

EIGHTEEN

Proxemics   288

PROXEMIC ZONES (PHYSICAL PERSONAL SPACE)
PSYCHOLOGICAL PROXEMICS   PROXEMIC TERRITORIALITY
PROXEMIC CATEGORIES   SUMMARY

NINETEEN

The Effective Use of Voice   295

INFORMATION FROM VOICE QUALITIES   VOICE QUALITIES AND EMOTIONS
SUMMARY

Part VI   SELF-MANAGEMENT SKILLS

TWENTY

Your Sales Career and Your Life   305

BALANCE   THE IMPORTANCE OF GOALS   FOUNDATION DEVELOPMENT
ASSUMPTIONS AND THEIR EFFECT ON BEHAVIOR   POSITIVE THINKING
SELF-CONFIDENCE   MODEL FOR ACHIEVEMENT
THE FILTER OF ONE'S SELF-CONCEPT
THE PROCESSES OF BRAINSTORMING, GOAL-SETTING, VISUALIZING, AND ROLE
MODELING   ROLE PLAYING   THE THOUGHT DIET CARD
SUMMARY

TWENTY-ONE

Time Management 324

Efficiency vs. effectiveness   The time log   Setting priorities
Menaces of time   Relaxation and stress reduction
Changing bad habits   Summary

Index 341

Preface

The field of professional sales can be the most challenging, rewarding, and interesting of all careers. Selling is more than a job; it is a people-business in which an understanding of human behavior is indispensable. The professional salesperson does more than develop an expertise in an industry to which he sells products or services; he also develops a far more profound expertise: the ability to communicate well with all kinds of people.

The successful salesperson possesses all the virtues necessary to be at the top of any profession: communication skills; the sensitivity and flexibility that enable one to create chemistry with people; and the ability to efficiently and effectively manage one's professional and personal lives.

If we could boil down the difference between salespeople who thrive and those who struggle to survive, it would be:

TRUE PROFESSIONALS THINK AND ACT
AS THE OWNERS OF THEIR SALES CAREERS.

Salespeople who merely survive act as representatives of their companies. They do as much as their job description demands and no more. There is a tremendous difference between the two. Both work for a company; the true professional, however, also thinks and acts as if he *is* the company. He thinks like the owner of a business, not like an employee. In fact, he is his own business and his best employee. He manages himself as efficiently as he would a subordinate, and with higher expectations.

A professional, regardless of his field of endeavor, is defined not by the business he is in, but by the way he conducts business. Professionalism belongs on every level of business, from the chairman of the board to the busboy in a local restaurant. The job itself is not important; it's how you do it that counts.

There is only one way to take pride in what you do; do the best job you possibly can. To do that, the professional salesperson does the following:

Takes pride in and full responsibility for his business.

Develops a long- and short-range plan for business growth.

Aligns his goals with those of his company or finds a company whose goals are compatible with his.

Makes a life-long commitment to self-improvement, which means acquiring, one by one, the skills needed for a high level of success.

Makes customer satisfaction his highest priority.

This text was written with one goal in mind: to meet the needs of the student who wishes to learn about and possibly adopt a philosophy and practice of sales that creates the highest level of professionalism.

The approach we advocate, Non-Manipulative Selling, has become the preferred sales philosophy of many Fortune 500 companies. It has done so because it is a customer-oriented philosophy that creates long-term good will and sound business relationships.

Non-Manipulative Selling views each customer contact as a custom-tailored, problem-solving process, not a one-size-fits-all approach on which persuasion is the primary motive. A non-manipulative salesperson, therefore, is not a pusher of products; he is a consultant and liaison between his company and his customers. A non-manipulative salesperson always has his customers' best interests in mind.

Non-Manipulative Selling is not only a philosophy of selling; it is also a philosophy of business. The principles and practices have all the hallmarks of good business: integrity, logical and practical application, customer service orientation, win-win values, and efficient/effective management techniques.

Whether you are guiding a company of one or one hundred, NMS is a true course you can navigate to success.

Acknowledgements

The authors would like to express their deepest admiration and gratitude to Lynette Cablk, the instructional technologist and writer who assembled many of our previous books and articles. She refined and combined them to make the book you are now holding. Her integrity, productivity, sensitivity and sincerity are truly amazing.

Richness and value were added to the text by the contributions of our fellow professional speaker, Rick Barrera.

Much of the material in the book originally appeared in our books, *Non Manipulative Selling* by Alessandra, Wexler, and Jerry D. Dean (Courseware, 1979 and Reston, 1981); *Non Manipulative Selling* by Alessandra, Wexler, and Rick Barrera (Prentice Hall Press, 1987); and *The Business of Selling* by Alessandra and Cathcart (Nightingale-Conant, 1985). Thanks again to all those who contributed to the creation and production of those works.

Serena Vackert and Paula Cathcart, both of whom we thank profusely, provided assistance in the preparation of the manuscript.

The Non Manipulative Selling approach evolved over years of refinement in hundreds of seminars and thousands of hours of consultation. We sincerely thank all the people who live and thrive in the world of sales and who put a great deal of thought and effort into selling better to live better.

SELLING
BY
OBJECTIVES

Part I

OVERVIEW

CHAPTER ONE

The Philosophy of Non-Manipulative Selling

CHAPTER OBJECTIVES

1 Provide an overview of the Non-Manipulative Selling philosophy.
2 Familiarize you with the guiding principles of NMS.
3 Introduce the six steps of NMS and briefly compare them to other sales techniques.
4 Introduce the self-management skills that complement and promote a successful career in sales.

When people hear the word "salesperson," different images come to mind. Some people think of the rude door-to-door salesman who immediately slips his foot in the door and fast-talks his way through the sale. Other people think of a courteous and helpful clerk in a department store who bends over backwards to make you happy.

These images reflect the experiences we all have had and the prejudices we all hold toward "being sold." They also reflect the changes that are taking place in the way people conduct themselves as salespeople. Professionalism, ethical standards, and ongoing relationships with customers are more important than being the top seller on the sales team. This should not imply that being professional and ethical is incompatible with top performance. On the contrary, high achievers are not only good at sales, but also have the highest standards of professional and personal integrity.

Sales is a common denominator of every business. No matter what business you are in, you must sell your product or service to customers. Even people whose careers appear to be furthest from sales have something to sell: themselves. Writers, dancers, artists, doctors, lawyers, and other professionals all must be paid by someone. That someone is a customer who must be sold one way or another.

Salespeople are an indispensable asset to the world economy. If you don't believe this, look at the financial statement or annual report of any corporation. The most important line of that report is not the bottom line (profits), but the top line (amount of sales). Obviously, without sales and salespeople, there are no profits and, therefore, no company.

The field of selling can be very exciting. It is an input = output career. In other words, you can have virtually any outcome you want if you put in enough effort. It is a career in which you can have your cake and eat it too. You can shape your career to enable you to do the things everyone wants to do:

Help other people solve problems
Be your own boss
Make a lot of money
Have a flexible work schedule
Travel and meet new people

Granted not every sales position offers all of these benefits, but many do. As you gain experience as a professional salesperson, you can change jobs and industries until you find the position that suits your needs and lifestyle. A good salesperson has one of the most flexible and adaptable careers possible.

THE FOOT-IN-THE-DOOR IMAGE

There is no denying that salespeople have gotten some negative press; but then every profession has its skeletons in the closet. If you talk to people about doctors, lawyers, or car mechanics, you will find some people love them, others hate them. The bottom line is that it is unfair to generalize about an entire group based on one bad experience. Certainly everyone in a particular business is not dishonest or exploitive. There are too many good business people in the world to let a few rotten eggs spoil your appreciation of the rest.

The reason the word "salesperson" carries some negative connotations is that inexperienced salespeople often create a lot of tension and distrust. No one likes to be sold in a way that is high-pressured, yet some salespeople use manipulative selling techniques because they are more interested in earning commissions than in earning the good will and loyalty of satisfied customers.

The salesperson is not always to blame. Many companies, especially small ones, hire salespeople and do not give them any training. They are allowed to begin selling with whatever resources they have and must scramble to bring in orders. By not training their salespeople, a company commits one of the gravest sins in the business. Unprofessional salespeople not only damage the company's reputation, they also ruin their own. It takes a great deal of effort to fix the bad feelings caused by offensive sales techniques. That effort, if it had been applied in a positive way before the sale, would be opening doors rather than slamming them shut. Salespeople who are not trained are forced to behave in the manner of the salesperson they have in their minds. All too often that model is the foot-in-the-door type or some variation thereof.

It is essential for a salesperson to be trained. That training should come from the employer. If it does not, however, there are many books, audio tapes, and video programs that a conscientious professional can use to improve himself or herself.

It is important to understand that training needs to be both adequate and appropriate to make it effective. Training should also be tied to an overall philosophy of doing business, as Non-Manipulative Selling is.

ADEQUATE TRAINING

It is not uncommon for a company to spend a lot of training dollars on only one aspect of sales competence: product knowledge. Being familiar with one's product is indispensable, but knowing it inside-out is going too far. The only time you have to know every nut and bolt is when you are selling a very technical product to people who think primarily in technical terms. This is a different type of selling than most beginning salespeople get into. It is very industry-specific and often requires an engineering or some other advanced degree. In that type of sales, the emphasis is on technical knowledge, not sales ability.

Most salespeople require only enough product knowledge to know how the product works and what its features and benefits to the customer are. Beyond that, the salesperson's expertise should lie in developing relationships and studying the prospect's business.

A salesperson whose training has put too much emphasis on product knowledge will tend to exhibit *technological arrogance.* The result is that the customer loses interest because the conversation revolves around the product and not his needs. A classic example of overtraining in product knowledge was experienced by Tony when he went into a retail computer store to look at a personal computer:

> I had great apprehension about going into the store at all because I wasn't sure I could really work with a computer. I wasn't brought up with computers and they seemed to be so technical and complicated—beyond my scope of comprehension. I was fearful, but I did want to go in and see what they were all about.
>
> Computer stores definitely understand retail merchandising. In the middle of the store they had this fantastic computer set-up with a color monitor and a program that was running with great color graphics and sound. I was mesmerized! All of a sudden a salesman walked up behind me and said something that I'm used to hearing at a used car lot: "It's a beauty, isn't it?"
>
> I couldn't believe it, but I was still so stunned at this computer marvel that I said, "Yes, it's incredible! I can't believe it. This thing is much better than I expected." The salesman responded with, "Guess what, it's 64K." I said, "My God, that expensive? Let's look at a more reasonable model." The guy roared, "No, no, no, that refers to its memory."

He then went on to explain the product in detail—how many bytes, how many bits, how many rams, how many roms, the storage capacity, the type of computer chips, and the add-on boards that can be put into the machine itself. He even took off the back of the computer to show me the inside. Now I was petrified. I politely excused myself and left the store, even more convinced that there was no way I could learn about computers.

This example illustrates two weak points of inadequate training: overwhelming the customer with product knowledge, and treating every customer in the same manner. Not every customer cares about the technical details; in fact, all most want to know is how the product will make life easier.

APPROPRIATE TRAINING

Training is appropriate when it serves the best interests of the customer, the salesperson, and the company. It is inappropriate when it only serves the profit motive of the company and the salesperson. Many people, from business students to top corporate executives, mistakenly believe the purpose of a business is to make money. That is only half (or even less) of the reason. A more enlightened and longer-lasting *modus operandi* is to have the purpose of the business be **to acquire and maintain customers.** If a company does this efficiently and effectively, it cannot help but make money.

Appropriate training, therefore, gives the salesperson a system for finding and evaluating prospects, contacting and interacting with them, discovering needs and opportunities, consummating the sale, and following up and maintaining that business relationship.

NON-MANIPULATIVE SELLING

Non-Manipulative Selling (NMS) is the name we have given our comprehensive, customer-centered philosophy of selling. There are six guiding principles of NMS that reflect this consultative, win-win approach:

1. **A professional salesperson is known not by the business he or she is in, but by the way he or she is in business.** Your expertise in an industry is lost when you change industries. Your professionalism, however, goes with you no matter where you are.
2. **If two people want to do business together, the details will not stand in the way.** On the other hand, if two people do not get along well and do not want to do business together, no detail will pull it together and make it happen.
3. **The sales process must be built on a foundation of trust and mutual agreement.** Relationships that are open, honest, and free of tension create long-lasting business associations that pay off in many ways for many years.

4. In selling, as in medicine, **prescription before diagnosis is malpractice.** A professional salesperson does not offer solutions before he completely understands his customer's business.

5. **The majority of the time, people buy because they feel understood and appreciated by the salesperson.** People rarely buy because they were made to understand a product by a pushy salesperson.

6. **People like to make their own decisions,** regardless of how smart those decisions are. This is called *autonomy*—the desire to control yourself and what you do. A salesperson can help a customer solve a problem, but should always do so in a way that makes the customer a partner in the solution. People resent the loss of control they feel when a solution is thrust on them.

Non-Manipulative Selling is not a new bag of tricks. Instead, it is a fresh way of looking at some time-proven and respected techniques used in clinical psychology, counseling, consulting, negotiating, sales management, and marketing. This eclectic sales philosophy can be thought of as more humanistic than the foot-in-the-door method of selling. With NMS, manipulation and pressure are gone, enabling the salesperson and the customer to relax and enjoy a mutually beneficial relationship.

THE NMS SALES PROCESS

Non-Manipulative Selling, like many other sales techniques, has four basic phases in the sales process: information-gathering, the presentation, commitment, and follow-through. Unlike many other sales techniques, NMS places the emphasis on the information-gathering phase.

Figure 1.1 illustrates the relative amounts of time spent in each phase of the sale. The wider the shaded area, the more time is spent in that phase. As a means of comparison, the middle column shows the amount of time spent by high-pressure salespeople in each phase of the sale. The phases are labeled with the words typically used by non-manipulative salespeople and by the foot-in-the-door breed.

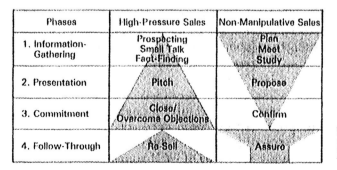

Phases	High-Pressure Sales	Non-Manipulative Sales
1. Information-Gathering	Prospecting Small Talk Fact-Finding	Plan Meet Study
2. Presentation	Pitch	Propose
3. Commitment	Close/ Overcome Objections	Confirm
4. Follow-Through	Re-Sell	Assure

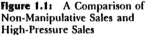

Figure 1.1: A Comparison of Non-Manipulative Sales and High-Pressure Sales

INFORMATION-GATHERING

How much do you want to know about your prospects? Enough to quickly sell your product or enough to fill their needs and make long-term customers out of them? Non-manipulative salespeople are interested in long-term customers. For this reason, they spend a great deal of time gathering information and laying the groundwork for an ongoing business relationship.

Planning

Planning is something you do before you even leave the office. It is the same as devising a winning game plan in the locker room that will give you an advantage once you are on the field or court (choose your sport). Planning involves managing your territory, your time, and all your accounts. It requires market planning and analysis, prospect planning, and preparation for the sales call. These activities, despite the way they sound to a beginner, are not very difficult and are worth the effort in the long run. The salesperson who figures, "I'll just start knocking on some doors," wastes a lot of time and becomes discouraged quickly. Systematic planning, on the other hand, increases your success ratio (number of sales to calls made) and puts more money in your pocket. It also gives you a better perspective of your prospects. The little bit of research you do on each prospect will give you confidence. You will be secure in the knowledge that you are calling on the right people.

Meeting

Meeting your prospect is the step that establishes the rapport and begins your business relationship. It is the point where you make a good impression with your professionalism, enthusiasm, and sincere concern for your prospect's business. Unlike the high-pressure salesperson, the non-manipulative salesperson does not aspire to making the sale on the first visit. Instead, the meeting is used as a time to prove your credibility and desire to be of service.

The meeting phase generally takes place in three mini-phases: contact by letter, then by phone, and finally in person. The logical sequence is to first send a letter to make the prospect aware of you and your product or service; follow up by phone to establish interest and set an appointment to meet; finally, meet and explore the possibility of doing business together.

Studying

As Figure 1.1 implies, the high-pressure salesperson operates on the unfair and fallacious assumption that everyone needs his product or service. But, as mentioned earlier, prescription without diagnosis is malpractice. When you meet a prospect, you must ask questions to see if your product or service is really needed.

The studying phase is a time to get the prospect involved in the sales process. It is an open, honest exchange of information that is spurred on by the well-thought-out questions that you ask. By digging deep into the prospect's business, personal goals, and current situation, you come away with a complete picture of what he has versus what he wants. You are then in the enviable position of being able to be a friend/consultant who can help him solve his problems and achieve his goals. If there is any persuading to be done by the salesperson, it is done from the standpoint of someone who understands his prospect's needs and is recommending the best solution to someone who perhaps cannot see the forest because the trees are too thick.

Every step of the way the salesperson goes as slow as necessary to be sure his client is in agreement with him. If his client is confused or does not agree on something being discussed, the salesperson finds out where their communication and agreement went astray. They then fix that problem and get back on the track of seeing everything eye to eye.

Proposing

After meeting with your customer, establishing a mutual interest in solving his problems, and studying his needs, the next step is to propose a solution to those needs. Since every client is different, many solutions will have to be custom tailored. Obviously this is not possible with every product or service, but with many it is. A computer system can be designed to meet the needs of various customers. A real estate agent can look for houses that fit the general needs of her clients.

No matter what the product or service, the benefits are always discussed in a way that illustrates exactly how they will solve specific problems. For example, if a home buyer enjoys swimming, a house does not necessarily have to have a pool. The agent could propose a house that is close to the ocean or in the same neighborhood as a community pool. There are many ways to skin a cat; knowing the prospect's needs gives the salesperson more options for satisfying them.

Just as no two customers are alike, no two presentations should be alike. The "canned" or memorized presentation used by the foot-in-the-door salesman is a thing of the past. It is essential to address the customer as an individual who is being given special treatment, no matter how many clients you have.

Confirming

One of the most dramatic differences between non-manipulative and high-pressure salespeople is the time spent confirming the sale. As Figure 1.1 illustrates, the amount of time spent in the confirming phase for the non-manipulative salesperson is the same as the amount of time spent in the information-gathering phase for the high-pressure salesperson. The reason for this is simple. By the time the non-manipulative salesperson gets to the confirming phase (or, as some call it, asking for the sale), it is natural to assume the customer will buy. Since he was involved in the sales process and agreed with everything discussed up to this point, the commitment becomes a question of **when** and not **if**.

The reason high-pressure salespeople have to spend so much time closing is that they have to convince the prospect to buy. Without laying any groundwork or gaining the prospect's trust, making the sale is an uphill struggle requiring a lot of time and effort.

Assuring

Non-manipulative selling is a philosophy that builds its strength on honesty, integrity, and the belief that long-term business relationships are the backbone

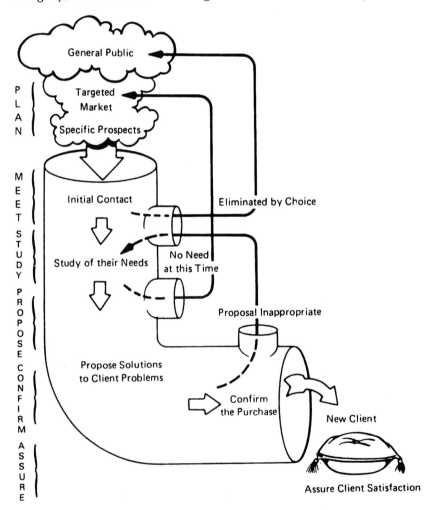

Figure 1.2:   The Sales Pipeline and the Six Steps of NMS

of success. Assuring customer satisfaction, therefore, is an ongoing activity that promotes repeat business.

Satisfied customers are an asset. To build up assets into a sizable investment that pays future dividends, it is necessary to occasionally change hats from "salesperson" to "customer service representative." Some of the things you'll do are: make sure the customer receives his order on time and in perfect condition; help the customer track his results and analyze the effectiveness of the product; and keep in touch to see if you can be of further service in the future. The business world is constantly changing and new needs can arise as quickly as old ones are satisfied.

By building a clientele of loyal and happy customers, the non-manipulative salesperson creates a network of people on whom he can call for help, and vice versa.

Another model that illustrates the non-manipulative selling process is the sales pipeline of Figure 1.2. The sales pipeline shows the flow of prospects through the sales cycle. First there is the general population from whom you target a specific market who can use your product or service. You then plan your territory, meet prospects, study their needs, propose solutions, and confirm the sale. Once they are clients, part of the salesperson's job is to assure their satisfaction and keep them happy.

It is essential for salespeople to continually feed new prospects into the sales pipeline. Without a steady stream of new prospects, a salesperson's productivity will suffer. You can see how this works if you imagine disconnecting the fuel line from an engine. The engine will run for a little while longer, but when the fuel line becomes empty, the engine will stop. Prospects are the fuel that makes the sales process run.

ENHANCEMENT SKILLS FOR SUCCESSFUL NON-MANIPULATIVE SELLING

The skills of Non-Manipulative Selling encourage *long-lasting,* trusting business relationships with your customers. NMS skills are most successfully used in conjunction with a variety of other personal skills that play a vital part in professional sales: self-management skills, relationship skills, communication skills, and sales management skills.

Self-Management Skills

To be professional, a salesperson must be proficient in self-management. Basic to self-management is managing your career as well as other aspects of your life. Building a successful career requires clarifying both your personal and career goals and developing an action plan for achieving those goals. Achievement comes easily when all aspects of your life—mental, physical, family, social, spiritual, career, and financial—are in balance.

Another essential of self-management is effective time management. By learning to eliminate time wasters, to identify the best use of your time, to determine what your time is worth, and to convert unproductive habits into productive ones, you will have better control over not only your sales career but all other aspects of your life as well.

These essential skills of self-management—managing all aspects of your career and life, and managing time effectively—are discussed in detail in Part VI, "Self-Management Skills."

Relationships Skills

Basic to effective non-manipulative selling is a sound understanding and the creative use of relationship skills. These include tension management, relationship strategies, and the characteristics of excellence.

In every relationship there is a degree of tension due to personal tension, relationship tension, and needs (for solutions). This tension may be positive or negative, depending on how much there is and how well it is handled. Identifying a customer's tension level and turning that tension into productive, relationship-building energy are techniques used by every successful professional salesperson.

In addition to being able to identify and control tension levels, the professional salesperson also develops skills in relationship strategies. He not only identifies his prospects' and customers' buying styles but is able to adjust his own selling style to fit the styles of his customers.

Using tension management and relationship strategies effectively are important skills within one's professional stage. The *image of excellence* has twelve characteristics which are shared by those salespeople found in the top 5 percent of the sales force: positive first impression, depth of knowledge, breadth of knowledge, behavioral flexibility, sensitivity, enthusiasm, self-esteem, extended focus, a sense of humor, creativity, willingness to take risks, and a sense of honesty and ethics. These characteristics are all under your personal control and can therefore be powerful assets in your professional sales career.

Managing tension and using relationship strategies skillfully and effectively, coupled with an image of excellence, are essential to successful Non-Manipulative Selling. Part III, "Relationship Skills," will give you specific direction in developing these areas.

Communication Skills

Effective communication, both verbal and nonverbal, is essential to successful selling. Without well-developed skills of communication both in sending and receiving messages, a customer's needs can be neither known nor understood, nor can your proposals and presentations be focused on those needs or well-communicated.

The verbal skills of questioning, listening, and feedback are rarely taught, and yet they are basic to effective communication and selling. When used properly, they determine prospects' needs, gather vital information, elicit prospect and customer participation, reduce potential objections, facilitate commitment, and keep customers sold.

When well-developed, the nonverbal communication skills of body language, proxemics, and the use of voice are invaluable to the professional salesperson. Such skills allow the professional to interpret nonverbal messages conveyed by the prospect and to control those he himself projects, to know what to do and what not to do in using space and territory when relating to prospects, and to glean important information from the prospect's voice qualities.

These verbal and nonverbal communication skills are indispensable for the professional salesperson, and Part V, on "Communication Skills," discusses them in detail.

Sales Management Skills

To be a successful professional salesperson, you must treat your career as a business and be your own sales manager. This requires developing the skills of proper territory management, effective prospecting, appropriate use of promotional strategies, and thorough preparation for each sales call.

Territory management is the skill of managing a market segment or territory like a business. This begins with a marketing plan which includes: doing a situation analysis, developing company and product knowledge, knowing market trends, doing competitive analyses and target marketing, conducting account analyses and classification, setting objectives, developing strategies, and keeping accurate records and controls.

The skill of effective prospecting involves knowing how to keep the sales pipeline full by developing sources for prospects, using promotional strategies, cultivating them, and setting up a system to qualify them.

Thorough preparation for a sales call requires diligent research to identify what vital information is needed and where to find it. It also includes setting call objectives and being fully prepared for all contingencies.

Part III, "Sales Management Skills," discusses each of these skills in detail, for they, too, are central to successful, professional non-manipulative selling. All of these skills are important enhancements to the central concept of Non-Manipulative Selling. Used in concert with each other, they allow a salesperson to exhibit a high degree of professionalism and develop a loyal and lucrative customer base.

SUMMARY

Non-manipulative selling avoids tension-inducing pressure; it does not attempt to manipulate people. Instead, it builds a relationship of mutual trust and increases sales while the salesperson and customer enjoy the process. NMS incorporates the time-honored nonexploitive techniques used in clinical psychology, counseling, consulting, negotiating, sales management, and marketing.

There are six guiding principles of non-manipulative selling: 1) It's not what you do in business, but the way you do it. 2) If two people do want to do business together or do not want to do business together, the details will not matter. 3) The sales process must be built around a relationship of trust which requires honesty and openness on the part of both the buyer and the salesperson. 4) Prescription without diagnosis is malpractice. 5) People buy most often because they believe that they and their problems are understood by the seller. 6) People strive to make their own decisions, even if they are poor ones.

There are four basic phases of every sale: information-gathering, presentation, commitment, and follow-through. The amount of time spent in each phase varies from one sales philosophy to the next.

Non-manipulative selling emphasizes the information-gathering and follow-through phases. In addition, the terms used in NMS imply a cooperative sales approach rather than a coercive approach. The steps of NMS are plan, meet, study, propose, confirm, and assure. High-pressure sales techniques use words such as pitch, close, and handling objections. Even though they are only labels, words reflect an attitude toward the customer.

In the first phase, information-gathering, the salesperson thoroughly plans his call, and, when meeting his prospect, his emphasis is on exhaustive study of the prospect's needs and situation through encouraging the prospect to become involved in the sales process. After such thorough study, if the salesperson determines that his product or service is warranted, proposing and confirming usually become a simple matter of mutual agreement. The last phase, follow-through, also receives substantial attention from the salesperson, for it is in this phase that he assures that the relationship established not only continues into the future but is mutually beneficial.

The skills of non-manipulative selling encourage long-lasting, trusting business relationships with our customers. Using those skills successfully requires their enhancement by a variety of other skills that play a vital part in professional sales: self-management skills, relationship skills, verbal and nonverbal communication skills, and territory and account management skills. By using all of these skills in concert with each other, a salesperson will be a professional, one who develops long-lasting customer relationships based on trust and mutual understanding.

DISCUSSION QUESTIONS

1. When you think of a salesperson, what words or images come to mind?
2. If you were in sales, how would you want to be different from the descriptions you thought of for Question 1?
3. From Question 1, which words would you want to describe you and your image as a salesperson?
4. In one sentence, describe the basic philosophy of Non-Manipulative Selling.
5. What are the six guiding principles of NMS?

6. For each of the guiding principles, think of a situation in your own life that illustrates it. How did you feel?

7. What are the advantages to the salesperson and to the customer of the Non-Manipulative Selling philosophy?

8. What are the four phases of any sales process?

9. What are the six steps of NMS?

10. What are the self-management skills that complement the use of NMS?

11. In addition to becoming a better salesperson, what are the other benefits of developing self-management skills?

Part II

RELATIONSHIP SKILLS

Remember: if two people want to do business together, the details will not stand in the way. The question then arises: if two people do not use the details of the business deal to decide, how do they make the decision to do business together? The answer is simple: personal chemistry. Do the two people get along or not?

Another truism in business is: "It's not only what you know, but who you know." Business is conducted by people, with people. It's an interactive, give-and-take process in which compatibility is the basic ingredient. Simply stated: Does the other person like you or not? If so, he'll do favors for you; if not, you're on your own. There is no denying the power of connections in the business world.

Building a successful career in sales, especially Non-Manipulative Selling, requires the cultivation of relationship skills. These skills will enable you to build trust and credibility, the foundations of long-term associations. Truly professional salespeople can get along with any type of customer. They have a gift that may be natural, but can also be developed. You can practice and learn to get along with people, but first you must see the advantages of doing so and motivate yourself to make an effort.

Relationship skills cover the following areas:

○ TENSION MANAGEMENT: This is the ability to reduce the destructive tension in a relationship so both parties can concentrate on the constructive task at hand—cooperation. Helping the other person relax is one type of tension management;the other is the ability to recognize and reduce the tension born out of a customer's need.

○ RELATIONSHIP STRATEGIES: This is a system that enables you to size up people quickly and accurately so you can practice the ultimate social skill—getting along with anyone. There are four behavioral styles with which people are comfortable. Once you have figured out a person's style, it is easy to create chemistry rather than conflict.

○ THE IMAGE OF EXCELLENCE: The two relationship skills above will help you get along with others, but what will those people think of you? You can stack all the odds in your favor and positively influence people by sharpening your image.

The way you carry yourself, the clothes you wear, your level of intelligence and awareness, your sense of humor, and many other factors affect the impression you make. Part of being a true professional is making an effort to cultivate in yourself the qualities that people like and admire.

Relationship skills are the beginning of the social side of selling. Other communication skills will be covered later in the book. Taken together, these skills will make you someone whom people enjoy being with—in business, at home, anywhere.

CHAPTER TWO

Tension Management

CHAPTER	**1**	Discuss tension and its relationship to productivity.
OBJECTIVES	**2**	Develop an understanding of customer perception of behavior.
	3	Discuss and illustrate the concept of tension management in a sales relationship.

"Is tension bad?"

Inevitably when asked this question, most people respond, "Yes, it's bad." In reality, contrary to the Anacin commercials, tension in and of itself is not bad. What determines if tension is bad or not, whether it is a negative or a positive force, is *how much* tension there is. Some people can handle more tension than others, but it is important to note that *every* person has a point at which he or she begins to handle tension poorly.

CATEGORIES OF TENSION

There are basically three categories of tension in the selling environment: personal tension, relationship tension, and need tension. Much of this book is dedicated to assisting you in understanding all three types and handling each of them effectively.

Personal Tension

Personal tension refers to the natural tension most salespeople feel when in the selling environment, whether they are preparing for sales calls, making appointments, or calling on prospects and customers. Such tension refers to the "butterflies" of the sales call, the stress of asking personal questions, the stress in general that can keep a salesperson from concentrating on what he should be doing—all of those feelings that contribute to what is called *call reluctance*.

Many factors contribute to call reluctance, all of which are due to a deficiency in one or more of the various skill areas needed in the selling environment: self-management skills, relationship skills, communication skills (verbal and nonverbal), sales management skills, and the non-manipulative selling skills.

Much of the call reluctance that many salespeople experience is due to *cold calling*, a popular term in sales which refers to making a sales call without an appointment on a person whom you do not know, with the intention of making a sale during that call. *The approach of cold calling is totally inappropriate in today's society*. There are several things wrong with this approach:

1. You have no reason to make the call other than your own desire to make a sale.
2. You may be an intrusion in that person's otherwise orderly day.
3. The person on whom you are calling may not need what you have to sell.

Cold calling is unjustified and inappropriate. By making calls with the sole purpose of making a sale without adequate prior preparation and research, you may feel like a defeated, nervous failure. Your prospects on the other hand will feel pressured and manipulated because you may press too hard.

Although cold calls may be inappropriate, *introductory* calls *are* appropriate. The purpose of introductory calls is to meet new people, expand your business base, and discover where new opportunities exist. The purpose is *not* to make a sale. If, however, when making an introductory call it becomes obvious that a need does indeed exist, then of course, make a sale. The important difference here is the purpose, or the intent of the call itself. Approaching sales calls with a clear purpose and with adequate preparation will do a great deal to reduce personal tension.

Personal Tension and Non-Manipulative Sales   The good news is that non-manipulative selling reduces the causes of personal tension inherent in the traditional sales approach. Taking them in order:

> Non-manipulative salespeople do not pressure their customers. The customer is an equal partner in the sales process, whose agreement every step along the way is solicited. When it is time to write up the order, it is a foregone conclusion, not a tactical close.
>
> Non-manipulative salespeople are not unsure of their skills, because they are prepared, practiced professionals. Their communication skills and the nature of their relationships with prospects make it easy for them to say, "Listen, I sense a misunderstanding; let me clarify this."
>
> Cold calls are not the norm for non-manipulative salespeople. There are times, however, when a cold call can be used, especially for a product that has a short sales cycle. The non-manipulative salesperson makes a cold call differently, however. He would only call on a prospect in his target market; he is more sensitive to the needs of the prospect; he enters with a different attitude and conveys it immediately by saying, in effect, "Some people I can help, some people I can't

help. Do you mind if I ask you some questions so we can both determine if I may be of service to you?" The non-manipulative salesperson is also sensitive to the fact that he does not have an appointment and may be there at a bad time.

In general, the nature of non-manipulative selling will eliminate most personal tension in both you and your prospects. It is important for professional salespeople to reduce their own tension so they can concentrate on managing the tension of the customer. This will make for a more productive working relationship.

Relationship Tension

Relationship tension refers to the normal, natural tension, either positive or negative, that exists between people. Managing this tension positively and effectively requires an understanding of behavioral styles and a flexibility in your own behavioral style to adapt to the style of the individual with whom you are meeting.

This practice of managing relationship tension—identifying the behavioral styles of others and adapting your own style to complement them—falls under the selling skills of relationship strategies discussed in detail in the next chapter.

Need Tension

Need tension is the stress you feel when your reality does not match your desired situation. This discrepancy between the real and the ideal creates what we call a *need gap.*

As Figure 2.1 shows, the larger the discrepancy between what you want and what you have, the greater your need gap. The more closely aligned the ideal and the actual, the smaller the need gap. This source of tension is based on expectations, wishes, and attitude versus current circumstances. Based on the need gaps in Figure 2.1, which person do you think will be more motivated to buy?

As a non-manipulative salesperson, part of your job would be to find out what your prospect's need gap is. Most prospects know they have a need gap, although they don't call it that. Some customers may require extensive questioning and discussion to make them aware of their existing need gap. A prospect who does not perceive a need gap will not be motivated to consult with you. That

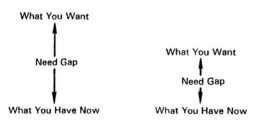

Figure 2.1: Two different-sized need gaps

is why it is important to ask questions such as, "What is your company's five-year goal?" or "What is your mission?" and then ask them to compare the present situation with the plan or goal. You can also ask, "What would you like to see happen to achieve that goal?" When a need gap is recognized by you and your prospect, you can then propose a solution that will close the gap and eliminate that source of need tension for your client.

Assuring customer satisfaction involves periodic follow-ups to see if the need gap is still closed. The ideal solution to a customer's problem will keep the gap closed for good; however, there are times when it will reopen in your absence. In this case, it is your job to propose a solution, which may be something as simple as providing additional training.

Part IV of this book, which is devoted to the non-manipulative selling skills, will discuss in detail the methods of effectively handling and managing need tension. In particular, Chapter 12 will discuss the many ways the professional salesperson can assure customer satisfaction and continue to manage tension after the sale.

TENSION MANAGEMENT AND RELATIONSHIPS

Tension and Productivity

The relationship between personal tension and productivity has been the focus of many theories, the most notable being that of Yerkes and Dodson. They found that people function best within a range of tension that has become known as the *comfort zone*. Figure 2.2 graphically depicts the relationship between tension and productivity.

As the figure shows, if there is no tension, there is no productivity. As tension increases, so does performance, to a point. Beyond that point, if tension continues to increase, productivity decreases. In other words, either a *lack* of stimulation or an *excess* of stimulation is bad for performance. In the middle of

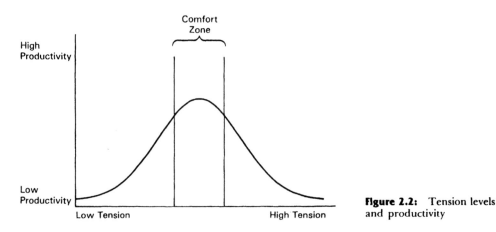

Figure 2.2: Tension levels and productivity

the two extremes is one's comfort zone or area of optimal productivity, which is different for everyone.

If we take the word "productivity" out of the Yerkes/Dodson law and substitute "communication," we get:

No tension → No communication

As tension increases, so does communication, to a point. Beyond that point, communication decreases.

We can again modify this law by taking out the word "communication" and inserting "productivity in the relationship." The new law reads:

No tension → No productivity in the relationship

As tension increases, so does the productivity in the relationship, to a point. Beyond that point, productivity in the relationship decreases.

Basically it is the object of each person in a relationship to try to keep the tension level within the comfort zone so that the relationship can be its most productive. It is human nature to want to be in the comfort zone. Any time one does something that helps another to be in his comfort zone, the relationship between them grows. On the other hand, whenever one does something that stands between another person and his comfort zone, the relationship deteriorates.

In one way or another, virtually every skill used in non-manipulative selling relates back to the management of tension toward the building of the business relationship.

Every salesperson has been taught, "Always sell yourself first." Most salespeople, however, begin selling their product as soon as they walk through a prospect's door rather than developing the relationship first. This creates a tension which literally prohibits the relationship from developing. Therefore, one could call a non-manipulative salesperson a "tension manager."

The Perception of Behavior

Let's take two words that are often associated with the word "salesman," and see how these words are affected by 1) the relationship and 2) the tension in the relationship between a salesperson and the prospect. The two words are pushy and aggressive.

Although some people use the word "aggressive" in a negative way, for the sake of this discussion, we are going to use it to describe behavior similar to "pushy" behavior, but with a *positive* connotation rather than a negative connotation.

When we ask people for the difference between these two words, pushy and aggressive, people give long lists of differences when in reality there is no difference between them in actual behavior. The only difference between the two is in the *perception* of the behavior.

For example, a salesperson could meet with a prospect in an organization, spend a bit of time with him, and be perceived by that prospect as aggressive in a very positive way. The prospect could say to his secretary when the salesperson leaves his office, "I really like that guy! He's a real aggressive salesman, and I like aggressive salesmen!" But, as chance would have it, this particular person is not the person in the organization that purchases the product that the salesman sells. Consequently, the salesman is sent to another person in the organization. The original prospect picks up the phone and says, "Hi, George. I've got Dick Adams in my office. He's a real aggressive salesman and we really like him, but he's selling widgets and you're the widget buyer. I'm going to send him over to see you."

When the salesman sees George, he spends 15 or 20 minutes with him. When he leaves George's office, George calls the original prospect and says, "Why did you send that pushy guy over here? You know I don't like pushy salesmen!"

Two customers in a 15-minute period of time—one perceives the salesperson as pushy; the other perceives him as aggressive. The difference is the *perception* of behavior, *not* the actual behavior.

Tension Management Techniques

A difference in perception can happen not only with two different customers in a short period of time, but with the *same* customer at two different times.

Let's imagine Dick Adams visiting Mr. Jones at 8:00 on a Monday morning for an appointment to sell him a training program. Dick shows up on time and the appointment goes very well. About one hour later, Mr. Jones says, "Dick, I'm really enjoying this meeting. We seem to have a lot in common, and there's possibly a lot of areas where we can be of mutual benefit to each other. But, frankly, I had not realized that this appointment was going to take this long, so I suggest we reschedule for Thursday and continue our conversation then. I have another appointment at 9:00 and it would be unfair to keep that gentleman waiting. Does that sound okay to you?" Of course, Dick agrees to return on Thursday.

After Dick leaves, the prospect turns to the secretary and says, "I like aggressive salesmen! That guy, Dick Adams, he's real aggressive. I'm looking forward to our meeting on Thursday."

Thursday morning arrives. Mr. Jones gets up, takes a shower, shaves, gets dressed, goes down to the kitchen, and unfortunately uses a cracked cup to pour himself a cup of coffee. As he picks it up to take his first sip, the cup falls apart, spilling coffee all over him. He goes back to the bedroom, changes his clothes, comes back down, and looks at his watch. It's getting late and he can't take time to have that first morning cup of coffee. He goes to the garage, gets in his car, tries to start the car and . . . his battery is dead! He opens the garage door, sees his nextdoor neighbor just pulling out, waves to him, and asks him for a jump start.

Finally he is on his way to the office. It's a cold, rainy, miserable day. About two and a half miles from the office, Mr. Jones gets a flat tire. He looks at his watch; he has about 25 minutes to get to the office before his appointment with Dick. He doesn't want to be late because Dick's coming back for the second time to visit him at his request. He'd like to be on time for the appointment. He knows that if he calls the Automobile Club, he *will* be late. So he gets out into the rain and changes the tire himself.

When Mr. Jones arrives at the office, he is cold, wet, and greasy. He says to his secretary, "Do you have those three reports that I need for Dick Adams this morning?" She says, "I have two of them ready, but not the third. I'm just finishing it up now." He says, "Give me the two you've got ready now. When you finish that third one, bring it in to me. I haven't had a cup of coffee yet this morning, so when you finish up that third one, would you please bring a cup of coffee with it?"

A few minutes later in comes the secretary with the third report. In her other hand is his cup of coffee. As she places the report on the table, she stumbles and spills the coffee on all three reports. Just as this happens, in walks Dick. "How are you doing, Mr. Jones?" he asks.

What do you think the prospect's perception is of Dick right now? He probably sees Dick as a pushy salesman. The question is: Did Dick's behavior change from Monday's appointment until Thursday's appointment? Of course not. Dick is the same aggressive salesman that he was on Monday. The only difference is that the prospect is now out of his comfort zone. When a person is out of his comfort zone, all of his perceptions change and all of the adjectives he uses to describe other people's behavior change. In this case, all of a sudden Dick Adams is a pushy salesman.

What do we do about this difference in perception? The first step is to recognize it when it happens. We find that excellent, professional salespeople always notice; they are always measuring the level of tension between them and the people with them. The mediocre salesperson, on the other hand, seldom even notices that there is a problem. In the rare case when he does notice that there is a problem, the typical attitude tends to be, "I took my time, my effort, my energy, and my gas to come out here and give a presentation. By George, I'm going to give a presentation!"

In contrast, what does the excellent, professional salesperson do? He responds in one of two ways that are considered proper and professional. The most typical response is something like, "Gee, Mr. Jones, it appears as though things are pretty hectic around here this morning. Would another day be more convenient for you?" Notice the phraseology. He doesn't say, "Gee, Mr. Jones, you look like you're in a bad mood. Would you like to reschedule the appointment?" It is important never to accuse anyone of being in a bad mood, for the response is always the same: "No, I'm NOT in a bad mood!" No one likes to be accused of being in a bad mood even when he is. The best method is to transfer the bad feelings from people to things: "Things look pretty hectic around here this morning. Would another day be more convenient for you?"

If the customer has bad feelings and his tension is either very deeply embedded or very high, the answer will be, "Good idea. Let's reschedule the appointment for another time." Once that happens, the customer feels better about you. He may hate the rest of the world, but he feels better about you. He is back in his comfort zone and it bears positively on your relationship with that customer.

Another way the salesperson can handle the situation is to use a psychological concept called the *intervention*. Occasionally, just asking the question solves the problem. For example, when the salesperson says to the customer, "Gee, Mr. Customer, things look pretty hectic around here this morning. Would another day be more convenient for you?" the customer may immediately relax just because he was offered an alternative. His tension level goes down, he comes closer to or actually returns to his comfort zone, and he realizes that whatever is happening isn't the salesperson's fault. He may turn to the salesperson and say, "I'm really sorry; things *have* been pretty hectic around here this morning and I shouldn't be taking it out on you. Why don't you and I go and have a cup of coffee, and discuss your proposal?" Just asking the question can act as an *intervention* between the customer's bad feelings and his relationship with the salesperson. But in order to accomplish this, the salesperson must always be aware of the tension level, constantly monitoring the level between himself and the customer.

Let's return to our mediocre salesperson, the one who takes the attitude: "I took my time, my effort, my energy, and my gas to drive out here to see this customer." His statement is actually correct: he *did* take his time, effort, energy, and gas to see that customer. In fact, when a salesperson makes an appointment with a customer, there is an implied contract. Essentially, the salesperson is saying, "I will be at a certain place at a certain time for a certain purpose with an open mind toward that purpose and in return, you, the customer, will be at that place, at that time, for that purpose, and you, too, will have an open mind toward that purpose." Such is the implied contract when one makes an appointment with a prospect or customer. If you, as a salesperson, meet *your* commitment for the appointment, don't you have the right to expect the customer to keep *his* commitment as well? Of course you have the right to expect this, but keep that wise old saying in mind: you don't want to "win the battle and lose the war."

Is there another way to deal with the situation that solves both problems: being able to give the presentation now without rescheduling and, at the same time, still getting the sale because you haven't hurt your relationship with the customer?

To answer these questions, we go not to the discipline of selling, but to the discipline of customer service. Consider a typical situation at a hotel front desk. The front desk clerk is standing by the front desk reflecting on the day so far. It's early, he's having a good morning, everything is going nicely. All of a sudden, Mrs. Daniels walks through the front doors of the hotel. She looks like a rhinoceros chasing a jeep and steam is coming from her ears. Immediately the desk clerk knows this is going to be a problem. He looks around to see if someone else is near the desk so he can go for a coffee break. Unfortunately, he is the only one there. Mrs. Daniels is *his* problem. She is yelling and screaming and banging on the desk. The front desk clerk can't turn to her and say, "Gee, Mrs. Daniels, thinks look pretty hectic around here today. Would another day be more convenient for you?" No, he has to deal with her problem on the spot.

How are customer service people trained to deal immediately with such situations and how can we transfer their training to the sales environment? Customer service people are taught a few simple—not easy, but simple—techniques. First, what is most important to Mrs. Daniels? She wants to be heard; she wants someone to listen. Believe it or not, she wants to be listened to more than she wants a solution to her problem. There may be lesser solutions that will be acceptable to her *after* she has had a chance to get rid of all of her bad feelings, solutions that would not be acceptable to her *before* she has had a chance to get rid of all of her bad feelings. It may be the 743rd time the desk clerk heard that complaint this week; but it is the first time Mrs. Daniels has given the complaint this week, and what she wants more than anything else is for the desk clerk to listen. This is called "dumping your bucket"—getting rid of all the bad feelings.

If, in fact, this technique works in a customer service environment, then how can this knowledge be used in the sales situation described previously? Instead of saying, "Gee, things look pretty hectic around here today. Would another day be more convenient for you?" what would happen if a salesperson said, "Things look pretty hectic around here this morning, Mr. Customer; what happened?" What would the customer do? In most cases, Mr. Customer will answer him and tell him what happened. He would begin by telling about the spilled coffee in the morning, the dead battery, and the flat tire. By the time he finishes telling his story, his entire persona will have changed. When the customer begins to tell the story of his bad day, his arms are crossed, his muscles are tight, his voice is strained, and his head is drawn. But, as he tells the story, the muscles relax, the arms uncross, and the voice tone becomes more mellow. Before long the customer is willing to talk about the salesman's product or service.

Tension Management—A Master Skill

Tension management is truly a master skill. It affects every aspect of our relationship with a prospect or customer. The excellent salesperson, the *professional* salesperson, is always measuring the level of tension between himself and the other person and using as many skills as he can to keep his prospects and customers within their comfort zones.

SUMMARY

The concept of tension and its effective management by the professional salesperson was the focus of this chapter. Tension, in and of itself, is not a negative force. What determines whether or not it is negative is the *amount* of tension there is for an individual.

There are three categories of tension in the selling environment: personal tension, relationship tension, and need tension. Personal tension refers to the natural tension most salespeople feel when in the selling environment. It is all of the feelings that many salespeople experience contributing to what is called call reluctance, which in itself is the result of a lack of skill in one or more of the various skill areas needed in the selling environment: self-management skills, relationship skills, communication skills (verbal and nonverbal), sales management skills, and the non-manipulative selling skills.

Cold calling is an approach that causes a great many salespeople to experience call reluctance. Cold calling is not appropriate for today's business world. The introductory call approach should be used instead; its purpose is meeting new people, expanding the business base, and discovering where new opportunities exist. Approaching sales calls with a clear purpose and with adequate preparation will do a great deal to reduce personal tension.

Relationship tension refers to the normal, natural tension, either positive or negative, that exists between people. Managing this tension positively and effectively requires an understanding of behavioral styles and a flexibility of your own behavioral style to adapt to the style of the individual with whom you are meeting.

Need tension encompasses the tension a prospect or a customer feels related to the difference between his or her *current* situation and his or her *desired* situation. The difference between those two situations is referred to as the need gap. The greater the person perceives that gap to be, the higher the need tension.

As a consultative salesperson, you discover through your communication skills of questioning and listening what the prospect's need gap is and then provide a bridge over that gap—the solution, which may be your product or service.

A study was conducted some years ago on the effects of tension on productivity. It was discovered that no tension caused no productivity. As the tension increased, productivity increased, to a point. At that point, if tension continued to increase, productivity decreased.

The area of optimum relationship between tension and productivity is a person's comfort zone. This is the point where we get the most productivity for our investment of tension. We can relate this to the sales environment by using the relationship: No tension, no productivity of the business relationship. As the tension increases, so does the productivity of the relationship, to a point. When we reach that point, if the tension continues to increase, the productivity of the relationship decreases.

As a salesperson who is a tension manager, it is important to try to keep the tension level within the prospect's comfort zone so that the relationship can be its most productive. Virtually every skill in non-manipulative selling relates back to the management of tension toward the building of the business relationship.

It is important to keep in mind the difference between perception of behavior and the actual behavior. Often our behavior remains the same from meeting to meeting with a prospect or customer. However, the circumstances of the day for that person may affect how he or she perceives us, making that perception positive or negative. By being aware of how perceptions can change, we must be prepared to recognize it if and when it happens. Excellent, professional salespeople always notice; they are always measuring the level of tension between them and the people with them.

Tension management is a master skill. It affects every aspect of our relationship with our prospects and customers. The excellent salesperson is always measuring the level of tension in the relationship and using all of the skills necessary to manage the tension present and keep it within the other person's comfort zone.

DISCUSSION QUESTIONS

1. What is the relationship between productivity and tension?
2. What is the relationship between communication and tension?
3. How does your personal tension affect your business relationships?
4. What can you do to reduce the tension level of the person you are talking to?
5. What is meant by a need gap?
6. Why is it important to understand the concept of perception of behavior?
7. What is meant by the expression, "Don't win the battle at the risk of losing the war"? What does it imply about your behavior in business situations?
8. Why is tension management referred to as a "master skill"?
9. How can you apply the concepts in this chapter to your personal life?
10. Identify a need gap of your own and find a solution.

CHAPTER THREE

Relationship Strategies

CHAPTER OBJECTIVES

1 Develop an understanding of the four basic behavioral styles and their influence on sales relationships.
2 Discuss methods of identifying the behavioral style of a prospect or customer.
3 Present guidelines on how to effectively practice behavioral flexibility—the adjustment of one's behavioral style to fit a prospect's behavioral style.

When meeting with other people, have you ever experienced a personality conflict? Most of us have! On the other hand, many of us have met someone for the first time and after 15 minutes or so, the *chemistry* was so strong that we felt as though we had known that person for many years. Instant rapport!

Your ability as a consultative salesperson to develop such a chemistry with all of your prospects and customers is crucial to your success in sales. In sales, the *first* thing that you have to sell before anything else is *yourself*.

You can create more chemistry than conflict in your sales relationships by practicing the Golden Rule: "Do unto others as you would have them do unto you." It is our contention, however, that if you practice this rule *verbatim,* you stand a much greater chance of creating conflict rather than chemistry with your prospects and customers. Literally translated, the Golen Rule says that a person should treat others from his own perspective, not *their* perspectives; that he should speak to people the way he likes to listen; that he should manage people the way he would like to be managed; and, most importantly, that he should *sell* others the way he would like to buy. Therefore, what we are proposing is that you learn to practice the *intent*, the spirit, of the Golden Rule: "Treat people the way they want to be treated," or, for our purposes here, "Sell people the way that they like to be sold."

In this chapter, specific "how to" material will be presented. This will include: developing an understanding of your style (how you deal with others)—its strengths and weaknesses—and the styles of your prospects and customers; providing some specific methods to quickly identify the behavioral style of a prospect or customer; and discussing how to practice sales flexibility, the adjustment of your selling style to fit your prospects' buying styles in order to decrease negative relationship tension and increase sales.

BEHAVIORAL STYLES

One of the most valuable skills in selling to others is the ability to "read" people. The people with whom you interact each day send signals on how to sell to them most effectively. By learning to visually and audibly pick up those signals, you will know just how to sell to them.

Everyone experiences the same basic desires, but with each individual some desires are more dominant than others. For example, a person like the TV character J.R. Ewing of *Dallas* is the type of person who measures his success by results. To him, the finished product is most important and he will do whatever it takes, within reason, to get the job done. His dominant need is for accomplishment.

Another example is the sensitive, supportive type such as Jane Pauley of *The Today Show.* In addition to her charm and good looks, she adds a warmth that makes viewers feel at home.

For a third type of personality, consider Robin Williams. His on-camera personality is that of an off-the-wall comedian. This type of person thrives on the recognition his humor brings. He measures his success by the amount of applause he receives.

Conversely, a character like Mr. Spock on *Star Trek* is more impressed with content than form. Spock's primary need appears to be regimentation. He is a systems expert; he enjoys putting things together in neat, logical packages that can be clearly understood.

Each of these four personality patterns requires a different type of sales appeal. The type of sales appeal that would work with J.R. Ewing would likely be totally inappropriate for Jane Pauley. Recognizing this factor is very important in conducting successful sales. Once you have learned the needs of each major personality pattern, you will then know how to more effectively sell to each person you contact.

When people act and react in social situations, they exhibit behaviors which help to define their personality patterns or behavioral styles. We identify behavioral styles by watching for the observable aspects of people's behaviors—the verbal, vocal, or visual actions that people display when others are present.

Without direction, one could observe and try to catalogue thousands of behaviors in any one person. But that, of course, would quickly become an exercise in futility. Identifying behavioral style is quite possible, however, when one begins by classifying a person's behavior on two dimensions: openness and directness.

Openness

Openness is the ease with which a person shows emotions and is accessible to others. It also encompasses the person's readiness to develop new relationships, whether he "jumps in" and gets involved interpersonally or remains aloof. Openness can be graphically illustrated on a vertical scale with the top of the scale representing open behaviors and the bottom of the scale representing self-contained behaviors.

Open

4

3

2

1

Self-Contained

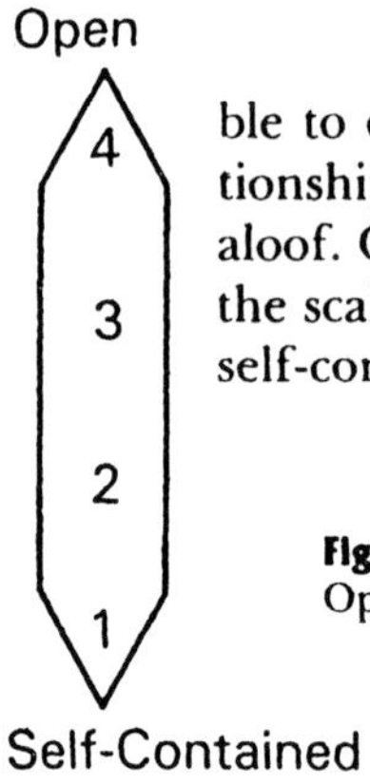

Figure 3.1: The Vertical Axis of Open vs. Self-contained Behaviors

The Openness Scale has four points indicating levels or degrees of Openness: #1 signifies very self-contained; #2, somewhat self-contained; #3, somewhat open; and #4, very open. As the behavioral descriptions of self-contained and open people are presented below, determine which behaviors are most like you most of the time in most situations with most people. In addition, consider a person you know who tends to be rather difficult and try to determine his level of openness. By the time you complete this chapter, you will have some significant ideas on how to improve that relationship and turn it into a more positive one.

SELF-CONTAINED BEHAVIORS. Self-contained people, those represented at the bottom of the Openness Scale, tend to display the following traits:

1. **Facial expressions and body language are not dramatic or animated.** Many very self-contained people are described as being stoic and hard to read. Statements such as "poker face" and "plays his cards close to his vest" are common descriptions of a very self-contained person.

2. **They like to keep a distance, both physically and mentally.** Physically, they actually stand farther away and sit farther away in their meetings with other people. They are much more desirous of having "their personal space." They are not touchers, do not like to be touched, and are likely to use physical barriers to separate them from other people, such as a desk or a table. They are more likely to have visitors to their offices sit on the other side of a desk or table rather than next to them. Such behavior does not mean that they do not like people; they just like their space and are not likely to open up or get close to other people unless they know them well. They also like to keep their distance *mentally*. They are more likely to remain on a formal basis, especially in business or unfamiliar social situations, keeping their feelings private and sharing them only on a "need to know" basis.

3. **They tend to focus their conversations on the issues and tasks at hand.** Self-contained people stay on the subject and are more likely to follow the agenda. When a person with whom they are talking gets off the subject, they will say things like, "Where's all of this leading?", "What's the bottom line?", "Can we summarize what has been said up to this point?", "How does this relate to your main point?"

4. **Self-contained people are more "guarded," showing less enthusiasm than the average person.** They may be enthusiastic but it doesn't show.

5. **They are objective decision-makers.** Being fact-oriented, they make most of their decisions based on evidence. They prefer to work independently and seem to be more responsive to realities, actual experiences, and facts.

6. **They are disciplined with time.** They prefer to follow an established schedule and are particular about how their time is used by others.

Classic examples of self-contained people would be Clint Eastwood, Captain Furillo on *Hill Street Blues*, and Charles Emerson Winchester III of *M*A*S*H*.

OPEN BEHAVIORS.   Open people are those represented at the top of the scale; they tend to display the following behaviors:

1. **Open people tend to be much more dramatic and animated than self-contained people.** They freely show and share their feelings and can be "read like a book." When they hear something exciting, they become very excited; when they hear something upsetting, they become visibly upset.

2. **They tend to show more enthusiasm than the average person.** You *know* how they feel because you can see it.

3. **They become close to other people both physically and mentally.** They are easy to get to know in business or unfamiliar social situations. They are more likely to shake hands in a warm, friendly manner. They are more likely to touch during communication, especially someone's arm or hand or by putting their arm around someone's shoulders. In other words, they initiate and accept physical contact.

4. **They are much more informal, wanting to get on a first name basis immediately.** Formalities make them uncomfortable.

5. **Their conversations may include many digressions.** They tend to bring up a lot of subjects and not bring many of them to closure. They are easily distracted.

6. **They tend to project more relaxation and warmth.**

7. **They are more flexible about how their time is used by others and feel cramped by schedules.** They go with the flow, not the agenda.

8. **They make most of their decisions based on inner feeling and intuition.** They are much more subjective and are more responsive to dreams and concepts.

Classic examples of open people are Muhammad Ali, Goldie Hawn, and Alan Alda.

Determining Openness From the behavioral descriptions above, determine your level of openness: Do you feel that you are very self-contained? In other words, do most of the self-contained adjectives apply to you most of the time in most situations? If so, you would choose #1 for yourself. If you feel that most of the open adjectives describe your behavior, you would choose #4. If you identify with both types of behaviors but more so with the open behaviors, you would pick #3. If you would identify with both sets of behaviors but more so with the self-contained, you would pick #2. Select a number on the scale for yourself, but be certain to choose a *whole* number, not a 1.3 or a 2.6.

Follow the same procedure for the person who tends to be difficult that we asked you to select earlier in the chapter: choose a whole number that best describes that person's behavior with you most of the time in most situations.

Directness

Directness refers to the amount of control and forcefulness a person attempts to exercise over situations and people. It also refers to how people make decisions and approach risk and change. Direct behavior can be visualized on a horizontal scale with indirect behaviors represented at the far left and direct behaviors at the far right.

Indirect〈 A   B   C   D 〉Direct   **Figure 3.2:**   The Horizontal Axis of Direct vs. Indirect Behaviors

The Directness Scale has four points, indicating degrees of directness: #1 signifies very direct; #2, somewhat indirect; #3, somewhat direct; and #4, very direct. As the behavioral descriptions of indirect and direct people are discussed, determine which behaviors are most like you. Do the same thing for that difficult person whom you considered for the Openness Scale above.

INDIRECT BEHAVIORS

1. **Indirect people approach risk, decisions, or change rather slowly or cautiously.**
2. **They tend to be rather inexpressive communicators.** They tend to be infrequent contributors to group conversations and make infrequent use of their gestures and voice intonation to emphasize points. They often make qualified statements during conversations such as "According to my sources," or "I believe so." They tend to reserve their expression of opinions and come across as being more patient and cooperative and more diplomatic and collaborative.
3. **They tend to shy away from conflict.** When they are not in agreement and the issue isn't very important, they are most likely to go along rather than argue. They tend to stand their ground only if they feel very strongly about an issue. In stress management, the classic "fight versus flight" response to tension and stress is often discussed. Most people have an immediate response to tension and stress of either "flight," trying to get away from it or avoiding it, versus "fight," confronting it and handling it immediately. Indirect people tend naturally to be flight-oriented people. They want to escape from or avoid tension, conflict, or stress.
4. **They come across in a rather understated and reserved manner.** Their initial eye contact tends to be intermittent and their handshake is gentle. At social

gatherings they are more likely to wait for others to introduce themselves rather than to initiate the introductions themselves.

5. **They tend to follow established rules and policies.** When something isn't clearly stated as to whether it can or cannot be done, they tend to ask permission before doing. They don't want to "rock the boat."
6. **They tend to be slower paced and low key.**

Classic examples of indirect people would be Mary Tyler Moore and Father Mulcahy on *M*A*S*H*.

DIRECT BEHAVIORS

1. **Direct people tend to be more forceful.** They come on stronger and they approach risk, decision, or change quickly and spontaneously.
2. **They tend to be expressive communicators.** They are frequent contributors to group conversations and often make emphatic statements such as "This is so, this is the way it is," or "Wrong!" They express their opinions readily whether others want to hear them or not.
3. **They tend to be less patient, more competitive, more confronting, more controlling.** They are more likely to maintain their position when they are not in agreement. They are obviously intense and assertive. Their initial eye contact is sustained and sometimes overwhelming. In social gatherings they are more likely to take the initiative and introduce themselves to others rather than wait for other people to take the initiative. They have a firm handshake.
4. **They tend to not be overly concerned with rules and policies.** When it comes to following the rules their attitude is, "Rules are guidelines." When something is not clearly delineated and sits in a gray area, it represents a window of opportunity for them. Their attitude is, "It's easier to beg forgiveness than seek permission."

Classic examples of a direct person would be Lee Iacocca, Bill Cosby, and James Bond.

Determination of Directness From the behavioral descriptions above, determine your level of directness. Choose a number that best describes how you come across to other people most of the time in most situations. Also choose a number for that difficult person in terms of how that individual comes across to you most of the time in most situations.

An example will illustrate how people fall into each dimension. Imagine walking into a prospect's office and finding him on the phone. He looks up and nods, but does not point you toward a seat. He makes no attempt to terminate his conversation. You seat yourself. Finally he hangs up, looks at you, says "Hello," and waits for you to begin the conversation. As you speak, he interjects specific questions and seems to ponder the answers thoughtfully. When you ask for feedback, he tells you his thoughts rather than his feelings. Instead of focusing on the overall idea you are presenting, he is more concerned with details such as costs, timetables, and so on. He lets you steer the conversation until the end when he sums up your presentation in a concise, efficient way and tells you that he will have to think about it. How would you rate this prospect in the two dimensions of openness and directness? (He is low in both.)

The levels of openness and directness vary among individuals, and any one person may be high in one, low in the other, or somewhere in between. In other words, each individual has some level of openness and some level of directness.

The Four Behavior Styles

When the Directness and Openness Scales are combined, they form four quadrants which identify different, recognizable, and habitual behavioral patterns. These four styles are the Socializer, the Director, the Thinker, and the Relater.

The Socializer   Socializers are high in both directness and openness, readily exhibiting characteristics such as animation, intuitiveness, and liveliness. But they can also be viewed as manipulative, impetuous, and excitable when displaying behavior inappropriate to the situation.

Socializers are fast-paced people with spontaneous actions and decisions. They are seldom concerned about facts and details and try to avoid them as much as practical. This disregard for details sometimes prompts them to exaggerate and generalize facts and figures. They are more comfortable with "best guesstimates" than with hard researched facts.

Socializers are idea persons and always seem to be chasing dreams. They have the ability to excite others about their dreams because of their good persuasive skills. Their emphasis is on influencing others and shaping the environment by bringing others into alliance to accomplish results. They seem always to be seeking approval and recognition for their accomplishments and achieve-

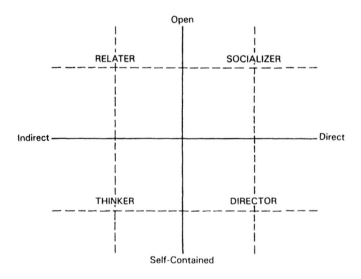

Figure 3.3: The Four Behavioral Styles and Their Positions on the Two Behavioral Scales

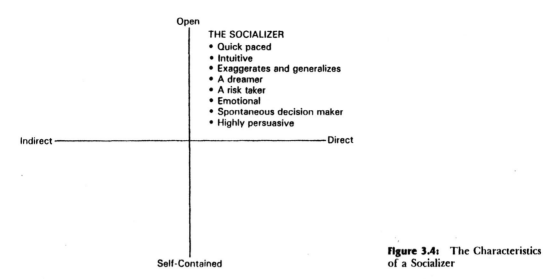

Open

THE SOCIALIZER
- Quick paced
- Intuitive
- Exaggerates and generalizes
- A dreamer
- A risk taker
- Emotional
- Spontaneous decision maker
- Highly persuasive

Indirect ———————————————————— Direct

Self-Contained

Figure 3.4: The Characteristics of a Socializer

ments. They are very creative and have that dynamic ability to think quickly on their feet.

Socializers are true entertainers. They love an audience. They thrive on involvement with people and tend to work quickly and enthusiastically with others. If they had a motto that would aptly describe their behavior, it might be, "When you're as good as we are, it's hard to be humble."

Socializers are stimulating, talkative, and gregarious. They tend to operate on intuition and be risk-takers. They are very enthusiastic and optimistic as well as emotional and friendly. They like involvement and their greatest irritations are boring tasks, being alone, and not having access to a telephone. They tend to question, "Who else uses this product?"

The primary strengths of Socializers are their enthusiasm, persuasiveness, and delightful sociability. Their primary weaknesses are their involvement in too many things, their impatience, and their short attention span.

In the business environment, they like people who are risk-takers. They tend to be alert, quick, and decisive. In a social environment they like people who are uninhibited, spontaneous, and funny.

Ideal occupations for Socializers might be public relations specialists, talk show hosts, trial attorneys, social directors on cruise ships, or even bartenders. Their ideal car would probably be a sports car or a convertible, probably in red. If Socializers had a theme song that best reflected their personality it might be "Celebration!," "Let the Good Times Roll," or "All Night Long." Some famous personalities who epitomize Socializers are Mohammad Ali, Burt Reynolds, David Addison on *Moonlighting*, and Hawkeye Pierce on *M*A*S*H*.

There are environmental clues that suggest behavioral style as well. The desks of Socializers may look disorganized and cluttered, but they know if something is missing. Their walls may contain awards, stimulating posters or notes, and motivational personal slogans. Their offices are decorated in an open, airy, friendly manner, and the seating arrangement indicates warmth, openness, contact, and activity. Because Socializers like contact, they may move to an alternate seating arrangement when talking with visitors.

To increase their flexibility, Socializers need to control their time and emotions; develop more of an objective mindset; spend more time checking, verifying, specifying, and organizing; concentrate on the task; and take a more logical approach to projects and issues.

The Director Directors are simultaneously self-contained and direct. They exhibit firmness in their relationships with others, are oriented toward productivity and goals, and are concerned with bottom line results. Closely allied to these positive traits are the negative ones of stubbornness, impatience, and toughness. Directors tend to take control of other people and situations and are decisive in both their actions and their decisions. They like to move at a fast pace and are impatient with delays. When other people cannot keep up with their speed, they view them as incompetent. The Director's motto might be: "I want it done right and I want it done now."

Directors are high achievers who exhibit very good administrative skills. They get things done and make things happen. They are like jugglers who like to do many things at the same time. They start juggling three things at once and when they feel comfortable with those three things, they pick up a fourth. They keep adding until the pressure builds to such a point that they turn their backs and let everything drop. They then immediately start the whole process over again. The theme of Directors seems to be, "Notice our accomplishments."

Because of their high achievement-motivation and their tendency toward workaholism, many doctors would say that Directors are in the high-risk category for heart attacks. Because of their impatience, a number of people believe that Directors are also prime ulcer victims. We tend to disagree with that view. We believe that they are *carriers* of ulcers; they *give* ulcers to other people!

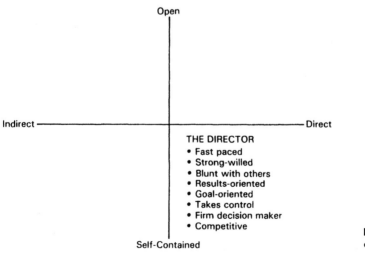

Open

Indirect ——————————————|—————— Direct

THE DIRECTOR
- Fast paced
- Strong-willed
- Blunt with others
- Results-oriented
- Goal-oriented
- Takes control
- Firm decision maker
- Competitive

Self-Contained

Figure 3.5: The Characteristics of a Director

Directors specialize in being in control. They tend to be independent, strong-willed, precise, goal-oriented, cool, and competitive. They accept challenges, take authority, and go headfirst into solving problems. They tend to exhibit great administrative and operational skills and work quickly and impressively by themselves. They tend to come on as cool, independent, and competitive with others, especially in a business environment. The emphasis of Directors is on dominance or shaping the environment by overcoming opposition to accomplish results. They prefer a maximum amount of freedom to manage themselves and others and tend to exhibit a low tolerance for the feelings, attitudes, and advice of others. They depend on their leadership skills and strive to be winners.

The primary strengths of Directors are: their ability to get things done, their leadership, and their decision-making ability. Their weaknesses, however, tend to be inflexibility, impatience, poor listening habits, and neglecting to take time to "smell the flowers."

In a business environment they like people to be decisive, efficient, receptive, and intelligent; and in a social environment they want others to be congenial, assertive, and witty. Their ideal occupation might be a newspaper reporter, stockbroker, independent consultant, drill sergeant, president/owner of a company, or dictator.

The theme song of a Director would be "My Way." Their ideal car would probably be a Mercedes, a Cadillac, or a BMW in "power colors" such as black or steel gray. Famous people who are most likely Directors in behavioral style are Lee Iacocca, Victor Kiam, Dr. Mark Craig on *St. Elsewhere,* Captain Kirk on *Star Trek,* and Maddie Hayes on *Moonlighting.*

Environmental clues of a Director personality are desks that appear busy: lots of work, projects, and material separated into piles. Their walls may contain achievement awards or a large planning sheet/calendar. Their offices are decorated to suggest power and control, and seating arrangements are closed, formal, and positioned for power. Their desks may be large to show success and to separate them from you.

To increase their flexibility, Directors need to practice active listening, pace themselves to project a more relaxed image, and develop patience, humility, and sensitivity. They need to develop a concern for others, use more caution, verbalize the reasons for their conclusions, and identify more as a team player.

The Thinker   Thinkers are both indirect and self-contained. They seem to be very concerned with the process of thinking and are persistent, systematic problem-solvers. They can also be seen as aloof, picky, and critical. Thinkers are very security-conscious and have a high need to be right, leading them to an overreliance on data collection. In their quest for data, they tend to ask many questions about specifics and their actions and decisions tend to be extremely cautious. Although they are great problem solvers, Thinkers could be better decision makers. They tend to keep collecting data even beyond the time a decision is due.

Thinkers tend to be perfectionists and to be serious, persistent, and

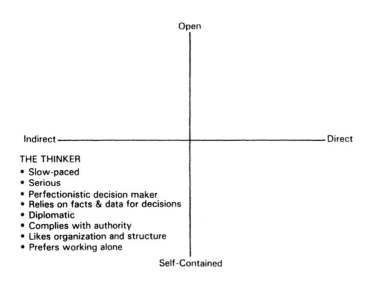

Open

Indirect ———————————————— Direct

THE THINKER
• Slow-paced
• Serious
• Perfectionistic decision maker
• Relies on facts & data for decisions
• Diplomatic
• Complies with authority
• Likes organization and structure
• Prefers working alone

Self-Contained

Figure 3.6: The Characteristics of a Thinker

orderly. They tend to focus on the details and process and are irritated by surprises and unpredictability, even when surprise and unpredictability are good. They question, "How does it work and how did you reach your conclusions?" Their theme is, "Notice my efficiency," and their emphasis is on compliance and working with existing circumstances to promote quality in products or service.

Thinkers like organization and structure and dislike too much involvement with other people. They work slowly and precisely by themselves and prefer an intellectual work environment that is organized and structured. They are time-disciplined and precise, concentrate greatly on detail, and tend to be critical of performance. They tend to be skeptical and like to see things in writing, which comes across as a "show me" attitude. They like problem-solving activities and prefer objective task-oriented, intellectual work environments and work best under controlled circumstances.

The primary strengths of Thinkers are their accuracy, dependability, independence, follow-through, and organization. Their primary weaknesses are their procrastination and conservative nature, which promote their tendency to be picky and overcautious.

The greatest irritation for Thinkers is disorganized, illogical people. In business environments, they like people to be credible, professional, and organized. In social environments, they like people who are pleasant and sincere.

Occupations that Thinkers tend to gravitate toward are accounting, engineering, computer programming, the hard sciences (chemistry, physics, math), systems analysis, and architecture. They like cars that are well-built, perform well, and are quite functional such as a Volvo or a SAAB, probably in brown, blue, or light gray colors. Famous people who would be classic examples of Thinkers are Spock from *Star Trek*, and Woody Allen.

Environmental clues of the Thinker behavioral style are desks that appear highly organized with a clear desk top. Walls may contain charts, graphs, exhibits, or pictures pertaining to the job. Their offices are decorated functionally for working with everything in its place. Seating arrangements suggest formality and noncontact.

To increase flexibility, Thinkers need to openly show concern and appreciation of others; try shortcuts and time-savers occasionally; try to adjust more readily to change and disorganization; improve timely decision-making and initiation of new projects; compromise with the opposition; state unpopular decisions; and use policies as guidelines only.

The Relater   The fourth and last style, the Relater, is open and indirect, relatively unassertive, warm, supportive, and reliable. However, relaters are sometimes seen by others as compliant, soft-hearted, and acquiescent.

Relaters seek security and, like Thinkers, are slow at taking action and making decisions. This procrastination stems from their desire to avoid risky and unknown situations. Before they take action or make a decision, they like to know how other people feel about the decisions to be made.

Relaters are the most people-oriented of all of the four styles. Having close, friendly, personal, first-name relationships with others is one of their most important objectives. They dislike interpersonal conflicts so much that they sometimes say what they think others want to hear rather than what they really think. They have strong counseling skills and are very supportive of other people. People usually feel good just by being with Relaters.

Relaters are also excellent listeners and, in turn, people listen to them when it is the Relater's turn to talk. This gives them the excellent ability to gain support from others when they need it.

The focus of Relaters is on getting acquainted and building trust. Their major irritation is pushy, aggressive behavior. Their theme is "Notice how well

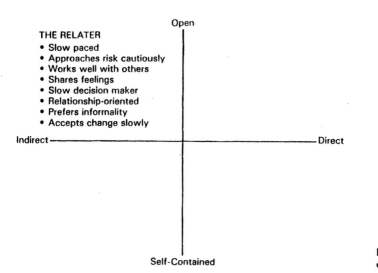

THE RELATER
- Slow paced
- Approaches risk cautiously
- Works well with others
- Shares feelings
- Slow decision maker
- Relationship-oriented
- Prefers informality
- Accepts change slowly

Figure 3.7: The Characteristics of a Relater

liked I am." They question, "How will it affect my personal circumstances and the camaraderie of the group?" They are outstanding team players and support specialists. Their emphasis is steadiness and cooperation. They work slowly and cohesively with others and "wear well."

The primary strengths of Relaters are listening to and understanding people, caring, and loving. As for their primary weaknesses, they are somewhat unassertive, overly sensitive, and easily bullied.

In the business environment, Relaters like other people to be courteous and friendly and to share responsibilities. In a social environment, they like others to be genuine and friendly. The ideal compliment a Relater could receive from another person is, "You are a fine parent or friend." The most painful criticism that they could receive is that they hurt someone else's feelings.

Relaters' ideal occupations tend to cluster around the helping professions such as counseling, teaching, social work, the clergy, nursing, parenting, and human resource development. The Relater's ideal car might be a station wagon or van (the more people, the merrier), beige in color, factory recommended tires and . . . no horn. (Relaters don't want to upset other people.) The songs that best reflect their personality might be "Feelings," "People," "Getting to Know You," or "You've Got a Friend." Famous people who would be classic Relaters are Dr. Donald Westfall on *St. Elsewhere* and Jane Pauley on *The Today Show.*

As for environmental clues, Relaters' desks may contain family pictures and other personal items. The walls contain personal slogans, family or group pictures, serene pictures or mementos. Their offices may be decorated in a relaxed, open, airy, friendly, soothing manner with seating arrangements open, informal, and conducive to building personal relationships.

To increase flexibility, Relaters need to say no occasionally; attend to the completion of tasks without oversensitivity to the feelings of others; be willing to reach beyond their comfort zone to set goals that require some stretch and risk; and to delegate tasks to others.

Is There A Best Style?

Of the four behavioral styles, there is no "best" style. Each style has its own unique strengths and weaknesses, and successful people as well as failures populate each group. All people possess traits from all four styles in varying degrees. Depending on circumstances, one style may be more dominant than any of the others on any given day. Most people, however, do have a single dominant behavioral style. Like a theme in a musical composition, one's *style* is a recurring and predictable component of behavior. But, like variations on a theme, people also possess other traits which vary from the traits of their dominant style. To be effective in sales, one must *always* be aware of the style that the other person is exhibiting during each and every contact.

Figure 3.8 summarizes the potential conflicts of pace and priority between the four behavioral styles. Problems of pace can be solved by either slowing down or speeding up for the other person. Priority problems relate to either tasks or relationships. If someone is task-oriented, don't spend time trying

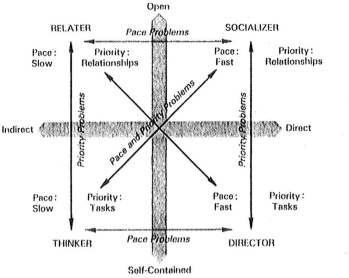

Figure 3.8: Pace and Priority Conflicts Between Behavioral Styles

to establish a friendship. The inverse is also true. For people who like to take the time to get to know you, don't rush right into the task at hand. Misreading a prospect's pace and priority often gets salespeople in trouble.

Behavioral Styles and Interpersonal Problems

Behavioral style characteristics become especially important when people of different styles meet. When that occurs and each person behaves according to the characteristics of his or her own style, negative tension often results, sounding the deathknell for the sales relationship.

Besides differences in openness and directness, the styles might differ in pace and priority preferences. Directors and Socializers are faster paced; Thinkers and Relaters are slower paced. Directors and Thinkers are more task- or objective-oriented; Relaters and Socializers are more people- and opinion-oriented. Consequently, when Relaters and Directors meet, they have *both* pace and priority problems as do Thinkers and Socializers. These pairings have a high degree of natural relationship tension. All other style pairings, other than styles of the same type, have either a pace *or* a priority problem. Such situations can also result in unproductive relationships. To avoid unproductive relationships when meeting with others, you must meet their needs, especially their behavioral style needs. In short, you must treat them in the way they want to be treated, sell them in the way they want to be sold. If they move fast, you move fast. If they like to take their time and get to know you, allow more time for the appointment. When you meet another person's behavioral style needs, a climate of mutual trust begins to form. As a trust bond develops, the other person will begin to tell you what he or she really needs. Instead of a contest, there will be a productive relationship and, hopefully, an eventual sale and long-term customer.

BEHAVIORAL STYLE IDENTIFICATION

You now have some knowledge of the four personality patterns and know how important it is to interact appropriately with a prospect's particular style. But how do you identify which of the styles your prospect respresents? And how do you do it quickly? To identify your prospect's style, you must observe what that prospect does; you must be sensitive to both verbal and nonverbal actions. Two procedures help you to quickly, accurately, and simply identify a prospect's behavioral style: 1) observe the prospect's actions, and 2) note the prospect's environment.

1. Observe the Prospect's Actions

The first method of identifying behavioral style is to observe it in action. This is the most crucial and accurate method. There is one catch, however. In order to observe someone's behavioral style, you need to observe a *range* of verbal and nonverbal behaviors. This may require you to *stimulate* more behaviors by asking questions and by "actively" listening.

Observable *open* behaviors include: animated facial expressions; considerable hand and body movement; flexible time perspective; story-telling and anecdotes; little emphasis on facts and details; sharing of personal feelings; and contact-oriented and immediate nonverbal feedback.

Observable *self-contained* behaviors include: little facial expression; controlled and limited hand and body movement; time-disciplined; focused conversation on issues and tasks at hand; facts and details required; little sharing of personal feelings; and noncontact-oriented and slow in giving nonverbal feedback, if given at all.

Observable *indirect* behaviors would be: soft handshake; intermittent eye contact; low quantity of verbal communication; questions for clarification, support, and information; tentative statements; limited gestures to support conversation; low voice volume; slow voice speed; little variation in vocal intonation; hesitant communication; and slow moving.

Observable *direct* behaviors are: firm handshake, steady eye contact; high quantity of verbal communication; more rhetorical questions asked to emphasize points or challenge information; emphatic statements made; points emphasized with gestures and challenging voice intonation; high voice volume; fast voice speed; and fast moving.

2. Note the Prospect's Environment

Notice the environment in which your prospect works. That may give you some clues to the prospect's behavioral style. How is the office decorated and arranged? What is on the desk, walls, and bookshelves? What is the seating arrangement between you and your prospect? For instance, if you entered a prospect's office and noticed family pictures on the desk and walls, nature post-

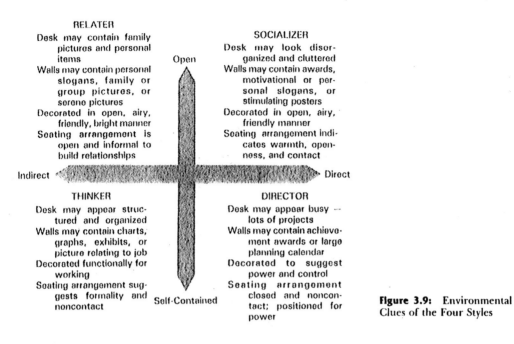

Figure 3.9: Environmental Clues of the Four Styles

ers with a personal relationship motif, a round desk, and a separate seating area with a couch and two side chairs, what would be your first impression of the prospect's behavioral style? By comparing these environmental clues against those discussed earlier, you have a fairly good initial indication that you are dealing with a Relater.

Such environmental indicators, however, are only *one* kind of clue to behavioral style. Do *not* use them as the sole determinant. Your client may have little control over the environment you see or may have changed the environment in order to meet other needs (e.g., an intense workload; a headstrong interior decorator, boss, or spouse; budgetary constraints; etc.).

Identification Process

To identify the behavioral style using the Openness–Directness Scales while on an appointment, first mentally locate the prospect's position on the Openness Scale, then determine the degree of Directness demonstrated. The result is a placement of the prospect into one of the four behavioral style quadrants through a simple process of elimination. For instance, if you determine that your prospect is exhibiting open behavior, you are automatically eliminating the styles with self-contained behavior: Director and Thinker. Likewise, if you determine that your prospect is also high in directness, you automatically eliminate the indirect styles: Relater and Thinker. Therefore, by the process of elimination, you are left with the Socializer style for your prospect.

The following examples from a seminar one of the authors conducted demonstrate that salespeople reflect as wide a divergence of styles as any other segment of the population. Try to identify these styles:

> The seminar was to begin at 8:30 A.M. following an 8:00 coffee and doughnut session. When I arrived at 7:45 A.M., a participant was already in the room, pad and pencils neatly laid out in front of him where he sat at the table. He said nothing until I approached, and we politely shook hands. He was totally non-committal. I asked a few questions for which I received polite, to-the-point answers.
>
> Around 8:15, with several other people in the room, a person stopped hesitantly at the door and softly asked, "Excuse me, am I at the training seminar for salespeople?" On being told, "Yes," the person breathed a sigh, walked in, and took a cup of coffee while stating how interesting the seminar would be for both business and home. He asked a few questions, listening intently to my remarks, and expressed some concern about role-playing in front of a group.
>
> At this moment, another participant strode in, loudly asking, "Hey, is this the sales seminar?" On hearing Yes, this person dramatized a faked sense of relief and started asking where the coffee was, explaining that she couldn't function without her "black poison." She had overheard our role-playing comments and leaped in on the conversation to say how she liked doing those things. She followed this with a tale of how she overwhelmed everyone in the last role-play situation in which she participated.

What would you call the styles of each of the persons described?

The first participant is clearly self-contained which indicated that he is either a Thinker or a Director. His low quantity of conversation and restrained gestures placed him as indirect; therefore, a Thinker.

The second participant volunteered information about personal feelings and gave rapid feedback in the form of a sigh and by his comments. These are open characteristics (Relater or Socializer). The soft voice, questioning for clarification, and hesitance all suggest indirectness, thus this person demonstrates a Relater style.

The third participant is high in openness, telling stories and responding quickly. Her directness is also on the high side—speed in responding, fast movements, high quantity of conversation, which are Socializer traits.

By checking the prospect's environment and observing and labeling his or her behavioral style, you can identify your prospect's style. For an example, if you have identified your prospect as a Director, you need to develop trust. You cannot expect the prospect to adapt to you. *You* therefore must adapt your selling style to your prospect's buying style which requires *behavioral flexibility*.

BEHAVIORAL FLEXIBILITY

Behavioral flexibility refers to your own actions, not those of others. It occurs when you step out of your own comfort zone, your own style preferences, to meet another's needs. It occurs each time you slow your pace somewhat for a Relater or a Thinker, or when you quicken your pace for a Director or Socializer.

It occurs when a Director or Thinker takes time to listen to a human interest or family story from a Relater or Socializer.

Behavioral flexibility is independent from behavioral style, and it varies greatly within styles. No one style is naturally more flexible than another. You can choose to be flexible with some people and inflexible with others. You can choose to be flexible with one person today and inflexible with that same person tomorrow. It is an individual decision to *manage* your own style in order to meet a prospect's style needs and reduce the possibility of that prospect experiencing negative tension.

Practicing behavioral flexibility means modifying your own style preferences when they differ from the preferences of your prospect. It isn't difficult to bite your tongue and refrain from telling the prospect about the latest news story if the prospect is a Thinker or Director who wants to get right down to business. Nor is it all that insufferable to hear about the Socializer's family vacation for awhile before getting down to business.

Before considering some specific guidelines on being flexible with each of the four behavioral types, let's look at some ways that you can modify both your openness and directness in general.

For Increasing Openness

Share your feelings; let your emotions show.

Respond to the expression of other's feelings.

Pay personal compliments.

Take time to develop the relationship.

Use friendly language.

Communicate nonverbally; loosen up.

Use a few more easy gestures like leaning back, smiling, or uncrossing your arms.

Be willing to leave the agenda to go more with the flow.

For Decreasing Openness

Get right to the task, the bottom line, the business at hand.

Maintain more of a logical, factual orientation.

Keep to the agenda.

Leave when the work is done; do not waste the other person's time.

Do not initiate physical contact.

Downplay your enthusiasm and body movement.

Use businesslike language.

Make more objective decisions.

For Increasing Directness

Speak and move faster.

Initiate conversation.

Initiate decisions.

Give recommendations rather than asking for opinions.

Use direct statements rather than circuitous questions.

Communicate with more intensity.

Take risks.

Act on your judgments.

Challenge and disagree when appropriate.

Face conflict openly.

Increase the frequency and intensity of eye contact.

For Decreasing Directness

Talk, walk, and decide less quickly.

Seek and acknowledge the opinions of others.

Share the decision-making responsibilities with others.

Allow others to assume some of the leadership.

Show less energy.

Do not interrupt.

When talking, provide pauses to give others a chance to speak.

Refrain from criticizing or challenging.

When disagreeing, choose words carefully and state opinions moderately.

Engage in participative decision making.

Do not push.

Use less intense and less frequent eye contact.

Guidelines for Implementing Flexibility

The following are guidelines in implementing flexibility with the four behavioral styles:

Sales Flexibility with Socializers   Because the Socializer likes to interact with other people, try not to hurry the discussion. Attempt to develop some mutually stimulating ideas *together*. Focus your conversation on opinions, ideas, and dreams, and then support them. Try to move the conversation at a pace that is both entertaining and stimulating. If, during the conversation, you come to some point on which you are not in agreement, try not to argue. You cannot win an argument with a Socializer. Remember that the Socializer deals in opinions and intuitions. Instead of arguing, try to explore alternative solutions you both can share with enthusiasm.

When you finally reach an agreement with a Socializer, iron out the specific details: what, when, who, where, and how. Make absolutely sure that you both agree on these specifics. Summarize in writing what you both agreed on, even though it may not appear necessary.

Keep in mind that Socializers want to enjoy and be entertained. They like presentations that are lively, stimulating, and fun. They like stories of triumph and disaster and prefer visuals and surprises. They like new ideas and thoughts and like to know creative, inventive solutions. They prefer to learn through examples and comparisons and like to see the big picture and not get bogged down in details. Make sure that you illustrate your ideas and concepts and point out the future prospects of any solution you propose. Their decisions are positively influenced by incentives and testimonials.

WHEN SELLING TO SOCIALIZERS

1. **Plan** to be stimulating and interested in them. Allow them time to talk.
2. **Meet** them boldly; don't be shy. Introduce yourself first. Bring up new topics openly.
3. **Study** their dreams and goals as well as their other needs.
4. **Propose** your solution with stories or illustrations that relate to them and their goals.
5. **Confirm** the details in writing. Be clear and precise.
6. **Assure** that they fully understand what they bought and can demonstrate their ability to use it properly.

Sales Flexibility with Directors   Directors are easy to deal with as long as you are precise, efficient, competent, time-disciplined, and well-organized. Make sure you keep the relationship businesslike. Do not attempt to establish a personal relationship unless that is one of the Director's objectives. Focus your conversation around the Director's goals. Remember that the Director is the most goal-oriented, achievement-oriented, and task-oriented of any of the four behavioral styles. If, during the conversation, you must take issue with the Director, argue the facts, not personal feelings. Make sure that you can back up your facts with solid, tangible proof. You should provide the Director with options. Directors like to make their own decisions.

Be sure to present the "meat" of the issue. Show the expected benefits and results now of any proposal you suggest to a Director. Make sure that the presentation is brief, clear, concise, and filled with facts and specifics. Any plan that you present should be logical and detailed and any humor should be pointed and relevant. Show the return on investment of any suggestion that you make. It is acceptable to use assertive, powerful gestures in a rapid, no-nonsense, delivery.

WHEN SELLING TO DIRECTORS

1. **Plan** to be prepared and organized, fast-paced, and to the point.
2. **Meet** them in such a way that you get to the point quickly. Keep things professional and businesslike.
3. **Study** their goals and objectives: what they want to accomplish; what is happening now; and how they would like to see things changed.
4. **Propose** solutions with clearly defined consequences and rewards that relate specifically to the Director's goals.
5. **Confirm** by providing two to three options with supporting analysis and let them make the decision.

6. **Assure** them that their time will not be wasted. After the sale, confirm that the proposals that you suggested did, in fact, provide the bottom line results that they expected.

Sales Flexibility with Thinkers   Try to be systematic, exact, organized, and prepared with Thinkers. Any contributions that you can make toward the Thinker's objectives should be demonstrated through actions rather than words. Thinkers may require that you send them solid, tangible, factual evidence that what you say is true and accurate. List the advantages and disadvantages of any plan that you propose to the Thinker and have viable alternatives for dealing effectively with the disadvantages. If you do not bring up the *obvious* disadvantages in your product or plan, the Thinker will certainly find them and will then believe that you are hiding things, thus ending the sales relationship. Try not to rush the decision-making process with Thinkers because they need time to verify your words and your actions. Above all else, be correct in your dealing with Thinkers. They demand it.

Thinkers want to learn, so present straight, pointed data backed up by solid tangible proof, substantiated facts, and evidence. Thinkers like an accurate, complete account of whatever it is you are selling. Make sure that you point out the pluses and minuses of the issue. You must build credibility before building rapport with Thinkers. They like presentations that are less dramatic, but more purposeful. In other words, give your presentation with a direct, straightforward, organized, logical delivery with slow deliberate gestures. They do not appreciate an overenthusiastic, "rah-rah" presentation that is wrought with hyperboles and exaggerations.

WHEN SELLING TO THINKERS

1. **Plan** to be well-prepared and equipped to answer all questions.
2. **Meet** them cordially but get quickly to the task at hand.
3. **Study** their situation in a practical, logical manner. Ask lots of questions and make sure that your questions show a clear direction. The better your questions fit into the overall scheme of things, the more likely that relevant answers will be received.
4. **Propose** logical solutions. Document the how and why; show how your proposal is the logical thing to do.
5. **Confirm** as a matter of course. Don't push; give them time to think. Offer documentation.
6. **Assure** them through adequate service and follow-through. Be complete and on time.

Sales Flexibility with Relaters   Try to support the Relaters' feelings and project your interest in them as individuals. Move along in an informal, slow manner, and constantly show the Relater that you are actively listening. If you must disagree, do not debate facts and logic. Discuss personal opinions and feelings. If you quickly establish an objective and come to a fast decision with a Relater, try to explore potential areas for future misunderstanding or dissatisfaction. Relaters like guarantees that any *new* actions will involve a minimum

YOUR STYLE

THEIR STYLE	RELATER	THINKER	DIRECTOR	SOCIALIZER
RELATER	• No change in openness or directness • Limit time spent in personal talk • Be responsible for initiating action • Establish deadlines/schedules	• Directness: no change • Openness: increase	• Directness: decrease • Openness: increase	• Directness: decrease • Openness: no change
	• General Strategies: support their feelings; show personal interest; accurately spell out objectives; when you disagree, discuss personal opinions and feelings; move along in an informal, slow manner; show that you are "actively" listening; provide guarantees that actions or decisions will involve a minimum of risk; offer personal assurances that you stand behind decisions. • To Motivate: show them how it will strengthen their position with others.			
THINKER	• Directness: no change • Openness: decrease	• No change in openness/directness • Take control of direction of process, let customer control decisions/destiny • Accept less than perfection	• Directness: decrease • Openness: no change	• Directness: decrease • Openness: decrease
	• General Strategies: support their organized, thoughtful approach; demonstrate through actions rather than words; give time to verify your words and actions; follow up personal contacts with a letter; provide solid, tangible, factual evidence that what you say is accurate; be systematic, exact, organized and prepared; list advantages and disadvantages of proposed plan. • To Motivate: appeal to their need to be accurate and logical; provide guarantees that actions can't backfire; avoid gimmicks.			
DIRECTOR	• Directness: increase • Openness: decrease	• Directness: increase • Openness: no change	• No change in openness/directness • Remain receptive; don't impose your view • Let customer feel in control	• Directness: no change • Openness: decrease
	• General Strategies: support their goals, objectives; keep your relationship businesslike; if you disagree, argue facts, not personal feelings; give recognition to ideas, not the person; be precise, efficient, well organized; to influence decisions, provide alternatives and probabilities of their success. • To Motivate: provide options; clearly describe probabilities of success in achieving Director's goals.			
SOCIALIZER	• Directness: increase • Openness: no change	• Directness: increase • Openness: increase	• Directness: no change • Openness: increase	• No change in openness/directness • Exercise discipline — establish agenda • Structure relationship by: note-taking, verification, follow-up • Summarize agreements in writing
	• General Strategies: support their ideas, dreams; don't hurry the discussion; nail down details verbally or in writing; be entertaining and fast-moving; use testimonials to positively affect decisions. • To Motivate: offer them incentives and testimonials.			

Figure 3.10: Behavioral Flexibility Chart

51

risk. Therefore, offer personal assurances and support. Try not to rush the Relater, but do provide guidance. Try to project genuine sincerity and concern in your relationship.

Relaters want to get acquainted. Therefore, make sure that you open your visit in a slow, friendly manner and with open, inviting gestures. Speak in a conversational tone. Discuss feelings and opinions and utilize frequent, friendly eye contact. Try to discuss the human side of issues and allow them to see the warm, personal side of you. Relaters buy from people that they trust and believe. It is critical that you develop that relationship with Relaters before you try to sell them anything. Take time in information-gathering with Relaters to get them to accurately spell out their needs and goals. Remember, in order not to rock the boat they may tell you what they think that you want to hear rather than what they really feel. Do not push or rush Relaters, but be assumptive and leading with them when it comes to making decisions because they need that gentle friendly push, especially from someone that they really trust.

WHEN SELLING TO RELATERS

1. **Plan** to get to know them personally. Be likeable and nonthreatening, professional but friendly.
2. **Meet** them by developing trust, friendship, and credibility at a more relaxed pace.
3. **Study** their feelings and their emotional and business needs. (Take time to encourage them to spell out what is really important to them.)
4. **Propose** by getting them involved. Show how your proposals affect them and their relationships with others.
5. **Confirm** without pushing or rushing. Provide personal assurances and guarantees wherever you can.
6. **Assure** by being consistent and regular in your communication. Give them the nurturing and reassurance that you would give those who are highly concerned about the purchase that they have just made.

IN CONCLUSION . . .

Your understanding of behavioral styles will provide you with the insight necessary to creatively handle *any* prospect that you encounter. Your skills will defuse the "personality bomb" inherent in some relationships and lead the way to a peaceful collaboration. The only way that this will come about is if *you* make it happen, if you go out of your way to be flexible by adjusting your selling style to fit your prospect's buying style. Less tension and more sales will be the rewarding results.

SUMMARY

Developing an understanding of the important concept of relationship strategies—the identification of behavioral styles and the practice of behavioral flexibility—was the thrust of this chapter. Our ability as consultative salespeople to develop a comfortable rapport with our prospects and customers is crucial to our success in sales, for the first thing that we must sell before anything else is ourselves.

We can create comfortable rapport rather than conflict by practicing the *spirit* of the Golden Rule: "Treat people the way that they want to be treated," or, for our purposes in this chapter, "Sell people the way that they like to be sold."

The basis of practicing this rule is an understanding of the four basic behavioral styles (personality patterns): the Relater, the Socializer, the Director, and the Thinker. When people act and react in social situations, they exhibit behaviors which help to define their behavioral styles. The behavioral styles are identified by watching for observable aspects of people's behavior—the verbal, vocal, and visual actions that people display when others are present. These observable aspects of behavior can be classified on two dimensions: openness and directness.

Openness is the ease with which a person shows emotions and is accessible to others. It also encompasses the person's readiness to develop new relationships. This dimension can be illustrated by a vertical scale with the top representing very open behaviors and the bottom representing very closed behaviors. There are four degrees or levels on the Openness Scale: #1 represents very self-contained; #2, somewhat self-contained; #3, somewhat open; and #4, very open.

Self-contained behaviors include: facial expressions and body language that are not dramatic or animated; a preference for keeping both a physical and mental distance from others; a focus in conversation on the issues and tasks at hand; a guarded manner, showing less enthusiasm than the average person; a very disciplined use of time; and objective decision making.

Open behaviors include: facial expressions and body language which are dramatic and animated; a preference to be close to people both physically and mentally; a very open manner, showing more enthusiasm than the average person; a preference for an informal, relaxed attitude; conversations which include many digressions; considerable time flexibility; and decision making based on intuition.

The second dimension is directness, which refers to the amount of control and forcefulness a person attempts to exercise over other people—their thoughts and their emotions—and over situations. It also refers to how people make decisions and approach risk and change. Directness can be illustrated by a horizontal scale with very indirect behaviors represented at the far left and very direct behaviors represented at the far right. There are four degrees or levels on this scale: #1 represents very indirect; #2, somewhat indirect; #3, somewhat direct; and #4, very direct.

Indirect behaviors include: a slow, cautious approach to risk, decisions, and change; infrequent use of gestures and intonation in verbal communication; a preference for avoiding conflict, tension, and stress; an understated, reserved manner; a preference for following established rules and policies; and a tendency to be slow paced and low key.

	RELATER	*THINKER*	*DIRECTOR*	*SOCIALIZER*
BEHAVIOR PATTERN	Open/Indirect	Self-contained/ Indirect	Self-contained/ Direct	Open/Direct
PERFORMAX EQUIVALENT*	Steadiness	Compliance	Dominance	Influencing of others
APPEARANCE	• Casual • Conforming	• Formal • Conservative	• Businesslike • Functional	• Fashionable • Stylish
WORK-SPACE	• Personal • Relaxed • Friendly • Informal	• Structured • Organized • Functional • Formal	• Busy • Formal • Efficient • Structured	• Stimulating • Personal • Cluttered • Friendly
PACE	Slow/Easy	Slow/Systematic	Fast/Decisive	Fast/Spontaneous
PRIORITY	Maintaining relationships	The Task: the process	The Task: the results	Relationships: interacting
FEARS	Confrontation	Embarrassment	Loss of control	Loss of prestige
UNDER TENSION WILL	Submit/Acquiesce	Withdraw/ Avoid	Dictate/Assert	Attack/Be sarcastic
SEEKS	Attention	Accuracy	Productivity	Recognition
NEEDS TO KNOW (BENEFITS)	• How it will affect their personal circumstances	• How they justify the purchase logically • How it works	• What it does • By when • What it costs	• How it enhances their status • Who else uses it
GAINS SECURITY BY	Close relationships	Preparation	Control	Flexibility
WANTS TO MAINTAIN	Relationships	Credibility	Success	Status
SUPPORT THEIR	Feelings	Thoughts	Goals	Ideas
ACHIEVES ACCEPTANCE BY	• Conformity • Loyalty	• Correctness • Thoroughness	• Leadership • Competition	• Playfulness • Stimulating environment

Figure 3.11: Behavioral Styles Summary

Figure 3.11 (cont.)

	RELATER	THINKER	DIRECTOR	SOCIALIZER
LIKES YOU TO BE	Pleasant	Precise	To the point	Stimulating
WANTS TO BE	Liked	Correct	In charge	Admired
IRRITATED BY	• Insensitivity • Impatience	• Surprises • Unpredictabil-lty	• Inefficiency • Indecision	• Boredom • Routine
MEASURES PERSONAL WORTH BY	• Compatibility with others • Depth of relationships	• Precision • Accuracy • Activity	• Results • Track record • Measurable progress	• Acknowledgment • Recognition • Applause • Compliments
DECISIONS ARE	Considered	Deliberate	Decisive	Spontaneous

*There are several other models of behavioral style. Performax is the most widely known.

Direct behaviors include: forcefulness; frequent use of gestures and intonation for emphasis in verbal communication; a tendency to be less patient, more competitive, more controlling, and more confronting; and a tendency to use rules and policies as guidelines rather than as strict requirements.

When the two scales are combined, they form four quadrants which identify different, recognizable, and habitual behavioral patterns: the Relater (upper left), the Socializer (upper right), the Director (lower right), and the Thinker (lower left). The Relater behavioral style is open and indirect while the Socializer is both direct and open. The Director behavioral style is self-contained and direct, while the Thinker is self-contained and indirect.

These behavioral style characteristics become especially important when people of different styles meet. When that occurs and each person behaves according to the characteristics of his own style, negative tension often results, sounding the deathknell for the sales relationship.

Besides differences in openness and directness, the styles might differ in pace and priority preferences. Directors and Socializers are faster paced; Thinkers and Relaters are slower paced. Directors and Thinkers are more task- and objective-oriented; Relaters and Socializers are more people- and opinion-oriented. Consequently, when Relaters and Directors meet, they have both pace and priority problems as do Thinkers and Socializers. These pairings have a high degree of natural relationship tension. All other style pairings, other than styles of the same type, have either a pace or a priority problem. Such situations can result in unproductive relationships.

To avoid unproductive relationships, you must adjust to the needs of each person (each behavioral style) you meet. Doing so encourages mutual trust. As the trust bond develops, so does a productive business relationship.

To identify a prospect's behavioral style, there are two procedures to follow: 1) observe the prospect's actions, and 2) note the prospect's environment. Environmental clues can give some indication of an individual's placement on the quadrant, but they should not be used exclusively to determine a person's style. The more crucial and accurate method is observing a person's actions, both verbal and nonverbal.

When on an appointment, you should first mentally locate the prospect on the Openness Scale, then mentally determine the degree of directness demonstrated. The result is a placement of the prospect into one of the four behavioral style quadrants through a simple process of elimination.

When a prospect's style has been determined, behavioral flexibility comes into play. Behavioral flexibility refers to your own actions, not those of the prospect. It occurs when you step out of your own comfort zone, your own style preferences, to meet the prospect's behavioral needs.

Behavioral flexibility is independent from behavioral style. It is an individual decision on your part to manage your own style in order to meet the style needs of your prospect and reduce the possibility of that prospect experiencing negative tension. Practicing behavioral flexibility means modifying your own style preferences, your own degrees of openness and directness, when they differ from the preferences of your prospect.

Your understanding of behavioral styles provides you with the insight necessary to creatively handle any prospect that you encounter. Skills in relationship strategies—identifying behavioral styles and practicing behavioral flexibility—will defuse any personality bomb inherent in some relationships and lead the way to a peaceful collaboration. The rewarding results of developing these skills will be less tension and more sales.

DISCUSSION QUESTIONS

1. What is the advantage of being able to "read" people?
2. Name and describe the two scales that determine behavioral style.
3. Name the four behavioral styles created by the two scales you named in Question 2 and list three characteristics of each.
4. How would you greet someone who is self-contained? How would you greet someone who is open?
5. Identify your own behavioral style.
6. What are the two procedures that enable you to quickly size up another person's behavioral style?
7. Identify the behavioral styles of your friends and family.
8. How can you change your behavior to make it more compatible with those friends or family members who are different from you?

CHAPTER FOUR

The Image of Excellence

CHAPTER OBJECTIVES	**1** Introduce the concept of the image of excellence.
	2 Discuss the twelve characteristics of excellence for which the top 5 percent of salespeople receive high scores.

In the first chapter, we touched on some of the images that come to mind when we think of the word "salesperson." Now shift your perspective. Assume business associates are talking about you as a salesperson. What words would you want them to use to describe you when you are at your best?

Many students and professional salespeople would like to be described with words such as these:

Thorough	Friendly	Competent
Professional	Prepared	Cool and calm
Confident	Self-assured	Sincere
Knowledgeable	Polite	Well-groomed
Honest	Creative	Caring

Interestingly, their lists almost always match the list describing a non-manipulative salesperson. In answering the question, "What is a non-manipulative salesperson?" we can safely say it is one who lives the words appearing in the list above.

When we developed the concept of Non-Manipulative Selling, we wanted to know what factors distinguish the excellent salespeople from the mediocre. A large number of people were asked, "Of all the salespeople that you have met, from the door-to-door peddlers of magazines and vacuum cleaners to the shirt salesperson at the local department store to the multimillion dollar mainframe computer salesperson, what percent of those salespeople would you classify as 'professional'?" The most typical response received was "less than 5 percent." It is that 5 percent that we then classified as the *Excellents;* the remaining 95 percent we classified as the *Mediocres.*

What are the differences between the Excellents and the Mediocres? For what characteristics do the Excellents receive high scores and the Mediocres receive low scores? And, of all of those characteristics, which can we choose to learn and practice?

A recent study shows that men who are more than six feet tall tend to be more financially successful than men less than six feet tall. Unfortunately, this knowledge gives no advantage to those under six feet tall, no matter how hard they may try. Therefore, the characteristics that are to be determined must be those over which the practitioner has control; those he can choose to learn, practice, and possess. Twelve specific skill characteristics have been identified that people of excellence share in common, but in which people of mediocre talents are weak, or, in fact, which they lack altogether.

People keep score on other people. Every time a person enters a new environment, the people of that new environment are evaluating him, giving him a score on various characteristics which they consider important. For an example, consider a social situation: a young man and a young woman sitting in a bar. Their eyes meet, they smile. He gets up and walks toward her. Halfway there, their eyes meet again, they smile again. What does she know? She knows that he is on his way over and she starts to size him up. She looks at the way he is dressed, his walk, his style, his physical appearance. Each of these factors wins or loses points.

When he arrives, he begins to speak. The sound of his voice wins or loses points. Soon is it not the sound of his voice, but what he is saying that wins or loses points: does he sound educated? intelligent? sophisticated? sincere?

At some point he asks for a minor commitment: "Can I buy you a drink?" At that point, what does she do? She hits the total button on her imaginary calculator and evalutes his score. On her personal rating scale, if he gets 60 points or less, her answer would be a definite no! If he scores 120 points or more, the answer would be an automatic yes!

In selling, an imaginary score of 120 points or more based on the twelve characteristics of excellence is called an automatic. You have done so well the customer would tug at your sleeve and ask, "Can I buy now?" For scores between 60 and 120 points, the customer would say, in essence, "Sell me. Don't go away, I need more information." And for 60 points or less, the customer probably would say, "I don't want to buy from you." At that point the answer would be a final no and mark the end of the conversation.

EVERYTHING counts in the customer's scoring process. In his book, *Dress for Success,* John Molloy writes that one should always carry a gold pen. How important can that be? you may ask. How many points can a pen be worth? Maybe 2 points. When do 2 points matter? They matter when you are winning by only 1 point! If a person has 150 points, it doesn't matter. If that person loses 2 points, she still has the sale. If she has 35 points, the pen doesn't matter because she can pick up 2 points and she still will not have the sale. But, what if (those magic words!) she had 121 points, an automatic sale, and the customer were ready to buy. She then pushes the contract across the table and pulls out her plastic pen. The pen has "Joe's Service Center" printed on the side; there is a little grease stuck in one end of it and the other end is a bit chewed. She may lose only 2 points, BUT she drops from 121 points to 119 points; from an automatic sale she has slipped down to the customer saying, "Gee, Susan, I like everything you've said to me, this is what we want to buy, but . . . but. . . ." A small detail tarnished her image.

Is it worth carrying a gold pen? Of course! The Point? EVERYTHING counts—every little image, every impression. In fact, it is usually not the big things, but the *little* things, that defeat our efforts.

There are things in life that we can control and there are things in life that we cannot control. Unfortunately, most people spend too much of their time, effort, and energy trying to deal with those things over which they have absolutely no control. If we exert all of our efforts in that way, we lose control over the things that we *can* control.

On the other hand, if we were to put our energy into the things that we *can* control, those things become managed, they improve, they become productive. As for things which we cannot control, those things may resolve themselves and they may not, but it doesn't matter because we had no control over them in the first place.

As a salesperson, would you have control over:

1. The economy? *No.*
2. Your competitors' prices? *No.*
3. Your competitors' quality? *No.*
4. The way you look when you dress in the morning? *Absolutely!*

THE CHARACTERISTICS OF EXCELLENCE

The importance of the twelve characteristics of excellence is not only that they are learnable and practicable, but they are also characteristics over which you have complete control. Every point that you earn from the customer in these twelve areas is a point that your product or service does not need in price, presentation, or competitiveness. It is, therefore, very important for you to win all the points possible in the areas over which you have 100 percent control.

The twelve characteristics of excellence are:

1. First impression
2. Depth of knowledge
3. Breadth of knowledge
4. Flexibility
5. Sensitivity
6. Enthusiasm

7. Self-esteem
8. Extended focus
9. Sense of humor
10. Creativity
11. Willingness to take risk
12. Sense of honesty and ethics

Let's now examine each of these characteristics to determine how to best achieve the Image of Excellence.

1. First Impression

First impression is the first characteristic for which people of excellence receive high scores and the mediocres receive low scores. When meeting someone, we can't help but form a first impression. We note them physically and also pick up subtle clues intuitively. We unconsciously gather information about them in order to answer the question, "What is this person like?"

When meeting someone for the first time, the first few moments can often make or break the sales call. Creating a favorable impression increases the possibility that your ideas or products will be accepted. An unfavorable impression, however, can thwart your efforts to even give things away!

Dress and Appearance   Many things make up a first impression, the first of which is the obvious: one's dress and appearance. There are many books on the market today on how to dress like a professional, depending on *what* your business is, *what* you are selling, *how* you are selling it, *to whom* you sell it, and *when* you are selling it.

The questions to ask yourself are: "How do I look? Do I think about my impression?" If you are selling in a professional environment, there are some standard rules: 100 percent wool suits (not sport jackets, but *suits*) and no dressing in only shirtsleeves. Other considerations are white and/or light blue shirt, tie, lace-up shoes, more conservative tones with darker colors and patterns such as pinstripes or very subtle plaids. A corresponding conservative type of business attire applies to women professionals as well.

There will be times when you can use your clothes to help build the rapport with your client. Table 4.1 offers guidelines for colors and styles of your clothes. You can take guidelines one step further by applying them to the behavioral style of your client. For example, if your client were a Relater who dresses very conservatively, you would make him feel better by dressing less expensively and by adjusting the colors you wear. A brown suit gives a friendly, down-to-earth impression. If you can, avoid the power colors of gray, dark blue, or black when meeting with Relaters. Of course, the opposite is true for meeting Directors and Socializers. For them, you should dress for power and prestige.

Many people are confused by the constant evolution of styles, especially when it comes to matching colors and patterns in their clothes. For men, it is

Table 4.1 Creating the Proper Image Through Suit Colors and Styles*

	Lt. Blue Solid	Med. Blue Solid	Dark Blue Solid	Med Blue Pinstripe	Dark Blue Pinstripe	Lt. Gray Solid	Med. Gray Solid	Dark Gray Solid	Med. Gray Pinstripe	Dark Gray Pinstripe	Dark Brown
To Appeal To Upper Middle Class	✓	✓	✓	✓	✓	✓	✓	✓	✓	✓	×
To Appeal To Lower Middle Class	✓	✓	✓	×	×	✓	×	×	×	×	—
For The Large Man Or Woman	✓	✓	×	—	×	✓	✓	✓	×	—	×
For The Small Man Or Woman	×	✓	×	×	✓	×	—	×	✓	—	×
For The Heavy Man Or Woman	×	—	✓	—	✓	×	×	✓	—	✓	✓
For The Thin Man Or Woman	✓	—	—	×	×	✓	—	—	—	×	×
Too Strong In Authority	✓	✓	×	×	×	✓	✓	×	×	×	×
Too Weak In Authority	×	✓	✓	✓	✓	×	—	✓	✓	✓	×
In Front Of The Public (Not On TV)	×	—	✓	—	✓	×	—	✓	—	✓	×
On TV	✓	✓	✓	×	×	✓	—	✓	×	×	×

Legend: ✓ - positive   — - neutral   × - negative

*Condensed from *Dress For Success* by John T. Molloy (New York: Warner Books, 1975), pp. 52–54.

important to select the right shirt, tie, and suit combination. For women, the suit, blouse, and scarf must complement each other. Table 4.2 summarizes the accepted and time-proven combinations that should be adhered to when dressing for business.

Depending on your product there may be environments where you can wear short sleeves or a sport jacket. There are even some products where you might wear coveralls as a salesperson. The important considerations are that your attire be appropriate for the environment in which you will find yourself and that your appearance always be clean, well-pressed, and neat. The big questions to keep in mind are: Do you think about your appearance? Do you work it through? Does your attire fit the circumstances in which you will be conducting your business? Does your appearance reinforce the impression that you want the prospect to have of you? To help you answer these questions, see Table 4.3. This checklist will help you make the best possible first impression with your clothes and accessories.

Other facets of first impression are:

Silent Messages   Body language, the popular term used to denote the silent messages that your body gives to people, is an important facet of your first impression. We all convey unconscious messages and give away our true feelings through the position and movement of our bodies. These unconscious messages disclose to the other person our attitudes and emotions; they indicate if we are nervous, distracted, open, relaxed, sincere, defensive, interested, phoney, bored, receptive, or distant.

It is therefore important for you to be as aware of your own body language as you are of your customer's. As you study body language and observe what people do with their bodies in different situations, you will notice that people sometimes project one message while their bodies and voices project another.

Eye Contact   Eye contact is another major characteristic of the first impression. Interestingly enough, what is considered *good* eye contact is culturally rather than universally defined. In our American culture, good eye contact is called the *glance away*. Americans don't like others to stare at them. If a salesperson locks eyes with a prospect, stares him right in the eye, never blinks, and never looks away, the prospect will begin to feel very uncomfortable. For Americans, it is best when with prospects and customers to let your eyes drift away from them occasionally. Doing so relieves the tension that can result from locked eye contact.

Posture   How do you walk? Do you stand tall, with shoulders back, stomach in? Do you stand straight or do you lean against your presentation material?

Handshake   Is your handshake a good one, that is, strong and firm but not overwhelming? The question is often asked, "When does one shake hands

Table 4.2 Appropriate Combinations of Suits, Shirts/Blouses and Ties/Scarves*

Shirts and Ties	Blue	Gray	Beige	Suits Pinstripe	Traditional Plaid	More Discernible Plaid
White Shirt/Blouse and Patterned Tie/Scarf	✓	✓	✓	✓	✓	×
White Shirt/Blouse and Solid Tie/Scarf	✓	✓	✓	✓	✓	✓
Blue Shirt/Blouse and Solid Tie/Scarf	✓	✓	✓	✓	✓	✓
Blue Shirt/Blouse and Patterned Tie/Scarf	✓	✓	✓	✓	✓	×
Other Pastel Solid Shirts/Blouses and Solid Ties/Scarves	✓	✓	✓	×	✓	✓
Other Pastel Solid Shirts/Blouses and Patterned Ties/Scarves	✓	✓	✓	×	✓	×
Patterned Shirt/Blouse and Solid Tie/Scarf	✓	✓	✓	✓	×	×
Patterned Shirt/Blouse and Patterned Tie/Scarf	✓	✓	✓	×	×	×
Plaid Shirt/Blouse and Solid Tie/Scarf	✓	✓	✓	×	×	×

*Condensed from *Dress For Success*, by John T. Molloy (New York: Warner Books, 1975), pp. 95–98.

Table 4.3 Checklist for Better Dressing*

---

1. If you have a choice, dress affluently.
2. Always be clean; it is not always necessary to be obsessively neat, but it is always imperative to be clean. Check the mirror whenever possible.
3. If you are not sure of the circumstances of a selling situation, dress more—rather than less—conservatively than normal.
4. Never wear any item that identifies any personal association or belief, unless you are absolutely sure that the person to whom you are selling shares these beliefs.
5. Always dress as well as the people to whom you are selling.
6. Never wear green (men)—seldom wear green (women).
7. Never put anything on your hair that makes it look shiny or greasy.
8. Never wear sunglasses, or glasses that change tint as the light changes. People must see your eyes if they're to believe you and trust you.
9. Never wear any jewelry that is not functional.
10. Never wear any item which might be considered feminine (for men) or masculine (for women).
11. Always carry a good quality attache case.
12. Always carry a good quality pen and pencil.
13. If you have a choice, wear an expensive tie (for men).
14. Try to wear, do, or say something that makes your name or what you are selling more memorable.
15. Never take off your suit jacket unless it is necessary.

---

*Condensed from *Dress For Success* and *The Women's Dress For Success Book* by John T. Molloy (New York: Warner Books, 1978).

with a woman?" Although the standard rule is that you shake hands with a woman when she extends her hand, the requirements of today's society are different. One should shake hands with a woman in any circumstance where one would normally shake hands with a man. This is especially true for groups. (Imagine being introduced to a group of four people; you shake hands and introduce yourself to the three who are men; for the fourth, a woman, you put your hands behind you, smile, lean forward, and introduce yourself. She would be highly offended, especially in a group.) How do you shake hands with a woman? The same way you would shake hands with a man: firmly but not overwhelmingly.

Smile   A smile is contagious and can be a powerful weapon. Imagine walking into a room with a big smile on your face: you are happy and you are having a great day. In that room you meet up with four unsmiling individuals sitting around a table. Within 30 seconds, one of two things will happen: either they are going to start smiling or you will begin to gloom. A smile is more powerful by far than a gloom. If you insist on smiling, eventually you will have four faces smiling with you!

Hygiene   It should be unnecessary to mention to adults in the business world about taking a bath, brushing one's teeth, and shampooing regularly. But there are two issues that do need mentioning: smoking and drinking on the job.

SMOKING.   When is it acceptable to smoke with a customer? Although the traditional rule is that it is acceptable if the customer is smoking or if the customer gives his permission, it is actually NEVER acceptable to smoke with a customer, especially on the customer's premises. There are three good reasons for this:

1. The smoke may bother the customer.
2. There is no such thing as a neat smoker. Not only can one's clothes be ruined, but accidents can happen, such as cigarettes falling out of ashtrays onto fine desks or carpets. With the accident may well go the sale! It is not worth the risk.
3. When you smoke, your movements add an unnecessary distraction to the situation which may cost you several points with the customer.

DRINKING.   This refers to the business lunch where it may be thought acceptable to drink on the job. Today there are many companies that absolutely forbid their employees, including their salespeople, to drink during the business day, even when they are interacting with customers over a business lunch. Drinking during the business day is a bad idea for two reasons:

1. The smell of alcohol stays on the breath for at least three hours, regardless of how much one has had to drink. Although the customer at lunch may also be having a cocktail, what will the customer at the 3:00 appointment think?
2. One's judgment is impaired with just one ounce of alcohol; even one drink can take away your ability to function at 100 percent.

Courtesy   Being polite is another important facet of first impression. All the common courtesies that have been taught to us all our lives absolutely apply in business today; such things as saying please and thank you and using the customer's name correctly and frequently are crucial to creating a good first impression. Be sure also to check both the spelling *and* the pronunciation of a customer's name. Mr., Mrs., and Ms. are appropriate. It is also best not to use a customer's first name unless permission has been given.

Punctuality   Be on time. Some people are naturally time-oriented and some are not. But it doesn't matter whether the customer is time-disciplined or not; it is still a requirement for you to be punctual. When a prospect or a customer gives you his time, you have an obligation to use that time well.

All of these facets of first impression blended together—dress, appearance, silent messages, eye contact, carriage, handshake, smile, hygiene, courtesy, and punctuality—result in the presentation of a good, strong first impression.

2. Depth of Knowledge

Depth of knowledge is the second component of excellence; how well do you know your business, your particular area of expertise? This includes knowledge of your industry, your company, its competitors, your company's strengths and weaknesses relative to its competitors', good management practices (if you are in management), and good communication skills.

The more you know about your area of expertise, the more professional you sound. It is therefore important to make every effort to learn as much as possible about your industry, your company, and its competitors. Know your product line—not just the products with which you are involved but all of your company's products, for an opportunity for lateral transfer may be the stepping-stone to your future advancement.

Study current situations and trends within your industry. Read trade journals and determine how your company rates within the industry compared to how its competitors rate. Take advantage of any training programs your company may offer. Whatever field, develop the reputation of being the person who knows the answers. Just being an expert is not enough to be in the top 5 percent category of Excellents, but it *is* a requirement.

3. Breadth of Knowledge

Breadth of knowledge, the third component of excellence, involves the *scope* of one's knowledge and determines the extent to which one can be conversant on a broad spectrum of subjects.

There are many problems with being a limited conversationalist. The most obvious problem is that it limits the number of people to whom you can relate and who can relate to you. To a salesperson this is a serious handicap.

Another consequence of having a narrow fund of knowledge is that it restricts the number of alternatives you have to converse intelligently. Uninformed people tend to be extremely repetitive and boring. A preoccupation with one topic, especially in conversation, merely shows how shallow the speaker is. Conversationally-limited people often assume that everyone can relate to complaining. These people will start tangents about the government, inflation, pollution, communists, and anything else worth complaining about. They do not discuss them intelligently; they simply whine about all of the injustices around us. Such "conversation" is definitely not conducive to establishing personal or business relationships. No one likes to share time with a malcontent.

Research has proven that, in purchasing, the primary motivation is to buy from those one likes, trusts, and with whom one is comfortable. The key to these factors is *perceived* common interests.

Salespeople who are experts in their fields but have little else to discuss may receive orders when specific materials/services are needed. But those salespeople who have gained a special status, those whom representatives of customer companies will always make time to see and to hear about new products or services even when schedules are hectic, are those who are liked. Common interest with those particular salespeople has been perceived by those customers. No matter what topic is brought up in conversation, they are interested, they know something about the topic, and they can easily become involved in conversation about it.

Imagine that you have just met someone new and you bring up something that is important to you. He knows a little bit about it, gets involved, and talks about it. A little switch closes in your brain. A few minutes later in the conversation, you introduce another topic and he knows about it, is interested in it, and can talk about it. Another switch closes in your brain. These common interests come up two, three, four, or five times in the conversation. If enough of these common interests are touched on, they close and complete the circuit. Your brain is saying, "I like this person; I feel comfortable with him."

On the other hand, if you had brought up a topic and he didn't know anything about it and he either had to change the subject back to something he knew, or at best, could ask only a few questions to find out why you have such an interest, a different switch closes. If enough of those switches close, the "I like you" circuit is not completed and you begin to feel uncomfortable, preferring not to be around that person.

People with a broad scope of knowledge make others feel relaxed. They perceive common interest. Such perceived common interest is the important difference between the salesperson who is merely an order-taker who gets an appointment only when the customer needs his product, and the creative salesperson whom people will see just to spend some time with him, giving him the opportunity for creative selling.

Unlike depth of knowledge, for which your company shares the responsibility to educate you, breadth of knowledge is your sole responsibility. Expanding your breadth of knowledge requires more than reading trade publications and other books in your area of expertise which only ensures greater depth of knowledge. One way of increasing breadth of knowledge is a faithful daily reading of a major city newspaper. Reading the daily newspaper to expand your breadth of knowledge means reading beyond the sections with which you are already the most comfortable. You need to read the newspaper from cover to cover. Although the classifieds and obituaries could be eliminated, if you live in a small town even the classifieds and the obituaries are relevant to your success. Should one of your customers experience a death in the family, knowing that fact will be very important in relating to him.

Reading the newspaper from "cover to cover" is not as horrendous a task as it may seem. Every single word of the newspaper needn't be read, but each headline and the first sentences of each story should be read to get its gist. If a story has special interest for you, finish it.

Find out what is happening throughout the world as well. Read one of the major news weeklies, such as *Time, Newsweek,* or *U.S. News and World Report,* on a regular basis. They summarize the major events in every facet of life from entertainment and people to the international scene. The weekly news magazines provide a perfect menu for a week's informed, casual conversation.

Reading is absolutely basic to expanding one's breadth of knowledge. And yet the statistics in this country on people's competence in reading, quality of reading, and frequency of reading are embarrassing. The importance of reading in our society cannot be emphasized enough; it is the primary source of information today as well as the primary source of our breadth of knowledge. Everyone should read a reasonable number of books each year. As the noted speaker Jim Rohn says, "When you start getting behind, you are in trouble. If someone is reading 2 books per week, after ten years he is 1,000 books ahead of you if you haven't read any." How would you like to enter the marketplace being 1,000 books behind the guy competing with you for your next job, that business loan, or that junior partnership in your firm?

If you are not a regular reader, become one. If you do not read regularly because you are a poor reader, most major city school systems in the United States have a remedial reading program for adults. One of the greatest gifts you can give yourself is the gift of learning to read. If you are not a regular reader, not because you can't read but because no one instilled the love of reading in you, take Maxwell Maltz' advice from his book, *Psychocybernetics:* It takes 28 days of discipline to establish or break a habit. Establish the habit of reading. Every night for one hour sit down and discipline yourself to read, if for no other reason but enjoyment. Not because it is the newspaper and you want to find out who won the baseball game, not because you want to see what is on TV, but just for pure enjoyment. After 28 days, you will find that the habit will be there. You will no longer have to force yourself because you will discover that reading is fun.

Establish the habit of reading. It not only rewards you personally, but it will give you a tremendous unexpected payoff in the marketplace by greatly developing your breadth of knowledge. Those of you who are already regular readers should know that most people read the same kinds of books consistently. To truly develop a breadth of knowledge, diversify your reading.

All of the above emphasis on reading may imply that television serves no useful purpose. Not so. What an incredible source of knowledge television is! As a source of breadth of knowledge, there has been nothing as powerful as television since the Gutenberg Press, which revolutionized printing and made the printed word available to everyone. For example, opportunities to see classic dramatic plays and movies and educational programs were not available to everyone until television appeared on the scene. Before television, historic events were only available to the relatively small numbers in attendance; now events can be seen not only as they occur, but they can also be replayed and made available to the generations to follow, thanks to film, television, and video.

There are more television sets in America than there are people. Who is watching them? The question should not be, "Do we watch television or do we *not* watch television?" The question should be, "How do we get the most, the best, out of television?" There are people who think that the producers, directors, and executives of the networks dictate what we watch, yet television is one of the last remnants of the free marketplace. If a program isn't watched, it is removed from the programming. If it gets attention, more of the same is put on the air. If television is of poor quality, it is a reflection of the tastes of the people who watch it. Think of that the next time you select a program to watch. Quality programming *is* available. In our major cities, if not everywhere, especially with the advent of cable, every thirty-minute slot has something worth watching on television.

Another excellent way to expand your breadth of knowledge is to use nonproductive time creatively. There are certain activities, such as driving a car, that require your autonomic nervous system—your brain stem and the spinal cord—but not your intellectual concentration. During such activities, listen to self-help audio cassettes, which are available on a tremendous variety of subjects. Frequently, salespeople ask, "Is there any way I can gain a few extra hours a day?" Amazingly, the answer is yes! By using your nonproductive time effectively, you use time that you would be using unproductively anyway and expand its use to include another area—learning, the expansion of your breadth of knowledge.

There are other ways to expand your breadth of knowledge. One is to keep informed about current movies, theatrical performances, and athletic events. If you have never been to a performance of the symphony orchestra or have never been to a baseball game, do so. Having such new experiences may provide three possible net results: (1) you may discover something you enjoy but wouldn't have anticipated you'd enjoy; (2) you may come into contact with a whole new circle of influence that may be of value to you at some future time; and (3) in the least, you will have expanded your breadth of knowledge.

All of these things—reading, doing, watching, listening—will make you the kind of person people will want to be around because they will perceive a common interest. *All* of the 5 percenters, the Excellents, have high scores in breadth of knowledge.

4. Flexibility

Flexibility, the fourth characteristic of excellence, is both the willingness and the skill of adapting your relationship style to the style of the other person with whom you are meeting.

Dr. David Merrill of Personnel Prediction & Research (Denver, CO) conducted research to establish the effect of flexibility on a person's success. The hypothesis was that people with low flexibility would perform poorly as managers and salespeople, or in any position that involved high quality communication skills. The presumption was that the higher one's flexibility, the more successful in "people jobs" one would be.

Imagine a line divided into four segments: W X Y Z; W represents the lowest flexibility and Z represents the highest. Dr. Merrill proved conclusively that W flexibility people made poor managers. The surprise, however, was at the other end of the line. People with Z flexibility were also poor managers and salespeople.

There are two well-known TV characters that provide excellent illustrations of these findings: Archie Bunker and Edith Bunker of the television show *All in the Family*. Archie Bunker illustrates low flexibility. Adjectives that would describe his character would be bull-headed, single-minded, rigid, nonnegotiable. Many would find working with or for that kind of individual very difficult. Edith Bunker, on the other hand, illustrates the opposite: extreme flexibility, perhaps to a fault. Adjectives that would describe her character would be unpredictable, two-faced, wishy-washy. There aren't many who would want to work for this type of manager or be sold by this type of salesperson.

The flexibility discussed here is vital to the "Relationship Strategies" concept presented in Chapter Five. Those in the top 5 percent—the Excellents—are professionals of high flexibility. The Relationships Strategies concept depends on flexibility and is one of the most powerful communication tools people have available to them.

5. Sensitivity

Sensitivity, the ability to feel and be affected emotionally and intellectually, forms the basis for all human emotions. We are all affected by the world around us, but the extent to which we are affected is determined by our sensitivity. Unfortunately, sensitivity is not taught in school along with the other basics of survival such as reading, writing, and arithmetic. Instead, we learn sensitivity from our parents and from society.

All of us are desensitized to a certain extent by the news media. As we watch the news on television, we turn off the feelings that we would normally extend to people experiencing hardships. We do this to protect ourselves, for we simply cannot drain ourselves emotionally every night in front of the television. Considering our upbringing and our desensitization as adults, it is no surprise that so many of us have a hard time knowing what we feel. But knowing what we feel is a prerequisite to feeling empathy or compassion for others.

Professional salespeople need to be sensitive. The give and take of a working relationship requires recognition of the other person's needs. An insensitive person cannot recognize that other people have needs. When communicating with people who are important to you, strive to be sensitive. Open yourself up to what may be happening inside of them. Be sensitive to what they are feeling as well as to what they are saying. This means being attentive and using good listening skills.

6. Enthusiasm

To project a professional image to prospects and customers, it is important to demonstrate a deep-seated commitment to them, their companies, their products, their customers, and the people with whom they work. Such a commitment is projected through enthusiasm, the fifth characteristic of excellence.

Consider an example from the entertainment world. Sammy Davis, Jr., a famous singer, dancer, and comedian who was popular in the 1960s, presents a tremendously enthusiastic image to his audience. If a couple went to a fancy nightclub where he was to perform and paid $100 as the cover charge and $10 per cocktail for a total investment of $140, what would be their expectation of their investment for the evening? A great performance!

The typical nightclub act is 12 to 14 songs, interaction with the audience, and some jokes. In Sammy's case, he adds some dancing and plays various musical instruments. On one particular evening, what if Sammy came out on stage, went up to the microphone, put his hands behind his back, sang his 14 songs, said "Thank you" to the audience, and walked off the stage. How would the audience feel about their investment? Probably quite cheated! What was missing? Enthusiasm! It would make no difference to those in the audience if Sammy hadn't been feeling well. Those are excuses that are worth nothing to those in the audience who have invested their time and a lot of money for an evening with Sammy Davis, Jr.

Excuses are what many sales managers hear in most sales offices in the country. For those offering the excuses, what are their chances of making a sale for the day? Quite small.

Many years ago, although he had pneumonia and was in the hospital, Sammy Davis left the hospital against his doctor's orders to meet a performance commitment. That night he projected more enthusiasm than a lot of entertainers project at their healthiest. What was his secret that night? He is a professional; he is consistent. He knows how to give the level of energy and enthusiasm that will make the audience feel good about their investment of time and money.

Whatever the level or the position, anyone in business should remain home for a day if he or she cannot generate enough enthusiasm for the day ahead. More credibility, more potential for the future can be lost because of a lack of enthusiasm than could ever be lost by staying at home for a day.

If a person experiences a lack of enthusiasm with regularity, however, a change is needed in some area of that person's life because it is a sign that something is definitely wrong. Everyone has a bad day; he wakes up less enthusiastic than he would like to be. Even on the worst days, however, within 20 or 30 minutes a person should be able to bring that level of enthusiasm up enough to get through the day. Exceptions to that should come only once or twice a year. If such exceptions happen more regularly, a review of that person's life—job, personal life, health, business—needs to be made.

Zig Ziglar, a well-known motivational speaker and author, says that every day is a great day! Just the fact that you are here to enjoy it gives you a leg up on the person who is not. If the day doesn't start out that way, make it a great day; *you* are the one in charge.

The professional experiences problems too, but he knows how to rise above them. When he walks into his office or when he relates with his customers, he knows how to bury his problems. He puts them behind him and works at eliminating them. A professional has a positive attitude, an important facet of enthusiasm. Ralph Waldo Emerson, the nineteenth-century poet and philosopher, once said, "People seem not to see that their opinion of the world is also a confession of character." The chances are that if you think this is a miserable world in which to live, then you are miserable. Your attitude will be reflected in everything you do. The same holds true of your attitude toward your customers. If you see them as people whom you can manipulate, then you will never be a truly professional salesperson. One way or another, your customers will pick up on your attitude and have nothing to do with you.

A healthier attitude is to see your customers as fellow business people with whom you probably have a lot in common. See your customers as people who are worthy of respect, if for no other reason than that they are human beings. Your customers are the people who will make it possible for you to be successful. Think of them as valves through which you must flow rather than as dams (obstacles) who will stop your progress. Only your positive attitude toward them as people will ensure the mutual trust which is so vital to doing business.

The only thing that we owe to the rest of the world is to be enthusiastic about sharing. Most managers like to see enthusiasm in their employees, and the enthusiastic employee seems to work harder, longer, and more efficiently than others. An enthusiastic person can spread the feeling to others. Similarly, if a person is unenthusiastic, that too is contagious.

7. Self-Esteem

The top 5 percenters, like Excellents, receive exceptionally high scores in self-esteem. Self-esteem is a unique understanding of ourselves, defining and judging ourselves as we relate to the world internally rather than externally, not by what others think of us but by how well we meet our own internal set of standards.

Years ago Dr. Norman Vincent Peale, the famous author of *The Power of Positive Thinking,* told the story of his walking every day from his home to his church. Each day he would greet the corner newsboy with a friendly hello, but the newsboy would never return his greeting. When Dr. Peale was asked how he could continue to be so friendly to this person, he responded with, "Why should I let him determine my attitude? If he chooses to be unhappy, that's his choice. I'd like to see his attitude change, but it's not a requirement. What *is* a requirement is that I not let him change *my* attitude. My good day or bad should never be determined by someone else's rudeness." For the excellent salesperson, this concept is very important. It is to easy for a salesperson to define his or her sales worth by whether or not a sale was made. Too often the feeling generated within a salesperson if a sale was made is that he or she is a good person; if the sale was lost, he or she feels a failure. This is definitely not the case.

No one's quality or value as a person should ever be judged by the results of a sales call. There are times when a salesperson can make an excellent presentation and still not win the sale, and there are times when a presentation can go quite poorly and the sale is won. The question to a prospect or customer when leaving a presentation should not be, "Did I make the sale?" but, "Did I do a good job?" If the answer is consistently yes, then success is virtually assured. If the answer is consistently yes and sales are *not* being made, then one's standards for judging the presentations are not high enough or not enough effort is being exerted.

Whether or not the sale is made, however, is not a basis to judge your worth as a person. The Excellent understands this concept. Our self-worth, our self-esteem as human beings, must always be based on a higher plane of standards: our standards of beauty, knowledge, justice, goodness, and equality, *not* on whether or not a sale was made.

8. Extended Focus

Focus is another characteristic of excellence for which the top 5 percent receive high scores. The Excellents of the world seem to have a great sense of where they are going. Their goals are specific and written, measurable and divided into easily attainable segments. They focus their energies into the plan they have set for themselves, are not easily distracted, and they reach resolution. They delegate details and follow through. In addition to focusing on the specific, the Excellents also look at the big picture. Our colleague, Rick Berrera, refers to their ability to simultaneously focus on the specific and look at the big picture as *extended focus.*

On the other hand, most people aim at nothing in life and hit it with amazing accuracy. Many talented people seem to float from one great project to

"Ha! We got him now!"

Figure 4.1: An Example of Not Seeing the Big Picture Reprinted with permission, Universal Press Syndicate.

another and never seem to achieve closure on any of them. In spite of their great talents, they seem to achieve only great levels of mediocrity. They lack focus.

9. Sense of Humor

> Conversation never sits easier than when we now and then discharge ourselves in a symphony of laughter, which may not improperly be called the chorus of conversation.
>
> SIR RICHARD STEELE

Humor acts as a social lubricant. It gives us something to share and helps create bonds of appreciation. We are automatically attracted to people who make us laugh.

Although the Excellents take their commitments and the task at hand seriously, they never take themselves or life too seriously. Above all, they have the ability to laugh at themselves. Prospects and customers, people in general, appreciate those who can see the humorous side of any situation, who can laugh at themselves, and who can see the humor in life.

As a professional salesperson, you would be wise to incorporate humor into your personal style. This humor should be the right kind, however, if it is going to be effective. Keep the following suggestions in mind:

Keep it in good taste. Know your audience and the type of material that they will appreciate. Some people are more inhibited than others. Respect their standards of good taste; use discretion.

Be sensitive to your customers' needs. Does this sound familiar? It applies to humor as well. If you are making them laugh, do not assume that your being "on a roll" justifies going on indefinitely. Be aware of your customer's body language (because his verbal language will sound like laughter), and if it indicates that it is time to get back to work, then get back to work! People appreciate digressions as long as they are short and sweet. You do not want to be known as "that clown who doesn't know when to stop."

Humor is not just telling jokes. If you rehash jokes that have been circulating for years, you will be regarded as a jerk rather than a person with a great sense of humor. The best humor is original and spontaneous, and flows with the conversation or the ideas being discussed.

Look for humor in everyday life. This is the best way to improve your sense of humor. Some people believe that comedic ability is a God-given talent, and some others believe you can cultivate it. There are numerous opportunities for you to increase your repertoire of humorous anecdotes and comments. Above all, be willing to laugh at yourself. If you make an awkward mistake, remember: Don't take yourself too seriously.

The advantages of humor in sales are numerous: customers will relax more readily with you; they will appreciate and respect you; and most importantly, they will remember you. As Romain Gray once wrote, "Humor is the affirmation of dignity, a declaration of man's superiority to all that befalls him."

10 and 11.   Creativity and Willingness to Take Risk

Two characteristics of excellence, creativity and the willingness to take risk, are particularly interrelated. To paraphrase Albert Einstein, "It is not the quality of ideas that makes genius. It is the frequency of ideas that you put into action." Albert Einstein felt that every man and woman, at some time in their lives, would have an idea that would change the world. Unfortunately, minutes after having this world-changing idea they would stare up at the sky, turn to their spouse, and say, "What's for lunch?" or "What's on TV?" and never mention the idea or think of it again. The genius has the idea, thinks the idea through, and experiments. He is willing to take the risk that it may be a bad idea, but recognizes that he is a good person in spite of the fact that the idea may not work.

Creativity is not the quality of the idea; it is the quality of the action that puts the idea into being. We are not born with creativity; it is a learned, acquired, practiced skill. Creativity is the ability to take many ideas, lots of individual bits of information, and repeatedly connect and reconnect those ideas to develop a new idea.

One of the facets of creativity is curiosity. As a Yiddish proverb suggests, "A man should live if only to satisfy his curiosity." There is so much to know and do that it is a wonder that we accomplish any work. The digressions are infinite; only the imagination is finite.

If we want employees to be creative, we cannot scold and criticize them every time they do something creative and it doesn't work. If we do, the chances are nearly nil that they will ever be creative again. We must learn how to support creativity, to stroke the attempt as long as it is well-thought-out and well-delivered, even if the idea doesn't work.

All those who are among the Excellents have these two characteristics. They are creative and they are not locked into doing things the way everyone else does. They are not even locked into the way that they were doing things the day before. They are always looking for new methods, new marketplaces, new applications, new ways to benefit their customers. Just as important, they do not just have ideas. They have the courage to put those ideas into action. This is creativity and the willingness to take risk.

12.   Sense of Honesty and Ethics

Having a sense of honesty and ethics is an essential characteristic for which the Excellents receive high scores. Honesty is the quality of being truthful, frank, and sincere. Ethics involves behaviors and can be thought of as honesty in action. Honesty leaves no doubt in people's minds when your word is as good as gold. Being ethical means answering to a higher law, and not waiting for a response; living ethically is its own reward.

In our day-to-day lives, the border between honesty and dishonesty is sometimes a wide one. There are many gray areas open to interpretation. Ultimately your conscience will have to live with whatever action you take. Being honest and ethical will bring you respect, and being respected is an important part of professionalism.

SUMMARY

According to a study conducted by the authors, most people polled believe that only 5 percent of all salespeople are professional. This 5 percent we have called the Excellents; the other 95 percent has been named the Mediocres.

The top 5 percent have been found to have twelve characteristics of excellence in common. All twelve are characteristics which an individual has within his own control.

First impression is made up of many things: one's dress and appearance, which should be clean, neat, and suitable for the business environment; posture; the handshake, which should be strong and firm but not overwhelming; a warm smile; good hygiene which includes, beyond the obvious, not drinking or smoking on the job; good eye contact; courtesy; and punctuality.

The second characteristic is *depth of knowledge,* which refers to how well a salesperson knows his subject, his area of expertise. Such knowledge covers a salesperson's industry, his company, his company's competitors, his company's strengths and weaknesses relative to its competitors', good management practices, and good communication skills.

Breadth of knowledge, the third characteristic of excellence, involves the scope of one's knowledge. This refers to knowledge which goes beyond the specific industry and product line or service. Research has proven that in purchasing, the primary motivation is to buy from those the client likes, trusts, and with whom the client is comfortable. The key to these factors is *perceived* common interest. A salesperson who knows something about a variety of different areas is better equipped to converse intelligently with his prospects and customers on a variety of different topics, thus tremendously aiding perceived common interest.

Flexibility is the fourth characteristic of excellence and is the willingness and the skill of adapting one's own relationship style to the style of the other person with whom one is meeting.

Sensitivity, which is the ability to feel, to be affected emotionally and intellectually, forms the basis for all human emotions and is the fifth characteristic of excellence for which professionals receive high scores. It is essential for professional salespeople to be sensitive, as it is a prerequisite to feeling empathy and compassion for others. The give and take of a successful relationship requires recognition of the other person's needs, a recognition which comes from a developed sensitivity.

The sixth characteristic is *enthusiasm.* To project a professional image to prospects and customers, it is important for a salesperson to demonstrate a deep-seated commitment to them, their companies, their products, their customers, and the people with whom they work. Such a commitment is projected through enthusiasm for life and work.

Self-esteem is the seventh characteristic of excellence. It is the unique understanding a salesperson has of himself as a concept. He defines and judges himself as he relates to the world internally rather than externally, not by what others think of him but by how well he meets an internal set of standards that he has created for himself.

Extended focus, the eighth characteristic, refers to a person's keen sense of direction. Professional salespeople, those in the top 5 percent, are specific in their goals, have them written, and have them divided into measurable, easily attainable segments.

A *sense of humor,* another essential characteristic, is especially important. Although the Excellents take their commitments and the task at hand seriously, they never take themselves or life too seriously. They have the ability to laugh at themselves and see the humor in life as a whole. Some suggestions concerning the use of humor that professionals keep in mind are: 1) humor should be kept in good taste; 2) salespeople should be sensitive to their customers' needs; 3) original jokes are better than the old standards; and 4) salespeople should look for humor in everyday life. The advantages of humor in sales are that customers relax more readily; they appreciate and respect the salesperson; and most importantly, they will remember that salesperson.

The two characteristics of *creativity* and *the willingness to take risk* are related. Creativity is not the quality of an idea but the quality of the action that puts the idea into being. It is a learned, acquired, practiced skill, and is particularly valuable when it is coupled with the willingness to take a risk—the willingness to try an idea to see if it works. Those who excel in this area are those who are always looking for new methods, new marketplaces, new applications, new ways to benefit their customers and have the courage to put those ideas into action.

The twelfth characteristic is a *sense of honesty and ethics.* Honesty is the quality of being truthful, frank, and sincere; ethics involves behaviors and can be thought of as honesty in action.

The importance of these twelve characteristics of excellence is that they are not only learnable and practicable, but they are characteristics over which an individual has complete control.

DISCUSSION
QUESTIONS

1. What are the characteristics of excellence?
2. What is the difference between depth of knowledge and breadth of knowledge?
3. How is flexibility related to relationship strategies?
4. Name three benefits of developing the characteristics of excellence and how they would improve your life.
5. For each of the twelve characteristics, rate yourself on a scale of one to ten (with ten being the highest score).

6. Next to each characteristic, list the activities that will help you improve that aspect of your personality.

7. Which characteristics can you improve by observing people you respect?

8. List five people who can be role models for you; next to their names list the characteristics you admire most about them.

9. Plan a convenient time to ask the five people you listed in Question 9 for advice and help in improving yourself. Some of the things you can ask for are: 1) Weekly "rap sessions," during which they will answer any questions you have about anything. 2) Suggestions of books or cassette tapes to learn from. 3) The opportunity to watch them in action doing what they do best in a business setting.

Part III

PERSONAL SALES MANAGEMENT SKILLS

Selling offers virtually unlimited opportunity for growth and income. Compared to other professions in which other people decide how quickly you climb the corporate ladder, in sales you decide where you want to go and how quickly. It's an input equals output business. The more time and energy you invest, the more it pays you back.

In addition to relationship skills, truly professional selling requires the ability to grasp the "big picture." The bird's eye view, as it were, is the perspective that shows you where the power and control lie: they lie with you. If you think about it carefully, you must realize that you are your best sales manager.

To manage your sales career, it is necessary to be organized so your efforts will be both effective and efficient. One without the other is not enough; you must have both to get to the top. The careful analysis and planning of your territory strategy will yield much higher results than simply pounding the pavement in search of a buyer. Personal sales management includes:

○ TERRITORY MANAGEMENT: If you fail to plan, you plan to fail. Territory management develops a game plan that takes into consideration the marketplace, your products/services, the competition, the potential business of your prospective customers, record keeping, and other procedures. These are the activities that make selling a science rather than an art. Territory management takes the guesswork and time-wasters out of your work.

○ PROSPECTING: Where do new customers come from? Prospecting is the method of finding them, and it's a lot easier than panning for gold. There are systematic ways for developing leads and aiming your sights on customers who are in the position to buy.

○ PROMOTIONAL STRATEGIES: Now that you know where your customers are, they need to know who and where you are. Being in business without advertising is like smiling in the dark; no one can see you do it. Promotional strategies include advertising, public relations, publicity, and sales promotions.

○ SALES CALL PREPARATION: Managing your territory and promotion will get you in the door, but once you are in you have to know what you are doing. Preparation ensures you will be informed and organized so you can make the most of each meeting with a customer.

The difference between people who excel and those who simply plod along is organization and planning. With a road map in front of you, the path becomes clear. Without one, you might as well be blindfolded. Personal sales management skills enable you to focus on your road to success.

CHAPTER FIVE

Territory Management

<table>
<tr><td>CHAPTER
OBJECTIVES</td><td>

1 Analyze the concept of territory management.

2 Develop an understanding of a company marketing plan and its relationship to a salesperson's sales plan.

3 Introduce the two-stage sales plan tool.

4 Discuss tools of analysis needed to accurately prepare a solid sales plan.
</td></tr>
</table>

PART ONE: Territory Analysis

The ingredients which most significantly affect your success as a professional salesperson are your *sales planning* and *territory management*. You may have a flawless presentation, excellent communication skills, and comprehensive product knowledge, but if you present your product to the wrong people, the sale will not be made. Effective territory management ensures that your time will be well spent.

Territory analysis is needed for many reasons. The most obvious is to reduce the inefficiency of going out into the field and making random calls. Although random calling may work in telephone sales where a large number of prospects can be called in a short period of time, it will work neither well nor efficiently in the field.

Over the years the cost of doing business has increased for everyone, including salespeople. Research has shown that although the cost of sales calls has doubled every ten years during the last twenty years, the amount of time that a salesperson spends with a customer has *diminished*. These two factors taken together add up to one thing: an increase in the cost of your selling time.

Inflation has also taken its toll on profit margins over the years. As profit margins slowly shrink and the cost of sales calls increases, the need for increased profitability per call becomes more urgent. This can only be accomplished by becoming more efficient through sales planning and territory analysis.

The process of territory management includes the activities that are required to cover the relevant markets in a given geographic area. Of these activities, the sales plan forms the skeleton upon which the rest of the system is hung. It identifies problems and opportunities, establishes priorities based on profits and the value of your time, sets objectives and strategies, and provides a means of evaluating performance over a given period of time. This is the *only* way a salesperson can hope to get a firm grip on his time, territory, and income potential. The sales plan must coincide with the company's marketing plan.

THE MARKETING PLAN

A marketing plan represents the overall strategy your company uses to identify and pursue promising markets. It includes the process of deciding the company's objectives, policies, resources, and strategies. An understanding of this process is invaluable to you for two reasons. First, it will show how your company approaches an entire market with the intention of penetrating it. Second, you will see what you must do to manage your sales territory. The principles of sales planning and territory management which you will apply are the same as those used by your company. Your plans, of course, will be on a smaller scale and affect specific accounts in a particular geographic area.

For each product manufactured or distributed, a company must determine the following:

1. *Who* and *where* are the buyers? In other words, what are the *target markets?* If a company manufactures Barbie Dolls, it certainly will not try to sell them to corporate executives.
2. *How* do we get to the buyers? What is the most effective way of letting the target know that the product exists? Is TV advertising, direct mail, or trade association participation most appropriate?
3. *When* is the best time to present your product to the target market? If it is a seasonal product, this will have an effect on sales planning. For example, you wouldn't want to sell wool sweaters in the summer *unless* there was something irresistible about them such as a very low price.
4. *How much* will the buyers pay? This must be looked at in absolute terms as well as in comparison with competitors' pricing.
5. *Where* and *how* will the buyers purchase the product? Will credit be extended? Can the items be leased? How will the distribution be handled?
6. Is the customer satisfied after the purchase? Did the product satisfy his needs? What kind of service will be needed in the future?

In order to answer these crucial questions, a great deal of research is needed. Marketing specialists compile data to guide them in forecasting potential sales, setting goals and action steps, and measuring the results. These plans are then passed on to other levels within the corporation for evaluation and execution. The market plan usually breaks down into four sections: *Situation Analysis, Objectives, Strategy,* and *Control.* Let's look at how this applies to the sales plan.

THE SALES PLAN MODEL

The sales plan is practically identical to the market plan except that it deals only with one salesperson's territory rather than an entire market. If you think of your territory as a submarket, you will see that you must perform many of the same steps as your company does in its market plan. The sales plan involves a two-stage planning process. The first stage revolves around the territory and all of its characteristics. The second stage is concerned with the individual accounts and the strategies for selling to them. Figure 5.1 depicts the layout of the sales plan.

Stage One: Situation Analysis and Objectives

In the first stage, assess your selling opportunities and problems just as the market plan does. In Step 1, your search for exploitable sales opportunities, study the following:

1. Your company and its products or services
2. The industry in general
3. The competition and their market penetration
4. The market potential in your territory
5. Business trends in different market segments

From this analysis, in Step 2 you can set some realistic territory and sales objectives. These goals would center around the following:

The most profitable products or services to be sold
The accounts of weak competitors to be pursued
Prime market segments in your entire territory
Groups of specific prospects to be contacted
Objectives of total sales or volume for your entire territory and individual accounts

Step 3 involves developing strategies to accomplish the objectives you have determined. These strategies will include time management (Chapter 21) and territory management. Territory management strategies include elements such as the frequency and priority of calls, methods of contacting, promotional aids (Chapter 7), and prospecting plans (Chapter 6). After all of this territory research has been completed, you can then move on to the second stage.

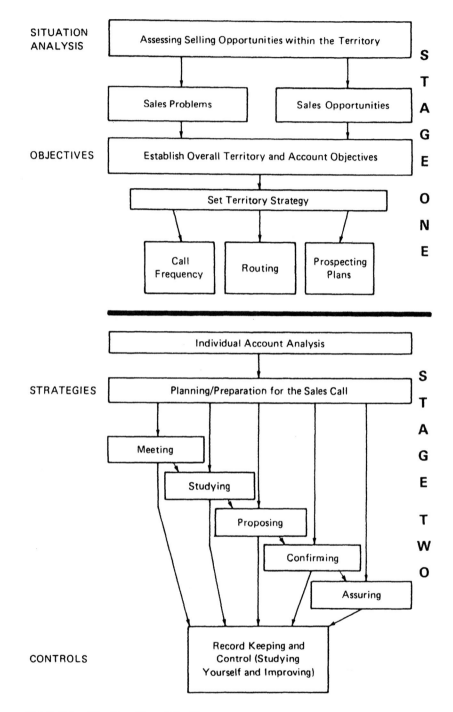

Figure 5.1: The Two-Stage Sales Plan

Stage Two: Strategies and Controls

Specific accounts are handled in Step 4. Here the sales opportunities and strategies are analyzed on an account-by-account basis, giving special attention to the following:

1. Prospect's purchasing behavior and needs
2. Characteristics of the prospect's company
3. Overall industry the prospect is in
4. Actual or potential competition

This research will uncover a wealth of information that can be used to great advantage when contacting a prospective or current customer. Naturally, sales and call objectives will be set for each account. These are both long-term and per-call goals. They can be as long-range as "sell $100,000 worth of product X in the next year" or as short-range as "introduce product at first meeting and schedule a demonstration."

Step 5 is the actual sales call itself. This involves meeting with the prospect or client, studying her needs, proposing solutions, confirming the sale, and assuring that the benefits will be effective solutions to her problems.

Last but not least in the sales plan is the control phase. This is a nice way of saying that you will be required to keep records of what you have done so that you can evaluate your performance later. Without the data provided by records, you will have no way of knowing if you have accomplished your goals for the territory or individual accounts. Without this feedback you will not be able to correct whatever problems you are having in achieving your objectives.

The two-stage planning process is a closed-loop system in which all stages depend on each other. All the information obtained in the control section is fed back to the situation analysis so that the process can begin again. This is a cycle that *every* non-manipulative salesperson goes through on an annual or semiannual basis. The time taken to carefully plan the strategies for a given period of time will pay off in increased sales and increased awareness of what is being done correctly or incorrectly. This will turn the art of selling into a science for you.

SALES PLANNING

Situation Analysis

Today's business climate is in constant flux, changing from week to week with the whims of a capricious economy. These rapid changes necessitate periodic assessments of the sales territory. The systematic and exhaustive assessment of sales problems and opportunities will arm you with the knowledge necessary to maximize your time and efficiency.

Company Knowledge Your company is the only entity which stands behind the product or service you are selling. Initially, prospects may be more interested in your company than in you and the product. You must be knowledgeable enough to educate your prospect if you want to gain his trust and confidence.

Company knowledge is independent of product knowledge. You need to be familiar with the history and development of both. If you are a sales rep carrying many products, becoming familiar with each company may seem like an arduous task. It should, however, be done conscientiously. The Company/Product Knowledge Worksheet (5-1) will test your knowledge and guide you in acquiring the facts that you should know about your company and product(s).

Often a company will describe its historical development and philosophy when you begin your employment. If not, you can approach the marketing or sales managers and ask them for the information. The same is true for product knowledge. If there are gaps in the information that your company has given you, seek out the knowledgeable people and tell them your needs. Often engineers, executives, and others in high-level positions know more than those who sell the products. You should also be aware of your company's operating activities. Is it buying new subsidiaries or creating new divisions? How well is its stock doing on the market? Have there been any significant managerial or executive changes lately? If so, how will this affect the company's policies? All of these things are worth knowing so that a prospect will not embarrass you by asking a question you cannot answer. Your knowledge will indicate to him that you care about your firm and that you do business in a professional manner.

Product Knowledge Every company provides its salespeople with information about the product or service they will sell. This takes the form of brochures, specification sheets, and other printed materials. In addition, many companies offer training sessions, workshops, and other informative classes to bring their people up to date on the latest developments in their products. All of this is extremely valuable and should be absorbed voraciously by the salesperson.

As technology develops at phenomenal rates, product cycles become shorter and shorter. What is new today is obsolete tomorrow. More often than not, the salesperson knows more than the customer about these changes. It is necessary, therefore, for the salesperson to introduce product changes to a customer in a way that will be informative as well as attractive.

As mentioned before, some sales representatives carry more than one product. For them, the task of organizing their products and becoming knowledgeable about each is made more difficult by a factor of n (n = the number of product lines carried). If a salesperson carries three lines, it is three times as much work to know all of those products. To help organize one's knowledge, a Multi-Product Knowledge Worksheet (5-2) is presented. This aid will uncover what you know and what you need to research further. It will also shed light on any product weaknesses you might not have recognized.

INSTRUCTIONS: Answer all of the questions below in as much detail as possible. Questions which you cannot answer will indicate areas that you need to research.

COMPANY

1. List the key personnel of your company and what their unique contributions are to the firm.

2. What unique capabilities or technical advantages does the company have?

3. What is the company's image and reputation among: a) present customers, b) prospects, c) the competition?

4. What are the relative strengths and weaknesses compared to the competition? How do these affect business?

5. What is the marketing philosophy of your company?

6. What are the present and future markets of your company?

7. What has been the company's sales history during the last 3-5 years?

8. What is your company's standard policy regarding: a) pricing, b) discounts, c) guarantees, d) service?

PRODUCT

1. What specific benefits do customers and prospects seek in your product?

2. How does your product compare to the competition's in providing those benefits?

3. Are there any features which make your product better than the competition's? If so, why?

4. How does your product compare with the others in your territory in the following aspects: a) quality, b) price, c) delivery, d) value, e) reliability?

5. What factor(s) might prevent a prospect from purchasing a product? What can you do about it?

6. Is your company a leader (developer) or follower (imitator) in its field?

Worksheet 5-1: Company/Product Knowledge

Product knowledge for_____as of_____
(your company)   (date)

INSTRUCTIONS: For each number below "Products," write in the name of one product you represent. Then answer Yes or No to the following questions for each product.

PRODUCTS

	1	2	3	4	5

Can you describe the
benefits, features,
and advantages of
each product?

Do you know all the
applications of each
product?

Can you explain the
company's marketing
plan and rationale for
each product?

Can you describe
how each relates
to other products?

Do you know each
product's competitive
position?

Can this product be used
with others to solve a
prospect's problems?

Can you project the
financial benefits to
be derived from this
product by the prospect?

Worksheet 5-2: Multi-Product Knowledge

Market Analysis

Knowing your own company and products is only one part of your job. You must also know the market of which your territory is a part. An analysis of your territory by *market segments* will simplify the process. A market segment is one category or type of industry or business. For example, if you are selling copying machines, some of the market segments would be banks, libraries, hospitals, law firms, doctor's offices, and so on. Each of these segments will be different but, within each category, the individual account's needs will be quite similar.

For each of your market segments you will want to know the potential demand for your product in terms of gross sales and number of units to be sold. This *quantitative* analysis will be done for a specified period of time, usually one year. Two types of data are needed for an accurate market analysis—*market potential* and *sales potential*. Market potential is the maximum sales possible for *all* companies in the market. For example, how many copying machines will be sold in your territory regardless of manufacturer? Sales potential is the maximum sales possible for a specific company during a given period of time.

You will be interested in the sales potential in your territory for each of your market segments. This will help you in many ways. First, you will see at a glance which market segments appear to be most promising. You will be able to rank the market segments in order of priority and budget your time accordingly. Second, seeing the relative fertility of different market segments, you will be able to set different (and therefore more realistic) objectives for each, as well as allocating different amounts of money for promotion and personal selling efforts in each segment.

To determine the make-up of your territory, divide it into segments. This is done by listing all possible uses of your product and the industries or businesses who will use it.

First, you must determine the number, location, and sales potential of each customer and prospect. This compilation will take research and creativity on your part. Be as thorough as possible. Names of present customers can be obtained from your company, other salespeople, and your own files. Prospects can be identified with the aid of trade directories (e.g., *Thomas' Register*), publishers of mailing lists (e.g., R. H. Donnelley Corp.), and other journals, magazines, and firms (e.g., Dun & Bradstreet).

After the customers are listed, make an assessment of the potential business from each. This is done by examining their past sales records, if available. For prospect estimates, the same sources mentioned can be used. After forecasts are made for each company, they should be ranked in order of their potential profitability.

Market Trends During this phase you should also be aware of any situations that may be affecting business. These can range from economic to political changes. For example, everyone is aware of the effect of interest rates on the economy. This is a trend worth considering when forecasting sales. The sooner you recognize a trend and figure it into your analysis, the more accurate your forecasts will be. Trends usually suggest areas of causation or of opportunities to be exploited. Being an aware, well-read salesperson is one of the best ways to get a jump on business trends.

Competition Analysis

There are very few products or services with no direct competitors. We need to be aware of competition. An important part of your territory analysis will be the evaluation of competitors. You will want to identify all of those who have a significant influence on the market segments in which you are interested. Analyze their share of the market, their strengths and weaknesses, and where they are headed in the future. The two worksheets that follow will help you organize your findings and rank your competitors on two criteria—their company/product strengths and weaknesses and their positioning/penetration in each target market segment.

The Competition Analysis Worksheet (5-3) compares your company with the competition in eight areas of criteria important to your prospects and customers. Feel free to add as many criteria as you wish to the list. To complete this analysis, simply rank your company *objectively* against the major competitors on *each* of the customer decision criteria. (Use a scale of 1 to 5 with 1 being the highest score.)

From this worksheet, you will quickly see which areas need improving and which can be emphasized in your selling efforts. For example, if your company is strong in pricing but weak in delivery, you should do what you can to improve delivery and emphasize pricing as a selling point. By knowing which competitor is highest in customer service, you will know who to study so that your sales can increase.

The Competitor's Market Share Worksheet (5-4) compares competitors' strengths in different market segments. This information is extremely valuable. For example, if one market segment seems to be neglected by practically all of your competitors, it could present a golden opportunity for you to penetrate a new market! You would, of course, find out why the others are not well-represented in that market segment. It is possible that a particular segment is not profitable for a number of reasons. If this is the case, you have a good reason not to pursue it. This determination requires more research but is well worth the effort.

On this worksheet, objectively rank each company on either its market share or its relative strength in *each* of the market segments that you have identified, using the same 5-point scale that you used before.

It is not enough to complete the worksheet and simply observe the standings of your company and its competitors. You must find out *why* these standings exist as they are. Then answer the next question: How can these standings be changed so that my company gets a bigger share next year in the segments we would like to penetrate?

After you have analyzed the competition and the various market segments, take a look at the factors that influence sales in each segment. This will show you which decision criteria can be emphasized for increased sales in each individual segment. The information for this analysis must come from the customers and prospects themselves. Survey the businesses or industries within the market segments to uncover their satisfactions and dissatisfactions. The Market Segment Needs Worksheet (5-5) can be used to organize your evaluation of this data and suggest opportunities to be pursued.

In showing you the decision-making criteria for different segments,

	Your Company	COMPETITORS A	B	C	D
Sales					
C U S T O M E R D E C I S I O N C R I T E R I A Reputation					
Pricing					
Quality Products					
Customer Service					
Market Share					
Growth Rate					
Financial Strength					

Worksheet 5-3: Competition Analysis

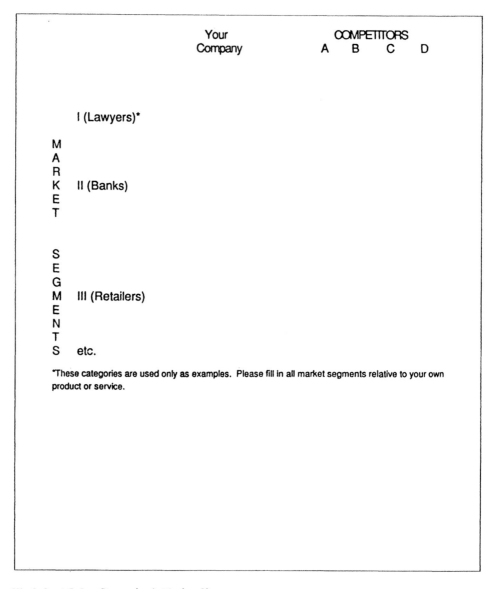

Worksheet 5-4:   Competitor's Market Share

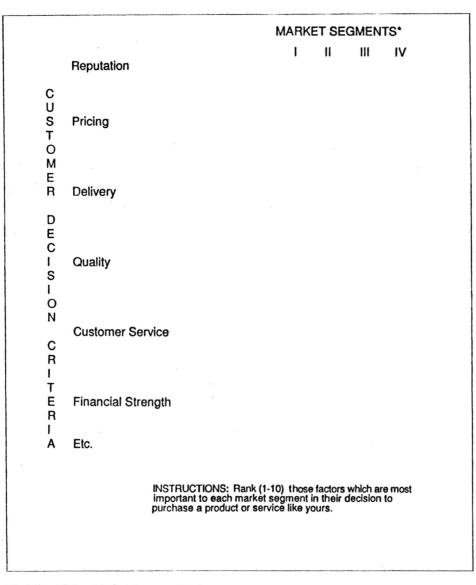

Worksheet 5-5:   Market Segment Needs

Worksheet 5-5 will help steer you towards a market which will capitalize on the strengths of your company and product. For example, if you sell an expensive but very reliable copying machine, you will want to know which market segment values reliability over purchase price. In your research you might find that banks and stationers buy those brands that are reliable. On the other hand, you may find law firms spending less for less reliable machines. Worksheets 5-3 and 5-5 will give you a good feel for your territory and what you have to do to strategically penetrate it further.

Customer Information

Now that you have some idea of the market segments you will pursue, you must learn more about the individual accounts. The first step is to list all the major customers and prospects in your territory for each market segment. By now you have done enough research to have uncovered the major segments. You may have to stretch your imagination and devote more time to finding specific prospects. Take the time to do this. As we will discuss in the following chapter, your need for prospects is continual. Worksheet 5-6 can be used to organize your customer and prospect list. Fill out a worksheet for every product and every market segment to which you sell. At this point the order is unimportant; after you have further analyzed each prospect, you can go back and list them in order of priority.

Although prospecting will be covered in the following chapter, it is appropriate to discuss some sources of prospects here. These sources will also provide invaluable financial and organizational information to be used in the individual account analyses which will follow. The following sources represent only a fraction of the available information on industry and business. For more references, contact your local reference librarian.

> *Standard & Poor's Industry Surveys*
> *Annual Report on Business* published every January by Forbes
> *Moody's Industrial Manual*
> *Dun & Bradstreet Reference Book of Corporate Management*
> *Standard & Poor's Corporate Record*
> *Encyclopedia of Business Information Sources*
> Periodicals
> Government publications from
>   U.S. Dept. of Commerce
>   U.S. Treasury Dept. (IRS)
>   Bureau of Census
>   Bureau of Economic Analysis
>   Dept. of Labor
> *Funk & Scott Index of Corporations and Industries*
> *Wall Street Transcript*
> Newspapers, trade journals
> Consulting firms

MARKET SEGMENT_____Product(s)_____Date_____

CUSTOMERS

PROSPECTS

Worksheet 5-6:   Market Segment Breakdown

Annual reports, stock prospectuses, stock performance guides
Personal contacts and observation
Company's resources, other salespeople, etc.
Trade associations

Sources are so numerous that there is never an excuse for being short of prospects. While doing your research, gather as much information as you can, but keep it relevant. To accomplish this, you need to know what is involved in the analysis of your accounts and prospects.

PART TWO: Knowing What Your Time Is Worth

ACCOUNT ANALYSIS

You have spent hours researching and analyzing, but what has it all been for? In one word—*priorities!* It takes knowledge to decide what to do and when to do it, or, in your case, on *whom* to call and *when.* The analysis of each customer and prospect will show you in hard figures which calls are worth your time and effort and which are not.

Pareto's principle of economics asserts that the top 20 percent of a country's population earns 80 percent of the money. This applies in sales as well. Twenty percent of your accounts will probably constitute 80 percent of your total sales. Your sales expenses for these key accounts are not much greater than for the smaller, less profitable accounts. For this reason you must identify and cater to the profitable 20 percent and make them grow. This is the beginning of setting your account priorities.

To set your priorities, it is necessary to look at your prospects and customers from two points of view. First, what will each account contribute to your overall sales profit? Second, what is the time investment necessary to cover that account and realize the profit potential? An important part of this second analysis is to determine what your time is worth on an hourly basis. The profitability of an account can be determined only if you have an idea of the overhead costs of your product. This cost includes your time as a salesperson.

There are several reasons why few salespeople analyze and classify their accounts. First, people generally tend to be lazy. We also tend to call on people who are pleasant to deal with even if their profitability as accounts is low. It feels good to have a warm chat with a customer on a cold day. Another reason is that salespeople prefer to sell easily moved products rather than the more profitable, slower moving ones. This is due in part to the fact that most of us feel more rewarded by short-term commissions than by long-term commissions. Most people focus on the short-term in their planning. The classification and prioritization of accounts requires a long-term outlook and a desire to build accounts over time. The rewards are eventually greater for those who can forego the short-term gratification in favor of the bigger long-term rewards.

Account Classification

The first step in classifying your accounts is to divide them into market segments. From these lists, take each account and analyze it on its own merits. The procedure is to make up an account profile; determine the profit margin; and estimate the cost of your time, the volume necessary to break even, and the return of your invested time. This will all lead to a rating of the account as an A, B, or C (high, medium, low) account. You will then be able to determine how much time to spend with each account, based on its expected return.

It should be noted that your accounts can be classified in terms of sales volume. This is not, however, the most efficient way. Sales volume is a one-dimensional measure which hides half of the truth. It is entirely plausible that you may have customers who are high in volume yet low in profitability. It could be that your expenses in reaching these customers are so high that your profit margin is cut significantly. In this case, ranking them as highly desirable or A accounts would be economically unsound. We advocate the use of profitability as a yardstick of the account's primary worth/value.

Account Profile

Your "bible" for each account should be the account profile. The Account Profile Worksheet (5-7) on pp. 98-100 is the one on which you will enter all information found during your research and analysis phases. The profile will be a permanent record to be used to refresh your memory about everything from sales volume to the buyer's name and personal style. Enter whatever information you feel is relevant to the account. A sample account profile is provided at the end of this section. Use it as a starting point to design and duplicate your own profit for each account and prospect you have. In doing so, remember to leave lots of space for new information.

As you can see on the profile, much of the information is straightforward. One of the first places to improvise on your own profiles is under the buyer's name. Here you can list little reminders such as personal style, best time of day to call, spouse's name, and so on. These things will help you add a personal touch to the sales call.

Company Name:_____

Street Address:_____

City/State/Zip:_____

Telephone:_____

Background:

Buyers (in order of importance):_____

_____

Products/Services Purchased:_____

_____

Buying Characteristics:

When does customer buy?_____

How often?_____Average order/call:_____

Gross Sales Volume (yearly):_____

Past Sales (last 4 yrs.):_____

_____

_____

Company Goals:

Short-Term (as perceived?):_____

_____

Long-Term (as perceived by?):_____

_____

Competitors (for this account):

Current Competitors:_____

Worksheet 5-7: Account Profile

Potential Competitors:_____

Your Company

Your company/product strengths:_____

_____

Your company/product weaknesses:_____

_____

Your Goals for Acct._____as of (date)_____

_____

Specific Account Needs:

_____Pricing _____Delivery _____Service

_____Credit _____Reliability _____Other ( )

PROFITABILITY ANALYSIS

Profit Margin_____Margin Percentage (GMP)_____

Number of calls necessary/year:_____

Average time per call:_____

Travel time per call:_____

Planning time per call:_____

Your Cost per Hour (CPH):_____CPH=$\frac{DC}{WH}$

Your Cost per Call Hour (CPCH):_____ CPCH=$\frac{DC}{CH}$

Worksheet 5-7 (cont.)

Break-even Volume:_____BEV=$\dfrac{DC}{GMP \; call}$

Break-even Volume/Call:_____   BEV/hr.=$\dfrac{CPCH}{GMP}$

Return on Time Invested:_____ROTI=$\dfrac{GM}{DC}$

Account Classification:_____

Worksheet 5-7   (cont.)

Our primary concern now is the determination of the profitability of existing accounts. Under profitability analysis is a space for profit margin. This figure comes from one of two sources. If you are in direct sales for a company like Avon, Amway, or Shaklee, then you know what the product costs you and what you sell it for. The difference between these two figures is your *gross profit margin*. If you work for a company and are not told what the profit margin is, you can find out by asking an executive in the accounting or marketing department. The number of calls and time required per call can be obtained from your past records. This is also true of your travel and planning time for each account.

The rest of the account profile is devoted to the calculations necessary for classifying the account as an A, B, or C. We will begin with the value of your time. This can be determined in two ways, both useful.

Cost Per Hour The cost method of deriving your time's worth takes into consideration the direct costs accrued in your pursuit of an account. These direct costs include your salary, bonuses, commissions, travel expenses, and other miscellaneous expenses. Knowing the profit margin of the product is not necessary to figure your *cost per hour* (CPH). The formula is:

$$CPH = \frac{DC}{WH}$$

CPH = cost per hour
DC   = direct costs
WH = working hours

For example, let's say a salesperson's direct costs are:

Salary	$15,000
Commissions	3,000
Travel	8,000
Miscellaneous	4,000
Direct Costs	$30,000

This is fairly typical because direct costs are usually twice the salesperson's salary. To figure CPH, you divide the figure representing direct costs by 2,000 working hours (based on 40 hours per week for 50 weeks of the year). If your working hours differ from our figure, be sure to use your own figures:

$$CPH = \frac{DC}{WH} = \frac{\$30,000}{2,000} = \$15/hr.$$

In this example, the salesperson's time is worth $15 per hour. This is not terribly accurate, however, because none of us is fully productive for 40 hours a week. It is nice to think we're being paid while we eat lunch, but in reality it's just not so. It's much more accurate to assume that your call hours are the only productive hours in your day. To know what your time is worth during the sales call (and later to determine whether you are wasting time or not), you need to divide your direct costs by the number of *call hours* (CH) in a year, rather than the total hours worked:

$$\text{Cost Per Call Hour (CPCH)} = \frac{DC}{CH} = \frac{\$30,000}{800} = \$37.50/\text{hr.}$$

The cost per call hour is important to remember so that you can aspire to earn more money for the company per call hour than you cost the company to keep you employed. Doing so will put you in the black rather than in the red or simply breaking even.

Break-even Sales Volume   Now that you know what your time is worth per call hour, you can figure out how much you have to sell in order to break even. In calculating your *break-even volume* (BEV), you must know the gross margin on your products. We will assume that you either know or can find out this information. For the purpose of illustration, consider the case of a salesperson getting a product for one price and selling it for another. The difference will be the gross profit margin. The formula for calculating break-even volume is:

$$BEV = \frac{DC}{GMP}$$

BEV = break-even volume
DC = direct costs
GMP = gross margin percentage

To illustrate, suppose a salesperson has gross sales of $100,000 in a year and the product sold cost $80,000. Subtracting the latter from the former would give you the gross profit. This can also be expressed as a percentage of the gross sales:

Sales	$100,000
Cost of Product	−80,000
Gross Profit	$20,000

$$\text{Gross Margin Percentage   (GMP)} = \frac{\$20,000}{\$100,000} = .2 \text{ or } 20\%$$

From this, the break-even volume can be calculated:

$$BEV = \frac{DC}{GMP} = \frac{\$30,000}{.20} = \$150,000$$

This figure tells you what your sales volume must be for the year in order to cover your direct costs and simply break even. Naturally you will aim to have gross sales far above your break-even volume so that you can contribute to the profits of your company (and be indispensable as a salesperson).

Knowing what your volume has to be for the year does not give you a feel for how you are doing on a per-call-hour basis. This can be worked out by the following formula:

$$BEV/CH = \frac{CPCH}{GMP}$$

Taking the numbers from the examples above, if your sales call time is worth \$37.50/hr. and your gross margin percentage is 20%, your break-even volume per call hour is:

$$BEV/CH = \frac{\$37.50}{.20} = \$187.50$$

This tells you that for every hour you make sales calls (based on 800 call hours/year), you need to make \$187.50 in sales in order to just break even.

Now that you know what your time is worth, you are much closer to making an objective evaluation of whether a particular account is worth your time to call on.

Return On Time Invested   The final step in evaluating an account before assigning it a priority is calculating your *return on time invested* (ROTI). This is basically a ratio of the results of your efforts and the amount of effort you put in:

$$ROTI = \frac{Sales\ results}{Sales\ efforts}$$

As with the value of your time, with ROTI there are several ways of measuring sales results and effort. Sales results can be measured in gross margin, gross sales, or number of units sold. The best method is to use gross margin, which we have available to us already. Sales effort can be measured in the number of calls, amount of time spent on the account, or the direct cost of your time. Since we have been working with direct cost, we shall continue to do so. The formula looks like this:

$$ROTI = \frac{GM}{DC}$$

ROTI = return on time invested
GM   = gross margin in \$
DC   = direct costs in \$

Let's say a salesperson has gross sales of \$30,000 in a year from Account A and knows her gross margin percentage is 20%. From this we can calculate her gross margin in dollars:

$$GM = Sales\ Volume \times GMP = \$30,000 \times .20 = \$6,000.$$

The question still remains: Was the account worth her time? She projects her direct costs for Account A to be three thousand dollars. Her net profit, therefore, is three thousand dollars. This can also be expressed in a ratio as ROTI:

$$\text{ROTI} = \frac{\text{GM}}{\text{DC}} = \frac{\$6,000}{\$3,000} = 2$$

The number 2 indicates that her return on time invested on Account A was two to one. Ratios provide a faster means of comparison than straight profit figures. The ROTI ratio takes into account both the factors of profit and time invested. It, therefore, keeps everything in the perspective we want. A ratio greater than one is profitable. A ratio of one means breaking even and a ratio of less than one means a loss, because more money was spent in costs than was made in profits for that account.

Classification   The last item on your account profile is the account classification based on your past ROTI. After you have calculated your ROTIs for all your accounts, you should divide them into three groups. For example, the highest 20 percent could be designated A accounts; these are the most worthwhile customers in terms of profitability. The middle 50 percent could be designated B accounts, and the bottom 30 percent classified as C accounts. You may want to use your own percentage breakdowns for A, B, and C accounts based on the specific ROTI scores that your accounts generate.

To further help you organize your classified accounts, the Key Accounts Worksheet (5-8) is provided. This worksheet simply categorizes the accounts, so that you can see them all in front of you.

Another interesting way of organizing your customer list is shown in the grid of Worksheet 5-9. This compares customers in terms of profit (ROTI) and sales volume. Evaluate each of your accounts in these areas and write their names in the appropriate squares. From this you will see which accounts require profit improvements, which require volume improvement, or both. For example, you will try to increase volume for those accounts which fall into the high-profit, low-volume area (upper left). For low-profit, low-volume accounts (lower left), you will try to increase both (without spending too much time on them because they would be considered poor C accounts). The difficult combination to improve is the high-volume, low-profit accounts. In this case, it is either the profit margin of the product that needs to be changed or the direct costs. Unless you have been inefficient, it is difficult to significantly lower your overhead. You might be better off trying to improve other accounts in the grid, keeping in mind that the desired direction of the improvement is from the lower left to the upper right side of the grid.

Having analyzed and classified your accounts into As, Bs, and Cs, you can now take a look at the problems and opportunities in your territory. This will suggest objectives and strategies for dealing with them.

DATE:_____through_____

Product/Service:_____

_____

 A Accounts

 B Accounts

 C Accounts

Prospects

Worksheet 5-8:   Key Accounts

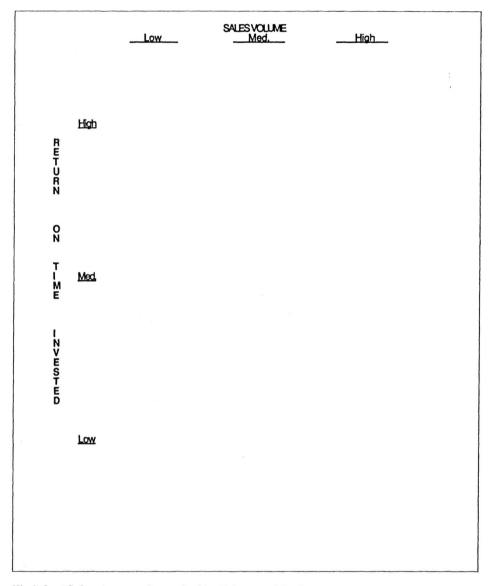

Worksheet 5-9:   Accounts Categorized by Volume and Profit

PART THREE: Territory Objectives and Strategies

TERRITORY OPPORTUNITIES AND PROBLEMS

Our world is in a constant state of flux. Changes in every facet of life occur so quickly that you would need a network of computers to keep track of them all. The business world is no different. Changes in manufacturing, commercial, and retail enterprises are mercurial. As a professional salesperson, you need to keep pace with the changes in your territory. Some of these changes will be to your advantage and others will cause headaches. The more aware you are, however, the fewer headaches they will cause.

Opportunities and problems can arise from both inside and outside the company. Environmental and market influences can affect sales as much as company policies, products, or services. Factors in the market which may cause increased opportunities include changes in consumer demand, fads, increased affluence due to social mobility, and the increased impact of technology. In fact, technology is such a strong influence on products that manufacturers estimate that over half of their existing products have been on the market for less than five years. This, obviously, will affect the salespeople handling those products.

Opportunities that stem from your company are the easiest to define and use. In our competition analysis you should have listed those strengths which put your company and its products ahead of your competitors. These can create strong selling points in market segments that will respond to them. Your company can also create opportunities through the introduction of new products or the improvement of old ones. New features and benefits often create renewed interest and sales. Promotional specials accomplish the same purpose by offering your customers a one-time-only offer which they can't refuse.

Every market segment and company has its problems. There is no denying that some problems out in the field exist because of things that the company has done. Sometimes poor management causes the company's image to be less than ideal. Sometimes a salesperson who starts working for a company which has just changed ownership may need to overcome a bad company reputation. This adds another challenge to the overall task of selling. The new reputation is built through the sales force and service, so the salesperson's role is essential in this metamorphosis.

Other influences from outside the company can cause problems: unfavorable market trends can shift business away from you; customers can be very fickle; a change in technology or fads may trigger a switch to another company. Although changing fads can create opportunities, they can also dry up a market. Stiff competition can also cause problems. There is no denying that some companies dominate a market segment; it requires an extra effort on your part to compete with them. The best way to do this is to carefully analyze your relative strengths and capitalize on them.

After completing a situation analysis for all your market segments, isolate the opportunities and problems and set up objectives for dealing with them. However, you cannot do this just once and leave it at that. Being aware of changes is a continuing part of being a successful salesperson.

Territory Objectives

As mentioned above, setting objectives is the next step in the overall management of your territory. The objectives you create should flow directly from your situation analysis as well as your observations of the existing territory problems and opportunities. Naturally, these goals will be aimed at overcoming the problems and exploiting the opportunities.

There are several other reasons for setting territory objectives. First, they serve as an incentive to motivate you. Only when you are challenged sufficiently will you seek new performance levels and strive toward loftier goals. Second, objectives define and control your activities. They take the randomness out of your calls by creating priorities. Objectives suggest action to be taken. Finally, concrete objectives give you something by which to evaluate your performance. They act as yardsticks by which you can gauge your effectiveness. From this feedback you will then modify your next set of objectives.

The objectives you set for your territory should include all accounts, market segments, products and services, and promotional and travel expenses. Some examples of territory objectives are:

1. Dollar volume for the entire territory
2. Percentage increase in volume over last year by a specific percentage range
3. Increase in sales of certain products by certain amounts
4. Increase in overall sales or specific product sales in particular market segments
5. Reduction by a certain percentage of overhead expenses for the entire territory
6. Addition of specific market segments to the overall sales effort
7. Increase in the number of new accounts over last year by a certain percentage
8. Increase in total dollar sales per customer
9. Upgrading a certain percentage of C accounts to Bs and B accounts to As
10. Seeing a certain number of prospects per week and turning a certain percentage of them into accounts
11. Reduction in expenses of sales calls by a certain percentage
12. Increase in the ratio of actual sales to sales calls
13. Addition of a certain number of qualified prospects to your files per month or year

One could go on and on listing objectives. The point is that your objectives will have to custom fit your customers, products and services, market segments, and territory. Your choice of objectives will make the difference between effective and ineffective management and sales in your territory.

Territory Strategy

Everything we do requires a strategy, no matter how simple it may be. If you are going to run an errand, you plan how you will travel, the best route to take, and how much time to spend doing it. When you have several errands, you usually figure out the most efficient way of accomplishing them all in the shortest amount of time. This is done so that you can save money, energy, and gas, and have some time left over for other activities. The same time management principle applies to territory management. Now that you have analyzed your accounts, classified them according to their profitability, and set objectives, you are in a position to decide when and how to call on them, how many to call on, and with what frequency.

There is no such thing as the "best" way to cover a territory. Every salesperson has a different combination of territory size, market segments, number of customers, and sales ability. There is, however, a general format which can be used and adapted by everyone in planning their territory strategy.

One of the first questions you need to answer is, "How many customers and prospects can I call on within the next planning period?" The Call Frequency Planner Worksheet (5-10) will prove invaluable to you in such an analysis. This is how it works:

1. Count the total number of A, B, and C accounts and prospects you wish to call on in your next planning period. In the Call Frequency Planner example shown, the plan covers the next six months. The numbers used in the Call Frequency Planner, Column 2, are 20, 50, 20, and 10.

2. From past experience and your account profiles, determine the average number of calls that you make on your accounts in each category. If you are planning for six months, such as in the example, you can think in terms of visits or calls twice a month, once a month, once every two months, or once a quarter. Column 3 lists the call frequencies for the six-month planning period.

3. Column 4 shows the total number of calls per category for the entire planning period. This figure is obtained by multiplying Column 2 by Column 3.

4. For each of your account classifications, calculate the average length of a sales call. This information should be available from your call records. The length of a call for customers can be estimated from your call records; the length of a call for prospects can be estimated from your past experience. As a rule of thumb, the time required for a prospect's call will be the same as other accounts within that market segment because their needs are so similar. Enter these averages in Column 5.

5. The time required for a call comprises more than the actual time spent face-to-face with a customer. It also includes planning (Column 6) and travel (Column 7) time. Both of these can be calculated from your records and field experience. In our example, a travel time of 20 minutes has been used for all types of accounts. Obviously, your numbers may be different. If your territory covers a large geographical area, you may want to fill out a separate worksheet for each area. This would prevent the differences in travel time from affecting the accuracy and realism of the planner.

6. Column 8 asks for the total time for each classification of accounts. This is simply

the sum of Columns 5, 6, and 7, multiplied by Column 4. For example, the total time for A accounts is:

Total time (Col. 8) = (40 + 30 + 20) × 240 = 21,600 minutes

This tells you that for the next six months you are going to spend 21,600 minutes on your A accounts.

7. Column 9 converts the total time from minutes to hours. This is done by dividing the total in Column 8 by 60 minutes per hour.

8. After arriving at the total hours for each type of account, add the figures in Column 9 so that you will know the total number of hours that you will have to work for the period. In the example, the total is 777 hours. Dividing this figure by 8 hours per day will give you the number of days required to cover all these accounts. In the example, 777 hours equals 97 days.

If you use a planning period of six months, they you have 120 days in which to work (based on 5 days per week). After filling out your Call Frequency Planner, if you find that your territory requires, for example, 97 days of work, then you can realistically manage your accounts in the next six months. However, if your total number of days exceed 120, then you need to go back and readjust your Planner. You could do this in several ways:

Plan to call on fewer accounts, especially fewer C and low priority B accounts.
Reduce travel time.
Use alternative methods of contacting accounts and prospects. For example, the less profitable accounts can be contacted by telephone or mail. This will save time that can then be devoted to the conversion of Bs to As, and so on.

If, as in our example, you find that you have planned for fewer than 120 days, you have two choices. You can increase any of the variables that seem too

Worksheet 5-10: Sample of a Call Frequency Planner

1 ACCT. CLASS	*2* NUMBER	*3* CALL FREQ.	*4* CALL TOTAL	*5* TIME/ CALL (MIN.)	*6* PLAN TIME	*7* TRAVEL TIME	*8* TOTAL TIME	*9* HOURS/ CYCLE
A	20	12	240	40	30	20	21,600	360
B	50	6	300	30	20	20	21,000	350
C	20	3	60	20	10	20	3,000	50
Prospect	10	2	20	20	10	20	1,000	17
Totals	100		320					777 hrs.

$$\text{Number of Days} = \frac{777 \text{ hrs.}}{8 \text{hrs/day}} = 97 \text{ days}$$

small. For example, you may want to increase call time or the number of prospects called on. Whatever you do, be sure to make the adjustment with profitability in mind. Your other choice is to leave the Planner as it is and use the extra time to cover the inevitable emergencies, unexpected delays, waiting time, cancellations, and added travel time. Although you do not want too much extra time on your hands, neither do you want to create stress by planning your schedule to the exact minute.

The Call Frequency Planner, in a condensed format, lets you know if your call objectives are possible within the time allotted. Let's say one of your objectives is to add 25 new accounts in the next six months. If you know from experience that for every 6 prospects you call on, 2 become customers, then you will have to call on 75 prospects. If you can only humanly manage to call on 300 accounts in six months, then one quarter of them will have to be prospects in order to reach this goal. You can see now how the Planner puts everything into the realistic perspective of available time.

Alternatives to Personal Calls

When mapping out your territory, evaluate Bs, Cs, and prospects for possible alternatives to personal calls. Obviously the cost of a telephone call is significantly less than the cost of a personal call. If a call can be made effectively over the phone, it should be considered for all classifications of accounts.

In covering your territory, try alternating between phone calls and personal calls for B and C accounts. You might also try contacting C accounts strictly by phone and doing all your prospecting, market research, and scheduling by telephone. To augment your calls, you can send personal letters with promotional literature to all accounts. This, too, will save your time over personal calls.

CONTROL

The statistical evaluation of your sales performance forms a major tool for improving sales and lowering marketing costs. The collection and analysis of sales activity data will tell you *what* you are doing as well as *why*. This is the only way of documenting your strengths and weaknesses and the means to doing something about them. The control procedure allows you to stand back and see your effectiveness objectively in the same way a manager would. Control guides you to being a better salesperson in the future.

There are four phases to the control of a sales territory: standards of performance, collection of data on actual performance, performance analysis, and corrective action.

Standards of Performance

Every experiment has a baseline with which the results are compared. The standards you set up for your sales territory and individual accounts are the objectives you set up previously. These range from total sales volume for the territory to small details about one particular account. This process will lead you to the design of forms that will measure your performance both quantitatively and qualitatively.

Data Collection and Record Keeping

Paperwork is an unavoidable part of our lives. In sales, it is part of an ongoing routine which simply becomes second nature. The records you keep serve to refresh your memory, evaluate your performance, and reflect trends in account and market activities. It is important that you know which records are valuable and which are a waste of time. Develop the ability to design your own forms so that you can collect data on your personal goals and objectives. You should keep certain standard records:

Customer files. These consist of cards or a database with customer information on them—name, address, phone, buying criteria, important salespeople, customer's personal style, past sales, needs, competitors, and so on.

Prospect files. These contain the same kinds of available information as customer files but they are kept separate until a sale is made. After the sale, the data is transferred to the customer file.

Tickler file. This file is simply an elaborate calendar. The cards or data file are arranged by month and day to cover an entire year. The cards for the coming three months are broken down into individual days, whereas more distant months are not as detailed yet. As time goes by, upcoming months are broken down into individual days so that specific notes can be made on each day's card.

The tickler file helps you plan your time and keep track of appointments. If you have to call on an account every other Thursday, you would write it in on the appropriate card in the file. In your planning time, you can pull the cards for the coming week and see what your commitments are.

You may want to use differently colored index cards to distinguish between customers and prospects; A, B, and C accounts; and even market segments or geographical locations. Keep in mind that too many colors can become confusing. Decide on the best system for you. The tickler file should be cross-referenced to the customer and prospect files so that you can go from one to the other quickly for pertinent information.

Sales and customer service report. This is a daily or weekly form that lists all of your calls and details about them. You'll enter things such as the type of call (personal, phone, letter), class of account, results, time required, necessary follow-up, and so on. At the time you should enter relevant data in your customer or prospect files and any new appointments in your tickler file. The master sheet lets you determine at a glance how you spent your week, giving you the overall picture.

Expense reports. Keep a record of all your expenses on a daily basis, coded as to the customers on whom the money was spent. In addition, the classification of the account and type of expenditure should be noted. Expenses will include things like gas, tolls, hotel, taxis, and meals.

Summary reports. These are reports that you make out at the end of the month and at the end of a planning period. They summarize the following areas:

1. *Sales.* Volume in units and dollars, volume by customer and market segment, percent increase or decrease over previous period, percentage of sales to calls.

2. *Accounts.* Number of accounts contacted, number of new accounts, percentage sold, number of accounts lost, number of new prospects.
3. *Profit.* Gross profit by market segment, overall territory profit, profit margins, ROTIs.
4. *Selling Expenses.* Total expenses, expenses per call, expenses per geographic locale, expenses per account classification.
5. *Qualitative Ratings.* Your strong points for the period in question, your weak points, areas of improvement, information needed for more effective sales.
6. *Miscellaneous.* Types of promotion used and their effectiveness, number of phone calls made and their outcomes, sales aids used, number of days and hours worked, and so on.

As you can see, there is plenty of room for expanding the summary report to suit your needs. Often your company will give you forms which they require on a periodic basis. If these suffice for all your data, then you are in luck. If not, make up your own forms and have them photocopied. The insight you gain will be well worth the effort required to keep these records.

Analysis of Records

Periodically you will sit down with your records, summarize them, and analyze what has happened while you were busy working. In this chapter the tools have been provided for you to determine your strengths and weaknesses from these records. You now need to determine the causes of any problems which may be evident. The analysis of your problems will allow you to head off trouble before it has a negative effect on sales or your reputation. Problems usually occur slowly, so your intervention at an early stage will occur only if you monitor your territory.

Correction of Problems

The type of correction required is usually suggested by analysis of the problem. In general, however, you can ask yourself some questions to try to pinpoint areas that need work. Some of those questions are:

1. "What unnecessary activities am I undertaking?" Under close scrutiny, many activities appear to be pursued for enjoyment rather than productivity. Often salespeople will call on a C account simply because they are in the neighborhood. The fact that the time could be better spent elsewhere occurs to them only after the fact. Try to think of the things in your day that you can eliminate without missing them.
2. "What am I doing that can be done by someone else?" If you are in a position to delegate tasks, do so whenever possible. It is important to be objective in your evaluation of whether the other person can do the job. We often operate under the assumption that only we can do a specific job, when, in fact, it can be done by someone else. This is especially important to keep in mind when you realize how much your time is actually worth compared to a co-worker's.
3. "What activities should I be engaged in that I'm not?" This includes things like promotional activities, PR, personal education, prospecting, planning, and time

management. This is a good time to set up goals for those activities that you should be doing.

4. "Have I set the right priorities?" That is, do you spend your time where it is most cost-effective? Do you think in terms of your ROTI when planning business activities?

The Five Commandments of Territory Management

The management of a territory can make or break a salesperson. It is as much a part of selling as the face-to-face sales process itself. Following are what are called "The Five Commandments of Territory Management."

1. Analyze your territory, products and services, market segments, competition, accounts, trends.
2. Set objectives based on your territory's potential.
3. Plan a strategy for the territory in general and for your individual accounts in particular.
4. Keep accurate records.
5. Analyze your records periodically and set new objectives based on this analysis.

SUMMARY

The ingredients which most significantly affect your success as a professional salesperson are your *sales planning* and *territory management*. You may have a flawless presentation, excellent communication skills, and comprehensive product knowledge, but if you present your product to the wrong people, the sale will not be made. Effective territory management ensures that your time will be well spent.

The process of territory management includes the activities that are required to cover the relevant markets in a given geographic area. Of these activities, the sales plan forms the skeleton on which the rest of the system is hung. It identifies problems and opportunities, establishes priorities based on profits and the value of your time, sets objectives and strategies, and provides a means of evaluating performance over a given period of time.

A marketing plan represents the overall strategy that your company uses to identify and pursue promising markets. It includes the process of deciding the company's objectives, policies, resources, and strategies. The principles of sales planning and territory management which you will apply are the same as those used by your company. The difference is that your plans will be on a smaller scale and will affect specific accounts in a particular geographic area.

A sales plan and a marketing plan are practically identical except that a sales plan deals only with one salesperson's territory rather than an entire market. The sales plan involves a two-stage planning process. The first stage revolves around the territory and all of its characteristics. The second stage is concerned with the individual accounts and strategies for selling to them.

The two-stage planning process is a closed-loop system in which all stages depend on each other. All of the information obtained in the control section is fed back to the situation analysis so that the process can begin again. This is a cycle that *every professional* salesperson goes through on an annual or semiannual basis.

Thorough sales planning includes several important activities: situation analysis, development of company and product knowledge, market analysis, awareness of market trends, competition analysis, development of customer information, and account analysis. Some of these activities are self-explanatory; some require some additional review.

Knowing your company and its products is only part of your job as a salesperson. You must also know the market of which your territory is a small part. An analysis of your territory by *market segments* will simplify the process. A market segment is one category or type of industry or business, such as banks, libraries, hospitals, law firms, and so on.

Two types of data are needed for an accurate market analysis: *market potential* and *sales potential.* Market potential is the maximum number of sales possible for all companies in the market. Sales potential relates to the maximum number of sales possible for a specific company during a given period of time.

An important part of analyzing your territory is conducting a competition analysis. You will want to identify all competitors who have a significant influence on the market segments in which you are interested. Analyzing their share of the market, their strengths and weaknesses, and where they are headed in the future, compared with the same information on your company and products/services, will help you to quickly see which areas need improving and which can be emphasized in your selling efforts.

All of the research and analysis that you conduct assists you in setting priorities. It takes knowledge to decide what to do and when to do it, or in your case, on whom to call and when. The analysis of each customer and prospect will show you in hard figures which calls are worth your time and effort and which are not. Remember Pareto's 80-20 Principle: 20 percent of your accounts will constitute 80 percent of your total sales. The sales expenses for these key accounts are not much greater than for the smaller, less profitable ones. For this reason you must identify and cater to the profitable 20 percent and make them grow. This is the beginning of setting your account priorities.

The business world, like every other facet of life, is in a constant state of flux. As a professional salesperson, you need to keep pace with the changes in your territory. Some of these changes will be to your advantage and others will cause headaches. The more aware you are, however, the fewer headaches they will cause.

Opportunities and problems can arise from both inside and outside the company. Environmental and market influences can affect sales as much as company policies, products, or services. Factors in the market which may cause increased opportunities include changes in consumer demand, fads, increased affluence due to social mobility, and the increased impact of technology. In fact, technology is such a strong influence on products that manufacturers estimate that over half of their existing products have been on the market for less than five years. This obviously will affect the salespeople handling those products.

Being constantly aware of change and the opportunities and problems that it can bring helps you set objectives for the overall management of your territory. The objectives you create should flow directly from your situation analysis as well as your observations of the existing territory problems and opportunities. These goals will be aimed at overcoming the problems and exploiting the opportunities.

There are several other reasons for setting territory objectives: 1) They serve as an incentive; 2) they define and control your activities; and 3) they give you something by which to evaluate your performance. Your choice of objectives will make the difference between effective and ineffective management and sales in your territory. They must custom fit your customers, products and services, market segments, and territory.

In addition to setting territory objectives, it is necessary to create a territory strategy, which is basically time management principles applied to your territory. Once you have analyzed your accounts, classified them according to their profitability, and set objectives, you are in a position to decide when and how to call on them, how many to call on, and with what frequency.

Having a system of control for your activities as salesperson is especially important. The statistical evaluation of your sales performance forms a major tool for improving sales and lowering marketing costs. The collection and analysis of sales activity data will tell you *what* you are doing well as well as *why*. This is the only way of discovering your strengths and weaknesses and the means to do something about them. The control procedure allows you to stand back and see your effectiveness objectively in the same way a manager would. Control guides you to being a better salesperson in the future.

There are five commandments of territory management to keep in mind: 1) analyze your territory, products and services, market segments, competition, accounts, and trends; 2) set objectives based on your territory's potential; 3) plan a strategy for the territory in general and for individual accounts in particular; 4) keep accurate records; and 5) analyze your records periodically and set new objectives based on that analysis.

DISCUSSION QUESTIONS

1. How does a marketing plan differ from a sales plan and what should the relationship be between the two?
2. What does the preparation of a solid sales plan require?
3. What is meant by a market analysis?
4. What is the importance of preparing a competition analysis?
5. Explain Pareto's 80-20 Principle and how it applies to your sales efforts.
6. What is involved in preparing an account analysis?
7. How do you determine the potential profitability of an account?

8. What is meant by account classification and why is the process important to your sales effort?

9. What is a market segment?

10. In planning your market strategy, would it be wiser to specialize in one industry and see fewer accounts, or to call on as many accounts as possible in many industries? Why?

11. How is a territory strategy prepared and why should one be prepared?

12. Why is it important to keep detailed sales records? What specific information can be learned by the periodic analysis of sales records?

CHAPTER SIX

Prospecting

CHAPTER OBJECTIVES	
CHAPTER OBJECTIVES	1 Introduce the process of the sales pipeline and its use.
	2 Recognize sources of prospects.
	3 Present direct mail techniques.
	4 Discuss the importance of qualifying prospects.
	5 Suggest systems that will avoid a "hit or miss" sales career.

The goal of every salesperson is to make sales. Unlike most other businesses, in sales the purchase represents merely the tip of the iceberg. What lies below the tip, or in this case, before it, is much research, preparation, and legwork. If you haven't done the advance work, you might as well be selling to a penguin with bad credit.

To conceptualize the need for preparation, imagine that you are in the plant business. You grow house plants and carry twelve varieties, each of which blooms in a different month of the year so that you have a different plant available each month of the year. Each of these plants, however, requires twelve months to grow from seedling to full bloom. In addition, each plant requires attention once a month. This attention includes feeding, watering, pruning, rotation, and "psychological counseling." Because of this you set up a schedule in which you plant the seeds a year in advance and then every month do what is required to continue or start the growth of each plant. The pay-off does not come until a year after you have started, but each month thereafter a new plant will be ready to sell. You will be all set, unless you forget a step some month. You will discover your oversight many months down the line. By then, however, it is too late. In the plant business, you can not plant the seeds on the thirtieth of the month and expect to have a sale on the first of the next month.

The development of your business as a salesperson also requires investing in a future payoff. The time lag between planting your seeds and reaping the rewards varies. Each month, however, you must do what is necessary to ensure a future yield. The maintenance and growth of your business requires that you:

1. Continually replenish your source of prospective customers.
2. Qualify prospects to determine their eligibility as customers.
3. Study the needs of each prospect.
4. Propose solutions to prospects' problems.

Developing the habit of engaging in these activities routinely will provide a smooth flow of income in the future. A failure to tackle these activities conscientiously will create a *sales slump.*

REPLENISHING THE SOURCE OF CUSTOMERS

A sales slump is usually due to negligence. Throughout the years we have found that salespeople who get lazy or ignore the cyclical nature of sales eventually experience slumps. Slumps can be avoided by maintaining an effective pipeline.

Figure 6.1 demonstrates the steps necessary in creating an effective sales pipeline. Starting at the top of the pipeline, you have an almost infinite source of prospects. Through the process of qualification, you reduce the infinite source to a realistic number. This group then enters the pipeline to be processed. You contact the prospects and study their needs to determine how your product or service can help them. After preparing an intelligent proposal, you suggest several alternatives to the prospective client and confirm the sale. You have then added yet another customer to your pool.

The flow from the reservoir of prospects to the pool of customers will be constant as long as you earnestly maintain each phase of the pipeline. This will result in a continual flow of income to you and make slumps a thing of the past.

QUALIFYING PROSPECTS

The failure to qualify a prospect will cause you considerable frustration, loss of time and money, and a decrease in your efficiency. Remember that a prospect is someone who has the need for your product or service. A *qualified* prospect not only has the need, but also the means to act. Your call-to-sale (closing) ratio will be much higher if you qualify each prospect before making your call.

Qualifying a prospect involves three basic steps:

1. Set the conditions for qualifying your prospects. Make a checklist of important prospect characteristics such as position in company, credit, and so on.
2. Determine if your prospect possesses those factors.
3. Decide if this is a good time to initiate contact with this prospect. Timing is often essential.

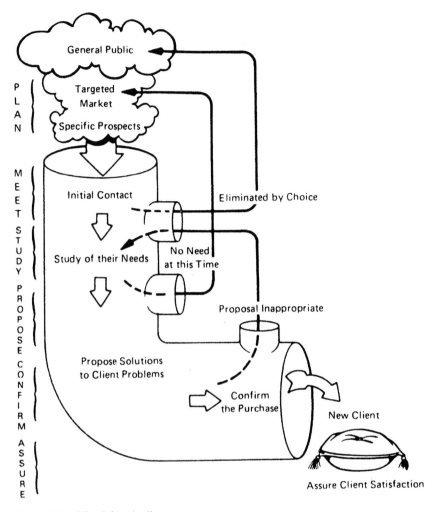

Figure 6.1: The Sales Pipeline

Sources of Prospects

Productivity, whether of a factory, a writer, or a salesperson, requires raw material. In the sales business, your raw material is people. You more than anyone else must be a "people person." You need to meet new people constantly in order to maintain a steady flow through your sales pipeline.

The sources of prospects are quite extensive; they are so extensive in fact, that many salespeople find them overwhelming. Having too many choices often makes decisions more difficult. As a salesperson, you need to be well-versed in all the proven methods of obtaining a prospect pool before choosing your best strategy. Only then can you professionally generate a virtually endless number of people to meet as prospects. The most accepted sources of prospects are depicted in Figure 6.2.

Prospects can be found in all walks of life. For every person you meet there is a chance that he or she may need your product or service. Getting to these people is just a matter of time, technique, and perseverance.

1. Customers Satisfied customers represent an excellent source of prospects for you. They will talk to their friends and associates about their new purchase and they may mention your name. Occasionally a customer will tell you the name of an associate, but this is rare. It is up to you to tactfully ask your customers for referrals. This is a habit you could cultivate after each sale or call. If you are always tactfully asking customers for referrals, perhaps they will think of some for you even when you're not there. If nothing else, they will be impressed with your enthusiasm and "stick-to-itiveness."

Most professional salespeople say the most effective way to obtain referrals is to ask specific leading questions. One way of doing this is to review your list of qualifying criteria for prospects. Choose one criterion and base your

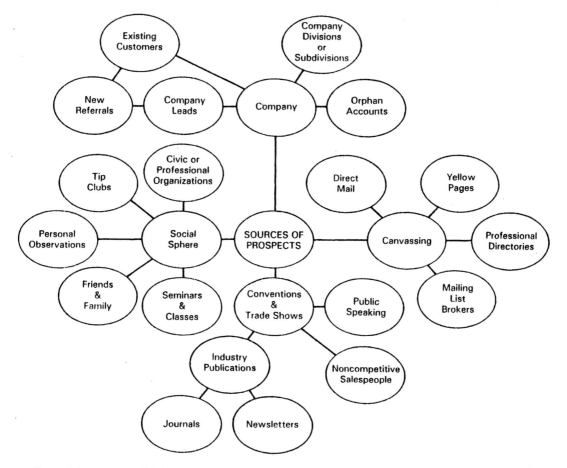

Figure 6.2: Sources of Sales Prospects

question on it. For example, one of your qualifying criteria may be that the prospect has been recently promoted. You would then ask your customer, "Who do you know who has recently been promoted?" You should then remain silent, giving your customer time to think. It is important to be quiet while customers think. If you keep on talking you will only distract him and will end up with fewer names, if any.

If your first question does not produce any leads, run down your list of qualifying criteria and ask similar questions. Be sure to phrase the question so that it is *open-ended* rather than requiring a yes or no answer. The example above is an open-ended question. A closed-ended question would be, "Do you know of anyone who has recently been promoted?" It is too easy for a client just to say no if he can not think of anyone off-hand. An open-ended question, however, requires that he think for a moment.

When a customer is giving you referrals, especially if there is more than one, jot them down without analyzing them. After he is finished, you can go back and question him on qualifying details.

Your customers are some of the most valuable resources for referrals that you have. They know other business people in their field and are in the best position to recommend you to them. For this reason, you should ask your customer if you can mention her name when contacting someone to whom she referred you. Through your customers you will find new branches to follow to tap prospects.

2. *Other Prospects* Prospects beget prospects. Many new salespeople assume that if a prospect does not buy, then there is no potential in the relationship. This is not so. A prospect can be asked for referrals in the same way that established customers are asked. With a prospect, however, it is paramount that you create a professional business relationship before asking for referrals. If you are perceived as being credible, trustworthy, and ethical, your prospect will have no qualms about referring you to others. In fact, the better your relationship with a prospect, the harder he will work to think of referrals for you. When they can, people like to help those they like.

3. *Company Leads* Your company can furnish you with some very high-quality leads. They procure their leads from mailing programs, telephone solicitation, existing customers, and other sources. Sometimes your company will have also done the qualifying for you.

Company leads have the advantage of giving you credibility simply by virtue of being associated with your firm. Thus, you can immediately establish a trusting relationship and work on studying the prospect's problems. The prospects who come directly to your company often do so out of need. They may be shopping around for a particular product or service. The first salesperson to get to them can often make the sale if he or she handles it right. This is also true with competitive bidding. The first person to contact the prospect has the advantage. She can get information to which others might not have access. Being first, she will find the prospect still tolerant and willing to answer a lot of questions. In addition, the salesperson will be more impressive, showing enthusiasm by being first.

4. *Friends and Social Contacts*   Your family and friends can provide a rich source of prospects. It is not uncommon to learn that a salesperson's friends and relatives have only a vague idea of what he does. Now is the time to enlighten everyone as to the exact nature of your business. This should be a two-way communication. Not only will you tell them what you do, you will also be sensitive to their needs. Whether you can sell to them is secondary. Like any prospect, they may be able to refer you to others. It is worthwhile to qualify your friends and relatives before contacting them. Let's say you are selling Lear Jets. Obviously, one qualifying criterion will be socioeconomic status. You would be wasting your time and embarrassing a friend or relative if you contacted them and *later* discovered that they are on welfare. It pays to do your homework. Worksheet 6-1 is designed to help you evaluate your opportunities among your friends. When filling out the tree, you will probably discover opportunities that had previously escaped you. This will happen often as you become more and more aware of the innumerable sources of prospects that exist.

Once you have contacted your friends and relatives, devise a method of maintaining that contact on a regular basis. Start a mailing list and send them something periodically to keep them up-to-date on you. Newsletters, brochures, direct mail correspondence, and birthday cards will all serve you well.

It must be stressed, however, that when you approach a friend or relative, do it in a low-keyed manner. Your sense of professionalism dictates that tact and sincerity are called for here. If you get the reputation of being overly aggressive, people will avoid you. Go about it in a matter-of-fact way at first. If they are interested, then put them on the mailing list and keep them informed. You have to be able to achieve a balance between social and business interests; otherwise, you will be left with only business.

5. *Membership in Civic and Professional Organizations*   As an individual, become involved with your family, friends, and different community groups. You will lead a more fulfilled life if you are active and interested in the world around you. From all of this will naturally come new social and business relationships. If you join a club or organization with the intention of milking it for its business, you will end up miserable. People can sense when they are being used. For example, assume that you are participating in a professional organization for the same benefits as everyone else. There is certainly nothing wrong with letting people know what you do and of your willingness to be of service to them. In the natural course of conversation you will frequently be asked, "What do you do?" The fastest way to turn people off is to launch into, "I'm glad you asked . . . this week we are having a half-price special on one-legged panty hose. May I interest you in a pair?" It is to your advantage simply to tell them what you do and leave it at that. Later, if you see that you may be of some service to them, you can approach them and discuss it in a relaxed and helpful way. You do not have to land every prospect as he or she appears.

Friends who know your capabilities and degree of professionalism make a good "tree" for potential customers.

Demographic characteristics of each friend should be evaluated to maximize your time and to avoid wasting their time. Age, occupation, length of time known, how well known, how often seen, ability to provide referrals, and how easy it is to approach this person are some factors to consider.

	TYPE OF FRIENDS	LIST TWO NAMES
School friends:		
Friends of family:		
Neighbors:		
Known through spouse:		
Known through children:		
Known through hobbies:		
Known through church:		
Known through social clubs:		
Known through community activities:		
Known through past employment:		
People with whom you do business:		
Other:		

Worksheet 6-1: The Friendship Tree
Source: Steve Curtis, Marketing Institute, Newport Beach, CA.

Once you get to know everyone in the organization (if it is small enough for you to do so), you can try to obtain a membership list or directory. You are then in a position to systematically contact each person, again in an informative, casual way. It is not advisable to send blanket direct mailings, unless you want to be the subject of organizational gossip. If people ask for brochures or information, by all means accommodate them. The idea is to enjoy the organization and the people in it. If you also broaden your prospect reservoir, then you have really lucked out. The chances are that you will. The organizations that you choose to join and participate in should be loaded with prospects within your priority target markets.

6. *Centers of Influence*   A center of influence (also called an opinion leader) is someone in a position to steer you to prospects and prospects to you. He or she is someone important to you for one reason or another. There are centers of influence in every facet of life and business. In order to ask a favor of someone who is going to influence the opinions of others, you must build rapport with that influential person. Opinion leaders as contacts are extremely valuable in any endeavor.

You will find the following suggestions useful in dealing with centers of influence:

1. Focus on building a trusting relationship (rapport).
2. Be sure that they know the benefits you have given other customers.
3. Let them know of your goals so that they can be aware of the kind of prospects you are looking for.
4. Make sure that they know that you sincerely want their help.
5. Give them a formal presentation describing your services or products.
6. Provide them with an extensive list of testimonials, personal and business references, and a professional resumé. Centers of influence are very concerned about referring only those salespeople who will not undermine their reputations.
7. Be sure that you report back to the center of influence after you contact the person referred.
8. Find some professional way to reciprocate or to say "thank you" (through your profession).
9. Get to know your center of influence. He or she might be a prospect without even realizing it.

7. *Canvassing*   We once heard a story about a very determined salesman. He was working in an amusement park canvassing everyone. He approached two 18-year-old kids with his pitch: "Hi, I'm with the Dreamland Funeral Parlor. We're having a special this week on balsa wood coffins. I know you're a little young, but . . . ." The kids walked away and he stood there wiping two scoops of ice cream off his face, calling after them, "We'll even throw in a custom stereo system!" Some people will do *anything* for a sale!

Most people think of sales in terms of a salesperson coming to the house, getting his foot in the door, and giving his pitch, even to deaf ears. Canvassing is the most criticized form of generating prospects, probably because it puts the prospect in an uncomfortable position.

To combat this discomfort we recommend making *introductory calls.* The purpose of these calls is, naturally, to introduce yourself and your firm and to determine when and whether it is appropriate to make a sales call. On some occasions you can make a sale then and there; on others you will determine the best time to call again and whom to see when you do call back. The introductory call is in direct contrast to the cold call discussed previously in which pushy salespeople drop in unannounced and begin to deliver their sales pitch.

As a professional salesperson, you should be extremely selective in calling on people at random. Unsolicited calls, when little or no homework has been done on the prospect, are a low payoff, high-anxiety undertaking. Canvassing can be a potential source of prospects if you follow the steps outlined in the pipeline.

Before you contact people or firms in your area, they should be qualified. Because they are unsolicited prospects, study their situation to determine any obvious need for your service or product. You can then approach them in an intelligent fashion. Doing your homework will make you a credible salesperson from the beginning. This alone opens more doors than simply having a strong foot. If done with sincerity, interest, and research, canvassing can expand your prospect reservoir significantly.

8. Conventions and Trade Shows Conventions and trade shows are to a salesperson like a candy store to a child. They are gold mines for prospecting. Attend as many trade shows and conventions as is practical. Whether you are sent by your company or go on your own, you will accomplish the same goals for yourself:

1. Increase your knowledge of your industry.
2. Appraise the quality and type of convention or show. (Analyze the show for possible individual or company participation in the future.)
3. Determine the level and type of executives who attend.
4. Impress delegates with yourself and your product or service.
5. Obtain as many prospects as possible.

Conventions are planned far in advance, often years. Therefore, you have plenty of time to do your homework before a convention or show. Find out who is attending or being represented. See if any of your company's present customers or prospects are planning to be there. Arrange to meet with them to solidify your current business relationships.

At the convention, try to meet as many people as possible. Determine why they are there and what they think of the convention and its various workshops. Discuss the latest developments in your field. Ask them about their companies and try to uncover their needs. Also attend as many workshops and seminars as possible. Be sure to take notes and save all handouts, programs, brochures, and literature. Plan to collect more business cards than you give away.

After the convention, follow up on your leads and prospects. Be sure to refresh their memories as to where and how you met. Often they will have pleasant recollections of the time you spent together at the convention.

Incidentally, when attending trade shows and conventions, save all of your receipts because they are often tax deductible!

9. *Directories* In addition to the Yellow Pages, your local library has directories on everything imaginable. Whether you are scouting out prospects in a particular area or creating a mailing list, directories will save you time and energy. Some directories list specific people to contact, such as corporate officers or department heads. Polk publishes a directory that is a reverse phone book for most major cities in the United States. You can look people up by their addresses. In some situations this can be very useful. For example, you may be selling dish antennas for satellite TV receivers. One of the things you will want to know is who in your area can afford one. In the directory, beside each address is the name and occupation of the resident. You are now in a position to send an introductory letter to as many people as you wish. The directory has given you the name, address, occupation, telephone number, and zip code of each person. What more could you ask for?

You *could* ask for someone else to make the initial contact to determine if prospects are even remotely interested. Many companies accomplish this by having a telemarketing team. These people call, ask certain questions, and set appointments if the prospect is interested. This saves everyone time and money.

10. *Tip Clubs* Many salespeople around the country have joined together to form small *tip clubs*. The purpose of these groups is to make each member aware of the resources available from the other members. This type of give-and-take results in a group synergism—the branches of each person's prospecting tree are extended farther outward. Each person is able to bring to the group his or her area of expertise, centers of influence, social networks, and business contacts. With everyone bouncing ideas off one another, a kind of professional kinetic energy develops in which everyone can gain information, cross-sell, obtain referrals, and increase the drive to achieve.

Most such groups meet on a regular basis over breakfast or lunch. They often have a short program during which a member can describe his or her product or service. Most tip clubs follow a few helpful guidelines:

1. *Establish a set of bylaws.* These can cover everything from the cost of lunch to ethical considerations of group interactions. An example of the latter might be that you do not use a member's name as a reference without having obtained permission.
2. *All expenses should be distributed evenly.* The fact that one member is a lawyer and another a telephone solicitor is irrelevant. The cost of meals, meeting rooms, speakers, and materials should be divided among the group on an equal basis.
3. *Shift the burden of running the group.* Periodically, the group should seek new volunteers to do whatever planning and arranging is necessary for the continuance of the meetings. This should be done in increments smaller than a year so that no one is unduly taxed with these chores.
4. *Limit membership to one representative in each field.* This will ensure that a cross-section of the community's resources are present while keeping the number of members manageable. The group could strive to have an accountant, sales reps from different fields, a lawyer, a banker, a writer, and so on.

11.   Study Groups   Study groups have become a very effective tool for strengthening a salesperson in his or her career. A study group is an assemblage of individuals involved in *similar* yet not identical activities. They form close, business-related friendships in order to help each other grow and develop as sales professionals. At each meeting, they bring one another up-to-date by comparing notes on recent events, types of strategies planned, obstacles encountered and overcome, and other insights. Each member tries to strengthen the other members by offering observations, assessments, feedback, and support.

Study groups become very creative, supportive environments in which each person can draw on the expertise and objectivity of others. A study group should always be kept noncompetitive. If the members are going after the same prospects, it is less likely that they will be open and supportive of one another. A study group could be viewed as your own personal board of directors.

12.   Direct Mail   Direct mail as a means of prospecting offers the major advantage of allowing you to reach a large number of people without being physically present. There are two basic kinds of direct mail strategies: one-time mailings and campaigns. The one-time mailing is aimed at generating an immediate response to an attractive offer. The *campaign* or *conditioning* method seeks to make the prospect increasingly more aware of you as a viable answer to her needs in a particular area. This involves a long-term campaign to create confidence and interest in your abilities as a professional salesperson. Many experts believe, as do we, that direct mailings should be followed by personal phone calls within two to four weeks after the mailing. Although this is time-consuming, it can significantly increase your "hit" ratio.

MAILING LISTS.   No matter how effective your direct mail letter is, if you send it to the wrong prospects you have wasted your time and money. *To whom* you mail is more important than what you mail to them. *What* you send, however, cannot be thought of as anything *less* than secondary.

Where will you get your mailing lists? In every major city there are firms that do nothing but compile mailing lists. You can rent these lists for $25 or more per thousand names. Renting a list from a list broker offers many advantages:

1. *Categorized lists.* Lists are classified by many different variables; some include geographic location, yearly income, demographics, age, interests, and so on. The larger the firm, the greater your choices will be. You may be able to save time in qualifying your prospects by asking for a specific type of list.
2. *Business expense.* Renting a mailing list is a business expense and therefore often tax deductible.
3. *Zip-code ordered.* When you are sending out a mailing to more than 200 addressees you can take advantage of bulk mailing rates. This requires separating the mail into groups by zip code. A rented list is already categorized by zip code, saving you hours of work. Bulk mail permits must be obtained from the post office but are worth the nominal fee.
4. *Computer-ready.* The mailing list you receive from a broker is available in a form which makes it ready to feed into a computer. You can then employ a typing

service with word processors to print out the address labels automatically.

5. *Clean and up-dated.* Most list brokers will guarantee that the list is current and has no "dirty" addresses on it. (Dirty addresses are those which cause the letter to come back marked "addressee unknown" or "return to sender.")

DIRECTORIES.   Depending on the size of your mailing, you may want to compile your own mailing list. This can easily be done by using the same directories we discussed as sources of prospects. In fact, whether you rent a list or not, you may want to go through local directories and add companies which may not be on your rented list.

PERSONAL MAILING LIST.   As a professional salesperson you should develop your own file of people to whom you will send mailings. This file can be accumulated over time and, like any list, needs to be cleaned periodically. Whenever you meet a prospect, trade business cards with him. Do not immediately throw that card into your mailing list, however, because he may not qualify. So qualify all new prospects for your personal mailing list just as you would if you planned to call on them in person.

When compiling your mailing list, it pays to be organized! Have separate lists with categories such as:

Customers already doing business with the company
High-potential prospects
Low- to medium-potential prospects
Centers of influence
Friends, relatives, and miscellaneous

You then need to determine when each of these groups should be contacted and how often. For example, you may want to contact pre-existing customers on a quarterly basis and low-potential prospects once a year. Mark your calendar and devise other systems for organization. It pays off in the long run.

Typically, direct mail yields a low percentage return. One to three percent is often good when you figure in the cost of developing the letter, postage, mailing lists, and so on. The sales on just one to three percent can be quite sizable. Be sure to measure the cost by average sale expected. You want people to be reminded of you and your ability to be of service to them in some way.

DIRECT MAIL TECHNIQUES.   What you send is second in importance only to whom you send it. When your prospect opens your mailing you want him to read it and to be interested in finding out more about you and your services. To increase the chances of this happening, you must design the mailing so that it will be attractive, easy-to-read, and informative.

Direct mail has become a science. In general the mailing should observe the following rules:

1. *Make it personal.* A letterhead should appear at the top of the page so the prospect can identify the mailer immediately. This may stop her from throwing it in

the trash. If your prospect is interested, your letterhead will prevent her from having to search the page for your name and address.

2. *Cover only one idea.* It is often tempting to cram in as much information as will fit on the page. The rationale behind this is, "As long as I'm going through the time and expense, I might as well get as much exposure as I can." This is not a sound advertising practice. You must keep the mailing as simple and straightforward as possible. Be satisfied to cover one idea well. As you will see, you will not have the room for more than one concept if you develop your mailing correctly. So aim for simple effectiveness (rather than complex chaos).

3. *Focus on benefits, not features.* This means that you should stress *what* effect you want. How the effect is achieved is important to you. That is, think of yourself as a consumer. If you are considering buying a food processor, you are more interested in all the things it can do than how or why it does them, which is the engineer's concern.

4. *Make it easy to read and attractive.* If you pick up a mailing that looks like a page of a book, the chances are that you will not read it. Let's face it, everyone is lazy sometimes. Your mailing must look attractive and draw your prospect in. For this reason it should not be solid text. This can be avoided by staggering the left-hand paragraph margin every couple of paragraphs. Use colors to emphasize different sections and important points. Arrange the page so that it looks interesting.

DEVELOPMENT OF AN EFFECTIVE MAILING.   Mailings should have a logical flow. They should aim to answer the reader's unconscious questions as they arise.

"What is it?"
"What does it do?"
"How would I use it?"
"Oh, yeah? Prove it!" or "Interesting, but I'd like a second opinion."
"If I'm interested, how do I get one?"
"How much does it cost?"

Your mailing should answer these questions in a way that impresses your prospects. The best way to impress is to adhere to the following five steps.

1. *Description.* Describe the product or service in a concise, attractive way, without claiming miracles. Be sincere and let the facts speak for themselves. For example, you might say, "We have a training program available which will make your salespeople much more aware of the number of prospects they can contact."

2. *Illustration.* Examples speak louder than descriptions. In this case, you might show a copy of a letter of appreciation from a customer, such as the one below. (Naturally the letter would have to be photo-reduced.)

Dear Dr. Alessandra:
   It is my pleasure to report to you that your Seminar on Prospecting was a complete success! Within a month, every member of our sales team had increased his prospect file by 25 percent and sales have increased an average of 14 percent. People are still talking about how effective your methods are once they adapted them to their target markets. . . .

3. *Claim on your behalf.* You are then in a position to promise the same results for your prospect. "Your company can see the same increase in sales and prospects after our three-hour seminar!"

4. *Proof.* This is the time to soothe the skeptical beast that afflicts most prospects. Your prospect may be thinking, "OK, that's *one* company that it worked for. Big deal. . . ." You can now dispense with humility and show how good you are. You may want to quote magazine articles or other reviews, as if advertising a movie.

"By far the most valuable seminar we've ever sponsored." KIRK STEELTOE, Mgr., Midwest Marketing Enterprises

". . . makes prospecting something tangible for a change." ROCKO GREEN, Chairman, Multi-National Multi-Level Marketing, Inc.

5. *Call for action.* Now that your prospect is interested, you need to use words which will spur him on to action. Using action words will help motivate. "Call our toll-free number now to find out more about how your sales team can gain the competitive edge!" Or you might encourage prospects to act by offering a special deal. "Increase your sales prospects! Send the enclosed postcard by November 30 and get 10 percent off our three hour seminar!" Both of these examples achieve three things. They repeat the claim, make it easy to respond, and use action words. To increase the ease of response in the second example, you would be sure to enclose a self-addressed stamped postcard.

After you have designed and laid out your mailing, double-check it for mistakes. You should also show it to someone who can react to it objectively. Often we are too emotionally wrapped up in our creations to see the mistakes in them. Make sure it is obvious to the reader how to contact you.

FOLLOW-UP. Needless to say, you will follow up on any responses to your mailing. Go one step further. Choose those companies that you wish that you had heard from and follow-up on them whether they respond or not. It is very possible that the combination of the mailing and a personal contact will prove advantageous.

RECORD KEEPING. This section will show you how a dull pain now can prevent a migraine later. Keeping records allows you to know what you are accomplishing and to do more of it in the future, if it is producing results. If you know your gross profit and expenses for any given mailing, you can determine your ROI and WIWMTM. Your ROI is the *return on your investment.* Did you make 5 percent, 10 percent, or 50 percent? If your ROI was low, could you have improved the mailing in some way? Would the money have earned you more interest in the bank? If so, you should figure out why your ROI was so low. Once you know whether you made any money, you will know your WIWMTM—Was it worth my time and money? Hopefully it was, but you will know only if you keep careful records.

Another reason to keep good records is for tax purposes. Every penny that you spend on a mailing is an expenditure for business and is probably deductible at tax time. Your accountant or tax preparer may need to see your records and the IRS certainly will if you are audited. Your records will save you money in the long run.

To take the guesswork out of cost analyses and to help you be more organized, we have included a worksheet for keeping track of your direct mail costs. The mail campaign budget breaks down your expenses from the development of the mailing to the sale of merchandise. It will give you a total of all your expenses to deduct from your gross profit. Keeping accurate records is one of the many habits cultivated by professional salespeople.

Worksheet 6-2: Budget for Direct Mail Campaign (one mailing)

NAME OF
MAIL PIECE:_____
OBJECTIVE:_____
DATE:_____
PREPARED BY:_____

A. DIRECT EXPENSES
1. Planning/Administrative/Operating
   Salaries (Man Hours x Hourly Rate) $_____
2. Creative Costs/Preparations
   a. Copy $_____
   b. Layout $_____
   c. Artwork $_____
   d. Photography/
      Retouching $_____
   e. Printing
      Preparation $_____
3. Other enclosure $_____
4. Envelopes $_____
5. Mailing list rental/purchase $_____
6. Mailing list maintenance $_____
7. Mailing piece preparation
   (folding, collating, inserting,
   labeling, addressing, metering
   sorting, typing, etc.) $_____
8. Postage
   a. Outgoing $_____
   b. Return $_____ $_____
9. If Selling Merchandise
   a. Cost of merchandise $_____
   b. Handling $_____
   c. Postage/shipping $_____
   d. Royalties $_____
   e. Refunds/cancellations $_____
   f. Refurbish returns $_____
   g. Bad debts $_____
   h. Storage $_____ $_____
10. Other $_____

TOTAL DIRECT EXPENSES $_____

13. Newsletters The rate of technical advancement in practically every field is so great that few individuals can keep abreast of it. If you are selling in one of these fields and have a thorough understanding of the changes as well as a knack for writing, you are in a prime position to issue a newsletter. For example, the home and small business computer market changes almost daily as new models and options are introduced. As an enterprising salesperson, you could develop a newsletter in which you call attention to new products, services, and technological improvements. Mailing a monthly newsletter of this type would certainly be a service to your customers and prospects. They would appreciate your saving them time and would keep you in mind as someone with whom to do business.

The most difficult part is finding the time to read, simplify, and rewrite newsworthy information. Keep in mind that a good newsletter should be:

1. *Sent out regularly.* Remember that consistency and regularity prove how serious you are.
2. *Brief.* No advertising, fish stories, or poetry for filler. Just meat.
3. *Clear.* Your writing must be concise, informative, and directed to the people to whom you are sending it.
4. *Accurate.* Your credibility is at stake. Make sure your facts are accurate.
5. *Personal.* Write your newsletter as if you were the reader's personal consultant. Giving advice and your opinion is fine as long as you make it clear that it is strictly *your* opinion.

14. Seminars and Classes For the professional salesperson, appearing as a lecturer or teacher is an exciting and rewarding way to gain exposure. You can offer to teach evening classes at local colleges and adult education programs. Large corporations occasionally hold seminars to improve their employees' skills. These all provide prime opportunities for you to become regarded as an expert in your field.

You may see the need for a seminar in a particular area but feel you do not have the expertise or time to conduct it yourself. In this case, hire a speaker under your sponsorship. When you sponsor a speaker, let it be known that you are doing so. After the seminar, provide a question-and-answer period in which you participate. Also, hand out product brochures and promotional materials to ensure your exposure.

The most valuable time after a class or seminar is when you socialize, listen to participants' individual needs, and schedule future contacts. This is the primary reason you are there.

15. Public Speaking Civic clubs, professional organizations, corporations, conventions, and church groups are constantly seeking effective speakers to address their groups. If you can develop your skills as a speaker, you will find this avenue to be highly rewarding and fruitful as a prospect generation source.

The speech you give as a public speaker needs to be much more general than the one you give as a lecturer or teacher. Remember not to be overly commercial! Focus on the broad subject in which your area of expertise lies.

There are two effective ways to gain prospects from a public speaking engagement. One way is to distribute response cards on which interested prospects fill in their names and phone numbers. Another method is to hold a drawing. Bring along a gift or offer a discount on your firm's product. To enter the drawing, the participants simply drop a business card into a box from which you will pick the winner. You will then have scores of names to qualify later as prospects. You can also offer to send a free article on your speech topic to those

Worksheet 6-3: Prospecting Action Plan

DIRECTIONS: Write out techniques to increase your exposure and generate more prospects
from these sources:

Source_____

1. A. _____

    B. _____

    C. _____

    D. _____

Source_____

2. A. _____

    B. _____

    C. _____

    D. _____

Source_____

3. A. _____

    B. _____

    C. _____

    D. _____

Source_____

4. A. _____

    B. _____

    C. _____

    D. _____

Source_____

5. A. _____

    B. _____

    C. _____

    D. _____

attendees who give you their business cards. When you mail the article, you can also include information about yourself, your company, and your products/services.

16. Personal Observation   Prospecting can take place whether you are wearing your three-piece suit or not. However, this is true only when it becomes *second nature*. Once you have conditioned yourself to recognize a prospect in any situation, you can act on the insight with a mailing, personal contact, conversation, and so on. You will find prospects in the newspaper, on TV talk shows, at parties, waiting in line, and in the doctor's office. The key is to have the qualifications firmly planted in your mind so that those types of people will jump out at you.

By now you see that prospects are ubiquitous—they are everywhere! Ways of contacting them are so numerous that they can be overwhelming. It is important for you to analyze your current sales situation and determine the sources that will be most productive for you. This will help you maximize the use of your time. The Prospecting Action Plan Worksheet (6-3) will clarify your prospecting goals and suggest action steps in achieving these goals. Take the time now to choose five sources (of the several we have described in this chapter) from which you would like to generate prospects. Think carefully about this; the five should be the ones that will yield the greatest number of qualified prospects. Under each of the five sources list the strategies to be used.

SYSTEMS OF SUCCESS

If you are scientific about your prospecting, you will increase your prospect reservoir and know exactly how you did it. This makes for future success rather than a hit-or-miss career. Adopt these systems for yourself:

> *Avoid confusion.* Be organized! Keep a good filing system. If necessary, get help in setting it up. When prospects are filed, make a log entry detailing where the prospect came from: referral, directory, introductory call, etc.
>
> *Monitor your results.* One of the great dangers in prospecting is the tendency to ease off as soon as the reservoir has swelled. Names alone are not enough; prospects must be qualified and moved into the pipeline for contacting.
>
> *Try different techniques.* Analyze and evaluate your prospecting system and your ROI. Discover which sources pay off best for you.
>
> *Follow up.* Imagine what not following through would do to your golf game. The effect is worse in sales. Having a file full of prospects' names makes you "prospect rich" but it does not increase your income.

There are literally acres and acres of diamonds (prospects) sitting out there waiting to be picked up. If you can cultivate an awareness of the sources and the discipline to pursue them, you will never have a sales slump and you will be handsomely rewarded for your efforts.

SUMMARY

The focus of this chapter was prospecting, the process of finding potential prospects and qualifying them in advance of the sales call. In order to be successful in sales, a professional salesperson must conduct a great deal of research, preparation, and legwork.

In developing your business as a salesperson, you must invest in future payoff, which means that you must do what is necessary to ensure a future yield. The maintenance and growth of your business depends on your: 1) continually replenishing your source of prospective customers; 2) qualifying prospects to determine their eligibility; 3) studying the needs of each prospect; and 4) proposing solutions to prospects' problems. Doing these activities routinely will provide a smooth flow of income in the future.

Qualifying prospects is an important step in prospecting. Failure to do so will cause considerable frustration, loss of time and money, and a decrease in your efficiency. A *prospect* is someone who has a need for your product or service; a *qualified* prospect not only has the need, but also the means to act, which is a significant difference.

Qualifying a prospect involves three steps: 1) set the conditions for qualifying your prospects; 2) determine if your prospect possesses those factors; and 3) decide if the time is right to initiate contact with that particular prospect.

For anyone in any business to be productive, raw material must be available. The raw material for a salesperson is people. As a salesperson, you want and need to meet new people constantly in order to maintain a steady flow through your sales pipeline.

The sources of prospects are quite extensive. Of all the sources available, the most accepted sources are those that follow:

Customers. Satisfied customers are an excellent source and probably the most valuable. A habit to cultivate is to regularly (and tactfully) ask those customers for referrals.

Prospects. Once a professional business relationship has been established with a prospect and you are perceived by him as credible, trustworthy, and ethical, you can ask him for referrals just as you would from established customers. This is true even if he does not buy from you.

Company Leads. Because companies frequently procure leads from mailing programs, telephone solicitation, existing customers, as well as other sources, they are an excellent source of prospects for their salespeople. Occasionally, the qualifying of these leads will already have been done. Company leads have the advantage of giving you credibility simply by virtue of being associated with your firm.

Friends and Social Contacts. Such a source can be quite valuable as a source of referrals. Regardless of the product or service that you sell, however, as with any other prospect it is best to qualify the prospect (relative, friend, or referral) prior to contacting him. A good tool for brainstorming this particular source is Worksheet 6-1. Filling it out will help you discover opportunities that had previously escaped you.

Membership in Civic and Professional Organizations. Becoming involved, active, and interested in the community will naturally bring new social and business relationships. However, you shouldn't participate in such activities with the intention of milking them for all the business you can get. Instead, you should enjoy the organizations and the people in them. Your business contacts will naturally expand in time.

Centers of Influence. A center of influence (also called an opinion leader) is someone in a position to steer you to prospects and prospects to you. It is especially important when dealing with centers of influence that you focus on building a trusting relationship (rapport) and that they gain a thorough understanding of what you have to offer in terms of benefits and services. This also includes providing them with an extensive list of testimonials, personal and business references, and a professional resumé.

Canvassing. This is the most criticized form of generating prospects, probably because it puts a potential prospect in an uncomfortable position. When using this method, you should be extremely selective in calling on people at random. Before contacting people or firms in your area, be sure to qualify them to determine if they indeed may have a need for your product or service. You can then approach them in an intelligent fashion; this will make you a credible salesperson in their eyes from the very beginning.

Conventions and Trade Shows. Attending such functions gives professional salespeople a virtual gold mine for prospecting. The focus should be on meeting as many people as possible and on attending as many workshops and seminars as possible. After the convention, follow up on leads and prospects that your attendance generated.

Direct Mail. The primary advantage of direct mail as a means of prospecting is that it allows you to reach a large number of people without being physically present. There are two basic kinds of direct mail strategies: one-time mailings and campaigns. The one-time mailing is aimed at generating an immediate response to an attractive offer. The campaign or conditioning method seeks to make the prospect increasingly more aware of you as a viable answer to her needs in a particular area. Many experts believe that direct mailings should be followed by personal phone calls within two to four weeks after the mailing.

Other good sources for prospects in addition to those listed above include directories, tip clubs, study groups, newsletters, seminars, speaking engagements, and personal observations.

If you are scientific about your prospecting, you will increase your prospect reservoir and know exactly how you did it. This makes for future success rather than a hit-or-miss career. To accomplish this, these systems of success should be adopted: 1) avoid confusion by being organized; 2) monitor your results; 3) try different techniques; and 4) follow up.

DISCUSSION QUESTIONS

1. What is meant by the sales pipeline?
2. Why is it important to keep the pipeline full?
3. Imagine you work for a school newspaper and are in charge of advertising. Name three specific sources of prospects for advertising in the paper.

4. How would you qualify the prospects you uncovered for the school newspaper?

5. As a salesperson, would you rather contact 100 unqualified prospects or 10 qualified prospects? Why?

6. If you were going to send out a direct mail letter to prospects to advertise in the school newspaper, whom would you target as a market and where would you get their names and addresses?

7. For the direct mail letter, answer the following questions about the school newspaper: What is it? How many students read it? How often does it come out? How can advertisers benefit from it? Offer a statistic to prove your claim of its value. How can prospective advertisers get a sample copy? How do the advertising costs compare to other local newspapers with similar circulations? (Make the phone calls necessary to get this information.)

CHAPTER SEVEN

Promotional Strategies

CHAPTER OBJECTIVES	1 Discuss the importance of *promotional strategy*.
	2 Describe the principal types of promotional strategies.
	3 Explain how you can put them to use in your own career.

In the sales profession, there are two ways of getting business. You can *go out* after it or it can *come to you*. The former is accomplished by prospecting, as discussed in the last chapter. Having business come to you is the primary objective of promotional strategies.

We would all agree that it is much more pleasant and less time consuming having prospects come to you. *Warm prospects*, that is, those who already have some interest in you and your company, make life easier by:

1. Being better qualified
2. Being ready to buy
3. Knowing more specifically what their buying needs are
4. Having decided that you and your product or services are worth their time to investigate
5. Being less price-sensitive than cold prospects

It's also very flattering when prospects knock on *your* door looking to do business with *you!*

Promotional strategies are techniques which give you positive exposure to your target market. Your prospects will know who you are, whom you represent, and what products or services you have to offer. This will smooth the way for setting up an appointment. If your prospect has been made aware of you in advance, you will find it much easier to establish a relationship, set up an appointment, and eventually consummate a sale. Promotion will give you, your company, and your product the *name recognition* that you need.

In selling, timing is crucial. Contacting prospects puts the control in your hands. You choose when to call on them. There is always the chance, however, that they will not be ready to buy. In this case, you make a note as to when to contact them again in the future when perhaps your timing will be better.

The beauty of promotional strategies is that they plant a seed in your prospect's mind. In effect, you have made a "reservation" to be considered for future business. When you are in the back of the prospect's mind, the chances are good that you will be called when he or she is in the market for your product or service. This does not guarantee that you will get the sale, but at least you will be able to compete for it. Prospecting does not necessarily create a lasting impression. So if your timing is off, you may never get another chance. Promotional strategies, therefore, increase your future chances significantly.

The professional salesperson will always be involved in promotion to augment and improve the effectiveness of day-to-day calls. A properly executed promotional program aims to accomplish the following objectives:

1. Introduce your service or product to new prospects and smooth the way for setting appointments.
2. Encourage more purchases by current customers.
3. Encourage off-season purchases.
4. Compete with competitors' promotional efforts and keep present customers.
5. Enlarge your market by encouraging activity in a wider geographic area.
6. Contact former customers with reminders of your services/products.

Ultimately all promotion is directed at increasing sales. Some strategies, such as advertising and sales promotion, are designed to do this directly. They are often bold, explicit forms of gaining the prospect's favor. Publicity and public relations, on the other hand, influence sales indirectly by encouraging the buyer to think highly of you and your company. Most people would rather buy from people or companies they have a favorable opinion of, even if they don't know them personally.

Salespeople generally think of promotional programs as being in the domain of their companies. Corporations usually have the resources available to develop and execute comprehensive promotional programs. As a professional salesperson, however, you should think in terms of being your own company. Promotion is as important to you as it is to a large corporation, but on a smaller scale. Become familiar with all of your promotional options in order to select those which will be most effective for you. The principal types of promotional strategies at your disposal are:

1. *Advertising*
   Ads in the Yellow Pages
   Ads in trade magazines and newspapers
   Direct mail
   Brochures and flyers
   TV
   Radio

2. *Sales Promotion*
   Sales aids such as pens, calendars, novelties
   Special events/open houses
   Exhibits at trade shows and conventions
   Discounts for off-season or special purchases (coupons, package deals)
   In-store demonstrations
3. *Public Relations and/or Publicity*
   Christmas, birthday, special occasion cards
   Membership in professional associations and clubs
   Donations of time or money
   Speaking engagements, seminars
   Press releases, interviews

In some fields, promotion is more important than the product being sold. Without promotion of some type, it is difficult to sell anything. Effective promotion, however, makes it possible to sell practically *anything!* The "pet rocks" which sold so well a few years ago are a case in point.

Advertising

Advertising is a paid, persuasive presentation which promotes you, your company, and your product or service. Advertising has become more and more sophisticated in its attempts to influence the buying behavior of its target markets. No matter how subtle or obvious the ad is, the desired outcome can be achieved only through:

Education. The prospects are made aware of you or your product, either for the first time or as a reminder.

Preference formation. After making prospects aware of your existence, you must form an attitude in their minds. You and your product must be liked. When there is competition, however, you must be *more* than liked—you must be *preferred.* You have to create the advantage that will cause your prospects to choose you over "them."

Affecting the purchase decision. You can educate your prospects and be so preferred that you will be remembered. If you do not get their business, however, your advertising has not been effective. Your ROI will be high only if you convince prospects that you are the best game in town.

Repeat business. Imagine how much more difficult your job would be if you sold to each client only once! You would need an infinite number of markets and prospects. Repeat business, especially when *they* come to *you,* is what makes the extra effort in sales worthwhile. An ongoing promotional program will strengthen and solidify your customers' preference for you.

Now that you know the objectives of the game, determine in which league you want to be. The size of your business and the nature of your target market will determine which advertising means you will use. If you're a sales consultant and professional speaker, it may not be as effective for you to advertise on TV or with fliers. A more effective medium would be trade journals.

In determining which sources would best fill your needs, you should ask yourself several questions:

1. What message do I want to convey? Should more emphasis be put on me or my product? With what themes am I going to try to associate myself and my product?
2. Who am I trying to reach? Who is my target audience?
3. Where will they be most likely to see my message? Should I buy a billboard in a subway car to advertise my karate classes?
4. How much can I afford to spend on advertising this year? Can I afford *not* to spend money on advertising? (Only you can determine the answer. There is no hard and fast rule for the percentage of gross sales which should be spent on advertising.)
5. When is the best time to schedule my advertising? (Did you ever notice how income tax services advertise less during the summer and fall? There is obviously a good reason for this.)

After thoroughly exploring these basic questions, you can then take your choice of the following available sources:

TV	Newspapers	Novelties
Radio	Direct mail	Handbills/fliers
Magazines	Billboards	Displays

Some of these are better suited for companies than for individuals, and vice versa. Over time, patterns have emerged which indicate that some sources are better for salespeople than others. Ranked in order of the highest to lowest value, the most proven methods are:

1. Person-to-person	High Value
2. Telephone	Medium Value
3. Personal letter	Medium Value
4. Form letter	Low Value
5. General promotional mailing	Low Value
6. Trade journal, newsletter, or publication	Low Value

As can be seen by their relative strengths, one good combination is a personal letter of introduction prior to personal contact.

In the United States billions of dollars are spent each year on advertising. Its effectiveness is undeniable. For example, Volkswagen was an unknown car manufacturer in the United States in 1947. By the early 1970s, Volkswagen was the largest selling imported car in the U.S.! The same can be said of Toyota, Honda, and Nissan. Advertising works!

Sales Promotions

Sales promotions include activities, other than personal selling and advertising, which directly affect sales. They differ from overall promotion in that they relate to one-time activities. Overall promotion is the marketing program or umbrella which includes sales promotions, advertising, and so on. Sales promotions themselves involve gimmicks, special sales, demonstrations, and other business stimulators that are temporary in nature. Some of the more common sales promotions are:

1. Demonstrations of new products, either live or on audiovideo displays
2. Exhibit booths at trade shows or conventions
3. Promotional packages, special year-end sales, and other discounts
4. Free calendars, matches, pens, and other novelties to be remembered by
5. Christmas cards
6. Attractions such as celebrities, raffles, etc.
7. Discount coupons

As an individual salesperson, you should create new ways to promote sales, especially if your company does not. Keeping an eye on the calendar and knowing when a product needs to be sold most heavily will allow you to plan ahead. Begin your sales promotion early so that the awareness has been established when the season arrives. You have probably noticed that the clothing and fashion industry begins advertising months ahead of time. Buyers in the clothing business plan their inventories at least one season in advance. Again, timing is important.

If your company is already involved with sales promotions, decide how you can take advantage of them. If the company is setting up a booth at a trade show or convention, volunteer to work the booth. This is a valuable place to prospect. At the show, give out your business cards and get one from everyone with whom you talk business. Try to set appointments while you are still at the show rather than calling everyone after the show.

If your company gives out calendars every year, you can stamp your name and phone number on the calendar. You can also have other items made up with your name, company, and phone number on them. Just make sure that whatever sales promotion item you distribute carries your personal and company image. It must be consistent.

Whether you are an independent or a representative of a large company, you can always create sales promotion ideas. Not only do they provide an immediate sales impact, but many sales promotional items have a long life and can remind your customers and prospects about you, your company, and your product throughout the year.

Public Relations

Public relations means relating to the public in a way which wins the public's appreciation. It involves good will, altruism, and community awareness. Its effect on sales is indirect and therefore difficult to analyze. Sales do improve, however, because people like to do business with firms that take an interest in the community. In determining your best public relations strategies, you should do an analysis through the use of several questions:

Who Are Your "Publics"?   *Publics* are groups of people who perceive you as a business person. Some of these publics act on their perceptions to increase your sales. Others just appreciate you. It is important for you to identify each of your publics and to develop strategies for improving your image in their eyes. For example, if you are selling real estate, your publics would be bankers, mortgage companies, customers, the community at large, other brokers, property managers, and so on.

What Methods Are Available to Reach These Publics?   There are many avenues open to you. Your choices will be determined by your personal interests and finances. Your company may engage in a wider range of PR activities simply because it can afford to do so. Then again, some companies do virtually no PR. For example, a defense contractor selling exclusively to the government does not need to be as concerned about public image, advertising, or sales promotion as a medical supplies manufacturer.

Public relations comes in many forms. Like advertising methods, some of these will be viable for you and some will not.

1. *Community activities.* Geared toward helping the community, these usually involve social functions, including benefits for underprivileged children, campaigns for community awareness and pride, contributions to a community event such as a carnival, and so on.
2. *Contributions of time or money* to a variety of groups. This includes sponsoring Little League teams, sporting events, cultural activities, charities, community development programs, and other worthy causes.
3. *Public speeches.* You, as an individual salesperson, can offer your service, free of charge, to a group who would like to hear you speak about your area of expertise. Large corporations also make speakers available as a public service.
4. *Public services.* Many TV and radio stations sponsor information services such as ski reports, surf reports, entertainment guides, medical tips, traffic reports, and other community services.
5. *Special events sponsorship.* Companies may sponsor picnics, anniversary parties, softball games, or other events. Your presence at these events gives members of the organization a chance to get to know you and feel comfortable with you in a relaxed setting.
6. *Trade associations.* Belonging to trade associations and interest groups provides good PR for individuals and companies. Your membership shows that you care about the industry. You can also generate many prospects from your participation.

What Is the Image You Want to Convey?   Public relations can be more important to an individual salesperson than to a company. A company has many resources for attracting business. You, the salesperson, have only yourself as a resource. Your *image* is an intangible asset which affects sales as much as your tangible assets (products). The image you should project through PR includes the following elements:

> You care about yourself, your company, your customers, and your community.
> You are an expert in your field.
> You are an accessible professional ready to be of service to customers and non-customers alike.

Public relations involves more than the methods discussed above. The way people see you on a day-to-day basis is also important. For this reason, public relations should be a way of life as well as a strategy for exposure. Professionalism is the best PR.

Publicity

Publicity means getting exposure through the news media. It involves announcements prepared by companies or by the media of newsworthy stories or events. It can also take the form of feature articles in trade magazines. This coverage or free advertising often has spectacular results. Publicity often succeeds where advertising fails because of three factors:

1. *Credibility.* When we read an article in the paper or hear a story on the news, we automatically assume it is authentic because it originated in the media. It gains believability simply because the company selling the product did not sponsor it.
2. *Subtlety.* Your message reaches people in an unobtrusive, indirect way. Publicity can, therefore, reach many prospects who would otherwise resist contact. Prospects ingest your message as news rather than as propaganda; they are therefore more receptive.
3. *Dramatization.* Advertising sometimes makes a product or service seem larger than life. Publicity dramatizes also, but in a different way. Publicity can convey the message that "We are your neighbors, struggling with you, and doing our part to improve life around us." Publicity, especially on a local level, helps create a feeling of community.

Publicity can take many forms. Articles about you or your company prepared by your company or a public relations firm are called *press releases.* They are brief, newsworthy stories that highlight the company in a way that is interesting to the public. The difficult step here is getting media representatives to use the story in the newspaper or on the news. To have your press releases published regularly you must have expertise in publicity as well as good connections in the news media. This, of course, does not apply to a good story submitted for the first time. An example of a newsworthy item would be your company's discovery of a cure for cancer or a new way to manage stress.

Feature articles are excellent sources of publicity. They are written by staff or freelance writers for trade magazines, professional journals, and special business sections of the newspaper. Feature articles cover your business in more

THE HOTEL ST. GERMAINE
1234 Place de Paris
New Orleans, LA. 99999
(555) 333-1144

DATE: FEBRUARY 20, 1987
SUBJECT: RESTAURANT OPENING
CONTACT: GARRY SCHAEFFER

FOR IMMEDIATE RELEASE:

The Hotel St. Germaine has completed the $1.6 million annex to its
waterfront location. The center of this high tech expanse of glass
and chrome is Le Bon Apetit, a 200-seat gourmet restaurant,
commanding a one hundred eighty degree view of Lake
Pontchartrain.

According to general manager Raoul LaBouche the new restaurant
will serve a variety of specialties ranging from traditional French
and continental fare to nouvelle cuisine and Cajun-style seafood.

There is much excitement around Le Bon Apetit as they prepare for
their grand opening celebration. Being billed as "The Classiest Party
in New Orleans History," this blow-out will feature three days of
food, music, wine-tasting, dance performances, and a chance to win
a brand new burgundy-colored Peugeot. The public is invited to tour
the restaurant and join in the festivities between 10 and 5 on March
2–4.

Chef Ronaldo MacDonaldo promises there will be enough food for
"every curious palate in New Orleans." MacDonaldo, originally the
head chef of Windows on the World, atop New York's World Trade
Center, is a graduate of the Culinary Institute of America and
Cordon Bleu in France. He has appeared on *Good Morning America*
and was featured in the January edition of *Gourmet Magazine*.

The gourmet fare of the restaurant is available for catered parties
both on- and off-premise. Adjacent banquet rooms are available for
groups of up to 600 people. After March 15, the restaurant will be
open for business and will feature live jazz six nights a week.

Figure 7.1: Sample Press Release

depth than press releases. If you are unique in some way as an individual, you may provide an interesting subject for a feature article. For example, let's say that when you were younger you were a professional baseball player, and now you are selling space age exercise equipment. You would provide an interesting background in which to set an otherwise boring article. In time, your business would increase due to the publicity.

Photographs are a good vehicle for publicity. Newspapers often print unusual, humorous, and interesting photographs. If you have a photograph which gives some exposure to you or your firm *and* is appealing from a jour-nalistic viewpoint, by all means send it to your local newspaper or trade journal.

Perhaps the most accessible form of publicity is the "Letters to the Edi-tor" section of the paper. If you are abreast of the issues in your town, especially those affecting business, you can express yourself in writing and derive a lot of exposure from it. You'd be surprised how many people read the letters to the editor.

Keep in mind that editors mercilessly cut and rewrite press releases. To avoid having your article butchered, be sure it is interesting, timely, factual, accurate, specific, informative, and humble, and keep the hype down to a minimum.

You should also keep in mind that advertising yields results more quick-ly than publicity. Advertising is a continual strategy, whereas publicity is usually only occasional unless you use a PR firm to mount an ongoing campaign for you and your company. When you advertise, you have some control over where the ad is placed. Publicity does not entitle you to choose. The editor makes that choice.

An excellent example of serendipity and effective publicity occurred several years ago when the rock star Alice Cooper was in London. The promot-ers mounted a billboard on a truck and instructed the driver to simply drive around town. As rush hour was approaching, luck would have it that the truck broke down in the middle of a busy intersection. Not only was the traffic tied up for hours, but the media came out to cover "the event." The promoters later acknowledged that they could not have bought better publicity had they tried.

YOUR PROMOTIONAL STRATEGY

As you can see, an effective promotional strategy is multifaceted. The question for you now is, "How do I go about developing a promotional program for myself?" The envelope, please! The answer is . . . brainstorming!

First, compile a list of all your publics. You must know whom you are going to reach before you determine how to reach them. Choose the most important prospects and brainstorm all the possible ways of influencing them or impressing them with your positive image. Use the Promotional Strategies Worksheet (7-1) to stimulate your imagination.

Once you fill out the Promotional Strategies Worksheet, choose the six

DIRECTIONS: Try to list as many creative ways as possible to use the following methods in your promotional program.

ADVERTISING

Radio:

TV:

Trade Magazines:

Newspaper:

Direct Mail:

Ads in Yellow Pages:

Other:

SALES PROMOTIONS

Displays:

Trade Shows/Convention Booths:

Novelties:

Demonstrations:

Other:

PUBLIC RELATIONS

Volunteer Work:

Donations:

Speeches/Seminars:

Holiday Greeting Cards:

Clubs//Organizations:

Other:

PUBLICITY

Letters to Editors:

News Releases:

Feature Articles:

Worksheet 7-1: Promotional Strategies

techniques that are most effective and affordable at this time. List them in order of priority, starting with those you can do immediately. Then write out your specific goals and the steps you will take to achieve them. Be sure to follow the rules of goal-setting to ensure that each one will come to fruition.

It is rare to find a product or service that speaks for itself and does not need to be promoted. As professional salespeople, we must recognize that fact and actively promote ourselves as well as our products or services. Promotional strategies will not only get you in the door, they will bring the business to you. Together with your prospecting strategies, you will get prospects *and* business coming and going.

SUMMARY

In the sales profession there are two ways of getting business: going out after it or having it come to you. The first is accomplished through prospecting; the second is accomplished through promotional strategies.

Promotional strategies are techniques which give you positive exposure to your target market and give you, your company, and product(s)/service(s) the *name recognition* that you need. Your prospects will know who you are, whom you represent, and what products or services you have to offer.

A properly executed promotional program, which is ultimately directed at increasing sales, will aim to accomplish the following objectives: 1) to introduce your product/service to new prospects; 2) to encourage more purchases by current customers; 3) to encourage off-season purchases; 4) to compete with competitors' promotional efforts and keep present customers; 5) to enlarge your market by encouraging activity in a wider geographic area; and 6) to contact former customers with reminders of your services.

Although salespeople see promotional programs as essentially the responsibility of their companies, a professional salesperson thinks in terms of himself being his own company. Therefore, promotion to him is as important as it is to a large corporation.

There are three principal types of promotional strategies at a salesperson's disposal: 1) advertising, 2) sales promotions, and 3) public relations and/or publicity.

Advertising is a paid, persuasive presentation that promotes you, your company, and your product or service. No matter how subtle or obvious the ad is, the desired outcome can be achieved only through education of prospects, preference formation, affecting the purchase decision, and repeat business.

There are a variety of outlets for the promotional message. Some are better suited for companies than for individuals and vice versa. Ranked in order of the highest to the lowest value, the most proven promotions or methods in the selling business are: 1) person-to-person; 2) telephone; 3) mail or personal letter; 4) form letter; 5) general promotional mailing; and 6) trade journal, newsletter, or publication.

Sales promotions, the second principal type of promotional strategy, include activities other than personal selling and advertising. They differ from overall promotion in that they relate to one-time activities. Overall promotion is the marketing program as a whole, including sales promotions, advertising, and so on. Sales promotions themselves involve gimmicks, special sales, demonstrations, and other business stimulators that are temporary in nature. As a salesperson, you should create new ways to promote sales, especially if your company does not. If your company does, decide how you can best take advantage of them.

Public relations and/or publicity is the third principal type of promotional strategy. Public relations means relating to the public in a way that wins the public's appreciation. It involves good will, altruism, and community awareness. Its effect on sales is indirect and therefore more difficult to analyze. Sales do improve, however, because people like to do business with firms that take an interest in the community.

Public relations comes in many forms, some being more viable for individual salespeople than others. They include: 1) community activities; 2) contributions of time or money; 3) public speeches; 4) public services; 5) special event sponsorship; and 6) trade association participation.

Publicity means getting exposure through the news media. It involves announcements prepared by companies or by the media of newsworthy stories or events. It can also take the form of feature articles in trade magazines. This coverage or free advertising often has spectacular results. Publicity often succeeds where advertising fails because of three factors: credibility, subtlety, and dramatization. As in public relations, publicity can take many forms: 1) press releases, 2) feature articles, 3) photographs, and 4) letters to the editor.

With all of the above in mind, an effective promotional strategy obviously is multifaceted. It is rare to find a product or service that speaks for itself and does not need to be promoted. Professional salespeople recognize that fact and actively promote themselves as well as their products and services.

DISCUSSION QUESTIONS

1. Define the following promotional strategies: advertising; sales promotion; public relations; publicity.
2. Name three methods of promoting a company using the four strategies in Question 1.
3. What is meant by "publics"? How does a company identify its publics?
4. What comprises a salesperson's image? How can this image be changed or enhanced?
5. Choose an industry (It can be a family business.). Identify your publics. List eight realistic ways to reach them using all four promotional strategies.

CHAPTER EIGHT

Preparation for the Sales Call

<table>
<tr><td>CHAPTER
OBJECTIVES</td><td>1   Describe the importance of thorough preparation for sales calls.
2   Discuss the methods of preparing thoroughly for each sales call.
3   Present a Sales Call Planning Guide to be used in preparing for each call.</td></tr>
</table>

Sales planning assesses opportunities in your overall market area; the preparation process assesses selling opportunities for a specific customer in your territory. Being fully prepared for the sales interview has a number of advantages for both you and your customer. By being prepared, you are better able to react to the demands of the sales transaction in the following ways:

1. You can talk about those service benefits that relate directly to the needs of the buyer.
2. You can bring the proper materials to the interview so that it progresses smoothly and efficiently.
3. You save the buyer's time because he is not burdened by an inefficient interview or salesperson.
4. You are able to set realistic call objectives and develop a sales strategy around them.
5. You impress the buyer with your knowledge, preparation, strategy, and confidence.

In other words, preparing for sales interviews leads to more, bigger, and better sales. It spells success!

Giving an effective presentation of your product or service to the prospect is a critical point in the marketing process. All the knowledge, skills, attitudes, and efforts you have developed are put into practice at this point. A sale doesn't just happen. An effective sales presentation is the result of thorough planning of all the factors which will influence the customer and motivate him to make a favorable decision.

Now you must develop a logical, intelligent presentation that will accomplish the desired goal—the sale. You need to plan *how* to reach the objective, *how* to influence the customer, *how* to make the sale.

Having a sales plan for each customer is nothing more than selling by objectives. You should plan before entering a sales situation, rather than reacting to whatever develops in the sales interview. This is not to say that if you pre-plan you can do without the skills necessary to spot a situation and react quickly. The chances of success in selling are much greater if selling instincts are combined with preparation.

You can achieve the highest degree of success in sales simply by planning! The most important planning you can do is the planning of the sales presentation itself, because that is where the final payoffs are realized. Planning a sales presentation involves nothing more than using common sales sense. You have something to offer your prospects which either provides them with a benefit or helps them prevent a loss. Therefore, you plan before the presentation to gear everything you say to achieving either or both of those two objectives.

Obviously, you should know all you can about the prospects on whom you are calling. Unless you do, you cannot hope to hold their attention to what you have to say. Figuratively, you must "walk in their shoes." You must relate what you say to their needs, their desires, and their objectives.

Get to know the *real* decision maker within the prospect's company, in addition to those who can *influence* the ultimate decision. This vital information should be ascertained as soon as possible. In addition, find out what the purchase decision process is. Does an individual make the purchase commitment or is it done by a committee? If an individual can make the purchase decision, can she make it only up to a certain dollar amount? Are there any external influences on the decision process, such as attorneys, accountants, consultants, or business advisors?

Once you have an accurate picture of the decision maker and the purchase decision process, you should learn all you can about the prospect, her company, and her industry. You should eventually be able to answer the following questions:

1. What are the prospect's personal style, idiosyncrasies, and temperament?
2. What are his hobbies, sports, and pastimes?
3. How about his family and their interests?
4. Does he buy on opinion or fact, friendship or reciprocity?
5. What is his present product usage?
6. What is your present or potential competition for this account?
7. What are his specific needs for your service?
8. Why should he purchase from you rather than one of your competitors?
9. What is his volume of business?
10. What type and quality of merchandise does he carry?

11. How does he market his merchandise?
12. What is his credit rating?
13. Are there any trends within his industry that might affect the purchase decision now or in the future?

The more questions you can answer, the better prepared you will be for your sales interview and the more likely you will be to achieve a successful outcome.

SALES CALL PLANNING GUIDE

Your primary activity in preparing for a sales call will be research. You will want to know whom to contact, her possible needs, her financial status, when she may want to buy, and who your competitors are. If you are well-organized, this task will be far easier. Be sure to take advantage of your company as a source of information. Your prospect may be a former or present customer of your company. In this case, a file will already exist, providing the information you need.

It is helpful to have a checklist or worksheet to use as a guide when doing research. After completing the worksheet you will know exactly where you stand with the prospect. Worksheet 8-1, the Sales Call Planning Guide, covers the information you need for planning and preparation. Adapt the guide to your needs and use one for each prospect that you research.

Information Needed Before a Sales Call

The more information you have about a prospect, the better your chances are of making a sale. The Sales Call Planning Guide provides you with information on the prospect's background. Whenever you do not have most (if not all) of the information listed on this guide, you are cold call selling, even though you may have made an appointment for a presentation. In this case, however, it is not the call that is cold; it is you.

In contrast, knowing as much as you possibly can about your prospects, their needs and wants, and the services you can provide will help you get a favorable commitment.

Some basic areas covered in the Sales Call Planning Guide need to be explored as part of your pre-call homework. These are covered step-by-step in the following sections.

Who is the Decision Maker? When you make your sales call, it is imperative that you meet with someone who is in a decision-making position. This person must also be knowledgeable enough to know what you are talking about. If you discover that this person does not have the authority to buy or to make decisions, you must diplomatically find out how the system works or whom you must see. Some company structures require the completion of a long chain of events before a decision can be made. If this is the case, ask your prospect, "Would you give me an idea of your company's decision-making process for a purchase such as this?" If that process involves more than one person seeing your presentation, try to arrange to show everyone at once. In some cases, however, it will be necessary for you to show your product to several people at different times.

Worksheet 8-1: Sales Call Planning Guide

Company_____Type of Business_____

Location_____Phone_____Date_____

Key Contact_____Title_____

Who is the decision maker?_____

Current Situation?

Goals and Objectives?

Potential Problem(s) or Need(s):

_____

What objectives should I seek to accomplish with this account?

Next Call:

Overall:

_____
If the key contact is not the decision maker, how can he/she influence the objective(s) I am trying to achieve?

_____
What questions can I ask to uncover, clarify, or amplify prospect problems, needs, and/or goals?

_____
What decision-making criteria are important to this prospect?

What is Your Prospect's Current Situation?   In order to get a feel for the climate of your prospect's business, you need to ask some general questions. You might start off by suggesting, "Tell me a little about your business." This is a safe, nonthreatening opener which can lead the way to more in-depth questioning such as, "What's happening with sales?" or "Are you encountering any special problems with your present product or service?" You will need to adapt

Worksheet 8-1   (cont.)

Possible benefits prospect is seeking:	Features I offer that provide those benefits:	Proof materials (Letters, testimonials) to be used if necessary:

How can I be of more benefit to this prospect than anyone else who has called on him/her?

Possible prospect objections:

1._____

2._____

3._____

Potential answers:

1._____

2._____

3._____

Based on my objective(s), what specific commitment will I ask this prospect to make?

Why should the prospect want to make this commitment?

By what criteria will the prospect judge whether or not my product/service was a satisfactory solution to his problem?

What methods, procedures, or forms can I use to measure whether or not the actual results did in fact meet the above criteria?

these questions to your industry, however. You can see that some delicate questioning can identify needs that might otherwise have remained hidden.

What Are Your Prospect's Goals?   Aside from making money, what are they trying to accomplish in business? Forget about your product or service for a moment and get a grasp of the overall picture. Once you understand a company's primary purpose in the marketplace, you will be able to relate to it in a more relevant way. This will also show them that you are interested in their business and well-being, in addition to making sales.

Does Your Prospect Have Potential Problems and Needs?   Once you determine your prospect's current situation, goals, and objectives, you can readily determine if a need gap exists, that is, when the prospect's *actual* situation is not living up to or accomplishing his *desired* situation (objectives or end results). The greater the need gap, the greater and more immediate the need is for the prospect to change what he is currently doing or purchasing. The greater the need gap, the greater the probability for you to make a sale.

You might also think about what the consequences could be if the prospect does not use your product or service. Having that insight, you can develop some very strong and well-thought-out selling points to use in your presentation.

What Are Your Call Objectives?   Every time you see a customer, you should have a reason for making that call. Dropping by to say hello is nice, but may be a waste of time. If you want to be sociable, you can use the phone. If you have not sold the prospect yet, your reason for stopping by should be one of the action steps that will move you closer to making the sale. For example, you might stop by to show the prospect the latest in your product line or a new service you have to offer. Each time you see your prospect you should try to learn more about his or her needs. Ideally, each call will produce tangible evidence that you are making progress with the prospect; otherwise, you are just going through the motions.

Questions to Uncover Needs   Although it is not generally advisable to have specifically worded questions that you will ask in a particular sequence, it is advisable to have a questioning strategy. This simply means that you should have a general idea of what you would like to ask in order to get the particular information you require. A questioning plan gives you a starting point but also allows you the flexibility to explore additional fruitful areas as they arise in the conversation. When you leave your planned questions to explore these other beneficial areas, you can use directive questions to bring you back on track. Remember that you need only a hazy idea of the type of information you desire as well as the types of questions you need to ask to get that information. You do not need specifically worded questions prior to your interview.

What Are the Decision-Making Criteria? Part of your research should uncover the reason(s) why your prospect might be interested in your product or service.

Once you have this information you can look for the criteria used by each person to whom you speak in the company. In general, you know that an executive will be interested in the long-term goals of the company or in increasing overall sales and profits; a middle manager will base his opinion on the cost effectiveness of your product; and the first-line supervisors will be concerned with installation and operation.

When you contact each of these individuals, be aware of their different perspectives and gear your presentation to the criteria on which their decision will be based. Everyone wants to know if the purchase will benefit him. If you can show everyone along the line how he, too, will benefit, then you will be a strong contender in the race for his business.

Decision-making criteria can also relate to constraints on the final decision, such as budget limits, quantity and size requirements, delivery dates, or other factors. It is crucial to determine these decision-making requirements as early in the sales interview as possible to ensure that you can meet them. For instance, if delivery must be made within 5 days and you normally deliver in 14 days, you have a problem. You can either attempt to negotiate this constraint to a mutually acceptable delivery time frame (e.g., 10 days), or you may have to walk away from the sale. As you can see, decision-making criteria are crucial prospect qualifiers that should tell you whether or not it is worth your time to pursue this specific account.

How Will You Have to Prove Your Claims? After you have presented your ideas and created some interest, many prospects will want you to prove your claims. They may ask you for a demonstration or an opportunity to try out the product in their business. An easier and less time-consuming way to prove your product or service is to offer testimonials from people the prospects know and trust. Being able to say, "Your friend Ajax, Inc., down the street bought one last year and is very happy with it. Susan James in accounting told me you should call her if you want to hear more about it." This can be very convincing to a prospect. If you can find out in advance what means will be necessary to prove yourself, you can spend time preparing to make your proof effective and appropriate to your prospect's needs.

What Is Your Competitive Edge? Is there something about you that is unique? Something which gives you the advantage over other companies and salespeople? If so, use it to your advantage. Often a minor detail will tip the balance in your direction. Many sales have been made based on the statement, "In addition to the product, you also get me. I come with the package. I'll be here when you need me to make sure that everything runs smoothly and that you realize the full benefits of the product." That kind of enthusiasm and sincerity makes salespeople winners!

During your presentation, highlight your unique selling factors. This is an excellent time to admit a limitation in your product as well. The customer will find out about it anyway, so you might as well score some points by being the one to enlighten him or her. When pointing out a weak point, contrast it with a strong point. For example, if you are selling dictation machines, say, "Yes, it's true that my machine will not take a standard cassette. The micro-cassettes are, however, much easier to store and take up less room in your briefcase. They're actually easier to carry with you." That's honest selling which shows you are different from the rest.

What Questions Are You Likely to Encounter? When you are rehearsing your presentation, either with someone else or in your mind, try imagining what the prospect's reactions will be. If you know the potential and questions, you then have time to prepare yourself. You can study your product and company until you have every possible question answered. By doing so, you will be able to quell your prospect's fears with smooth, confident, and truthful answers. You will find this to be time well spent because there is nothing worse than stammering and struggling to answer a prospect's question. When you do, your credibility often takes a nose dive.

What Commitment Will You Ask? It is essential at the end of a sales call to know what action will follow; you must confirm it with the prospect in the form of a verbal agreement. There are all kinds of things you might ask for: more information, a referral, permission to give a demonstration, or best of all, the order itself!

Regardless of the commitment you seek, before you make the call you should have in mind a specific end result for the meeting. This is the most important part of your call objectives.

How Will You Know the Success Criteria? Many products, such as business computers, serve different functions for different customers. If your product or service falls into this category, how will *you* know if it is benefiting the customer or not? You may know some of the improvements he or she wants to make, but you can't know them all. So ask your customer, "What are the criteria that you will use to judge the effectiveness of this product?" Your customers will tell you what they are looking for and when they hope to see results. You should make a note of this and follow up at the appropriate time. Even if the followup is months later, you must carry through in order to keep your professional reputation intact and your customer happy.

There's an old adage: "If you fail to plan, then you are planning to fail." In sales, this couldn't be more true. Your research and preparation will educate you so that you *will* be of service to your customer. If you do not prepare yourself, you might as well be calling on everyone cold without even knowing their names. It is not a very attractive alternative. Preparation and planning are like studying a map: you will know which road to take with your prospect to get where you *both* want to go.

SUMMARY

The preparation stage of the selling process assesses the selling opportunities for a specific current or potential customer in a salesperson's territory. Being fully prepared for a sales interview has several advantages: 1) service benefits that directly relate to the need of the prospect can be discussed; 2) the proper materials can be brought to the interview; 3) the prospect's time is saved because he is not burdened by superfluous information; 4) realistic call objectives can be set and a sales strategy developed around them; and 5) the prospect is impressed by the salesperson's knowledge, preparation, strategy, and confidence.

An effective sales presentation is the result of thorough planning of all the factors that will influence the customer and motivate him to make a favorable decision.

Having a sales plan for each customer is nothing more than *selling by objectives*. You should plan before entering a sales situation, rather than reacting to whatever develops in the sales interview.

The primary activity in preparing for a sales call will be research. You will want to know whom to contact, their possible needs, their financial status, when they may want to buy, and who your competitors are. If you are well-organized, this task will be far easier. To conduct this research, it is a good idea to use a worksheet or a checklist, such as the one suggested in this chapter. The Sales Call Planning Guide is your pre-call homework. It provides you with a guide to getting the information needed to be well-prepared for the sales interview. Whenever you do not have all or most of the information listed on the guide, you will be doing cold call selling—you will be unprepared.

Information necessary for you to be solidly prepared includes: 1) who the decision makers are; 2) the prospect's current situation; 3) the prospect's goals; 4) the prospect's potential problems and needs; 5) your own call objectives; 6) an idea of questions to ask to uncover prospect's needs; 7) the prospect's decision-making criteria; 8) what you will need as proof to back your claims; 9) knowledge of your competitive edge; 10) objections that the prospect may have; 11) the commitment that you will request; and 12) what the success criteria will be.

Your research and preparation will educate you so that you *will* be of service to your customer. If you do not prepare yourself, you might as well be calling on everyone cold without knowing even their names. Preparation and planning are like studying a map: you will know which road to take with your prospect to get where you *both* want to go.

DISCUSSION QUESTIONS

1. What are the advantages of being prepared for a sales call?
2. What are several call objectives you could have for a meeting with a customer?
3. List all the information you should have about a prospect and the sources of that informatin.

Part IV

NON-MANIPULATIVE
SELLING SKILLS

As we have discussed, Non-Manipulative Selling is a comprehensive philosophy that incorporates relationship and communication skills, personal sales management skills, and later in the book, self-management skills. Many of these techniques are not unique to NMS, but certainly fit well into the framework of the non-manipulative philosophy.

The core of NMS is the six step sales process discussed briefly in Chapter 1. This process differs from many sales philosophies in that it places the emphasis of the sales relationship on the information-gathering phase. The reason for this emphasis is simple: you cannot solve a customer's problem unless you know what it is. To provide the best solution to a problem, you must fully understand every facet of the problem. That takes time and effort. Hence, the non-manipulative approach is practiced by salespeople who really care about their clients.

In addition to the planning step discussed in Chapter 8, Non-Manipulative Selling skills include the following five steps:

- o MEETING: In this phase, you contact prospects by phone, letter, and in person. There are advantages and disadvantages to each, and strategies to optimize your contacts will be discussed.
- o STUDYING: Your questioning skills come in handy once you've met your prospect and are studying his or her business. Studying involves building trust and seeking information on every facet of their business. One thing you look for is a need for your product. If none exists, you acknowledge that and part friends. If a need does exist, you continue studying as long as necessary and then move on to the proposing phase.
- o PROPOSING: After studying, you should have a good idea of your prospect's needs and opportunities. You are then in the position to help by proposing a solution to problems and ways to take advantage of opportunities.
- o CONFIRMING: By conducting the sales process in an open give-and-take manner, you will keep your prospect involved every step of the way. Confirming the purchase is the step in which your customer agrees to move forward and adopt the solution you proposed.

o ASSURING: Customer satisfaction is the most important part of your business. Without happy customers, you have nothing. Assuring their continued satisfaction with your product/service is a part-time job that becomes a natural part of your other daily activities.

As you read about the six steps of NMS, you will see the logic behind the philosophy and why it is a truly professional, consultative approach.

CHAPTER NINE

Meeting the Prospect

CHAPTER OBJECTIVES	**1** Introduce the three methods of meeting the prospect: face-to-face, telephone, and letter.
	2 Provide guidelines for the successful use of each method.

Up to this point in the book we have discussed everything you need to know to prepare for your sales call. These topics included territory management, prospecting, promoting, preparing for the call, and the communication of selling. We will now discuss the meeting phase of the sales process.

Meeting prospects, like every other facet of the selling profession, must be accomplished in ways that are:

1. Conducive to business
2. Cost-effective
3. Image-effective
4. Tension-reducing
5. Trust-building

When done with these goals in mind, contacting prospects becomes less frightening and more fruitful for the beginning salesperson.

CONTACTING A CUSTOMER

There are three ways that you can contact a customer, each of which varies in impact: face-to-face calls, telephone calls, and letters. Of the three ways, face-to-face calls carry the most clout because you can communicate both verbally *and* nonverbally and use visual aids. The telephone is the second most effective method. Although you can communicate only verbally over the phone, you can use your vocal qualities and command of the language to increase your impact. The third and least dynamic way to contact a prospect is by letter, in which only words convey your message. Letters can, however, be augmented by enclosures such as brochures, specification sheets, and so on. All three methods have their advantages and disadvantages. The professional salesperson should be adept at each and incorporate combinations of the three into his contacting activities.

We are often asked which of the three primary ways of contacting a customer is the best way. The answer can best be given by describing the effectiveness of these three types of contacts. We measure their effectiveness in two ways; one is based on quality and one is based on quantity.

Let us first look at quantity. By which of the three ways can we contact the most people at any one time? The answer, obviously, is by letter. Theoretically you can mail a letter to every man, woman, and child on the face of this earth all at one time. Not very practical, but theoretically possible. So let's give an A to the letter in quantity. Now consider the phone. Surely you can call more people a day on the telephone than you can visit in person. Let's give the telephone a B. Then in-person contact deserves a C for the fewest contacts we can make in a day.

Now let's look at the qualitative aspect. We're going to use two criteria to measure quality. The first is the ability to get feedback from the customer. In other words, when we say something to the customer, how quickly can we get feedback from them, that is, how fast can we confirm that they understand what we said and get some response from them. The second criterion is the ability to reach some closure, the ability to get a confirmation from the customer. It need not necessarily mean the confirmation to buy. It could be an appointment for the next meeting, or it could be an agreement to provide certain material. But how quick and how immediate is that ability to reach closure? With these criteria in mind, which of the three primary ways of contact is the best in terms of quality? If we look at our A of quantity, the letter, we find that it is a C in quality. There's no opportunity for feedback and there's no opportunity for closure. It always requires at least one more contact, either by letter or by phone, to reach any type of closure and to get any feedback from the customer. Our B from before, the telephone, remains a B. We can get some feedback from the customer immediately, but it generally requires another step to reach some form of closure—another contact. In person, however, we can get both immediate feedback and reach closure right up to and including closure of the sale—the big commitment of the sale. That gets an A for quality. Looking at Figure 9.1, we see the telephone gets two Bs for an average of B. The letter gets an A and a C for an average of B, and in-person calls get a C and an A for an average of B. Which is

TYPE OF CONTACT	QUANTITY	QUALITY	
In-Person	C	A	
Telephone	B	B	
Letter	A	C	**Figure 9.1**

the best? All three! To quote sales trainer Nido Qubein, the smart salesperson has as many things going for him as possible in his prospecting. He's consistently feeding the pipeline. He's consistently creating new and different ways to reach customers; the more things he has going for him the better. Qubein calls that the *synergistic approach* to marketing. If you only have one prospect source and it fails, you're out of business. If you have ten prospect sources and one of them fails, you're still in business. So, basically, in order to constantly feed the pipeline we recommend the combination of mailed material going out to prospective clients consistently, telephone calls following through on those letters, and in-person calls. I want to make a distinction here between letters going out in a mass-marketing approach and letters going out from an individual salesperson. Many companies do mass-marketing: they constantly send out large volumes of direct mail to thousands or hundreds of thousands of customers for a response. That is not what we're talking about in this chapter. What we're talking about is a salesperson's individual mailings to potential clients for that salesperson. And for this reason we recommend that only as many of these letters go out daily as can be followed through on three to four days later.

1. Letters

As we mentioned in Chapter 7, it is essential for a prospect to have seen or heard your name before you contact him. This will avoid the awkwardness of the prospect asking "Who?" Instead it will be, "Oh, yes, I received your letter recently." For this reason, letters are often a logical precursor to phone calls and personal visits.

Letters can be used as introductions and are especially effective if they include a third-party referral. Whenever you can obtain a referral or a recommendation, you are stacking the odds in your favor. Don't be afraid to be an honest name-dropper because names can open doors.

Letters can also be used to:

1. *Secure an appointment.* Confirmations for long-distance appointments can be done by letter.
2. *Answer questions.* Providing information or asking further questions of a customer costs less by mail.
3. *Contact busy people.* Doctors and other extremely inaccessible people often find it impossible to come to the phone.
4. *Follow up on a sales call.* It is helpful to summarize with a letter the key points which were agreed on during the face-to-face call. This will provide you and your customers with a written record of what transpired and demonstrate that you do business in a professional way. "Thank you" letters are also appropriate after a sale.
5. *Provide updates.* A brief letter with enclosures will keep your customers informed of new developments or changes in your field.
6. *Stimulate business.* Mailing notices of promotional specials and introductory offers can increase sales. In addition, direct mail is a viable and profitable technique for some salespeople.

7. *Relate a conversation.* Often you will want to relate to a customer a conversation you had with a third party.

No matter what the purpose of the specific letter, they all serve to establish or cement the trust bond, create or maintain interest, and keep the lines of communication open.

Personal Letters Whenever possible, a personal letter should be written. In our computerized, impersonal business world it is like a breath of fresh air to receive a personal rather than a form letter. A personal letter addresses an individual within a company and seeks to provide him or her with a product or service. "To whom it may concern" becomes "Dear Jim," or "Dear Mr. Cathcart."

The art of concise letter writing is one that requires practice. A good letter will always follow these guidelines:

1. *Use good stationery.* Your letter is an extension of you and your professional image. Use paper that looks good and is of good quality.
2. *Personalize your letters.* Use a letterhead on your letters. When designing a letterhead, be conservative but different. You should also enclose your business card for your customer's convenience.
3. *Type your letters.* Unless they are brief notes, handwritten letters look amateurish. If you don't have a typewriter, beg, borrow, or steal one. If you can't type, beg, borrow, or steal a secretary.
4. *Break up the text.* Write in short, yet sharp paragraphs. Avoid long sentences and keep your ideas separate. Use one paragraph for each idea and develop the idea fully. Letters are easier to read when written in this way.

These guidelines are the basics of how a business letter should look physically. What it says is more involved. Practice writing letters that are polite and to the point. Develop a style that is informative and personal. Try to include the following:

1. *Refer to the customer by name.* Don't just refer to his company or department.
2. *Identify yourself and your company.*
3. *Mention who referred you to him,* if appropriate.
4. *State the purpose of the letter.* Be honest.
5. *Make an initial benefit statement.* Capture your customer's attention.
6. *Identify an area of probable interest,* which you discovered in your pre-call preparation.
7. *Write in the language of your customer's industry.* Use words and phrases to which he can relate and which will show that you are knowledgeable.
8. *State one or two reasons for the customer to see you.* Make the reasons relevant to the person's job or business.
9. *Include a brochure,* if appropriate, to increase interest.
10. *Indicate when you will follow up with a phone call or a personal visit.* Be sure to schedule the personal call.
11. *Be brief.*

All of this may seem like a lot to cover in one page, but it can be done quite easily. On the following pages we have included both a good and a poor example for you to compare. Refer to the good example and note how each point is covered. Then look at the poor example. We are sure that you will see a significant difference.

When writing your letter, it's best to talk in terms of your prospect's interest rather than your own. Doing so will convey sincere concern for your prospect's needs, making it more likely that you will have a strong business relationship. If you were to focus on your needs and interests instead, there would be a good chance that you would never get in the prospect's door.

One way to ensure a selfless letter is to do an "I" count. Read the letter that you have written and count the number of times that you use the words "I," "me," "my," or "mine." You will be surprised at how often they show up. Rewrite the letter and focus its emphasis on your prospect and his needs. Instead of saying, "I have a product which . . ." say, "You'll be interested to know that . . ."

Avoid hype in your letters. Your sense of professionalism should tell you that enthusiasm, when carried to extremes, can be repulsive. Convey your enthusiasm in a sincere, meaningful way rather than with glowing hyperboles.

In evaluating your letter, ask yourself if it will accomplish what you had planned. Is the purpose of the letter clear? Does it sell the product or service without giving too much of your presentation? This is important particularly because you want to pique your prospect's interest without giving enough information to allow him to jump to a conclusion.

Always keep a copy of your correspondence. This will help you document your progress with the prospect as well as evaluate your letter-writing ability.

Let's take a look at the good sample letter and analyze why it is effective:

1. The first paragraph is straight and simple, and reminds the prospect of the referral.
2. The second paragraph shows that the salesperson did his homework by reading the paper and then gets to the point of the letter.
3. The third paragraph says something about his company and makes a subtle benefit statement.
4. Lastly, a meeting is suggested and a tentative time is proposed.
5. A brochure was included with the letter as well as a promise to have more information when they meet.
6. The letter closes with a promise to follow up on a specific date with a phone call.

The poor example of a letter is obviously pedantic and vague. It sounds like the writer is more in love with his verbal prowess than with communicating in a simple manner. Letters like these can only alienate prospects. The poor letter also uses the prospect's first name in the salutation. This is acceptable only if you have established an informal first-name relationship. If there is any doubt, it is safer to be formal. When addressing someone informally, be sure to sign the letter with your first name. You should also be careful in your use of the words

GOOD SAMPLE LETTER

Tom Tapehead
SUPER-TECH RECORDING
1234 Hi-Fi Avenue
Los Angeles, CA 90021

March 2, 1986

Mr. Allan Ears
Multi-Hit Records
33425 Hollywood Boulevard
Hollywood, CA 90087

Dear Mr. Ears:

Our mutual friend, Jim Cathcart, told me he spoke to you about my ability to help in the expansion of your business.

I recently read that Multi-Hit Records plans to open three "satellite" studios in order to be more accessible to the many undiscovered, "struggling" recording artists. I think this is an exciting concept and feel that Super-Tech could be of service to you in the project.

As you know, Super-Tech is the most widely used and respected manufacturer of 16-track recording equipment in the country. I'm certain that we can design a system that will enable your smaller studios to produce the high quality, low cost recordings that you desire.

I'd like to talk further with you about this. Would the afternoon of Thursday, the 8th, be convenient? By then I will have consulted our Engineering Department and will have all the information pertinent to your specific needs. I have enclosed a brochure of our new digital delay line for your perusal.

Thank you for your time. I'll give you a call on Tuesday, March 6th, to see when an appointment would be convenient.

Sincerely,

Tom Tapehead
Sales Representative

TT:sr

POOR SAMPLE LETTER

Tom Tapehead
SUPER-TECH RECORDING
1234 Hi-Fi Avenue
Los Angeles, CA 90021

March 2, 1986

Mr. Allan Ears
Multi-Hit Records
33425 Hollywood Boulevard
Hollywood, CA 90087

Dear Allan:

I wanted to tell you that I felt our lunch was mutually beneficial. I discerned an inordinate amount of information and hope that you did as well.

These are arduous years for every business. I admire the tenacity of your company and the courage you manifest in expanding your horizons. It is inspiring to see a young company such as Multi-Hit defying the statistical configurations in their ascension to the top of the recording industry.

Your concept of satellite studios is efficacious and I'm certain Super-Tech Recording can help you implement the modularity you are seeking.

Perhaps we can meet again at a time that is convenient for both of us.

Pedantically yours,

TOM TAPEHEAD
Sales Specialist

Mr., Mrs., and Ms. "Dear Sirs" is an obsolete salutation. The best bet is to invest some extra time to find out exactly to whom you are writing so that you can address him or her properly.

DICTATION.   Many people find dictation to be a valuable time saver. If you have a pocket dictation machine, you can utilize your travel or waiting time. For example, after a sales call, you can dictate a thank you letter that your secretary can type later. This should only be done, however, if you can think in an organized way. Many people find it difficult to organize their thoughts and speak simultaneously. For this reason, we recommend that you write an outline first. Your outline should incorporate all of the key ideas and how you will communicate them. Make notes on examples, prices, data, times, dates, and other details that you will need to include.

After your dictation, be sure to listen to what you have recorded. Keep in mind that a letter should sound different from a conversation. Letters must be written in proper English rather than in the loose grammatical style that most of us use verbally. Unless you have a secretary who can rewrite your letters, you need to give it to her in the same form as it will appear on paper.

Form Letters   The advantage of form letters is that they accomplish the maximum amount of contacts in a minimum amount of time with a minimum amount of rewriting. The disadvantage is that they are impersonal and, therefore, not always appropriate.

Form letters are most appropriate when the circumstances are the same for each contact. Some introductory letters, direct mail compaigns, and market surveys lend themselves well to form letters. In these cases, the letters are carefully written to accomplish a specific purpose and then bulk-mailed to large numbers of people.

Form letters follow the same principles that govern personal letters. The following questions will help you evaluate your writing of form letters:

1. Does the lead sentence immediately get in step with the reader?
2. Is your lead sentence no more than two or three lines long?
3. Do your opening paragraphs promise a benefit to the reader? (Don't waste too much time introducing.)
4. Have you fired your biggest gun first?
5. Is there a big idea behind your proposition?
6. Are your thoughts arranged in logical order?
7. Is what you say believable? (It may be true, but is it believable?)
8. Is it clear what you want the reader to do and did you ask him to do it? (Take note: This is an extremely important point.)
9. If there is an order form included, does the letter's copy tie in with it and have you directed attention to the order form in the letter?
10. Does the letter have a "you" attitude all the way through?
11. Does the letter have a conversational tone? (Try to write as easily as you talk. Write as you would if you were visiting with the person by phone.)
12. Have you connected one paragraph to the next while gently leading your reader through the copy?
13. Does your copy have between 70 and 80 five-letter or less words for each 100 words you have written?
14. Are there any sentences where you could have avoided beginning with "a," "an," or "the"?

15. Are there any places where you have strung together too many prepositional phrases?
16. Have you eliminated wandering verbs?
17. Have you used action verbs instead of noun construction? ("We will be glad to send you a bill at a later time.")
18. Are there any "thats" which you don't need?
19. Does your letter look the way you want it to look as far as these items are concerned?
    a. Placement on the page
    b. No paragraphs over six lines
    c. Indentation and numbered paragraphs for emphasis
    d. Underscoring and capitalization used sparingly
    e. Punctuation for reading ease

The purpose of these guidelines is to make your letter look interesting and read smoothly so as to capture the reader's interest. An effective letter will convey professionalism and motivate people to contact you. The interest you stimulate through your letters will be strengthened by your personal and phone contacts. Letters provide a necessary introduction and follow-through that are an indispensable part of doing business. Business, however, can rarely, if ever, be conducted solely through the mail.

2. The Telephone

From a cost-benefit standpoint, the telephone is an extremely valuable communication tool. This is especially true for contacting established customers in the B and C categories. It has been estimated that the cost of a letter is $5–$10. This figure includes the time of the secretary who types it and the cost of materials and postage. The cost would be even higher if this figure included the time of the person who prepared the letter. A face-to-face call has been estimated to cost well over $130. Obviously, a telephone call is significantly cheaper than both. Phone calls are more personal than letters but less personal than face-to-face calls.

Being such a time and money saver, the telephone is well-suited for contacting customers and prospects about everything from scheduling an appointment to making sales. The use of the telephone for business does require skills that differ from those used in face-to-face selling. It is interesting to note that the skills you learn for effective phone calling will also improve your personal face-to-face selling.

The primary disadvantage of the telephone is that you are limited to the verbal aspects of the interaction. For this reason, some salespeople find it difficult to relate to people over the phone. Therefore, it is helpful to try to create a mental image of the other person. Obviously this is much easier if you already know the person. If you do not know the prospect, imagine someone you know and relate to him or her in the relaxed, friendly way that you normally would. By doing this, you will find that your mental image affects your attitude.

As we discuss in the chapters on communication skills, your attitude is conveyed through your vocal quality. If you are in a bad mood, your voice will convey it. Because of this, many telephone sales offices use mirrors on their employees' desks, which allow the salespeople to see themselves as they talk on the phone. Research has proven that smiling while you are talking will affect the person on the other end of the line because the listener can actually hear a difference in your voice when you are smiling.

Test Your Vocal Quality   The way that you sound on the phone is an important factor in determining the outcome of the call. One valuable tool for improving your vocal quality is to record your conversations with a cassette recorder, using, if possible, a phone adapter so that you can hear both sides of the conversation. Then call some friends, tell them what you are doing, and either have normal conversations with them or go over one of your presentations. Afterward, listen to your voice and analyze your vocal style.

Save the tapes so that you can compare them to the ones you will make after you have worked on improving your vocal quality. By listening to the tapes you will be reminded constantly of those aspects of your speech habits which need to be improved. If you cannot judge your vocal quality, ask a co-worker or friend to listen to the tapes and evaluate your effectiveness. Often an objective listener will hear things that you miss.

You may find it useful to refer to the chapters on verbal communication skills. The same principles apply to your voice over the phone. Listen to your enunciation. Are you easy to understand or do you mumble? Are you repeating phrases like "you know," or "like"? Do you say "uh" before every new thought? All of these conversational idiosyncrasies cause distractions which dilute the potency of your message.

Background Noise   Have you ever called someone and tried to have a conversation while kids were screaming in the background on the other end of the phone? If so, then you know how irritating background noises can be. The distraction becomes even greater when the other person interrupts the conversation to yell at the kids. You can overlook these things when talking to friends, but a business call should be free of all background noises.

In addition to being distracting, background noises also say something about you. If you make business calls when there is a lot of background noise, you are telling your customer that you don't care enough to eliminate distractions. Naturally, there are extenuating circumstances in which you must call from a phone booth, but routine business calls should be made where it is quiet. If not, your customers will infer that you are inconsiderate and unprofessional.

Telephone Phobia   Some salespeople are afraid of using the phone. They feel uncomfortable because they cannot see the other person to create the personal atmosphere which is necessary in sales. They also feel that it is easier for prospects to give them the brush off over the phone.

It is helpful to ask yourself, "What is the worst thing that could happen?" The worst thing is that the person on the other end of the line could say something nasty or hang up on you. The best thing that could happen is that you could make a sale, perhaps a large sale! Between the best and worst ends of the continuum, there are many possibilities. Certainly the gains outweigh the possible losses with the risk well worth it, especially when you consider that a phone call could help you save time and money, obtain a referral, expand an account, or avoid a cancellation.

Be Organized   If you have a large number of phone calls to make every week, it is an absolute necessity to do it in an organized fashion. The first step in being organized is to establish a time once a day or once a week (depending on your needs) that you will devote exclusively to phone calls. You should then force yourself to sit at your desk until you have completed all of your calls or made enough sales to reach your goals. Not only will this develop self-discipline, it will also make the calling sessions easier as time goes by. Calling prospects and customers is like most things that take practice: the more you do it, the better you become.

During your calling sessions, it is important to maintain your momentum. When you have completed a call, don't stop to fill out your log or order forms. Make rough notes and then make another call. You will have time later to go back and fill in the details. If you have just made a sale you should carry that momentum and feeling of accomplishment into the next call rather than let it dissipate by filling out the order form. Enthusiasm and success feed on themselves.

When preparing for your calls it is important that you have all the information at your fingertips. If you were to set aside an hour each day for calls and spend twenty minutes looking for phone numbers, you would only be cheating yourself. Another item to have on hand before you start your calls is a calendar. It sounds awfully foolish if you have to say, "Hold on, let me get my calendar," everytime you set an appointment. Whether you prefer a large appointment calendar or a pocket calendar is unimportant as long as you have it in front of you during your telephone session.

When planning your calls, it is helpful to categorize them by the objective of the call. For example, you might make calls to collect money, survey needs, offer promotional sales, follow up a complaint, or make a presentation (in the case of telephone sales). You should then make all the calls in one category at the same time. This will establish a "mind set" from which to operate. Making similar calls one after another helps you maintain your momentum because you know what you are going to say and are warmed up for it.

You can also categorize your calls by determining when it is best to call. This time you should group them by the type of people to be called, because different groups answer the phone at different times. Here are some suggestions on when to call:

TYPE OF PEOPLE	BEST TIME TO CALL
Engineers, Chemists	4:00–5:00 P.M.
Clergymen	Anytime after Tuesday but before Saturday
Contractors, Builders	Before 9:00 A.M.–After 8:00 P.M.
Dentists	Before 9:30 A.M.
Druggists	Between 1:00–3:00 P.M.
Executives and Businessowners	Before 8:30 A.M. (before they leave for work)
Housewives	11:00 A.M.–12:00N—2:00–4:30 P.M.
Attorneys	11:00 A.M.–2:00 P.M.
Physicians	9:00–11:00 A.M.—1:00–3:00 P.M.—7:00–9:00 P.M.
Professors, Teachers	At home—7:00–9:00 P.M.
CPAs	Anytime except between January 15–April 15
Publishers, printers	After 3:00 P.M.
Butchers, Grocers	Before 9:00 A.M.—Between 1:00–2:30 P.M.

Monitor Your Calls   In order to improve at anything, you need a baseline with which you can compare your progress. In order to increase your effectiveness on the telephone you should keep track of your calls. The Telephone Prospecting Log will help you structure the data to keep on each calling session. This log is not concerned with individual accounts. It is a day-by-day tally of what happened with each call you made.

The importance of keeping a log can be seen in the analysis of the results. Let's say, for example, that you started off using a different time of day to call every day for two weeks. At the end of that time, your log will show you which times were productive and which were not. If you found that for every contact you dialed an average of three times, you may be choosing the wrong time to call. If you find, however, that you are getting through to your prospects but not getting results, you may need to analyze your telephone habits or make more face-to-face calls. Without a record, however, you would not be able to track your results and analyze your performance.

Brevity   If you value your prospect's time as much as your own, you will want to make your calls as short as possible. This does not mean you should talk in shorthand, but don't waste time either. It is important to remember that your call is an interruption. It may not be an irritating interruption, but you are breaking the flow of the prospect's activities. For this reason, it is helpful if you "take the curse off the call" as soon as you can. This involves finding out if you called at an inconvenient time. If so, find out when you should call back. The idea is to have the prospect's full attention rather than his partially resentful attention.

TELEPHONE PROSPECTING LOG

Date	Company	Contact	Phone	Time Called	Outcome of Call	Source of Lead
3/2/87	GMS ENT.	Bill Smith	302 541- 8709	9:30	Set up Appointment	Yellow Pages
3/2/87	ACME Electric	Tony O'Neil	415 777- 1800 X 491	10:00	Send Brochure Call Back 2 weeks	Electrical Supply Catalog
3/2/87	Belmont Hotel	Randy Jones, MGR.	735- 8104	11:30	Out to Lunch Call at 2 pm	Jim Weinberg

Worksheet 9-1:   Telephone Prospecting Log

Pre-Call Planning   In order to make your calls short and to the point, plan ahead. Imagine how much time would be wasted if you improvised during each call. Instead, you need to know where you are going and how you are going to get there. To help you with your pre-call planning we have devised a Telephone Planning Sheet. This worksheet will summarize everything you need to know to make the call. Fill out the planner in advance and have one for each call to be made.

TELEPHONE PLANNING SHEET

Target Segment for these calls:_____
_____

My purpose for these calls (objective):_____
_____

Best time of day/week/month for making these calls:_____
_____

Initial Benefit Statement (Opening):_____
_____

Key points I should cover:_____
_____
_____

What commitment will I ask the other person to make:_____
_____
_____

Potential Objections/Answers:_____
   Objection:_____
   _____
      Answer:_____
   _____
   Objection:_____
   _____
      Answer:_____
   _____

Worksheet 9-2: Telephone Planning Worksheet

The items on the planner are straightforward and in the order you will need them. The first thing to note is the objective of the call. Every call you make should have an objective which is realistic and specific (like a goal). You should never make a call simply to say hello.

After you know the call objective, outline the call by starting with an initial benefit statement or other opening.

After the opening you need to know what important points will be covered, what information you should ask for and so on. This will prevent you from hanging up and saying to yourself, "Oh, I forgot to mention. . . ." This is especially important when calling long distance.

If you are going to ask your prospect or customer for a commitment or course of action, make a note of this on the telephone planner. This way you will not lose sight of your call objective.

Many beginning salespeople prepare for their calls in another way as well. They like to think of possible objections to their proposal and answers that are fitting. This is primarily done in telephone sales. At the bottom of the planner a space is provided for some objections and answers. Even if you are not in telephone sales, it is a useful exercise to think of objections and answers. This helps you see things from your prospect's point of view.

Correct Information   Part of your homework before contacting a prospect is to find out exactly whom to call. This can often be done by calling the prospect's company and asking a switchboard operator, secretary, or receptionist. The advantage of finding out directly is that you will also hear how the person's name is pronounced. All too often we have to call a prospect whose last name is a tongue-twister. It's embarrassing to ask someone how to pronounce his name. It is even worse if you assume that you know how to pronounce it and you are wrong. So make sure that you find out how to pronounce it correctly and whether it is preceded by Ms., Mrs., or Mr. Remember, names such as Pat, Joe, Lou, and so on, can belong to either a man or a woman.

Dealing with Secretaries   In preparing for your calls, it is invaluable to have a strategy for getting past secretaries. Sometimes it seems like secretaries are recruited from college football teams because they are so good at running interference.

If you run across a skeptical secretary, there are several things that you can do. First, it is often a good idea to ask for your prospect by his first name. This will imply a familiarity that may melt the secretary's skepticism. If the secretary persists by asking, "And who are you with?" you can say, "I'm with the XYZ Company. Would you connect me please?" Bear in mind that although as you want to be firm and assertive, you do not want to antagonize anyone by sounding hostile and pushy. A gentle persuasiveness is called for here. You will undoubtedly run into secretaries who ask, "And what is this regarding?" You should simply state that you would like to discuss business with Mr. Prospect and you need to talk to him for only a few minutes.

When calling long distance, it is highly advisable to tell the secretary that you are doing so. People tend to give long distance calls a higher priority than local calls. If they say, "Do you mind if I put you on hold?" be careful. Being put on hold can mean being ignored for two or three minutes. Some people are not in the habit of checking back with the caller every 30 seconds or so to make sure the caller is still breathing. Your best bet is to tell the secretary that you can only remain on hold a short time, otherwise you will have to hang up.

This also applies to you. If you have a hold button on your phone and are in the habit of using it, be sensitive to the fact that your caller is waiting. It is a good business practice to check back with your caller every 30 seconds to give some feedback as to what is happening on your end of the line.

The best solution to putting someone on hold is to return the call. If you are busy or need to get some information, simply ask if you can call back in a few minutes.

When you find a secretary who is friendly and cooperative, ask for her first name. In the future you can refer to her by name and create a rapport which can only help you.

Choose Your Words Carefully   Because the prospect has only your words from which to get your message, the way you say things over the telephone is even more important than when meeting in person. In person, if there is any doubt as to your meaning, you can sense it from the person's nonverbal feedback. Over the phone, however, you may unintentionally insult your prospect and never know it. For example, when you say, "As I said . . . ," or "To put it another way . . . ," you are repeating yourself with the implication that the other person did not understand you for the first time. Another common phrase is, "Let me ask you a question." It may be subtle, but this is a command not a question. A command immediately puts someone on the defensive. A better way to say this is, "May I ask you a question?" or "Do you mind if I ask you some questions?" This involves them in the conversation and makes them want to talk to you instead of defensively following your commands.

In addition to choosing your words carefully, you should also choose your attitude carefully. The idea is to come across as natural as you can. Be neither overly friendly nor too cautious. Talking on the phone is just like making a personal face-to-face sales call: you do your best when you are relaxed and courteous.

Listening   Effective listening is required on the phone as well as in person. We discussed active listening in Chapter 8, but effective listening over the telephone requires more effort on your part.

When you are on the phone with a prospect, ask as many open-ended questions as possible. Listen to *what* is being said, not just to the words that are being spoken. When long pauses occur, try not to interrupt unless you sense that the prospect is finished with her thought. Reinforce the prospect's participation by giving verbal feedback about the things being said. A simple "Yes," or "I see," will suffice. Make sure you understand what the prospect is saying and avoid jumping to conclusions. Toward the end of the call, arrange for the next call and express your sincere gratitude.

Let Them Hang Up First   Have you ever concluded a conversation with someone and just as they were hanging up you thought of one more thing to say? This often happens because we think so quickly. To avoid cutting off your prospect's thoughts, it is a good practice to let the prospect hang up first. Stay on the phone during the silence until you finally hear the click and dial tone on the line. This is easily done unless the prospect has also been trained to hang up last. In this case, you had better pack a boxed lunch and a couple of books because it could be a long time until you hear the dial tone again.

Call-ins   When you answer the phone in the office, immediately identify your company and department and give your name. If you are self-employed and have an office at home, simply answer by stating your name.

The true wisdom of using the telephone is that it gives you control over your sales career. When you phone for appointments and orders, you save money and increase the profitability of that account. You also gain control of your time and manage your day more effectively. The telephone is such an integral part of our lives that it is inconceivable how people conducted business before its invention.

Personal Face-To-Face Contacts   There is nothing like meeting someone in person. Phone conversations and letters only reveal an inkling of someone's personality. Because sales is such a personal business, it is no wonder that the most highly valued form of contact is face-to-face.

The easiest in-person call to make is the one made through a referral or previous introduction. This is why the professional salesperson always precedes a personal call with a letter and a phone call. And the professional always has an appointment! Traditional salespeople often experience *call reluctance* before calling on a prospect whom they have never met. This is not a problem for professional salespeople because they have done their homework, contacted the prospect, and secured an appointment before they showed up. The professional way decreases the tension for both the buyer and the seller.

Personal face-to-face calls can be made for any number of reasons: to introduce yourself to the prospect; to gather information; to give a presentation; to confirm the sale; or to follow up on a sale. After the business relationship has been established, personal calls become easier. For this reason, we will center our discussion on the introductory call.

The introductory call is designed to be an information-gathering session for you and your prospect. Before business can be transacted, both of you need to know and trust each other. Basically, the procedure is as follows:

1. *Enter and introduce yourself.* This is a time when you should be conscious of your image, body language, and eye contact. At this point you are relating to each other on a personal rather than a business level. Your prospect is sizing you up (on strictly superficial terms) to determine if he can trust you.

2. *Establish the purpose of your call.* Early in the sales process you need to make it clear why you are there and to capture the prospect's attention. An initial benefit statement is useful at this point. It will draw the prospect in by stating, in a nutshell, what you have to offer him. The closer your statement is to his needs, the better your chances are of holding his interest. This is where your homework begins to pay off.

3. *Uncover needs.* After you have established the reason for the call and created some interest, you need to have a reason to continue. You should explore the prospect's business situation by asking him questions. This is best accomplished by first asking permission to inquire into his business and then asking him questions which will require narrative answers. At the same time, you need to be an active listener so that you can begin to develop the trust bond. When asking questions, encourage your prospect to talk freely by asking open-ended questions that are specific. It may be helpful for you to refer to Chapter 7, which deals with the art of questioning.

4. *Propose a solution.* Many times a sale will require a number of calls before a solution can be proposed and the sale confirmed. You may have to do more studying or the prospect may need time to think about your product. There are situations, however, in which a proposal can be given during the first meeting. Chapters 20 and 21 discuss the proposing and confirming phases of sale.

Brevity, Again   Remember that time is money, so be careful how you spend your prospect's time. Imagine yourself as having a meter running while you are meeting with your prospect. The more time you spend with your prospect, the more it will cost both of you.

When setting up an appointment with a prospect, it is helpful to tell him that you will only need a small amount of his time. Try to impress on him that you recognize that he is busy. You do not want to carry this too far and imply that you yourself are unimportant, but do respect his time and schedule. If, during the call, you are running over your allotted time, ask your prospect if he minds if you continue. If you get the feeling that continuing would be an inconvenience, then ask him when a more convenient time would be and set another appointment. It is better to come back than to overstay your welcome.

Look for Sales Opportunities   When you walk into a prospect's place of business, be observant and look for sales opportunities. Browse through the inventory or make note of how things are done. As an objective observer you may see things that go unnoticed by the management. Pointing them out in a diplomatic way can earn you the respect and credibility that you need in order to establish a strong relationship.

Stumbling Blocks   It is interesting to note the reasons why more sales are not confirmed by salespeople. Many executives have indicated that these include:

Complacency Among Established Salespeople	26%
Insufficient Preparation	25%
Improper Prospecting	14%
Inadequate Training	12%
Fear (New Salespeople)	3%

As you can see, the professional salesperson has the edge because she has taken care of all of the above. The process of studying, proposing, confirming, and assuring is so strong that it cuts down wasted time and money more than any other sales technique. But professional sales is more than a technique; it is a way of life.

SUMMARY

Meeting prospects, like every other facet of the selling profession, must be accomplished in ways that are conducive to business, cost-effective, image-effective, tension-reducing, and trust-building. There are three methods in which a salesperson meets (contacts) his prospects and customers: by letter, by telephone, or by a personal face-to-face call. Although all three methods have their advantages, the most effective of the three is the personal face-to-face call because it provides the opportunity to communicate both verbally and nonverbally and to use visual aids.

There are a number of reasons for using letters to contact prospects and customers. They are an excellent means of introducing yourself prior to calling for an initial appointment. They can also be used to answer questions, contact busy people who are frequently inaccessible, follow up on a sales call, provide updates, stimulate business, and recount pertinent conversations of interest to a prospect. Whatever the purpose of the personal letter, it basically serves to establish or cement the trust bond, create or maintain interest, and keep the lines of communication open.

Writing concise personal business letters that accomplish a planned goal is an art and requires practice. Among the several things to keep in mind when writing a successful business letter are the following: use the name of the customer; identify yourself and your company; mention who referred you; state the purpose of your letter; make an initial benefit statement; identify an area of probable interest; write in the language of the prospect's industry; state one or two reasons for the prospect to see you; include a brochure, if appropriate; indicate when to expect a follow-up call; and be brief.

Form letters, although impersonal, do have an advantage. They accomplish the maximum amount of contacts in a minimum amount of time with a minimum amount of rewriting. They are most appropriate when the circumstances are the same for each contact and lend themselves quite well to introductions, direct mail campaigns, and market surveys.

From a cost-benefit standpoint, the telephone is an extremely valuable communication tool. It is particularly well-suited for contacting customers and prospects for everything from scheduling an appointment to making sales. Its primary disadvantage is that you are limited to the verbal aspects of the interaction with the other person.

When using the phone for telephone sales, it is absolutely necessary to approach the task in an organized manner. This means establishing a specific time in a day or week to make the calls, giving yourself the needed discipline to accomplish the task successfully. Also be sure to maintain the momentum by just jotting significant notes during and after each call, leaving the completion of your phone log to the end of the calling session. In this way, you are able to maintain your momentum. Organization for the calling session also includes: having all the information necessary at your fingertips; having a calendar with you for appointments that can be made; and categorizing your calls by objective. Before making telephone sales calls, it is best to do some pre-call planning. This includes knowing the target segment for the calls you will be making; the purpose of your calls; the best time of the day/week/month for the calls; the initial benefit statement you plan to make; the key points you plan to cover during the call; the commitment you plan to request; and the potential objections that may be raised with the responses you can provide.

The most effective contact with a prospect or customer is through the personal face-to-face contact. The easiest in-person call to make is the one made through a referral or previous introduction. That is why the professional salesperson always precedes a personal call with a letter and a phone call.

The personal face-to-face call can be made for a number of reasons: to introduce yourself to the prospect; to gather information; to give a presentation; to confirm the sale; or to follow up on a sale.

The introductory call is designed to be an information-gathering session for you and your prospect. Before business can be accomplished, both of you must know and trust each other. The procedure for such a call is to enter and introduce yourself; establish the purpose of your call; uncover needs, and, if appropriate in that meeting, propose a solution.

Stumbling blocks for traditional salespeople tend to be complacency, insufficient preparation, improper prospecting, inadequate training, and fear. The professional salesperson has taken care of all of these stumbling blocks, for the process of studying, proposing, confirming, and assuring is so strong that it cuts down wasted time and money more than any other sales technique. Professional sales is more than a technique; it is a way of life.

DISCUSSION
QUESTIONS

1. What are the three ways of contacting a customer?
2. Rate each method in terms of the quality of contact and the number of contacts possible.
3. What are some uses of a personal letter?
4. When is a personal letter inappropriate?
5. What elements give a letter a professional appearance?
6. The telephone is a useful tool for what kind of calls?
7. Is it ever appropriate to try to sell someone by phone?
8. Is there a way to organize phone calls to make the task easier?
9. What kind of records should be kept for phone calls? What are the benefits of keeping these records?
10. Give all the reasons an in-person meeting is the strongest.
11. Why should the introductory call be seen as an investment of time?
12. What is the most important reason for getting together with a

prospect? (The answer is not in this chapter. Think about what you have learned so far.)

13. What is an initial benefits statement?

14. Pretend you are applying for a job. If an employer asked for an initial benefits statement about you, what would you say? Write such a statement, containing at least four sentences.

CHAPTER TEN

Studying Needs

<table>
<tr><td>CHAPTER
OBJECTIVES</td><td>

1 Describe the process of thoroughly studying the prospect's needs.
2 Suggest topics about prospects that require study.
3 Provide guidelines to follow for the studying phase when meeting with the prospect.
</td></tr>
</table>

Every situation requires studying before you can make a judgment, propose a recommendation, or draw a conclusion. Hasty decisions often prove to be reckless. The greater a decision's importance, the more time people like to take in making it.

Can you imagine visiting your doctor and having him prescibe a medication without first diagnosing your problem? How would you feel if he spent two minutes with you without asking any questions and then suggested a treatment on the basis of that "examination"? The chances are that you would feel very uncomfortable. In fact, you would feel offended, unimportant, and exploited. This would not create a trusting relationship.

The sales relationship is no different. You cannot go into a call with the intention of selling a customer without first learning her needs. The truly professional salesperson recognizes and respects the importance of this studying phase. It is one of the things that differentiates a professional from a charlatan.

A healthy attitude is to see yourself and your prospect as being experts. You are an expert in your field, specifically about your product. Your prospect is an expert in her business, especially regarding the needs which she is presently experiencing. You cannot be condescending by assuming that your product will solve her problems without first studying those problems. Rather than telling her what she needs, treat her as an equal by taking the time to discover her buying motives and the benefits she seeks. This will also allow you to structure your presentation to meet her buying criteria.

The only way to effectively study a prospect's situation is to put her in a frame of mind which is conducive to self-disclosure. This is necessary because the prospect's thoughts, feelings, and business details will be the basis of your studying. The best way to encourage your prospect to open up is to establish a trusting relationship. After you have accomplished this, you can assess her situation and uncover her goals and objectives.

ESTABLISHING TRUST

Building trust in a relationship is first accomplished by lowering your prospect's tension level. When meeting with another person, tension is caused by the other person suspecting that you have ulterior motives. In a sales situation, a suspected ulterior motive would be your determination to sell your product whether the prospect needs it or not. If your prospect picks this up from you, then she will be tense and defensive. If, on the other hand, you are sincere and take an interest in her and her business, her tension and defensiveness will be reduced.

The first factor in creating trust is the image you project. As soon as you are seen by your prospect, she immediately infers things from the way you look. Everything we discussed in Chapter 4—grooming, wardrobe, body language, eye contact—have their effect on the tension level your prospect initially feels. If your image is positive, sincere, and nonthreatening, you will have an easier time building trust.

Another important factor is your behavioral flexibility. Remember that it is important to determine your prospect's personal style and to blend with it. Your top priority is to facilitate a working relationship with your new customer. It will serve you well to refrain from voicing your opinions or venting your frustrations if this is inappropriate for the type of person with whom you are dealing. Think of the business relationship as being a chemical reaction. You are not only an ingredient, but also the catalyst. As such, it is in your power to create either an explosive reaction or a stable mixture. There is no doubt that the latter is by far the more preferable.

Being an active listener is another important factor. You should give verbal and nonverbal feedback and ask open-ended questions to draw out your prospect and make her feel comfortable with you. As you communicate with her you should periodically reassure her that you want only what is in her best interest.

ASSESSMENT OF SITUATION AND GOALS

In order to determine if your product or service will be of any value to your prospect, you must know her current situation, all of its attendant problems, and the goals and objectives that she has in mind. For example, if your prospect has a very unorganized payroll but no desire to be more organized, there is no sense in trying to sell efficiency to her in the beginning. Note that we said, "in the beginning." At first you should accept your prospect's goals (or her lack of goals). As you develop your relationship, however, you will be in the position to bring up new needs that she might not have previously addressed. Having a strong trust relationship, you could mention the unorganized payroll and show her a way to not only clean it up, but also how to save time and money in the process. If she has confidence in your expertise at that point, the chances are good that she will be open to your suggestion.

Since you need to know about the prospect's situation and goals, which do you explore first? At first glance, it may appear that the order is unimportant. This is not the case. Consider the fact that the current situation deals with something concrete: the present. Goals and objectives deal with something abstract: the future. Different behavioral styles prefer talking about different things. A Relater prefers relationships to tasks, so your discussion should first revolve around the present situation and how the prospect feels about it. With a Relater, you should also move slowly rather than rushing to the topic of goals and objectives. After you have completely talked about her current situation, you can then move on to the future. Gentle, effective questioning can lead the way to discussing the Relater's more task-oriented goals.

How would you handle a Director? Would you discuss the situation or his goals first? You know that Directors are very task- and goal-oriented. To be well-received, therefore, you should center your discussion on goals and objectives. A Director is also well-organized and fast, so he is able to give you the information you need quickly. You can then move on to discussing the current situation. Keep in mind, however, that you should discuss the situation from the perspective of the goals he has outlined. If you couch everything in the terms he perfers, you will get much more cooperation and information from him. You will also gain more respect and confidence as well as business.

Reality as a Selling Tool

Studying a prospect's situation and objectives may take many calls and much outside homework. On the other hand, you may accomplish it all in one call. Each account is different. After you have completed your studying, you will have a picture of the actual conditions versus the desired conditions. This will enable you to analyze all of the variables to see how they compare.

This comparison, in the form of two lists, can be used as a tool to show the prospect how things really are. Often customers feel that their goals are being met when, in reality, they are not. This happens because they are too close to the situation to see it objectively. Customers also become defensive about their businesses, especially if they are owners. After you have established a good working relationship, it is your job as a consultant to analyze the situation and its possiblities to point out any deficiencies in the system.

If you find the actual situation to be fairly close to the desired goals and objectives, then your product or service can offer little or no improvement. In this case, you would not advise your prospect to buy. When this happens, you should wrap up the call so that you will not waste either your time or his. You will then put your prospect's name on a *follow-up* list. As time goes by, needs change and you may find your prospect ready to problem-solve with you again. At this point, you will already have established the trust relationship, especially because you were honest in the past. It is very convenient to have already laid down the groundwork for the relationship so you can pick things up from where they left off.

In the majority of cases, after analyzing your prospect's actual and desired situation, you will find large discrepancies. By pointing these out, you can work with him to clearly define his needs. It will take the two of you to effectively solve the problem.

This is the time to look for the deeper causes of the problems. All too often a cause is assumed to be one thing when it is another. The obvious is sometimes overlooked and at other times blamed. Great care must be taken in diagnosing a prospect's problem. If necessary, call in a specialist or do more homework to help with the analysis. This is analogous to having migraine headaches. If you work on the symptom with drugs, the cause (psychological stress) is still untouched. The remedy, therefore, is only temporary. Business problems are the same way. If a customer needs better service, is it due to a lack of service calls or ineffective communication? It may require some deep questioning to find out, but that is your job if you want to do it right.

BE ORGANIZED

Part of your pre-call planning involves the establishment of call objectives. These can range from confirming a sale to simply introducing yourself and gathering some information. In any case, having a brief outline of topics to be covered and questions to be asked will keep you on target. It is easy to lose your train of thought when a conversation becomes convoluted, so refer to your outline rather than letting the conversation go astray. It is also a good idea to jot down some notes during the call. You can only be of service to your customer if you have the facts straight.

Topics to Study

Every prospect will be different, but there are many things that you will need to know about all of them. Although you may have the topics to be covered listed in your notes, you should not question your prospect as if you were interviewing him. Some of the areas to inquire about are:

1. the psychology of the situation
2. your prospect's feelings
3. key decision maker(s) and the buying process

4. time factors
5. political considerations within the company
6. relevant past experiences
7. product specifications
8. budgetary constraints

Naturally, you will think of your own topics to include. Our list will stimulate your thinking of others.

1.   *The Psychology of the Situation*   In analyzing the current situation, you need to consider the psychological determinants of the sale. These will take a little closer scrutiny than the more obvious physical or business needs. A prospect's ego is often involved in his decision to buy. This could be happening for many reasons, some of which may be:

Fear of not conforming
Fear of losing the esteem of others
Fear of making less money
Desire to be efficient
Desire to have the best
Fear of wasting time and energy
Desire to please
Fear of rejection

There are many reasons why people buy and most of them have nothing to do with need. This is something you should be aware of and look for in your calls. A psychological need can be just as strong as a concrete business need. There is nothing wrong with a customer wanting to buy for superficial reasons, but you must be certain your product or service will satisfy this need. A small sampling of some of the emotional reasons why people buy would be:

1. *Prestige.* People buy in order to gain distinction, influence, or admiration from others. The prestigious product indicates that they have reached a level of success which puts them a cut above most people. We see this every day in the form of homes, automobiles, club memberships, clothes, and even designer chocolates.

2. *Love.* We buy things to express our feelings, to protect or to share with someone we love. Everything from diamond rings to smoke alarms can be bought with love as a motive. Sometimes love and prestige enter into the same purchase. This can be seen in a case where someone feels that he will be loved more if he buys her a Porsche instead of a Toyota.

3. *Curiosity.* We are all curious by nature. Many things we buy are packaged in ways to make them appeal to our curiosity. We buy them just to satisfy that need. Of course, there is more of a limit to our willingness to spend money due to curiosity than to prestige or love.

4. *Imitation.* Not only are we curious by nature, we are also imitators. This is not entirely bad, especially if we are imitating successful, positive people. Often we

will buy similar clothes or other things that we associate with them. The hope is that we will acquire some of their good qualities through imitation. This can work well between competing companies. The underdog may try to emulate the other's success through imitation.

5. *Fear.* Fear is a very strong, although sometimes a subtle, emotion. We may buy things because we have physical or psychological fears. Physical fears would be those concerning health, property, life, freedom, or death. For these reasons people buy health and life insurance, security systems, diet books, and so on. Psychological fears include growing old, loss of self-esteem, poverty, criticism, loss of love, unemployment, or lack of fulfillment. These fears are sometimes assuaged by buying "how-to" books, vitamins, investment plans, and psycho-therapy, to name a few.

6. *Rivalry.* Rivalry and rebellion are closely related. Here, people buy because someone else did not. This is the opposite of imitation. Rivalry between com-petitors is common in some retail businesses such as audio and video equipment. This should be kept in mind in case you run across competitors who are always trying to "one-up" the others.

7. *Self-Preservation.* For most people the instinct to survive is stronger than any other need. People simply want to live as long as they can. If someone says he doesn't really want to live past age 70, wait and ask him when he is 69. People buy items that will help them to live longer such as health foods, vitamins, exercise equipment, diet books, and doctors' advice.

8. *Variety....* is the spice of life. People like new things, even if they are only slightly different than what they already have. Proof of this lies in the fashion industry. It thrives on the fact that people tire of their clothes after wearing them twice, especially if they have to be ironed!

2. Your Prospect's Feelings How your prospect feels about her situa-tion is something you should know. If she is ambivalent about spending money, take this into consideration. It is better to postpone a sale than to confirm it only to have it cancelled later. You want your prospect to be happy with her purchase. This may require your stimulating some excitement in her, which çan be done by learning as much as you can about her situation, analyzing it, and then present-ing the problems and solutions to her. Once she sees the possibilities, she may become enthusiastic about your product or service.

You also want to learn what your prospect's feelings are toward you and your company. Her perceptions will undoubtedly color her feelings about doing business with you. If she is part of a large corporation and sees you as a "Mom and Pop" business, she may not trust your company with her business. If she is a small business and sees you as a conglomerate, she may fear a loss in personal service. There are all kinds of combinations and possibilities. Your knowledge of how she feels will enable you to assure her that all will be well if she chooses to do business with you.

3. Key Decision Makers and the Buying Process Many companies, es-pecially large corporations, have several people who must be sold on an idea before they buy it. It is important for you to learn the names and positions of the other people whom you will need to see. Simply asking, "Who, besides yourself, will be making the final decision on this?" will move you one step closer to those people. Sometimes it is difficult, if not impossible, to get to the key decision-makers. In this case, the person to whom you sell will, in effect, become *your* sales representative in presenting your case to the higher ups. If this is unavoidable, then do your best to educate your rep. Provide him with statistics, brochures, visual aids, charts, lists of benefits, testimonials, and so on. Then keep your fingers crossed.

You will also want to know what the procedure is for the sale to take place. Find out what steps are necessary and how you can help expedite them. In your willingness to help, convey that you are trying to help them save time and work rather than rushing the sale through.

There is a better way to ask the question "Who besides yourself will be making the final decision on this?" For example, "Could you draw a picture for me of how decisions like this are made in your company?" enables your prospect to include himself in the decision-making process while still telling you who the real decision maker is. The typical question posed by most salespeople, "Who's the decision maker?" puts the customer in an uncomfortable position. If he is the decision-maker, he feels insulted that you had to ask; if he is not the decision-maker, he feels insulted or embarrassed. Most likely, he will feel the need to say yes whether it's true or not. Thus, asking him to draw a picture of the decision-making process, putting the emphasis on a process rather than a person, makes it easier for the person to answer the question. The most important fact here is that we should not ignore everyone except the major decision-maker. Sometimes there are people who are major influencers of the decision-maker who must be sold before we ever get to a decision maker. You still get a commitment from this person; it's just a different kind of commitment. Instead of asking him to buy something, you're asking him what he would do if he were the person who could buy something. If he says, "Yes, I'd buy this," then you have an ally to help you sell to the decision-maker. The next step becomes, "Since you are going to be giving this presentation and you are going to be pushing my product and selling for me, wouldn't it be a good idea for me to be there?"

4. *Time Factors* While you are asking about the procedure, find out how quickly they would like the purchase to transpire. It is helpful to know if they are in a hurry to implement the changes that your product/service will provide. If they are not in a hurry and seem rather noncommittal, you might ask if there are other companies bidding for the sale. Obviously, if there are other bidders, you will need to be extra sharp in your analysis and proposal of solutions.

A time factor could make or break a sale. If a prospect wants a delivery on a certain date and you cannot provide it quickly enough, you might lose the sale. If there is ever a doubt as to your ability to meet a time constraint, don't give a negative response right away. Tell your prospect that you will look into it, then do your best to convince your company to speed up the process so that you can accommodate your prospect. This is often a difficult balancing act in which you must work with the demands and limitations of both parties.

5. *Political Considerations Within the Company* Everyone knows that politics are sometimes stronger than knowledge, talent, and every other lofty virtue which deserve recognition. That's life. Knowing we can't fight it, we have to work with it. In the sales situation, try to ascertain what the politics are and how you will have to work with them. This overlaps into the realm of knowing who the key decision makers are. Key decision makers usually have their egos wrapped up in their decision-making status. If you can identify the political game being played, it will be much easier to become a player. One way you can use this knowledge to your advantage would be to meet with the politically powerful party(s) and sell your product/service to them based on their behavioral style(s) *and* buying criteria. Not only is this professional selling, it is also very shrewd. By saying this is shrewd, we are not advocating pulling the wool over their eyes. We are simply saying you should recognize the system and play within the rules. Since politics often dictate the rules, you will have to conform to them.

Another form of politics is loyalty. You may run across a situation in which a prospect's brother-in-law presently supplies a similar product. You will immediately be the underdog in this race. If you hope to pick up the account, you will have to look long and hard for several good reasons why they should buy from you instead of the brother-in-law. You will have to take each area (pricing, quality, service, etc.) and analyze how you compare to your competitor. Hopefully you will uncover some strong selling points.

6. *Relevant Past Experiences* We have all encountered customers who have a negative attitude about our product because of a past experience with something similar. This can be a difficult obstacle to overcome. It would be especially difficult if the customer had a bad experience with your company. Dealing with a prospect whose mind is closed can be very frustrating.

In these cases, you must proceed very slowly in the development of the relationship. Establishing trust will be of the utmost importance. Without trust you are sunk. Talk with this prospect about anything except the thing he has his mind set against. It may require several calls before you can hope to break the ice. Naturally you would not waste your time with this prospect if he were not a top prospective account. If he is, patience will be a virtue.

7. *Product Specifications* If you are selling a technical product or service, you may have to be concerned with specifications. This is an accepted fact of life for businesses dealing with the military or the government. Products or services which are custom-made for a customer will also require gathering data on specifications.

These types of products sometimes need to be certified, approved, or endorsed by a third party. This is important for you to know for two reasons. First, this approval may take a lot of time or red tape. Certainly you will want to know this so you can fit this account and the time factor into your overall plans. Second, this will affect the chances of the sale occurring at all. For example, if you know there is no way that your product will be approved by the military, then you can stop pursuing the account immediately. On the other hand, if the product has been approved or certified already, then you can save time by providing proof of this and obviating the need to repeat the procedure.

Knowing the prospect's specification needs will also help you judge other things. For example, if a prospect needs a large quantity of a certain color or size of product, the manufacturer may have to make a special run to accommodate him. This will certainly affect the delivery time and possibly the price. These are all things you will have to know. The decision to buy may be based on these details.

8.   Budgetary Constraints   In qualifying a prospect, establish his credit and buying power. As thorough as your investigation might have been, it is entirely possible that things have changed for the worst for him. This is an area where you will have to question in a subtle, nonthreatening way. As we mentioned earlier, it is not wise to immediately bring up the subject of money.

Often a prospect will mention his lack of funds in the beginning of the call. You can acknowledge that money is tight for everyone, but that alternatives do exist. The two of you can approach his needs from the perspective having only *X* number of dollars to spend, which is one viable approach. Another is to see if the product can be presold for next year. You can also suggest breaking down the desired results into smaller increments, each of which would cost less to remedy. Your prospect could then resolve them one by one. It is helpful to know what your options are before you go into a call so that you can handle any budgetary obstacles which may arise.

SETTING PROBLEM-SOLVING PRIORITIES

After having gathered all the information you can, you may find that you have uncovered more than one problem or more than one cause of a problem. If this occurs, you and your prospect should set priorities based on the severity of the problems and your ability to solve them. You may find that some problems are out of your field and others are not of great importance. Of course, there will always be a few that you can solve which need to be handled as soon as possible. Take these relevant problems and set priorities which are in your prospect's interest.

Studying a prospect's business needs is like any course of study. You must define the area to be explored; collect as much information as possible; analyze the data; make sense out of the analysis; and come to some conclusions. All of this work will save you from making incorrect assumptions, treating only the symptoms and recommending the wrong solutions.

There is no denying that studying can be a lot of work. It will be much easier if you keep these guidelines in mind:

1. Begin by creating the proper image.
2. Identify your prospect's personal style.

3. Establish trust.
4. Encourage your prospect to communicate by using open-ended questions.
5. Use developmental and clarifying questions.
6. Use verbal and nonverbal feedback for understanding and support.
7. Take notes and be organized.
8. Discuss each topic fully with your prospect.
9. Set priorities.
10. Agree on the courses of action to be taken.

The studying phase of a sales relationship establishes you as a consultant and an expert in your field. In order to be effective for your prospect, you need to conduct this work in a professional manner. A strong studying phase will prove invaluable when you move on to proposing solutions to your prospect's problems.

SUMMARY

The building of a sales relationship is much like a relationship that exists between a doctor and a patient. When a patient visits a doctor, he expects the doctor to ask questions before prescribing treatment. For the doctor to do otherwise would make the patient feel not only very uncomfortable but quite distrustful as well.

The sales relationship is much the same. The professional salesperson recognizes and respects the importance of the studying phase which significantly differentiates him from the traditional salesperson.

In order to effectively study a prospect's situation, it is necessary to build trust in the relationship. That is accomplished by lowering the tension that initially exists in a new sales relationship. If you are sincere and take a true interest in the prospect and his business, tension and defensiveness will be lowered considerably. Important factors in creating trust are: 1) the image you project; 2) your behavioral flexibility; and 3) your ability to actively listen.

In order to determine if your product or service will be of any value to your prospect, you must know his current situation, all of its attendant problems, and the goals and objectives that he has in mind. Determining which of these areas to explore first rests on the behavioral style of the prospect, for different behavioral styles prefer discussing different things and have different priorities.

After completely studying the prospect's situation, you will have a picture of the actual conditions versus the desired conditions. This will enable you to analyze all of the variables to see how they compare. You may find that the actual situation is fairly close to the desired goals and objectives, thus your product or service is not needed at this time. More than likely, you will find significant discrepancies between the two. It is then necessary for you to look for the deeper causes of the problems.

When doing pre-call planning, it is important to establish call objectives.

These can range from confirming a sale to simply introducing yourself and gathering some information. Whatever the objective, be organized and have a brief outline of the topics to be covered and questions to ask that will keep the conversation on target.

There are several topics that are important to study, in addition to others that you may add that are important to you. These topics include: 1) the psychology of the situation; 2) your prospect's feelings; 3) key decision-makers and the buying process; 4) time factors; 5) political considerations within the company; 6) relevant past experiences; 7) product specifications; and 8) budgetary constraints.

Studying a prospect's business needs is like any course of study. You must define the area to be explored, collect as much information as possible, analyze the data, make sense out of the analysis and come to some conclusions. All of this work will save you from making incorrect assumptions, treating only the symptoms and recommending the wrong solutions. The studying phase establishes you as a consultant and an expert in your field.

DISCUSSION
QUESTIONS

1. Why is it important to study a prospect's needs?
2. During the studying phase, what information are you looking for?
3. What are the three primary keys for developing a trusting relationship?
4. What should you do if a prospect does not want to answer questions about his business?
5. What information will help you determine if a need gap exists?
6. What are the eight areas that must be covered during the studying phase? What are two areas *you* would add to this list?
7. How will you know what kind of pace to use when asking questions? Similarly, how will you know how much socializing will be appropriate during the call?
8. What should you do if you run out of time before all your questions are answered?

CHAPTER ELEVEN

Proposing Solutions

CHAPTER OBJECTIVES	**1**	Introduce the process of proposing solutions to prospects.
	2	Present instruction on delivering effective presentations to prospects and customers.

The sales process, from prospecting to the confirmation, can be like a good movie. It slowly builds in suspense until the point of climax, after which the outcome is known. In sales, the long hours of preparation and studying lead up to the big moment—the presentation of your product or service. After having done all the studying and preparation in hope of a sale, you will undoubtedly place a great deal of importance on the presentation, and for good reason. The presentation is the time when you give the sale your best so that you can convince your prospect that your product or service will be a sound investment.

In the studying phase, you analyzed your prospect's problems and determined her goals and objectives. Now that she has acknowledged a need for improvements, the next step is to convince her that your product or service is the means to attain those changes. Unless your prospect sees your product or service as the answer, your efforts will have been less than profitable.

The presentation phase has two parts. You have to *remind* your prospect of his needs and then *prove* that your product or service is the one that will have the best results. Up to this point you devoted all of your efforts to uncovering the prospect's dissatisfactions. Now you have to show the path to satisfaction and convince him to take that direction with you.

TRUST, AGAIN

Trust and confidence are critical to the sales relationship and the presentation. Many sales are made solely on the basis of confidence. A prospect may take your word for something and buy blindly because she believes you are looking out for her best interests. Without trust, however, the best products or services in the world cannot be sold.

Credibility is the key to confidence and trust. You must carry yourself and speak in ways that are believable. It has been said that even one statement which the prospect finds unbelievable is like one drop of ink in a glass of water—it colors (darkens) the entire contents. By now you know that the only way to be professional is to be honest.

If, during your presentation, you sense that your prospect is losing confidence in you, perhaps you have said something that she did not believe. It is best to stop and clarify any misunderstanding or doubts that she may have. In this way you are checking and maintaining the trust bond that exists between the two of you. The level of trust may fluctuate, depending on the content of your presentation. Prospects are more suspicious about some things than others. It is important for you to pay attention to your prospect's body language and other cues. Before moving from one phase to another, make sure that you still have her with you. It is a waste of time and energy to establish trust and proceed through the sales process only to find out that you lost it somewhere back in an earlier stage. The trust bond, like a marriage, requires constant attention and work.

THE PROCESS OF PROPOSING SOLUTIONS

Confirm Decision-Making Criteria

Decision-making criteria serve to identify specific, measurable, attainable criteria which, when met, indicate that the problem is solved or the need satisfied. For example, the decision criteria may be, "I need to reduce scrap material waste by 10 percent, avoid a reduction in product quality, and increase production by 5 percent at a minimum." If a prospect were that specific, wouldn't he be easier to help? If the figures were dream figures or unreasonable for some other reason, your help with making them more realistic is needed as much as your help in meeting realizable goals.

A prospect's decision criteria will lead the way to concrete *solution objectives*. A solution objective is the measurable change that will be seen after the implementation of your product or service. Notice the characteristics of a good solution objective:

1. *It is specific.* "I want to increase productivity by 5 percent," not just "I want to increase productivity."
2. *It must be measurable.* To say that you want to increase employee morale is not as good a solution objective as saying that you want to increase employee morale and will recognize it by a reduction in the number of sick leave days taken of 4 percent over the next three months.
3. *It must be attainable.*

4. *The set of objectives must be complementary.* To achieve one objective, a person should not eliminate the achievement of any other. For example, if you wish to serve your customers better, you might achieve this by a monthly contact with every customer and a weekly or biweekly contact for those who need more. But this may prevent you from meeting another goal which requires a large time commitment. Each goal is attainable in itself, but taken together they are unlikely to be met. Strive for complementary goals which can all be met when considered together.

Part of your role as a consultant is to help your prospect define his solution objectives. This requires breaking down his problems and reasons for buying (if he buys) into solution objectives which meet all of the criteria mentioned above.

Solicit and Suggest Potential Solutions

Armed with solution objectives, you and the prospect are ready to explore potential solutions. These are direct responses to the solution objectives and grow out of the information discovered during the initial information-gathering phase.

Whether you or the prospect first suggests the solution, or whether you exchange ideas, look at the product or service with an eye toward the customer's needs and the criteria by which those needs will be met. This is done by matching the benefits of the product to the needs you've uncovered. *Notice that you match benefits, not just features, of your product or service.* The *features* are basically the various parts that make it up. They are (physical) characteristics that exist regardless of who buys it or even whether it is bought or not. They answer the question, "What is it?" On the other hand, a *benefit* is how an individual feature helps satisfy a specific need or problem of the prospect. The benefit is the most important part of your product or service. In reality, a prospect does not buy a product; he buys what it will do for him—the benefit. Products or services are means to goals, not ends in themselves. For example, the prospect does not view an advertisement as paper and ink alone. It is an investment for future gain or a means for self-esteem. Similarly, a movie theater is not just a building, projector, and screen. It is the means toward the benefits of relaxation, pleasure, and social interaction.

You raise the value of your product or service simply by allowing the prospect to discover the *benefits* received from owning it. Naturally, this means that you must be prospect/customer-oriented, sensitive to your prospect's needs. You should ask yourself, "Why would I purchase my product or service?" "How would it satisfy my needs?" "How would my product benefit me more than my competitors' products?" By having good, solid answers to these questions, and the honest belief that you and your product or service can truly benefit your prospect, you will be well on your way toward consummating more and more sales.

Your prospect's contribution to the suggestion process is twofold. First, as you suggest solutions, the prospect needs to respond and assist. Second, the prospect should suggest solutions. Many times, it is good to have the prospect do this *before* you make suggestions. In this way, more of the solutions that eventually work may be the prospect's, not yours. Moreover, the prospect may come up with a fresh solution otherwise lost as you direct the effort down a different path.

You, as the salesperson, have the job of presenting the features and benefits of the product or service which directly meet the needs identified and satisfy the solution objectives. Ideas that are short and set apart are easiest for your prospect to remember and provide the time to think about each one. Therefore, present your features and benefits one at a time and in order of their importance. The first feature/benefit should be the one that would have the most personal or professional meaning to the prospect. Before discussing the next most important feature/benefit, get feedback to make sure that the prospect understands how it can help. This is actually the process of *testing product acceptance.* Have these feature/benefit feedback statements take the form of open questions. For example, "How do you feel this will help you meet your objectives?" "What importance does this have to you (or your company)?" or "What benefits do you think you might derive from this?" The feedback gives you some excellent clues about the readiness of your prospect to make a commitment.

View the presentation as a discovery process and not as a time for you to do all of the talking. The whole idea of presenting features and benefits one at a time and getting feedback on each one before proceeding to the next fosters the two-way communication process. To ask your prospect how a specific feature can benefit him or her adds personal meaning to the presentation process and keeps your prospect involved in the buying process.

When you are satisfied that your prospect fully understands and accepts or rejects the importance of a given feature/benefit in solving a problem, you can then move on to the next feature/benefit, going through the same process. Present as many features and benefits as necessary to comfortably determine that your prospect is ready to make a commitment (to buy, not to buy, continue the search, etc.).

Do Remember the Preliminaries

Of course, before you get into a sales situation you must prepare for it. As preparation, compare your product or service to your direct and indirect competition. What unique, positive features does your product have that competitive products do not have? What features does your product have that are of higher quality than those same features in your competitors' products? After compiling this strategic product (service)/feature list, determine all of the benefits that each of these features provides for your prospects. In completing this exercise, remember that often one feature can satisfy more than one prospect need. In other words, any one feature can have many associated benefits. In addition, any one prospect need can be satisfied with more than one feature.

Keep in mind the critical importance of benefits. They build value into your product or service in the mind of the prospect.

Maintain the attitude that the solutions to be suggested are indeed potential and not final. This avoids pressure on the prospect and the problems associated with picking THE solution prematurely, only to discover later that it does not fit.

This phase, like all others in professional, non-manipulative selling, is uniquely tailored to the specific needs of the prospect. It has to be, for the benefits that you present and the order in which you present them are dependent on the information that you received earlier from your prospect. Each problem, each need, each prospect, the influence of time, and each set of priorities is different; therefore each presentation must be different.

Agree on the Best Solutions

When the solutions are analyzed and any solution is mutually acceptable to you and your prospect, it becomes, in effect, a psychological commitment on the part of the prospect. However, this commitment by the prospect is only one step toward the consummation of the sale. The implementation of the solution is the other crucial part; it is the physical part of the commitment. Until the prospect puts the new plan into action, do not count on your commission.

When all solutions are acceptable to both you and your prospect, and when all solution objectives look like they have been matched with a solution—or reanalyzed and eliminated—you are ready to implement the solutions, the commitment. But before moving on to the commitment phase, let's look more closely at the presentation itself: the types of presentations and the methods and tools of demonstration.

THE PRESENTATION

Pre-Call Planning

The vast majority of salespeople agree that the planning and preparation of the sales presentation are indispensable to successful selling. This pre-call work has many advantages: 1) it saves the buyer and the seller time; 2) it aids the neophyte salesperson; 3) it assures an effective, cohesive presentation; and 4) it increases sales volume.

1. It Saves Time   We have already discussed the fact that most of your time will not be spent facing the prospect in a sales call. It is ironic that one of the most important parts of selling is allocated only a small percentage of your time. This is unavoidable due to the logistics of making calls. With this as a given, you can see that it is paramount for you to make the most of every minute of the sales call.

Buyers appreciate a salesperson who enthusiastically delivers a well-thought-out, researched presentation. Prospects are often inundated with salespeople trying to sell them things. They not only respect a salesperson who takes the time to study their business, but who also proposes a product or service in a quick, concise, and professional way. You should respect your prospect's time as much as you do your own; it is a scarce commodity for both of you.

2. It Helps Organize the Neophyte Salesperson Most salespeople, especially beginners, are under varying amounts of nervous tension. This tension would be even greater if the salesperson did not know what to say or how to say it. A well-planned presentation will go a long way in relieving much of this tension. It will also help the beginner establish credibility and confidence in himself.

Planning the sales presentation takes the trial and error out of the delivery. You can practice and smooth out the presentation so that it flows from one sales point to another; weak points can be discovered and fixed; and you can anticipate a prospect's objections and be prepared to answer them with valid, informative statements.

3. It Assures an Effective, Cohesive Presentation The more effective the presentation, the fewer lost calls there will be. An amateurish, unconvincing presentation can only result in a waste of selling time and a decrease in professional image.

This is not to say that all presentations have to be "canned." On the contrary, the more natural your presentation appears, the more credible it will be. Because your knowledge will be put to the test during a presentation, you must be able to digress and improvise. Flexibility is the key here. You must be flexible enough to meet the demands of your prospect and his individual needs.

4. It Increases Sales Volume The better your presentation is, the more sales you will confirm. For all of the reasons we have cited above, you will have a distinct advantage if your proposal is well-planned. The alternative is almost frightening if you think about it. Can you imagine demonstrating a product to a prospect and not knowing where to start it or how to work it? If you were lucky, you would be booted out of the store. If you weren't lucky, you would have to stay and fumble your way through the presentation.

Four Characteristics of an Effective Presentation

An effective presentation should encompass the following four characteristics:

1. *It should be comprehensive.* This means you should cover all of the problems that your prospect is having and demonstrate how your product or service will solve them. You should also go beyond this to features and benefits which have not

been discussed but are also relevant. However, you do *not* have to talk about *all* of your features and benefits—only those relevant to each specific prospect.

2. *It should eliminate the competition.* Point out how your product is the best solution for the problem. This can be done by highlighting your *unique* features versus the competitions'. *Never* knock the competition, however; only focus on your competitive strengths.

3. *It should be clear.* Leave no doubt in the prospect's mind and never use technical jargon which can cause confusion. Be open to questions, even if this means being interrupted by your prospect during your presentation.

4. *It should win the confidence of your prospect.* Impress upon her that what you are saying is the truth. Substantiate your statements with data, charts, visual aids, and so on, when appropriate.

Types of Presentations

The type of presentation that you use will be determined by your level of experience and by the type of selling in which you are engaged. As your experience increases, you may change styles or use more than one approach. It is helpful for you to know the types of presentations and their appropriate uses so that you can customize your presentation for maximum effectiveness.

1.   The Memorized Presentation   The memorized, or "canned," presentation is a carefully written paragraph or two, containing all of the effective ingredients needed to captivate the interest of the prospect. It spells out exactly what the salesperson will say and gives standard answers to objections and questions. If the salesperson is working in phone sales, the presentation is written on a card from which it is read. In a door-to-door situation, the salesperson would memorize the presentation word-for-word.

In general, the memorized presentation will be written by the company for which you work. The company may have had it prepared by experts who have studied the psychology of sales, know the product, and have a creative way with words. It is their expertise which makes the memorized presentation so effective in the right context.

The memorized presentation is a general rather than a specific one. It does not address the individual needs of a specific prospect. Instead, it tries to appeal to a broad spectrum of people. For this reason, it is used for selling to large groups. For individual prospects, the canned presentation can be used as an introduction to the product or service, but should be disbanded or made more flexible once the ball is rolling.

There are many arguments for and against canned presentations. As with any controversial issue, these advantages and disadvantages are worth considering.

ADVANTAGES OF MEMORIZED PRESENTATIONS

1. They guarantee that the salesperson will tell a complete and accurate story about the product, service, or company.

2. They employ the best techniques and time-honored methods.

3. They aid the new, inexperienced salesperson.

4. They eliminate repetition and save time for everyone.

5. They assure effectiveness by arranging the sales points in the most logical sequence.

6. They give the salesperson confidence by providing answers to possible objections.

DISADVANTAGES OF MEMORIZED PRESENTATIONS

1. They are too inflexible and artificial and therefore cause the salesperson to lose enthusiasm and originality.

2. They cannot be used in the types of selling where repeat calls are made on a customer.

3. They limit or discourage the prospect from entering into the sales conversation. This creates a sales monologue wherein the prospect cannot disclose his needs and objectives.

4. They create a rigidity that becomes awkward if the salesperson is interrupted.

5. They do not lend themselves to the sale of many products.

It should be obvious that the memorized approach, in and of itself, is not suitable for the salesperson who is acting as a consultant to his prospect.

2. *The Outlined Presentation* The outlined presentation differs from the memorized presentation in that it is more flexible and not memorized. It consists of an outline of all the important topics to be covered. The salesperson rehearses the presentation by becoming thoroughly familiar with the selling points. The order of the outline can be rearranged to suit the needs of the prospect without confusing the salesperson.

The outlined presentation is often the responsibility of the salesperson. It allows her to say things in her own words rather than follow someone else's script, thus enhancing her image of being knowledgeable, credible, and honest. The outlined presentation is also more conducive to relaxing with a prospect and having him relax in return.

This type of presentation is used extensively in cases where the product is complex or fulfills many different needs. It is used by salespeople who sell to many different types of market segments, all requiring different handling. Lastly, it is used by salespeople who sell many products or services.

The professional approach which we advocate is basically the outlined presentation. As opposed to the memorized presentation, this technique allows you to uncover the needs of your prospect before proposing a solution. It necessitates the gathering of pertinent information and the development of a logical solution. Like the memorized presentation, there are some advantages and disadvantages.

ADVANTAGES OF OUTLINED PRESENTATIONS

1. They are more natural and informal.
2. There is more of a dialogue; therefore, the prospect's needs will be considered.
3. They are more flexible.
4. Interruptions do not upset the salesperson.

DISADVANTAGES OF OUTLINED PRESENTATIONS

1. Speaking in your own words may not be as effective as having a proven, prepared speech.
2. There is a greater chance that the salesperson will digress and not return to the outline.
3. The preparation may not be as complete because it wasn't committed to memory.

Most experienced salespeople are able to overcome the disadvantages of the outlined presentation. As experience and confidence are gained, outlined presentations become more preferred than those that are memorized.

3. The Program Presentation   The program presentation is a more detailed type of individual selling. It is developed from an in-depth and comprehensive analysis of the prospect's business needs. A program presentation is comprised of four steps: 1) obtaining permission for a survey; 2) conducting the survey; 3) preparing the proposal; and 4) presenting it to the prospect.

1. *Obtaining Permission to Take a Survey.* In order to develop a program presentation, you must first convince your prospect that it is a desirable thing to do. The use of testimonials is helpful to point out the satisfaction that others have derived from surveys and subsequent sales. The use of examples, statistics, and other sales aids increase your credibility and the chances that your idea will be approved.
2. *Conducting a Survey.* Surveys vary from single interviews to complex analyses in which specialists or technicians are brought in. The nature of the prospect's business will determine the type of survey used. An insurance salesperson only needs to interview a prospective buyer in order to collect data. An industrial machinery salesperson, on the other hand, may call in psychologists, statisticians, engineers, and whoever else is necessary to help him do the job. After the research has been done, the salesperson or his assistants analyze the data and diagnose the problem(s). This analysis answers the question, "Can our product/service solve the prospect's problem?"
3. *Preparing the Proposal.* After the data has been analyzed, a written and/or illustrated proposal is prepared. This proposal contains a statement of the prospect's problem, a proposed solution, and a breakdown of what the solution will cost. Ideally, the program presentation will also include a section on cost effectiveness. The use of graphs, charts, tables, and illustrations is highly recommended for the written proposal.
4. *Presenting the Proposal.* The last step is the selling of the proposal to the client. All of the work that has come before will be a waste if it is not convincing to the

prospect. It is essential, therefore, that the salesperson who presents it to the prospect does a first class job. It is not unusual in some industries for proposals to cost thousands of dollars to prepare.

ADVANTAGES OF THE PROGRAM PRESENTATION

1. It gives the salesperson the opportunity to determine the needs of the prospect.
2. It provides sufficient time to gather and analyze the facts and to prepare an effective solution to those problems.
3. It gives the salesperson the time to develop a polished, personalized presentation.
4. It enhances the image of the salesperson and her company. The prospect comes to think of her as a consultant who wants to help.
5. It saves time by eliminating sales calls. Normally, permission is obtained during the first meeting and the presentation is given during the second.

DISADVANTAGES OF THE PROGRAM PRESENTATION

1. It is time-consuming and relatively expensive. There is no guarantee of making the sale, despite the investment.
2. Salespeople are not always qualified to conduct surveys.
3. The prospect may object to the salesperson conducting the survey because he feels that the salesperson cannot be objective.
4. In the past, many salespeople have been granted interviews under the false pretense of conducting a survey. As a result, many prospects are suspicious of people requesting permission to conduct surveys.

The three types of presentations discussed are the basic tools of the presentation phase. Which type you choose to employ will change from situation to situation and from job to job. It is important to know the impact of each as well as how it will affect the profitability of a call. The more time invested on a prospect the greater your ROTI (return on time invested) should be.

One demand that all presentations have in common is that they must be effective. Effectiveness requires attention to many details within the presentation. If you hope to see your prospect using your product or service, you need to be unlike all of the others who make demands on his time. Your presentation must be a gem which you polish constantly in order to impress your prospect with your professionalism. To do so, you should take advantage of all of the techniques at your disposal.

Getting Attention and Holding It

Whether you are meeting a prospect for the first time or seeing an established customer with whom you are familiar, you should avoid boring him. You can never tell what your customer's mood or energy level will be on any given day. You must, therefore, be entertaining and informative and deliver your presentation in a way which will captivate his interest and hold it. Some of the ways that you may want to use are:

1. *Refer to specific problems when you open the call.* This is a strong way to begin, because you will have your prospect's attention. Things which hit home rarely bore us. Of course, this will require some studying on your part so that you can uncover your prospect's problems.

2. *Offer compelling data which is both convincing and attractive.* Statistics, comparisons to competitors, and facts about the industry will interest a prospect more than allusions to unfamiliar companies or obscure industries.

3. *Use interesting exhibits as a part of your opening.* Models are excellent attention-getters because they are so much like toys. This is especially true if the model is one with which the prospect can experiment, a method frequently used at conventions. Combining visual and oral presentations reinforces what is being said and helps to hold the prospect's attention.

4. *Use showmanship if it will not look foolish.* If a picture is worth a thousand words, then a memorable demonstration is worth *ten* thousand words! On the other hand, a demonstration which is all showmanship and no substance will only make you and your product look foolish. As much as you want to impress your prospect with your sales ability, you should not resort to juggling your products.

5. *Use third party opinion questions.* You will be surprised at how quickly your prospect will perk up if you say something like, "I just spoke to Jerome Stevens over at XYZ Company and he said that our new product has increased productivity 15 percent in only a month!" Third party opinion questions and testimonials lend credibility to your product.

Although there are some ways that you can get attention in the beginning of your presentations, what do you do if you lose it? After all, the setting is rarely ideal for giving your presentation. You may have to compete with ringing phones and other distractions. When these arise, simply stop and give your prospect time to attend to the other matters. When he returns, you can quickly review the last few points that you covered before continuing with new information. It is important not to show your annoyance or to say anything about the intrusion. If the interruptions become too distracting, you might suggest that the two of you take a coffee break or talk elsewhere. In getting away from the hectic environment, you both will be able to clear your minds and concentrate on the subject at hand. If need be, you can reschedule the presentation for a better time. Consider meeting with your prospect before or after business hours when all is quiet.

The Demonstration as a Powerful Tool

Why demonstrate something when you can describe its use verbally? One reason was mentioned above—a memorable demonstration is worth ten thousand words. But demonstrations are more than that. Demonstrations bring into play other human dynamics which make your presentation more effective. Those dynamics are auditory and visual learning, selectivity, learning principles, and forgetting.

Auditory and Visual Learning   In planning your presentation, you should think of ways to visually demonstrate all of the key points of your proposal. If you want to stress the ease of understanding the product, you can show a drawing or other diagram as proof. To hold interest you can use a miniature model of the product. There are many supplements to your oral presentation that will facilitate learning. The combination of visual and auditory input is far superior to oral-only presentations. A visual input is more readily accepted as proof.

Selectivity   When you engage the prospect's eyes and ears with a demonstration, you have a greater chance of getting your message firmly implanted in her mind. Without a demonstration, it is too easy for her to look around the room while listening to you; at the end of the presentation she may find that she heard less of what you said than she thought. By keeping her eyes glued to your demonstration, you are eliminating one very distracting variable—the environment.

Learning Principles   Visual and other stimuli add a realistic dimension and help facilitate learning. They do this through participation, association, transfer, and insight.

1. *Participation.* The more active our learning is, the more long-lasting it will be. Prospects who are actively engaged in the demonstration will retain more. This is why many presentations are designed to get the prospect involved. Listening is adequate, seeing is better, but hands-on experience is best.
2. *Association.* We learn best by associating new information with things that we already know. Past experiences and knowledge are convenient hooks on which to hang novel stimuli. It is therefore helpful if you know something of the prospect's background. You can then relate a point in your presentation to an experience that the prospect has had.
3. *Transfer.* To help a prospect imagine the use of a product in her business, it is a good practice to show her pictures of the product in use. A better way is to demonstrate the product under actual working conditions in the prospect's business. If this is not possible, devise an alternative such as a field trip to a facility where the product can be observed. This acts as a transfer of learning. What works in one situation will work in another. This is especially useful for technical and industrial products.
4. *Insight.* The demonstration serves another useful purpose that is apropos to learning principles: it provides insight. The verbal presentation alone may provide details and statistics, but the demonstration cements it all with impact by showing the total picture. The demonstration consolidates everything that is known into one sharply focused picture.

Make a Lasting Impression   There is a time lag between the presentation and the point where the prospect uses the information he hopefully learned. This requires the salesperson to devise ways of increasing the amount and length of time that ideas will be remembered. Many salespeople are given items to leave with the prospect so that their memories will be jogged whenever he sees them. Calendars, rulers, notepads, pens, and other promotional novelties serve as reminders to those who use them. The type of promotional gifts that you give will have to be appropriate for the prospects that you have. It certainly would not make sense to give a corporate executive a cheap pen with your company name on it.

Demonstration Tools

There are many materials and tools to be used during a demonstration. Your company may furnish you with some, but you should be aware of the possibilities that follow so that you can construct your own as well.

Pictures. Color pictures are better than black and white. The pictures should be realistic in scale and do the product justice. It is best to show a product in use rather than simply on display. For emphasis, enlargements of specific parts can be used to show details.

Mechanical or Schematic Drawings. For the technically minded prospect, these are very helpful in explaining the operation of an electronic or mechanical apparatus. The use of color in different parts of the drawing will separate the components or circuits from one another. These can be printed on transparent sheets and laid on top of each other in sequence. In this way, you can start with the basic chassis of the equipment and work your way up to the complex interconnections in steps.

Mock-ups. Mock-ups are three dimensional models of the product without the detail of an actual model. Their advantage is that they portray more than pictures and cost less than models. They are helpful to people who have difficulty imagining a three-dimensional object from a two dimensional picture.

Models. Models are exact replicas of the product scaled down for use in a demonstration. They provide greater realism but cost more to produce than mock-ups. There are some cases where models are indispensable, as in the sale of an airplane or boat design.

Samples. There is nothing like selling the real thing. If you are selling small consumer and industrial products, samples are easy to carry and give away. You should keep your freebees down to a limit, however, so that small users of your product will not accept them in lieu of a purchase. After all, why pay for what you can get for free!

Tests. As previously mentioned, tests, statistics, and other impressive findings serve to hold attention as well as convince. In many markets, test results are required before a product is even considered. This is true in the pharmaceuticals, military, industrial, and chemical fields, among others. Ideally, the prospect should use his own facilities as a testing ground; in this case, you should be present for the test to ensure that it is performed properly. You should also request that all of the key decision makers are on hand to observe. If the test goes well, you are in a strong position to ask for an order. If the test does not go well, you will at least know why and be able to prevent the same thing from happening in the future.

Full-Scale Demonstrations. Tests can also be considered full-scale demonstrations. The most immediate question is, "Where will the demonstration be held?" The least expensive way is to take your prospect to a current customer's place of business to see the product in use. This has the added advantage of letting the prospect hear the customer's testimony. Another possibility is to conduct the demonstration on the premises of the salesperson's firm. This will be less expensive than doing it at the prospect's business. In addition, by bringing the prospect to your company, you can treat him like a VIP and control the demonstration fully.

If the expense is reasonable, it is often most effective to demonstrate at the prospect's facilities. There are four important things to strive for in this situation:

1. Be certain that all the key decision makers are present.
2. Produce something of value for the account. For example, if you are selling a copying machine, do a specific job for them such as duplicating an office memorandum.
3. Give the prospect a chance at hands-on operation. This will help him learn better by engaging him through his eyes, ears, and hands.
4. Press for an order if everyone is impressed with the demonstration.

The Art of Demonstrating

The art of demonstrating is very much like the art of public speaking. Both require 1) a clear understanding of the audience; 2) a precise purpose; 3) a well-organized approach; and 4) effective delivery and proper length.

1. Understanding the Audience In order to tailor your presentation to fit a group, you must have an understanding of that group. This includes the group's personal styles, buying criteria, level in the company, decision-making capacity and technical knowledge. Obviously, a presentation to a group of engineers would be different from one to a group of executives or purchasing agents. Other important facts to know are how long the prospect has been doing business, who the competition is, how the prospect feels about your company versus the competition, and so on.

2. Precise Purpose The demonstration, like the overall presentation, needs to be focused in order to be interesting. It has to be more than, "Let me show you how this works." The demonstration should address the solution to the specific need that you are trying to fulfill.

3. An Organized Approach The demonstration is only part of the show. As a single act, however, it must be as tight as the entire presentation. The organization of your speech will be related to your use of visual aids. Both visual and oral facets of your demonstrations must be designed to move the audience forward toward a climax. One point should build on another and each should be an integral part of the whole. It may be helpful to think of your demonstration and presentation as having a beginning, middle, and end. Like any good story, at the end, your audience should be glad that they sat through it.

*4. **Effective Delivery and Proper Length*** The way that you speak and look affects your presentation significantly. This, again, points out the importance of everything that we cover in the communication chapters. A salesperson who speaks in a monotone will not win the endorsement of his audience or get the sale.

The length of your demonstration is also critical. You have to consider people's attention spans and the value of their time. A demonstration which is too long will be an imposition and annoy them. One that is too short will seem half-hearted. In practicing, you should get your demonstration down to a time that will make it short yet significant. Try to make it direct, enthusiastic, and unique.

As part of your delivery, you should keep in mind that certain words have emotional blindspots for buyers. To avoid them, you should substitute other words for sensitive ones. Some of the words are:

SENSITIVE WORD	SUBSTITUTE
Deal	Opportunity
Sell, Sold	Involve
Buy	Own
Pitch	Presentation
Cost, Price	Total Investment
Down Payment	Initial Installment
Monthly Payment	Monthly Investment
Contract	Agreement, Forms, Paperwork
Sign	Authorize, OK, Endorse, Approve

Your avoidance of these sensitive words will take the shock out of buying. Remember, too, that prospects buy less when money is tight. They can be even more defensive toward salespeople during tight times and may require more finesse to sell.

Remember that there is another way to make the buying decisions easier. As we discussed earlier in this chapter, it is helpful to get the prospect involved in making little decisions throughout the presentation. Most people have the tendency to postpone making decisions, especially about money, so including them in the discussion is particularly important. This avoids the discomfort of the big question at the end. Each successive agreement builds up momentum for the commitment, the next phase of the selling process.

Proposing solutions to problems and needs of prospects and customers (the presentation phase of the selling process) is one of the most important parts of the selling process, yet it is allocated only a small percentage of your time. It is built on thorough planning and preparation and, when conducted properly, results in a business relationship founded on trust and confidence.

SUMMARY

The focus of this chapter was on the presentation phase of the selling process, the proposing of solutions to prospects' and customers' problems and dissatisfactions.

The presentation phase has two parts: 1) you must remind the prospect of his needs, and then 2) prove that your product or service is the one that will have the best results.

It should be remembered that trust and confidence are critical to the sales relationship and the presentation. Credibility is the key to confidence and trust. You must carry yourself and speak in ways that are believable. If during your presentation you sense that your prospect is losing confidence in you, it is important to discover immediately the reasons for the loss of confidence through feedback. Otherwise, you may end your presentation only to discover that you lost the prospect long before.

When developing a presentation, it is best to confirm the decision-making criteria. These are specific, measurable, attainable criteria which, when met, indicate that the problem to be handled is solved or the need addressed and met.

The prospect's decision criteria will lead the way to concrete solution objectives, which are the measurable changes that will be seen after the implementation of the product or service. There are several characteristics of good solution objectives: 1) they are specific; 2) they are measurable; 3) they are attainable; and 4) they are complementary. Part of your role as a consultant is to help your prospect define his solution objectives. This requires breaking down his problems and reasons for buying (if he buys) into solution objectives which meet all of the criteria mentioned above.

Once you have defined the solution objectives, you and the prospect are ready to explore potential solutions. These are direct responses to the solution objectives and grow out of the information discovered during the initial information-gathering phase.

Whether you or your prospect first suggests the solution, or whether you exchange ideas, you take a look at the product or service in light of both the needs and the criteria by which the needs will be recognized as met. The solution is the matching of the benefits of your product or service to the needs. Notice that you match *benefits*, not just features of your product or service. Remember that features are basically the various parts that make up the product or service. They are the (physical) characteristics that exist regardless of who buys it or even whether it is bought or not. They answer the question, "What is it?" Benefits, on the other hand, are how individual features help satisfy a specific need or problem on the part of the prospect and are the most important part of your product or service. By allowing your prospect to discover the benefits of owning your product or using your service, you raise the value of your product or service in his mind.

The presentation should be viewed as a discovery process and not as a time for you to do all of the talking. The whole idea of presenting features and benefits one at a time and getting feedback on each one before proceeding to the next fosters the two-way communication process. To ask your prospect how a specific feature can benefit him or her adds personal meaning to the presentation process and keeps your prospect involved in the buying process.

The presentation phase, like all the others in professional, non-manipulative selling, is uniquely tailored to the specific needs of the prospect. It must be, for the benefits that you present and the order in which you present them are dependent on the information that you received earlier from your prospect. Each problem, each need, each prospect, and each set of priorities is different; therefore, each presentation must be different.

Planning and preparation are essential steps prior to giving your presentation. Such pre-call work has many advantages: 1) it saves the buyer and the seller time; 2) it helps organize the neophyte salesperson; 3) it assures an effective, cohesive presentation; and 4) it increases sales volume.

An effective presentation has four characteristics: 1) it should be comprehensive; 2) it should eliminate the competition; 3) it should be clear; and 4) it should win the confidence of your prospect.

There are three types of presentations: 1) the memorized ("canned") presentation; 2) the outlined presentation; and 3) the program presentation. These three types of presentations are the basic tools of the presentation phase. Which type is used will change from situation to situation and from job to job. It is important to know the impact of each as well as how it will affect the profitability of a call. The more time invested on a prospect, the greater your ROTI should be.

One demand that all presentations have in common is that they must be effective. Effectiveness requires attention to many details within the presentation. If you hope to see your prospect using your product or service, you need to be different from all the others who make demands on his time. You must impress your prospect with your professionalism. To do so, you should take advantage of all of the techniques at your disposal.

Your presentation should be entertaining and informative and should hold your prospect's interest. Some of the ways to do so are: 1) refer to specific problems when you open the call; 2) offer compelling data which is both convincing and attractive; 3) use interesting exhibits as a part of your opening; 4) use showmanship if appropriate; and 5) use third party opinion questions.

Demonstrations are a powerful tool in presentations. They bring into play other human dynamics which make your presentation effective. Those dynamics are visual and auditory learning, selectivity, learning principles, and making a lasting impression.

Giving a demonstration is very much like giving a speech. Both require a clear understanding of the audience, a precise purpose, a well-organized approach, and effective delivery and proper length.

Proposing solutions to problems and needs of prospects and customers (the presentation phase of the selling process) is one of the most important parts of the selling process, yet it is allocated only a small percentage of your time. It is built on thorough planning and preparation and, when conducted properly, results in a business relationship founded on trust and confidence.

DISCUSSION
QUESTIONS

1. What are decision-making criteria? Who decides what they will be?
2. What are solution objectives?
3. Why should decision-making criteria and solution objectives be established for each customer?
4. What is the difference between a product's features and its benefits?
5. How are features and benefits discussed during a presentation?
6. Should a salesperson explain all of a product's features in a presentation? Why or why not?
7. In Non-Manipulative Selling, the presentation is referred to as a "discovery process." Explain why.
8. What research should be conducted as a preliminary step before giving your presentation?
9. What are some of the methods used to hold a prospect's attention and ensure he will remember what is said?
10. Pretend you are going to give a presentation to sell advertising space in your school newspaper. Outline the steps you would take, the features and benefits you would present, and the visual aids you would use.

CHAPTER TWELVE

Confirming the Purchase

CHAPTER OBJECTIVES

1 Discuss the difference between closing and confirming.
2 Discuss the confirmation phase of the selling process in detail.
3 Present a method of self-evaluation in order to improve performance with each successive sales call.

The confirming phase represents a significant milestone in the sales process, for you have completed a tremendous amount of groundwork up to this point. You are now finally at the stage where you hope to get a commitment from the prospect.

At this stage, most traditional salespeople would probably take a Valium and pray for success. On the other hand, professional salespeople who follow our game plan can be much more relaxed. If you have been conscientious along the way in working with your prospect, the two of you will progress naturally into the commitment phase. Because it is a more personal form of selling, professional selling takes the awkwardness out of confirming the sale. Unlike a traditional salesperson, the professional does not find it necessary to maneuver his prospect like a cowboy lassoing a steer.

CONFIRMING VS. CLOSING

Closing implies that your hard work is over and that you are now free to reap the rewards. This is only half true. You *will* reap the rewards, but your work has only begun! To maintain a profitable relationship with your customer, you will have to follow up, service, promote, satisfy, and continually communicate with him. You first focused on winning the sale; now you must avoid losing the account. Being a professional salesperson and everything that it entails takes much of the worry out of sales.

Another distasteful aspect of traditional sales is the overemphasis placed on the "close." It is ascribed so much importance that it reeks of manipulation, trickery, and a disregard for the prospect's needs. The end does not justify the means in professional selling.

For the professional salesperson, the emphasis is not on the confirmation of the sale but on the entire sales process. The confirmation is just the beginning of a mutual commitment to have an ongoing business relationship. The professional salesperson sees the customer as more than a source of orders and commissions. She sees the customer as an important building block in the foundation of her sales career. The confirmation therefore is not a time to sigh in relief; it is a time to feel happy about having developed another (hopefully long-term) account.

You may have already noticed that the separation between selling and closing is barely perceptible in professional non-manipulative selling. If the studying process and the proposing process have been done well, the customer has clearly specified his needs and problems and knows how your product or service will specifically meet or solve them. You have had adequate chance to use verbal and nonverbal feedback to see how the customer perceives your product or service as the means to his end results. In fact, before you enter the commitment phase of the sales process, you and your customer should have mutually agreed on acceptable solutions to his problems. Therefore, the commitment is not an "if" but a "when." Closing techniques are unnecessary, in the sense of radical, complicated, or manipulative techniques used to turn a sales situation around.

Therein lie the differences between confirming and closing. It is primarily a qualitative distinction that embodies both attitude and behavior. Despite their differences, the two schools of thought have many things in common. In the confirming phase, regardless of your philosophy, you must be tuned into your prospect and her reactions. She will determine what you do and when by her level of receptivity. If she is ready to commit herself in the presentation, then you need not finish your presentation. If you do, you run the risk of overselling and boring her. On the other hand, a prospect may want all of the information that you have before agreeing to anything. You then must elaborate on your presentation. Any attempt to gain a confirmation too soon would be pressuring her. All of this emphasizes the importance of being cognizant of verbal and nonverbal buying signals that your prospect is projecting.

Recognizing Confirming Opportunities

By the time that you reach the proposing stage you will know your prospect's personal style, typical body language, and ways of accepting and rejecting things that you say. During the presentation, this knowledge will aid you in determining what your prospect is thinking or feeling. There will be times, however, when you do not know the prospect all that well. For example, your prospect may ask you to give a final presentation to someone else whom you do not know. In this case, you will have to infer these buying signals from the more obvious signals being given by that person. Therefore, it is valuable to know the general indicators of buying decisions. These will take both verbal and nonverbal forms and can be positive and negative in nature. These buying signals can take the form of red (negative), yellow (neutral), or green (positive) signals. At the end of the presentation, dominant color signals projected by the prospect generally dictate the type of commitment question that you would choose. We will discuss this further later on. For now, let's look at the various verbal and nonverbal buying signals.

Prospect's Questions The questions that are asked will tell you a great deal about a prospect's thoughts. Some questions are more neutral than others and have to be evaluated in the context of the prospect's other signals. Some typical questions are:

1. "Could I try this out one more time?"
2. "This machine is supposed to be more reliable than mine?"
3. "What sort of credit terms do you offer?"
4. "How soon can you deliver?"
5. "How can I even think of buying with interest rates so high?"

Questions which are concerned with terms, delivery, quantity, benefits, and service usually indicate a positive buying attitude. Questions that ask about product features, ease of use, and maintenance are more neutral. Questions which are negative are usually pretty obvious.

Prospect's Statements A prospect may comment about a product or service and in this way indicate a buying tendency. You may hear statements like:

1. "That's very interesting."
2. "We could probably afford that."
3. "Hmm, I just don't know about this."
4. "Yes, I've seen these before."
5. "Things are tough these days."

Body Language We give away a lot of information through our posture, facial expressions, and hand and arm movements, which we will discuss in more detail in the sections on verbal and nonverbal communication. If you watch your prospect carefully you will see many correlations between their body language and their intentions. Keep these clues in mind:

1. If the prospect is sitting, open arms indicate receptiveness; tightly crossed arms show defensiveness.
2. Leaning forward and listening carefully shows that she is interested.
3. Supporting her head with one hand and gazing off into space means that you have lost her attention.

4. Increased tense postures are not a positive indicator. People tend to relax when they have made a decision to buy.

5. Happy, animated facial expressions show you that the prospect is relating well to you and to your product/service.

Because you are developing a working relationship, you will want to do more than simply monitor your prospect's buying signals; you will want to know the whys behind them. This is especially true if the indicators are negative. With a trust bond established, you can feel comfortable in asking your prospect why she feels the way she does at this time. Each successive stage of the sales process is based on a mutual agreement to continue towards solving her problems. If you see that her questions or body language indicate disinterest, you should say something like, "I get the impression that I have lost you. Is there something I can do to get back on track?" You can think of your relationship as a walk through the woods. Both of you are walking side by side down the same path. If your prospect starts to lag behind, you turn to find out why. If she speeds up, you do the same.

When to Seek Confirmation

The walk in the woods analogy takes us to the next question. When should you try to confirm the sale? Unfortunately, there are no definite answers. The best approach is to watch your prospect's interest level and buying signals. Is she side by side with you, slowing down, or speeding up? If, during your presentation, your prospect is acting and speaking in ways that indicate that she is ready to place an order, you should stop the presentation and do just that—confirm the sale. You would tie up everything that had been said with a benefit summary and then take the order.

When the buying signals are appropriate or you are at the end of the presentation process, you and your prospect are ready to proceed to the key stage of the confirmation phase—the commitment question. To do this, ask the prospect an open question that requests direction, such as, "Where do we go from here?" "When do we proceed?" "How would you like to proceed?" "What's our next step?" Because of all of the previous preparation, this question is an open, straightforward request, lacking the pushy, tricky, and manipulative characteristics of other closing or assumptive questions under other situations. Since your prospect has participated fully in the entire sales transaction and has had a major hand in arriving at the solution, you will generally be answered with a time, date, or other relevant reference. If there is something for concern, your prospect will generally by this time feel comfortable and trusting enough to speak out. You are, after all, problem solvers working together. There is no "Objection Game" when the mutual trust level is high.

So far, this is all very simple. You ask an open question or an assumptive question and the prospect positively commits. What happens, however, if the prospect does not commit at this point? In the past, salespeople have typically reacted in an aggressive manner. Get the objection, overcome the objection, ask for the order—and on and on and on. This does not seem right. Such a method raises defenses, increases tension, and reduces trust. Instead, manage the problem.

MANAGING OBJECTIONS

An objection is anything that creates an obstacle that blocks the smooth flow toward the completion of a sale. Objections often surface when you least expect them and come in many shapes and sizes.

Typically, the traditional salesperson reacts to objections by becoming tense and feeling threatened. He interprets objections as being barriers to the close of the sale. Thus, he overreacts and defends his product and his presentation relentlessly. He is more concerned with his need to make the sale than the prospect's need for self-expression or clarification.

A professional salesperson learns to view objections in a different light. He sees them as valuable signals that warn him that he and his prospect are no longer on the same wavelength. The prospect is not putting an end to the sales relationship; he is just expressing his desires. If we use the analogy of the walk in the forest again, an objection can be thought of as a point where many paths cross. The two of you stop at the intersection and decide which way to go. If the prospect wants to go right, you go right. It would make no sense to proceed straight ahead if the prospect wants to go elsewhere. The prospect's objection, then, is saying, "Don't go *that* way; let's go *this* way."

Objections can also be seen as positive opportunities. The prospect is letting you get to know him better and helping you uncover his needs even more. A customer who objects to something is participating in the relationship instead of remaining aloof. This is what a professional wants—a mutual exchange! Only through this exchange can you mold your efforts to solve your prospect's problems.

Types of Objections

Objections can take many forms (questions, statements, and body language) and mean different things. Often it is difficult to ascertain the exact reason for an objection because people sometimes use excuses to cover up their true feelings. You are actually lucky when someone is straightforward and tells you where you or your product has failed. This is one type of feedback from which you learn and improve yourself.

Occasionally a prospect's attitude will change between the last sales call and the present call; sometimes it may be difficult to find out why. People do odd things sometimes and being inconsistent is one of them. In such a case, you might gently question your prospect, keeping in mind that her objections may be caused by one or more of the following reasons:

1. She no longer has a need for your product or service due to changes of which you have not been informed.
2. She lacks the ability to buy. This could be due to lack of authority, high interest rates, or financial problems which are beyond your control.
3. Her trust in you has diminished. Perhaps you have misjudged her personal style and have been treating her incorrectly.
4. There is no urgency to buy. Time pressures usually motivate; a lack of pressure or the perception of no need can cause complacency.
5. She has a lack of interest in your presentation. You have somehow failed to uncover needs or tailor solutions. You might have been working with incomplete data or wrong information.
6. There are technical problems over which you have no control.

A review in greater detail of some of the above reasons may be helpful. If the reason for an objection is incorrect or insufficient information, you need to determine where and why you went wrong. Did you gather the wrong information, give erroneous or incomplete information, or was there simply a breakdown in the feedback process? In any of these cases, you have to go back to the point of communication breakdown, start all over, and use this new information to design a new plan that may better suit the needs of your prospect.

Objections stemming from wrong or insufficient information can usually be corrected simply by providing new information. The four-step process to use in dealing with easy objections is:

1. *Listen* and intently observe both the verbal and the nonverbal message of the prospect. (What is really being said?)
2. *Clarify* the objection so that there is no misunderstanding about what issue (concern) you are addressing.
3. *Respond* to the objection using one of the objection answering techniques that seems to be most appropriate. (Be tactful and honest.)
4. *Confirm* the prospect's acceptance of your answer to assure that your response was on target before you proceed further into the sales process.

For instance, a prospect may say that your service is desired only if you can implement it immediately. You may want to clarify what "immediately" is before you go any further. Depending on this clarification, you may be able to meet the immediate requirements. In that case, you directly answer the concern. Finally, you confirm your response to make sure that it fully and satisfactorily answered the concern.

Other objections which lead to an unsold prospect are more difficult to handle. Some of them occur when the trust bond is broken or if you mistakenly identify the prospect's behavioral style. If trust is lacking, try to use your communication and trust-building skills to reestablish that bond (if it is not already too late). If you misjudged your prospect's style, you probably have been interacting inappropriately. Start treating the prospect according to the prospect's style needs. It may reestablish your rapport and salvage the sale.

Even with high trust sales situations, technical problems may be beyond your control and result in a lost sale. For instance, you may be expected to provide a color or style of an item that is no longer available. Unless the color or style can be changed, the sale cannot be consummated; it is beyond your control. These problems are the *difficult* ones. When appropriate, use the following four-step process in dealing with difficult objections:

1. Listen and observe.
2. Clarify the objection.
3. Answer via the *compensation* method.
4. Confirm your answer.

In this approach, Steps 1, 2, and 4 are similar to Steps 1, 2, and 4 for easy objections. The difference between the two approaches lies in Step 3. The compensation method acknowledges deficiency in a particular area, but tries to compensate for it by using other features that are unique or of equal quality to outweigh the shortcomings. If you cannot meet a delivery date, suggest other times and stress the other *advantages* of the sale. If you do not have a requested style or color, present options that you do have and identify the benefits of using the product that you sell. This method is especially effective when the shortcoming of the service or product is not an item that is high on the prospect's priority list. Suggested alternatives will often appear attractive.

Sometimes you can use the classic "Ben Franklin Balance Sheet." This is a sheet of paper divided into two columns with "Reasons For" at the top of the left column and "Reasons Against" at the top of the right column. Using this balance sheet, you list the reasons for going ahead with the purchase in the left column and the reasons against going ahead with the purchase in the right column. You add as many reasons as you can to those for going ahead with the purchase and you acknowledge the negative reasons against the purchase. It quickly becomes obvious to people using this method whether or not they should take action. In many cases where they initially thought it was not a good idea to pursue the purchase of your product, this written balance sheet persuades them to go ahead.

It is not inconceivable that, during the development of your relationship with a prospect, she may have misunderstandings or concerns which were not vocalized. The relationship and sales process may have proceeded fine until suddenly she has an objection which comes as a complete surprise to you. Despite all of your communicating thus far, everything was not as positive as you had thought. How are you going to handle this objection?

Handling Objections

In sales, there are two ways to handle objections: the traditional way and the professional way. These methods are very similar to the modes of negotiating in which you see the other person as either an adversary or a colleague. How you perceive the other person will affect your attitude and the outcome of the dilemma. The two attitudes are incompatible. For instance:

ADVERSARY	*COLLEAGUE*
Goes for the "win"	Seeks solutions to problems
Competes	Cooperates
Withholds information	Discloses/shares information
Uses power	Uses openness and honesty

Professional salespeople relate to their prospects as colleagues. As a consultant, you can only be of service if you cooperate with people. Your prospects are on your side. When objections arise you should try to get the prospect to open up so that you can uncover and solve the problem. To do this, you can use some methods which have been adapted from counseling and listening techniques.

Methods   One of the most therapeutic processes is talking to someone. Often we can discover the answers to our problems simply by listening to ourselves speak. You should always be a listener and allow your prospect to express what is on her mind. The following methods will help you respond to her objections, perhaps bouncing them back from a different angle for reconsideration.

1. *Use "Feel-Felt-Found."* It is important to acknowledge how people feel and point out that the feeling is not unusual. A helpful thing to say is, "I understand how you *feel*." This conveys your empathy to the prospect. "Many people have *felt* that way," reassures her that she is not alone. You might then offer a solution to the problem by saying, "However, it has been *found* that. . . ." This will sound fine to Relaters and Socializers, but Directors and Thinkers are not impressed by the words "feel" and "felt." For those behavioral styles, you can say, "I understand your *thinking*. I *thought* the same thing at first. However, it has been *found*. . . ." Directors and Thinkers also prefer more concrete answers to their concerns.

2. *Convert to a Question.* When the customer makes a statement, many times it is difficult to answer the statement. However, you can convert the statement into a question that allows you to answer it more easily. Example: "I don't think I could use that product." Your response could be: "There is an important question I perceive in your statement and that is, 'How can you gain maximum use from a product like this?'" Then you proceed to answer *the question*, not rebut the statement.

3. *Echo and Listen.* It is helpful to *show* people what they feel because they sometimes do not know. This is where good communication skills come in. If you listen to your prospect's voice quality, observe her body language, and hear her words, *you will know how she feels*. You are then in a good position to reflect this back to her to encourage further discussion. This is especially helpful if a prospect's objection does not give you enough information. She might say, "The price is too high." Through your observations you might see the emotion behind the words and respond, "You feel frustrated about the price?" The prospect then might

say, "Sure, I feel frustrated; have you tried to get a loan lately? How can I do business when money is so tight!" Your response can then save the day: "That's not an insurmountable problem, for we have several credit plans from which you can choose." In the case of a vague statement with no emotion, you can act as an echo. Prospect: "The price is too high." You: "Too high?" This will encourage the prospect to explain herself.

4. *Break the Objection into Smaller, More Manageable Increments.* In this case, you take an objection which seems to have enormous proportions to your prospect, and reduce it to a smaller, more reasonable and less objectionable concept. Prospect: "Three hundred dollars is too much for that." Your response: "You might look at it a different way. Consider the fact that you will probably use it 3 thousand times a year. That reduces your cost to $.10 per use. Now where can you have it done for $.10 each? You should also consider the added convenience, time saved, and profitability of the product. If you look at it that way, is the price still unreasonable?"

5. *Use the Boomerang Method.* Think of what a boomerang does. It is thrown out, makes a wide arc, and returns to the person who threw it. You can do the same thing in response to an objection, *if appropriate.* Imagine a prospect saying, "We are too busy right now to put your product into service." The boomerang approach returns their objection to them in the form of an answer. Your response: "The fact that you are so busy makes time-saving all the more important to you. My product will save you 50 percent of the time it takes for you to do this, that, and the other. If you spend a little time now to install it, you will find yourself with more time at the end of the month than you ever thought you would have." Prospect's response: "OK, prove it to us." Your response: "My pleasure."

6. *Change the Base.* In this case, you take the basis on which the prospect is founding his or her response and change it so that he or she can see things in a different light. For example, the prospect says: "This won't accomplish the ABC process." Your response: "The main reason that you inquired about this product was to increase convenience. An added benefit, naturally, would be that it *would* accomplish the ABC process, but the point to bear in mind is that it does bring you the convenience that you require and, therefore, the ABC process should be secondary to any other consideration."

Which Method to Use In any given situation, two things will determine which method to use. The most obvious is the appropriateness of the answer. The other determinant is the prospect's personal style. With time and experience you will learn which methods work best with different types of people. In addition, when you find the need to handle an objection, remain observant and note the person's reactions—both verbal and nonverbal. This will tell you if you were on target and if you should continue along the same vein.

Avoid Feeling Dishonest by Being Honest

Many salespeople feel dishonest and coercive when they try to overcome an objection. Perhaps they feel that learning the methods implies that they will use them as trickery to close a sale. This is not the case. As a consultant, you have been working with your prospect to solve her business problems as only you can. You would not have gotten this far if both of you did not think that you were right for the job. If an objection arises at this point, it could be because the prospect, her need, or her financial situation has changed. Handling an objection is simply a way of trying to clarify it for *both* of you. You never can tell what extenuating circumstances have caused the objection. For all you know, your prospect might have spent too much time in the sun over the weekend and her judgment may be peeling. Your handling of her objection could gently point out the fallacy in her thinking for which she will hopefully thank you later. After all, you are looking out for her best interest in addition to your own. Another possibility is that things have changed and she is no longer interested in your product. This being the case, your response will at least bring out the real reasons why the sale is not being consummated. So it is not manipulative for you to respond to objections. On the contrary, it is helpful to the sales relationship.

If, after discussing your prospect's objection, you find that she is still opposed to the sale, you can put the ballgame in her hands by asking, "Where do we go from here?" This conveys your continued desire to be of service but gives her the choices. She may make another appointment with you, ask you to explain an unclear point, provide you with more information, or simply terminate the relationship.

CONFIRMING THE SALE

Ultimately, one of two things can happen when you attempt to confirm the sale. You can succeed and get the order or the confirmation can be postponed or rejected. We will explore the latter possibility first.

If You Don't Make the Sale, Evaluate

Let's face it, you are not going to confirm every sale, nor are you going to lose them all. *Regardless of the outcome,* you should make notes following each call so that you can evaluate your effectiveness. Doing so after *confirmed* sales will point out your strengths. For those sales not consummated, you will learn your weaknesses by evaluating what transpired and how it affected the outcome.

In situations where you will be returning to the prospect, you should always use the final minutes of the call to pave the way for the next call. Obtain further information that you may need to improve your knowledge and help you prepare a more beneficial proposal for a later date. You should reiterate your desire to be of help and express your appreciation for your prospect's time.

After leaving the call, write down everything new that you learned about the prospect and her needs. Summarize what transpired and include any mistakes that you made and how to correct them. Note the objections that arose, how you handled them, and whether you could have done things differently. Also note any verbal commitments such as price quotes, delivery dates, or terms discussed. You should also enter the call-back date in your tickler file.

The best way to learn by your mistakes is to systematically record the positive and negative aspects of the call. Our Post-Call Checklist will guide you

POST-CALL CHECKLIST

Account Name: _____

Address: _____

Phone: _____

Person Contacted: _____

Product/Service: _____

Date: _____

DIRECTIONS: Circle how you rate yourself for each of the areas below:

	Rating				
	Excellent				Poor
YOUR IMAGE:					
Appearance	5	4	3	2	1
Attitude	5	4	3	2	1
Interest Level	5	4	3	2	1
Eye Contact	5	4	3	2	1
Body Language	5	4	3	2	1
Listening Level	5	4	3	2	1

Comments: _____

_____

STUDYING/PLANNING:					
Knowledge of Prospect's Needs	5	4	3	2	1
Knowledge of Personal Style	5	4	3	2	1
Knowledge of Buying Criteria	5	4	3	2	1

through a thorough examination of what transpired during the call. You should fill out a similar form while the events are still fresh in your mind. Doing so creates a written record of what happened, which is far more useful than fading memories. In fact, if you do not write down what happened during the meeting, there is a good chance that you will not learn from the experience at all.

As you can see on the checklist, everything from soup to nuts is covered, including the tip. To make it particularly relevant to the calls that you will make, be sure to add to the list whatever items that you feel will specifically help you in evaluating your calls.

(continued)

PRODUCT/SERVICE:

Company Image	5	4	3	2	1
Company Reputation	5	4	3	2	1
Price	5	4	3	2	1
Delivery	5	4	3	2	1
Service	5	4	3	2	1

Comments: _____

_____

_____

PROSPECT:

Receptivity	5	4	3	2	1
Mood	5	4	3	2	1
Consistency with Past	5	4	3	2	1
Freedom from Distractions	5	4	3	2	1
Initial Interest	5	4	3	2	1
Final Interest	5	4	3	2	1
Validity of Objections	5	4	3	2	1
Reasons for Refusal	5	4	3	2	1

Comments: _____

_____

_____

Let's review each category on the list beginning at the top with the personal impact and image category:

Appearance: Were you dressed properly? Did you look well-groomed?

Attitude: Did you have the proper frame of mind for the call or were you resentful that you had not had a vacation in two years?

Interest Level: Were you concentrating on the presentation or daydreaming about Pago Pago?

(continued)

Knowledge of Key Decision/Makers	5	4	3	2	1
Knowledge of Competitors	5	4	3	2	1
Knowledge of Product/Service	5	4	3	2	1
Overall Preparation	5	4	3	2	1

PROPOSAL:

Presentation Length	5	4	3	2	1
Organization	5	4	3	2	1
Demonstration/Organization	5	4	3	2	1
Demonstration/Focus	5	4	3	2	1
Relation of Features to Benefits	5	4	3	2	1
Prospect's Reaction	5	4	3	2	1

Comments: _____

_____

_____

CONFIRMATION:

Handling Objections	5	4	3	2	1
Benefit Summary	5	4	3	2	1
Open with Direction	5	4	3	2	1

Eye Contact and Body Language: Was your nonverbal communication telling the customer something different from your words?

Listening Level: Were you an active listener? Did you give the prospect time and encouragement to discuss her situation?

The next category deals with your preparation for the call. It always pays to do your homework, for many times an inadequate job of preparing will ruin a call.

Knowledge of Prospect's Needs: Needs change from day to day and week to week. Were you up on the latest changes in her situation? Were you and your prospect on the same wavelength regarding her present needs?

Personal Style: Did you judge your prospect's personal style correctly? You would certainly get in trouble treating a Director like a Relater.

Buying Criteria: This is a lot like personal style. If your prospect is buying for efficiency and you talked about status, it would be no wonder that you lost the sale.

The rest of the items in the section are straightforward. You know if you did your homework well.

The proposal category on the checklist deals with your ability to be convincing.

Presentation Length: How long did you take to propose your ideas? When you looked up from your presentation, was your prospect with you? Length is very important to presentation quality.

Organization: How logical was your presentation? Did you start at the beginning and go to the end or did you start in the middle and wander around aimlessly?

Demonstration/Organization: Your demonstration has to flow logically also. Can you imagine entering someone's home to demonstrate a vacuum cleaner, dumping a pound of dirt on the rug, and then finding out that the electricity is temporarily off! That's a good way to lose a sale!

Demonstration/Focus: Good demonstrators are like good stories, they both make a point.

Relation of Features to Benefits: During your demonstration did you show your prospect the different features and explain how they will take care of her specific problems?

Prospect's Reaction: Was she impressed or depressed by the demonstration? As you were talking, did someone come on stage with a shepherd's hook to haul you away?

The confirmation section of the checklist reviews your handling of the confirmation phase of the selling process.

Handling Objections: Were you able to handle the prospect's objections smoothly? If not, what were the difficulties?

Benefit Summary: Did you sum up the benefits of your product/service at the appropriate time? Were you able to read your prospect's buying signals?

Open with Direction: What commitment questions did you use? Were they appropriate? What kind of response did you receive?

The items under Product/Service relate to the *prospect's* perception of these things. Since you tried to correct any misconceptions that she may have had, did you succeed? When you left, what were her impressions of all of the items listed?

The last category of the checklist, Prospect, deals with the prospect's affect of the outcome.

Receptivity: Was the prospect happy to see you and looking forward to your presentation?

Mood: What kind of mood was she in and how did it affect the sale?

Consistency with Past: Was the prospect's overall attitude toward you and your product the same as in the past? Were there any unexplainable changes in behavior compared to previous calls?

Freedom from Distractions: Was the prospect's full concentration with you? Were there interruptions during the proposal? Did these affect the customer's ability to absorb what you were proposing?

Initial Interest: What was her interest at the beginning of the call?

Final Interest: What was her interest at the end of the call? If there was a wide discrepancy in interest, you must evaluate to determine why.

Validity of Objections: If your prospect had objections, were they valid or merely excuses?

Reasons for Refusal: This is tied in with the validity of objections. Were the reasons for refusing to confirm the sale good reasons or superficial excuses?

This worksheet, in and of itself, will provide you with a great deal of useful information about yourself and your prospect. In a nutshell, it will evaluate your performance and the frame of mind of the prospect so that you can determine whether it was your shortcoming or hers that prevented the sale from being confirmed.

Visualization Tool   There is another invaluable use for the checklist. When you have time at the end of your day, you can sit, relax, and reflect on the call. This is a prime opportunity to use your visualization skills to improve your performance. Visualize the call and focus particularly on the part with which you had problems. Run the "tape" through your mind and envision what you did. Then imagine the scene again, only this time see yourself doing what you should have done. Imagine the prospect's conversation and reaction to your new behavior and see the outcome as positive.

You should visualize your successes as well as your failures. By doing so, you will reinforce the effective things that you do because in your mind you are practicing them over and over again. The repetition of productive behaviors creates strong working habits. In the same way, the substituting of new behaviors for the unsuccessful ones will help you include the new ones in your behavioral repertoire in the future.

Whether or not you will be returning to the prospect, the Post-Call Checklist will be especially useful to you and other salespeople who may be calling on the account in the future.

Making the Sale

The joy of the positive outcome! Imagine it! You have given your presentation and asked for the order, and you received it! Not because you were shrewd, but because you were professional and did your work well (including your homework). Now what do you do before you go out and celebrate?

You need to verbally clarify and confirm what each of you will do to make the proposed solution work. This includes delivery dates, installation details, criteria for judging success, service agreements, and so on. This information should be put in writing and is independent of the contract associated with the sale itself. The written agreement between you and your customer will serve to remind each of you of your commitment and will impress your customer with your professionalism.

The drawing up of the contract of mutual responsibilities should be handled carefully with some personal styles. Relaters and Socializers, if you remember, prefer relationships to tasks. They may feel that personal, informal agreements are good enough. You should, however, diplomatically insist that everything be put in writing for the protection of both parties. You can blame it on yourself by saying that you have a terrible memory and that *you* need it in writing. It would then be helpful for you to intentionally forget your pen when you leave. People who are primarily Relaters and Socializers tend to overlook structure and deadlines. It is therefore up to you to provide the structure so that the tasks will be done.

When writing out tasks and responsibilities with Directors and Thinkers, be sure to give them the freedom to contribute to the list. Remember that Directors like to call the shots and feel like they are always right. Thinkers will be less assertive but equally as interested in being methodical about the confirmation and implementation of the sale. They will also want guarantees that everything will go smoothly.

The commitment process must be consistent with the rest of your treatment of your prospect. The process stems from trust and cooperation and is handled with sensitivity and respect for his personal style. Getting a commitment from a prospect does not have to be perceived as the point where the sale begins and ends, as the traditionalists see it. The professional salesperson keeps the confirmation in perspective and realizes that it will follow if everything that comes before is done earnestly and without deception. From the confirmation comes the need to assure client satisfaction, the topic covered in the following chapter.

SUMMARY

The third phase of the selling process is the commitment phase. In professional, non-manipulative sales, the process differs significantly from the traditional method in that the sale does not have to be "closed." Rather, the sale is *confirmed*, following an extensive information-gathering phase and a customized presentation phase. The emphasis of the professional salesperson is on the entire sales process, not merely on the sale's confirmation, for the professional sees the confirmation as just the beginning of a mutual commitment to an ongoing business relationship.

There are several ways which will guide you in recognizing opportunities for confirming sales. Most often, by the time you reach the presentation phase of the sales process, you will know your prospect fairly well: his style, typical body language, and his ways of accepting and rejecting what you say. There will be occasions, however, when this will not be possible, such as when you are requested to give a final presentation to a person who has more authority to make a buying decision. In such a situation, you will have to infer the unknown person's style from the more obvious signals being given by that person. Some of those signals come in the form of the prospect's questions, statements, and body language. Within their context, all three forms can indicate positive, neutral, or negative signals.

The timing for seeking a commitment—for confirming the sale—depends on your reading of the buying signals. When they are positive and strongly indicate the prospect is ready to buy, even if you have not completed your presentation, it is time to wrap up the presentation with a benefit summary and take the order. This is accomplished by asking an open question that requests direction.

There are times, however, when the prospect is not ready to commit at the end of your presentation. Objections, which are anything that creates an obstacle preventing the smooth flow toward the completion of a sale, can occur. Professional salespeople are not threatened by a prospect's objections, but see them as opportunities to better understand the needs of the prospect. They also are signals indicating that they and their prospects are not on the same wavelength.

Objections take several forms (questions, statements, and body language), can mean many things, and stem from several reasons. Because of this, it is important for you to question your prospect so that you can understand the reason(s) behind his objections.

In handling simple objections, the basic method is a four-step process: 1) listen, 2) clarify, 3) respond to the objection, and 4) confirm your prospect's acceptance of your answer. In handling more difficult objections, the basic method is the same except for the third step. In this case, the response is given using the *compensation* method, which acknowledges the deficiency in a particular area but tries to compensate for it by using other features that are unique or of equal quality to outweigh the shortcoming questioned.

When handling objections, it is best to cooperate and to be of service, perceiving your prospect as a colleague rather than an adversary. Doing so will encourage your prospects to open up, thus helping you to uncover the problem and to help suggest a solution.

There are several methods to use in handling objections: 1) use "feel-felt-found"; 2) convert to a question; 3) echo and listen; 4) break the objection into smaller, more manageable increments; 5) use the boomerang method; or 6) change the base. The method you choose depends on the appropriateness of the answer and on the prospect's personal style.

Regardless of whether or not a sale is made in a meeting with a prospect, it is extremely valuable to evaluate your own performance to learn not only from what you believe you did correctly, but more importantly, from what you believe you did incorrectly. This evaluation is best done by completing a post-call checklist immediately following the call. Doing so will provide a written evaluation, which is far more accurate than fading memories.

When a sale has been confirmed, there are two steps that follow: 1) verbally clarify and confirm what each of you will do to make the proposed solution work, and 2) follow up this clarification and confirmation with a written agreement between you.

The commitment process must be consistent with the rest of your treatment of your prospect. The process stems from trust and cooperation and should be handled with sensitivity and respect for his personal style. Getting a commitment from a prospect does not have to be perceived as the point where the sale begins and ends, as the traditionalists see it. The professional salesperson keeps the confirmation in perspective and realizes that it will follow if everything that comes before is done earnestly and without deception.

DISCUSSION QUESTIONS

1. What is the difference between "closing" the sale and "confirming" the sale?

2. How will you know when to seek confirmation of the sale?

3. What are some questions that can be used to ask for a commitment?

4. What would it mean if you demonstrated your product, asked for a confirmation, and still received no commitment?

5. Explain what an objection is. How does a Non-Manipulative Salesperson interpret objections? How would this treatment differ from the treatment by a high-pressure salesperson?

6. What is the benefit of a self-evaluation after each sale?

7. What should be done following a sale's confirmation and why?

CHAPTER THIRTEEN

Assuring Customer Satisfaction: The Follow-Through Process

CHAPTER OBJECTIVES

1 Discuss the process of assuring customer satisfaction.
2 Define the salesperson's value to the customer in terms of service following the sale.
3 Present methods of maintaining customer satisfaction.
4 Outline methods of expanding current business.

> Those who enter to buy, support me. Those who come to flatter, please me. Those who complain, teach me how I may please others so that more will come. Only those hurt me who are displeased but do not complain for they refuse me permission to correct my errors and thus improve my service.
>
> MARSHALL FIELD

Marshall Field's statement perfectly sums up the attitude of the professional. It establishes the customer as the person to whom you as a professional are responsible. Customers support you; therefore, they deserve VIP treatment. When your customers are happy, you are happy. You are unhappy when they complain, but you examine their complaints calmly and see them as opportunities to learn as well as to satisfy their needs. The quote above echoes the fear that customers will not vocalize their dissatisfaction, but will instead take their business elsewhere.

The follow-through process, the last phase of the sales process, can also be called assuring customer satisfaction because it is something that you must do continually. It requires servicing your accounts, maintaining the accounts that you have, and expanding your current service.

SERVICING YOUR ACCOUNTS

In analyzing prospects, one of the questions that you might ask yourself is: "Is this prospect satisfied with his present supplier and, if not, how can I capitalize on this dissatisfaction?" You actually seek out areas in which the competition is weak so that you can move in and coax the customer away. In assuring customer satisfaction, however, the proverbial shoe is on the other foot. *You* are in the position of having to keep a customer satisfied in order to fight off the competition. You would be naive to think that your competitors are not using the same prospecting tactics that you are. Therefore, a major reason why you should be diligent in your maintenance of customer satisfaction is to protect your investment from the wolves. The other reason, which should be obvious, is that a professional salesperson cares about his customers and endeavors to maintain his working relationships. Although this often takes an extra effort on your part, it is very rewarding in every way.

When your customer bought your product or service, he received an extra bonus: *you*. As a salesperson, you have the ethical and professional obligations to be a part of that customer's life as long as the account is active. This commitment begins as soon as you confirm the sale. From this point on, your value to the customer takes many forms:

1. You are a person rather than a company with whom the customer deals. People prefer relating to individuals rather than to large customer service departments.
2. You are an open, concerned person who will listen and understand. You can be reached for even the most minor questions.
3. You have a depth of knowledge that can be helpful in solving specific problems. You also have the means to obtain additional information to save the customer time.
4. You are accessible and make your company accessible. You are a conduit through which customers can reach other people in your company. If a customer wishes to consult with an engineer, for example, he can arrange to do so through you more easily than on his own.
5. You represent security. The customer knows that you have a vested interest in his business. He also knows that you can be relied on for consistency and performance. You are a known entity whereas another rep is not. Remember how much more comfortable people are with familiar things.

The commitment to an ongoing relationship is more appropriate to complex sales relationships than to simple ones. A simple sale would be selling a consumer item in a store either once or periodically. The need for a conscientious follow-up program is unnecessary. The account simply has to be serviced for reordering. A complex relationship occurs when the sale involves installations, training, tracking, and analyzing results and technical services. Complex relationships require more customer knowledge and a longer period of time to develop the relationship and make the sale. It is on this particular type of sales relationship that this book is focused.

Identify Criteria for Satisfaction

After the confirmation of the sale, but before the implementation of the solution to your customer's problem, the two of you need to discuss and put in writing exactly what the expected results are. This is much like goal-setting in that the criteria must be specific, measurable, and within realistic ranges. For example, let's say that you are selling a jellybean maker to Presidential Jellybeans, Inc. In the past, they have been able to produce 500 pounds of jellybeans per month by hiring migrant jellybean workers. You claim that your machine could make 1,000 pounds of jellybeans a month with only one person running it. You and the buyer would then set up the criterion of 1,000 pounds per month as being satisfactory performance.

When to Measure Results

After you have determined how to measure the improvement, you must decide when to measure the results. Your customer in the example above may want to base his measurement on the first month's performance. You, however, may prefer to take the average of the first three months of production to allow for a break-in period and minor adjustments. Unless the two of you agree, you will lose your common ground for judging the success of the implemented solution.

Another reason to agree on the measurement of success criteria is that there are so many ways to measure successful results. In your discussion, you can weigh the advantages and disadvantages of each method of measurement to find the most accurate one. Some examples of criteria by which to measure sales are:

1. Sales volume in dollars
2. Sales volume in units sold
3. Sales volume by type of customer
4. Sales volume by type of product or service
5. Number of new accounts sold
6. Gross profit of salesperson's territory
7. Average order size
8. Net profit of territory
9. Number of calls required per sale
10. This year's gross sales vs. last year's sales

This list could go on and on. As you can see, there are many ways to measure. More than likely your customer will have a preference with which you should concur if it will measure the results accurately.

Monitor the Results

After the time period that you and your customer have agreed on, the results should be compared with the desired objective. If the performance meets the standards set, then all is going well. You should arrange with your customer to periodically monitor and measure the continued operation at specified times in the future. This will ensure that the desired standards are maintained.

On the other hand, if your test results are not acceptable, you need to determine the reason(s). This should be done with your customer and any other technical assistance that you deem necessary. Once the problem is isolated, correct it and set up new success criteria again. Then repeat the above process until the customer is satisfied.

MAINTAINING CUSTOMER SATISFACTION

Since your first concern is customer satisfaction, you should be aware of some emotional stumbling blocks in your path: selective perception, user error, and buyer's remorse.

Selective perception is the process in which only selected details of the whole form the entire picture. This attention to detail is sometimes petty. For example, a customer may have a new copying machine that works like a charm, but he is irritated by the sound of the motor. He focuses only on what is wrong rather than all that is right.

This selective perception occurs because buyers expect their purchases to be perfect. Regardless of the purchase price, they figure that for what they spent, they deserve perfection. When you encounter someone who is practicing selective perception, evaluate the situation to determine if his complaint is reasonable or exaggerated. If it is exaggerated, try to resolve the problem by pointing out benefits and features that compensate. Put the negative detail in a different perspective for your customer so that it becomes one small part of the total picture.

Many sales involve the installation of a new system or piece of equipment, and the buyer or his employees must be trained to use it. The successful use of the equipment depends on the effectiveness of the training, and it is imperative that the salesperson follow through after the training period to ensure that they are using their purchase properly. It is not uncommon for people to forget 75 percent of what they hear after two days. This can cause *user error*, which will significantly affect the outcome of your tests and may prevent your customers from reaching their success criteria. Often customers will be unhappy about a purchase and not realize that it is due to improper operation. The more complex something is, the more training it requires to use it properly. In the interest of implementing the solution quickly, users may settle for incomplete training or become sloppy in their application of good training. In any case, look for user error whenever a customer's success criterion is not being reached.

Buyer's remorse refers to the regret that a buyer feels after making a purchase. It could be caused by selective perception, user error, or the customer's error that he will not realize the full benefits of the product. Buyer's remorse can also be caused by the economics of the purchase. Until the benefits prove themselves to be cost-effective, a buyer regrets having made the purchase. It is the responsibility of the salesperson to assuage these fears by assuring the customer that his investment is wise and sound. Reiterate some of the selling points which convinced him to buy it originally, present data, and put him at ease.

Handling Customer Complaints

Whether your customer's complaint is legitimate or not, follow it up with a service call. Whenever possible, do it personally instead of sending someone from the customer service department. First, it provides the personal service that your customer appreciates. Second, it may obviate the need for a technician or serviceman to call. As an alternative, both of you can go together in handling customer complaints. Keep the following guidelines in mind:

1. *Don't procrastinate in making the call.* Often a problem is not as serious as it sounds. Some customers "read the riot act" when they call about a complaint. A delay in responding will only irritate the customer all the more.
2. *Admit mistakes and apologize.* Just because you made the sale does not mean that you should become defensive about your company, product, or service. Even the most reputable companies make mistakes and have problems with their products.
3. *Show compassion for your customer.* Whether the complaint proves to be true or false, show your customer that you are concerned and investigate the problem immediately.
4. *Listen actively.* Listen to your customer's complaint; talking will make him feel less anxious about it. Let your customer vent his feelings before you react to the situation.
5. *Don't pass the buck to your company or someone else within it.* This may take the blame off of you, but it undermines the integrity and organization of the company, and your customer will lose confidence in your firm.

The follow-through after the sale is necessary for the continuation of a sound business relationship. Naturally, your service cannot stop there. From the post-confirming service phase you will make a smooth transition into the maintenance phase.

The philosophy behind maintaining your customers is simple: now that you have them, do not lose them! Your customers are assets who need to be preserved. In the same way that you would not neglect caring for a prized show horse, you cannot neglect attending to your accounts. When you consider the amount of time and money invested in your customers, you cannot afford to lose them. This investment goes beyond your personal expenditures. It also includes your firm's advertising and marketing costs to reach that particular market segment. Your customers, therefore, should be treated as if the life of your business depended on them—which it does!

Fifteen Ways to Keep Your Customers Satisfied

1. Show your customers that you think of them. Send them helpful newspaper clippings or articles, cartoons related to their business, and "Here's an idea I thought you'd enjoy" notes as well as Christmas/New Year's cards, birthday cards, and thank you notes.
2. Drop by to show them new products and brochures and offer additional services. Always make an appointment before making your call! Respect your customers' time as you do your own.

3. Offer a sample gift to enhance the use of your product. See how they are utilizing your product or service and suggest other ways that they can benefit from it. They may not be realizing its full potential.

4. Offer customer discounts on new products or services to encourage additional business.

5. When new employees are hired, offer to train them free of charge in the use of your product.

6. Repay or compensate them for lost time or money caused by problems encountered with your product.

7. Be personal. Record details about your customers and enter these into your file. It is so much nicer to say to someone, "How's Bob?" rather than, "How's your husband?"

8. Tell the truth; lies have a way of coming back to haunt you.

9. Accept returns without batting an eyelash. In the long run, they are much less expensive than finding new customers.

10. Be ethical. Keep all of your information about your accounts confidential.

11. Be certain that your company follows through on its commitment. This includes delivery, installation, packaging, and so on.

12. Show your appreciation for your customers' referrals by reporting back to them on the outcome.

13. If your company has a newsletter, obtain permission from your successful customers to write about them in the newsletter. Naturally you would send them a copy.

14. Keep track of your customers' results with your product and meet periodically to review the entire picture (their business, industry, trends, competition, etc.).

15. Always keep the lines of communication open. As in any relationship, you must be able to exchange grievances, ideas, praises, losses, and victories.

What all of this comes down to is that you should be willing to go the extra mile for your accounts. The extra effort that you expend now will be repaid handsomely in the future.

How and When to Call

The maintenance of your accounts requires scheduling them for periodic calls. The classification of the account determines the frequency and type of call. You might consider calling on A accounts twice as frequently as B accounts, and so on. You may decide to contact less profitable accounts by telephone or mail. The logistics of calling on your accounts must be both planned *and* flexible. Monitor your customers and be sensitive to their needs. Be alert to the concrete *warning signals* of customer dissatisfaction:

1. Changes in purchase volume: unless external variables have a bearing on a product's sales volume, a decrease in volume should be interpreted as a warning signal.

2. An increase in the number and frequency of complaints about your product, customer service, company policies, pricing, or delivery.

3. Repeated comments about the merits of the competition.

4. A decrease in rapport: a less cordial atmosphere during your sales calls, with a simultaneous breakdown in communication.
5. The hiring of managerial personnel who are not familiar with your product or service and seem to have no desire to become familiar.
6. The absorption of your customer's company by a larger firm: often they will start over by accepting bids on different products or services; you may find yourself back at square one again.

Winning Back Lost Customers

A fact of life in sales is that customers are lost. A customer's needs may change so that your product or service no longer suits him. A competitor wins the account with lower prices or better service. Whatever the reason, try to regain the account.

When it comes to your attention that an account is lost or close to being lost, you should conduct an immediate and thorough investigation. Contact the customer and respond to his complaints in a realistic, calm fashion.

The answers that you receive will determine the objectives and strategies that you will use to try to regain the account. If you are lucky, it will just involve the effective handling of the complaint. On the other hand, winning back lost customers can take you through the entire process of establishing trust, identifying needs, determining solutions, and assuring the customer that things will improve in the future. This can be a time-consuming job, and you must decide if the account is worth your time and effort.

Annual Reviews

Annual or periodic reviews are valuable tools for evaluating the activities of an account, the industry in general, competitors, company strengths and weaknesses, and so on. Evaluate each account, both privately and in conference with your customer.

Reanalyzing your market segments and accounts periodically will help you reclassify and prioritize accounts if necessary, and allow you to gain insight into new markets and trends.

In addition to analyzing this information for yourself, meet with your accounts to discuss where you have been and where you are going together. This special meeting will give you feedback about your customer's level of satisfaction, will give you the opportunity to introduce new products or services, will convey to him that you care, and will strengthen the trust bond between you.

The following guidelines will help produce an effective meeting:

1. Arrange a breakfast or luncheon meeting, if possible.
2. Select a place that is well-lighted and conducive to conversation.
3. Invite all of the necessary people participating in the account. If there are two buyers, take them both to lunch.

4. You and your customers should bring all of the records needed to discuss the previous year's business.

5. Allow an adequate amount of time for the meeting, but do set limits. As much as you do not want to rush the discussion, you also should not let it continue beyond a reasonable amount of time.

6. Be organized. Know what you want to talk about and proceed in a logical manner. Take notes if necessary, and send a clean, typed copy to the other participants.

7. Listen carefully for implied needs and concerns.

8. Reiterate your desire to be of service and maintain an open, trustworthy relationship.

9. After the review, offer a new idea, service, product, or special promotional deal whenever possible. This is an excellent opportunity to spark their interest in something new.

10. During your conversation, look for opportunities above and beyond their immediate horizon. Ask for referrals and letters of testimony, if appropriate.

EXPANDING YOUR SERVICES

It is not sufficient to service your present accounts; you must also provide for the future. This means continually adding new qualified prospects and turning them into active accounts.

Acres of Diamonds

Perhaps you have heard the story about a nineteenth century farmer who sold his farm and traveled the world in search of his fortune. After he exhausted his resources, he lost hope and threw himself into the ocean. Meanwhile, back on the farm he had sold, diamonds were discovered which yielded untold fortunes!

Opportunities are available to us every day, but we may miss them in our anxious search for new horizons. The professional salesperson will recognize that his current customers represent the best source of new business. If you have a strong relationship with your customers, you can feel comfortable asking them for referrals which may bring you additional accounts. There are several ways to expand your business through your customers:

1. *Look for referrals within a customer's company.* Whenever you talk to a customer, keep an ear open for clues that may indicate needs within his company. For example, a new office or branch might open which may need your product or service. Ask your customer for a referral, either verbally or in writing. Keep your eyes open for new pockets of opportunity within your customer's company.

2. *Ask for referrals outside a customer's company.* It is important to ask your customers if they know of anyone else who may have a need for your services. In doing so, it is helpful if you can get a testimonial letter or an introductory note. Something in writing has more credibility than simply saying, "Ms. Jones of Real Time Systems sent me." And always ask your customers for permission to use them as

3. *Sell more of the same.* If, during your servicing of an account, you see that the company has the capacity to buy larger volumes of your product, suggest that they buy more. In this way, B accounts can sometimes be turned into A accounts. Under no circumstances, however, should you try to sell them more if they do not need it.

4. *Sell additional products or services to your accounts.* Again, if you see the need or the capability, offer new products/services to your present customers. If they like your original product, they will listen to your ideas about expanding into other products.

5. *Upgrade your customers.* If a customer uses a medium-priced product, you may be able to upgrade it to a higher-priced, higher-quality product, especially if the company is growing and its needs are changing. For example, a company which uses a copying machine may find that it needs one with more capabilities such as photo-reduction and collating. If you are aware of the increased needs, you can suggest the upgrade before your competitor does.

Assuring customer satisfaction is like working at keeping a marriage stable. It requires communication, a sensitivity to the other's needs, and a commitment to grow together. As a salesperson, you need to exert an extra measure of effort to ensure the continuation of the relationship. Unlike a marriage, however, your customers can walk out on you anytime that they feel dissatisfied. The divorce process in business is much less complicated and much less emotionally traumatic than in a marriage. The relationship, therefore, is definitely not 50-50. If you accept this, you will go the extra mile for your customers and find that they appreciate you more because of it. This will undoubtedly be reflected in your increase in sales, self-esteem, and growth as a professional salesperson.

SUMMARY

The follow-through process, the last phase in the selling process, can also be called assuring customer satisfaction because it is a process that a professional salesperson does continually. It requires servicing your accounts, maintaining the accounts that you have, and expanding your current business.

Servicing an account is your primary responsibility on completion of the sale. As a salesperson, you have an ethical and professional obligation to be a part of that customer's life as long as the account is active. Your value to the customer is extensive. It includes you as a personal liaison with your company; as a concerned person who cares about the account; as one with a depth of knowledge that can help solve problems; as one who is accessible when needed; and as one who represents consistency, performance, and security.

After confirmation of the sale, but before the implementation of the solution to your customer's problem, you and your customer need to discuss and put into writing exactly what the expected results are. This is much like goal-setting in that the criteria must be specific, measurable, and within realistic ranges. After you have determined how to measure the improvement, you must determine when to measure the results.

Maintaining customer satisfaction is another facet of the follow-through process. There are several stumbling blocks that you should be aware of. Three such stumbling blocks are: selective perception, user error, and buyer's remorse.

Handling customer complaints is another part of maintaining customer satisfaction. There are several guidelines to keep in mind when customer complaints arise: 1) don't procrastinate; 2) admit mistakes and apologize; 3) show compassion for your customer; 4) listen actively; and 5) don't pass the buck to your company or someone within it. Your customers are assets who need to be nurtured. In the same way that you would not neglect caring for a prized show horse, you cannot neglect attending to your accounts. When you consider the amount of time and money invested in your customers, you cannot afford to lose them. There are several warning signals of customer dissatisfaction of which professional salespeople need to be aware so that they can act immediately to preserve their accounts.

Annual or periodic reviews are valuable tools for evaluating the activities of an account, the industry in general, competitors, company strengths and weakness, etc. These evaluations should be done both privately and in conference with the customer.

Reanalyzing your market segments and accounts periodically will help you reclassify and prioritize accounts if necessary, and allow you to gain insight into new markets and trends.

It is not enough to service your present accounts. You must also provide for the future. This means continually adding new qualified prospects and turning them into active accounts.

Assuring customer satisfaction requires communication, a sensitivity to the other person's needs, and a commitment to grow together. As a salesperson, you need to exert an extra measure of effort—go the extra mile—to ensure the continuation of the relationship.

DISCUSSION QUESTIONS

1. What does it mean to "service an account"?
2. What is your role and value to your customer after the sale?
3. Explain what criteria for satisfaction are and why they are important.
4. How is drawing up criteria for satisfaction similar to goal-setting?
5. How often should you contact your customers to monitor their success criteria?
6. What is buyer's remorse? What are the causes of it? What should you do to help?
7. Describe how customer complaints are professionally handled.
8. What are some ways to let your customers know you care about them and their business?
9. Name some of the signs of customer dissatisfaction.
10. How can satisfied customers be helpful in expanding your business?
11. What is an annual review? How is it conducted? What are its benefits to you and your customers?

Part V

COMMUNICATION SKILLS

Communication is power. In a world in which money has become a secondary asset, specialized knowledge and the ability to communicate it are the primary measures of a person's value in the business world. Our information-hungry society has discarded experience as a gauge of credibility.

If you are skeptical about knowledge taking precedence over money and experience, consider the fame and fortune enjoyed by entrepreneurs in their 20s who started companies such as Apple Computer, Microsoft, and Herbalife, to name a few. Most people would argue that it takes millions of dollars to start a computer company. Not true. It takes knowledge and first rate communication skills. With those two assets, money will be forthcoming from venture capitalists and other investors.

If you were to choose only one skill to cultivate in yourself, you would be wise to choose communication skills. The gift of gab and a flair for quickly and genuinely creating a closeness with different types of people will get you further in business than three Ph.D.s. Add to that a firm grasp of a saleable body of knowledge and your road to success will be smooth and straight.

Selling is many things, but first and foremost it is a process of communication. It is a "people" business in which you establish relationships, give and receive information, solve problems and build mutually beneficial associations with many people. Non-Manipulative Selling is one of the most communication-dependent forms of selling. Salespeople who truly want to excel will work on their communication skills as diligently as their product knowledge, prospecting strategies, promotion, and so on.

Communication skills can be divided into two categories: verbal and nonverbal. Verbal communication skills, covered in Chapters 14 through 16, involve the giving and receiving of spoken information. These skills include:

O QUESTIONING. The ability to ask the right questions so your customer gives you useful information that will allow you to be of service.

O LISTENING. The ability to accurately and courteously receive and understand the information given.

O FEEDBACK. A verbal technique to double-check your understanding of the message and convey that you are not only listening, but also on the same wavelength as the other person.

Nonverbal communication, covered in Chapters 17 through 19, involves a fascinating yet subtle form of interaction. We've all heard the expression, "Actions speak louder than words." What this means is that people reveal their thoughts and feelings not only through words but also through physical gestures. Nonverbal communication skills allow you to observe and interpret the subtle messages people give with their bodies. Your understanding will allow you to control the nonverbal messages you give so people will interpret you correctly. Nonverbal communication includes:

O BODY LANGUAGE. This is the study of the emotions conveyed in the movement of one's hands, eyes, head, face, and posture.

PROXEMICS. This is the study of the physical and psychological closeness people are comfortable with.

O USE OF VOICE. Just as physical movements can be observed and interpreted for emotional content, so too, voice inflection can be studied for better understanding and communication.

The fascinating study of human communication will increase your insight and make you more appreciative of people's needs and motives. In a nutshell, you will become a better communicator, which will increase your understanding and control of your personal and business lives.

CHAPTER FOURTEEN

The Fine Art of Questioning

<table>
<tr>
<td>

CHAPTER OBJECTIVES

</td>
<td>

1 Discuss in depth the effective use of questioning to promote successful sales relationships.

2 Introduce the various types of questions and illustrate their uses.

</td>
</tr>
</table>

Do you ever envy the salesperson who picks just the right questions to get at the core of a prospect's situation? Questioning is an important communication skill essential to selling, for it not only simplifies the salesperson's job but also helps to increase sales. Well-phrased questions help prospects to open up. When a prospect reveals feelings, situations, motives, needs, and desires, a salesperson knows better how to help that prospect.

Amazingly, the essential questioning skills are seldom taught. Law schools typically instruct students on productive ways to use questions within the courtroom where a witness has sworn to tell the truth, but these cases have little bearing on the world outside the courtroom where people are not obliged to answer. In the sales world, finely honed questioning skills must be applied in order to obtain valid and useful information.

By questioning appropriately, you initiate and maintain conversation that will lead to a successful sales relationship. Whether your prospect is reluctant to talk or leads the conversation, your questioning skills help you in four specific, sales-related ways: 1) they identify behavioral styles; 2) they uncover needs; 3) they build trust; and 4) they develop the relationship. In other words, a question does more than get the prospect to respond. Appropriate phrasing and content of questions promote a good sales relationship.

Before contacting a prospect, a salesperson should determine his call objectives. Based on the purpose of the visit, he should plan a number of questions to be asked during the call. This is an important step for it helps him focus his call on an end result. It is also important, however, that he remain *flexible* during the call by not leading the prospect in his planned direction if the prospect's responses indicate that he wishes to go in another direction.

QUESTIONING STRATEGIES

As you select and use questioning, keep the following general strategies in mind:

1. *Ask permission to ask questions.* Asking for permission will help the prospect relax and will explain why you are asking the questions you will be asking. You might say, "Would you mind if I asked you a few questions so that I can better understand your situation?"

2. *Start with open questions on broad topics and narrow with subsequent questions.* "Tell me a little about your business" is an example of a broad, open question. If you dislike asking such a question, think for a moment of the benefits: the question gives prospects total autonomy to go wherever they wish. Letting the prospect go where he wishes without pinning him down also acknowledges implicitly or explicitly his ability to take the conversation in a direction meaningful to his needs. Questioning is liable to be intimidating if the questions are too specific too soon.

   The broad response opportunity also allows the prospect to reveal behavioral style more readily than using a narrower question. In other words, prospects are freer to talk about goals or other concerns in their own ways. As the prospect provides an answer, listen selectively for that information for which you can provide help. Thus, broad questions allow responses that provide clues to prospect needs, problems, goals, or things that generally make the prospect feel good. Your ability to listen will also guide you to your next question, a question which further focuses your inquiry based on the prospect's response.

   The second question should be a little narrower. It might be, "What do you do in terms of training?" or "Can you elaborate on . . . ?" Questions that follow are in the same vein, moving into still narrower and more defined areas, each based on clues provided by the responses to earlier, broader questions.

3. *Build on previous responses.* Simply stated, listen before questioning. Rather than becoming preoccupied with what you want to ask next and thereby missing most if not all of what your prospect is communicating to you, concentrate on what your prospect is saying. With this information, you can easily frame your subsequent questions based on his previous responses. This technique has many advantages. First, you concentrate on listening rather than letting your mind wander. Second, the questioning process is orderly, logical, and focused. Third, building on the prospect's previous responses, you show through actions that you are, in fact, listening to what he is telling you. Fourth, you have the opportunity to explore areas of prospect interest that you might not have chosen on your own.

4. *Keep questions free of buzz words, jargon, or technical terms that may confuse.* If a does not understand the question, how can the response be accurate or complete? To avoid breakdowns in communication, carefully structure your questions to promote understanding and avoid confusion.

5. *Keep questions simple; one idea at a time is the most effective.* Discussing one idea at a time allows the prospect to concentrate on one main subject. Questions which contain multiple ideas lead to misunderstandings. Such questions force a prospect to choose between topics. Furthermore, sometimes you forget to come back to the other topics. An example of questions containing too many thoughts is:

"Would you mind telling me a little bit about your personal and professional objectives, as well as some of the things you find have been helping or hindering you in accomplishing those goals, as well as some suggestions that you might have to overcome some of the hindrances, as well as. . . . " Instead, proceed logically through each topic separately.

6. *Keep questions focused.* When the *subject matter* is too broad, the prospects' answers may be irrelevant. Initially a broad question is used but one which is within the range of a pertinent subject. When questions wander, responses may be either far off the topic or interesting but hardly useful. Instead, pursue one topic to its conclusion. In that way, your prospect will know better why you are asking certain questions and where your questions will lead. People like to know where they are going; they dislike being led into the unknown. Expecting a prospect to continue a conversation with an unclear understanding of the logic behind your questions is similar to going to an airport and getting on a plane without knowing its destination, when it is leaving, how long the flight will take, or if the plane has enough fuel to arrive at its destination.

7. *Keep questions nonthreatening.* Threatening questions, such as, "How much money do you want to spend?" (when asked at the start of a sales interview), raise tension and decrease trust. Other sensitive areas involve economic stability, health, age, and political affiliations. Questions in these areas may threaten your prospect. Moreover, you prospect is generally under no legal obligation to be truthful, and questions which embarrass (if answered truthfully) encourage avoidance of the truth. Therefore, despite a prospect's tendency toward answering honestly, be wary of answers to questions that touch on sensitive areas.

8. *Explain why you are asking a question and indicate what the benefits are for the prospect to answer forthrightly, especially when questions must touch on sensitive areas.* For example, the ability to meet financial obligations is one area which may cause embarrassment for a prospect, yet supply you with crucial information. In such cases, be straightforward and businesslike. Prospects respect this and usually are willing to provide the necessary information. If a prospect hesitates at disclosing the minimal information necessary to check credit, you may be wasting time. Aside from personal questions about income and ability to meet financial obligations, queries about age and medical problems may make a prospect anxious and uneasy. If you *must* know about these potentially embarrassing subjects, take time to prepare your prospect with the rationale behind the questions and phrase the question in as nonthreatening a manner as possible. "We require our applicants to earn or have $5,000 minimum available within a week. Does that apply to you?" works much better than, "I can't issue this until I know how much you're good for. What could you accumulate in a week?" With proper preparation, the prospect can anticipate the question and be prepared to answer it. Suspicions vanish and anxieties fade. For example, a loan officer at a bank was told that the bank was having trouble collecting loans from underage borrowers; therefore, future applications required the person's age for processing. Faced with a middle-aged customer, the loan officer said, "Mrs. Jones, the bank loan committee requires a statement of a customer's age so that we know the person is of legal age to make a loan. Some of my customers prefer to say 'twenty-one plus.' Is that all right with you?" He received quite a few laughs, and most people just told him their age. He didn't offend customers, and he met the loan committee's need.

If a prospect remains anxious, back off a bit, explain your purpose, and ask a second time. Be sure, however, that you need the information that is causing the prospect uneasiness. Otherwise, change to another, less threatening subject.

9. *Structure questions to ask about general benefits sought.* Questions that ask for specific

features or benefits desired in a product or service can put a prospect on the spot. A prospect may not fully understand the needs met and problems solved by your product or service. To ask him about general benefits allows the prospect to speak knowledgeably and, at the same time, gives you more latitude in satisfying needs, since general benefits are easier to provide than specific features.

Consider two people selling real estate. One tries to solve customer problems early in the sales relationship, by asking specifics such as, "Do you want a fireplace?" The other keeps the questions more general: "Do you like a romantic feeling in your home?" What's the implication? Note that if the first one cannot show a house with a fireplace, an awkward situation exists unless the prospect's needs are renegotiated. The second salesperson maintains wide latitude: a fireplace, a cozy corner, a den, a patio, a pool, and so on. The more general request will not limit or terminate the sale too early in the sales relationship.

10. *Phrase questions that allow a prospect some latitude in answering rather than forcing a specific answer.* "How do your mornings look for an appointment this week?" is better than, "Would you prefer to see me at 10:00 A.M. on Tuesday or 8:30 A.M. on Thursday?" The latter is manipulative, and manipulation, even if unintended, violates the prospect's sense of dignity and insults the prospect's intelligence.

11. *Maintain a consultative atmosphere.* You are an assistant to your prospect, not an attorney who is questioning the prospect on the witness stand. Interrogative, rapid-fire questions will not pressure your prospect into answering—at least not over the long (and sales-prosperous) haul. Use a relaxed tone of voice. Give your prospect time to contemplate the question, even if it means a period of silence. By pausing and allowing him time to think, you will likely receive a more accurate and complete reply. Do not interrupt. Proceed only after the answer is complete.

12. *Phrase questions so that they are easy to answer.* Research has shown that people prefer to agree to something rather than to voice objections. Therefore, if you sense your prospect has a preference, phrase your questions to allow for this preference. Say, "Would you like the large size?" if you sense that is the case. It is easier to agree to the large size by saying yes, than to specify objections to a smaller size.

As you question, be careful that easy-to-answer questions are what you *want.* Some questions, called closed-ended, are easy to answer in that they require only a yes or no or some other short reply. Such short replies can quickly terminate a flow of conversation when used inappropriately.

13. *The pause.* Encourage pauses in the conversation. Americans tend to believe that silence must be filled with conversation, therefore we have an impulse to fill in pauses with words that are not necessarily important: If you can discipline yourself to allow those pauses to exist, the quality of your conversations will improve. How? They will give both your prospective clients and yourself a chance to reflect on what has been said, determine the true meaning of what's been said, and allow you to compose what you're going to say next. They also give the customer time to respond thoughtfully.

TYPES OF QUESTIONS

After the preliminary "how-do-you-dos" and other easy conversation openers, the real questioning begins. Even though you know your questioning strategies, you still must decide how to phrase questions to promote those strategies. A properly selected and phrased question can dramatically further the relationship between you and your prospect. Questions take on two basic forms: *open-ended* and *closed-ended.* Below are some guidelines for this selection.

Open-Ended Questions

Open-ended questions are phrased in a way that requires the prospect to answer narratively or with description. They increase the prospect's involvement in the conversation by asking for knowledge, feelings, or opinions, and allow her to reveal her personal style.

In general, open-ended questions are preferred to closed-ended questions, especially when getting to know someone. Examples of open-ended questions are:

> "What type of billing schedule would meet your needs best?"
> "What kind of features do you most like on your TV?"

Open-ended questions usually have the following characteristics:

1. They cannot be answered by a simple yes or no.
2. They usually begin with what or how.
3. They do not lead the prospect in a specific direction.
4. They increase dialogue by drawing out the prospect's ideas or feelings.
5. They encourage the prospect to elaborate on objectives, needs, wants, and problems.
6. They help the prospect to discover things for himself or herself.
7. They can be used to stimulate the prospect into thinking about your ideas and product or service.
8. They allow the prospect to exhibit his or her behavioral style more readily than closed-ended questions.

Closed-Ended Questions

Closed-ended questions allow the prospect to answer quickly and to the point. Typically, they require a yes or no answer, offer a choice, or ask for a specific short response. Some examples are:

> "Do you know anything about small business computers?"
> "Does your office have a lot of paperwork?"
> "Would you like the large or the small size?"

Questions of this nature perform the following functions:

1. They allow specific facts to be obtained quickly.
2. They are simple to answer.
3. They are useful in the feedback process where the salesperson desires to check the accuracy or completeness of his understanding.

4. They may be used to gain commitment to a definite position.
5. They can be used to reinforce positive statements.
6. They can be used to direct the conversation to a desired topic or concern.

STRATEGIC USES OF QUESTIONS

In addition to knowing the two basic forms questions can take, you should be familiar with their strategic uses. Questions can be used to effectively draw out particular information you seek from prospects. The use of the following types of questions will help you fully diagnose a prospect's situation.

Clarifying Questions

Clarifying questions restate the prospect's remarks or refer directly to them. They generally are accompanied by a rising inflection in the voice which implies a question, even if one is not directly asked. "So, you will be here on Tuesday" is a statement, but with a rising inflection implies the additional, "Isn't that so?" These questions do not insist that what was heard and included in the question was what the prospect actually said. Rather, they feed back what was understood by the prospect's remark. Examples of these questions are:

> "If I hear you correctly, you're saying that you need at least one copy for each secretary. (Is that so?)"
> "Are you speaking about peripherals or just the central processing unit?"

These questions may be successfully used to:

1. Express in different words what the prospect appears to have meant. This checks your understanding.
2. Invite the prospect to expand or clarify an idea previously expressed.
3. Help clarify ambiguities and broad generalizations.
4. Uncover what is on the prospect's mind.

Developmental Questions

Developmental questions ask the prospect for further details on specific subjects. In the case of a vague word or broad generalization, the developmental question will ask the prospect for more definition in the picture she is trying to convey. An example of a developmental question is:

> "We have quite a few homes that have room for family activities. Tell me, what does each member of your family like to do in or around the house?"

Notice that a fairly narrow topic—family-related activities—is open to a relatively unpredictable and long list of responses.

Developmental questions help in the following ways:

1. They ask for additional information in a more detailed form.
2. They encourage the prospect to expand and elaborate on the topic being pursued.

Directional Questions

As the word implies, directional questions steer the conversation into other directions. As a consultative guide, you are navigating your way through the prospect's problem to a destination which will reveal his needs. Directional questions are appropriate when you want to move from one topic area to another. Consider these examples:

"How does the office's inefficiency affect your job?"
"Are you aware of the affect of stress on job performance?"

Well-used directional questions help:

1. Direct the conversation and sales presentation through logical steps. ("As you see here, what is the third step?")
2. Provide a means of supplying necessary information to the prospect. ("From my viewpoint, I see three conditions for us to have a successful relationship: good quality products with service to back them up, fair and reasonable prices, and assurance that the delivery dates can be met. Do you agree?")
3. Give the prospect an additional way to participate in the information exchange. ("Many people in your industry have found that using this product has saved them money. How do you think the product will save you money?")

It should be noted, however, that directional questions, if not used carefully, can be perceived by prospects and customers as leading them to respond in a manner that they do not intend. Such a practice can then be perceived as manipulative and will give you very negative results in your sales efforts. Be sure then that your use of directional questions follows the guidelines given above.

Testing Questions

Testing questions allow you to determine where the prospect stands on an issue or if she is keeping up with you in the discussion. At the end of a sales call, testing questions give the prospect an opportunity to express any additional thoughts that may have arisen. Some examples of testing questions are:

"How do you think that might help you?"
"Does that sound reasonable?"
"What's our next step?"

Third Party Opinion Questions

Third party opinion questions combine a statement and a question. They question indirectly by relating to the prospect how others feel or react to a particular subject. They then ask the prospect to give his opinions and reactions concerning the same subject. Research indicates a greater acceptance of a statement if a well-known and respected person or corporation endorses that statement, so long as the mention is not perceived as name-dropping. Third party opinion questions, therefore, are used to:

1. Increase prospect confidence in the way problems or needs can be met by suggesting that others of name or note have solved a similar need in a similar way. ("*Consumer's Union* has rated this product as the best available for its price range. Is this the price range you're interested in?")
2. Increase prospect pride in a decision or perception. ("That's a good selection. Mr. Jay at Beech Manufacturing, the president of the national manufacturers' group, has used this product successfully to cut his downtime by 30 percent. Do you have similar downtime considerations?")

In conclusion, there are many questions that you can ask to elicit responses from your prospect. Questioning skills are most effective with the right questions used at the right time for the right purpose. Accomplishing this, of course, hinges on a solid understanding of the product or service being offered and of the conditions the prospect faces which make a product or service attractive, even necessary. Then questioning strategies are built on this foundation—strategies that lead to uncovering and solving prospect needs in the shortest, least-threatening manner.

SUMMARY

Questioning is an important communication skill which is rarely taught in schools and yet is an essential part of selling. By questioning appropriately, we can initiate and maintain conversation that will lead to successful sales relationships.

Skillful questioning helps us in two sales-related ways: 1) we can better identify the behavioral style of each of our prospects, and 2) we can uncover the prospects' needs by obtaining valid and useful information. This simplifies our job and helps increase sales because we will know how best to relate to and help our prospects.

There are several strategies involved in effectively using questioning in selling. They include: 1) asking permission to ask questions; 2) starting with open questions on broad topics and narrowing with subsequent questions; 3) building on previous responses; 4) keeping questions free of jargon and technical language; 5) keeping questions simple—one idea at a time; 6) keeping questions focused; 7) keeping questions nonthreatening; 8) explaining reasons for questions when touching on sensitive areas; 9) asking about general benefits sought; 10) allowing prospects to answer rather than forcing their answers; 11) maintaining a consultative atmosphere; and 12) phrasing questions so that they are easy to answer.

To use questioning effectively, we should understand the forms that questions can take and their strategic uses. Questions are basically of two forms: open-ended and closed-ended. Open-ended questions are phrased in a way that requires the prospect to answer narratively or with description. They increase the prospect's involvement in the conversation by asking for knowledge, feelings, or opinions, and allow her to reveal her personal behavioral style. In general, open-ended questions are preferred to closed-ended questions when getting to know someone. Closed-ended questions allow the prospect to answer quickly and to the point. Typically, they require a yes or no answer, offer a choice, or ask for a specific short response.

Questions can be used to effectively draw out the particular information that we seek from our prospects. The strategic use of the following types of questions help us fully diagnose the prospect's situation: clarifying questions, developmental questions, directional questions, testing questions, and third party opinion questions.

Clarifying questions are used to: 1) express in different words what the prospect appeared to have meant, which checks our understanding; 2) invite the prospect to expand or clarify an idea previously expressed; 3) help clarify ambiguities and broad generalizations; and 4) uncover what is on the prospect's mind.

Developmental questions are used to: 1) ask for additional information in a more detailed form; and 2) encourage the prospect to expand and elaborate on the topic being pursued.

Directional questions when well-used help to: 1) direct the conversation and sales presentation through logical steps; 2) provide a means of supplying necessary information to the prospect; and 3) give the prospect an additional way to participate in the information exchange. It should be remembered, however, that directional questions, if not used carefully, can be perceived by prospects and customers as leading them to respond in a manner that they do not intend. Such a practice can then be perceived as manipulative and can have a negative influence on our sales efforts.

Testing questions allow us to determine where prospects stand on an issue or if they are keeping up with us in our discussion with them. At the end of a sales call, testing questions give prospects an opportunity to express any additional thoughts which may have arisen.

Third party opinion questions combine a statement and a question. They question indirectly by relating to the prospect how others feel or react to a particular subject. They then ask the prospect to give his opinions and reactions concerning the same subject. This type of question 1) increases prospect confidence in the way problems or needs can be met by suggesting that others of name or note have solved a similar need in a similar way; and 2) increase prospect pride in a decision or perception.

Using questioning skills effectively depends not only on a thorough understanding of questions and their uses, but also on a solid understanding of the product or service being offered and of the conditions the prospect faces which make a product or service attractive or necessary.

Let's compare the art of questioning to the art of painting. When a painter begins a picture, he first uses a wide brush and broad strokes to paint the background. As the painting progresses, he uses smaller and smaller brushes until the fine details of the painting are finished.

Discussing a prospect's business is done in the same manner. You start off with broad, general questions. As the conversation continues you eventually narrow those questions to finely focused ones. Done in this way, you will not only uncover the specific needs of your prospect, but also you will see the big picture as it pertains to his business. This approach will build trust, develop the relationship, relax your customer and give you time to identify his behavioral style.

DISCUSSION QUESTIONS

1. Why is questioning an indispensable part of the sales process?

2. What are open-ended questions? When are they most appropriate to use?

3. What are closed-ended questions? When are they best used?

4. Give three reasons why questions should start general and slowly become more specific.

5. When dealing with certain behavioral styles, questions should be direct and to the point, rather than general. What are those styles and why?

6. Define and give examples of the following types of questions: clarifying; developmental; directional; testing; third party opinion.

7. Imagine a family member is shopping for a new car. Write five questions you could ask that would help her focus on the family's needs.

CHAPTER FIFTEEN

The Power of Listening

CHAPTER OBJECTIVES

1 Develop an awareness of the three levels of listening.

2 Discuss the skills that promote *active* listening.

3 Review listening habits to identify and eliminate those that can be irritating to others.

The National Society of Sales Training Executives conducted a survey among purchasing agents throughout the United States to determine what those agents perceived to be the major shortcomings of today's salespeople. The results of that survey indicated that in terms of selling skills, the number one shortcoming perceived was *the inability to listen effectively*.

If selling involves information exchange, then the exchange cannot be one way only. Listening is, by definition, part of the process. Prospects and customers provide information about problems in exchange for information about potential solutions. Not listening to them effectively has at least two detrimental results. First, solutions tend to be faulty or inappropriate. If you don't listen carefully to your prospect's problems, how can you effectively present solutions? Second, a prospect is likely to turn the tables and not listen to you. In contrast to these are the cooperation and understanding that arise through active listening. In fact, active listening is the master skill in tension management.

Unfortunately, however, listening skills are very often ignored or just forgotten in sales training. While businesses may be willing to spend the money to send executives to sales courses, they rarely direct personnel to courses designed to improve listening habits, even though effective salespeople spend the majority of their sales time listening. The reason for this may be due to the misconception, held by many, that listening is the same as hearing and everybody does it. This just is not so. Nichols and Stevens, in their book *Are You Listening?*, point out that a person listens with approximately 50 percent efficiency and that information loss is compounded as the message is passed from person to person. In other words, people may hear an entire message and still lose or distort its meaning. It is much like the childhood game of "Telephone," where children pass a message by whispering it from person to person around a room. The fun results when the last person to receive the message repeats it aloud and compares it with the original message. The two messages may not even be in the same language anymore. Without adequate listening skills, what is understood is not necessarily what has been said.

In fact, while the normal, untrained listener is likely to understand and retain only about 50 percent of a conversation, this relatively poor retention rate drops after only 48 hours to an even less impressive 25 percent. Think of the implications. Memory of a conversation which took place more than two days ago will always be incomplete and usually inaccurate. No wonder people can seldom agree about what has been discussed!

Effective listening is hard work. It not only involves considerable concentration, but it also causes noticeable physical changes. During active listening, heart action increases, body temperature rises slightly, and blood circulates faster. You can actually learn to sense these changes in yourself just by being aware that they occur when you are actively listening to someone.

The focus of this chapter is on the skills that you can use to actively listen to prospects and customers. It also presents ways to avoid misunderstanding or irritating your prospects and customers through ineffective listening habits. The net result of this chapter, if you implement its ideas and suggestions, is that your prospects and customers will feel understood, feel good about you, and sense that you listen to them. An additional benefit to active listening is that when you listen to someone, that person tends to work harder at listening to what you have to say, too.

LEVELS OF LISTENING

Whenever people listen, they are at one of three basic levels of listening or attentiveness. Each requires a particular depth of concentration on the part of the listener. As you move from the first to the second and on to the third level, the potential for understanding and clear communication increases.

Marginal Listening

PROSPECT: What I need, really, is a way to reduce the time lost due to equipment breakdowns.

SALESPERSON: Yeah, OK. Let's see, uh, the third feature of our product is the convenient sizes you can get.

Marginal listening, the first level, involves the least concentration and attention. The listener is easily distracted by his or her own thoughts and fleeting impressions. During periods of marginal listening, a listener will exhibit blank stares, nervous mannerisms, and gestures that tend to annoy the prospect and cause communication barriers. The salesperson toys with the message but doesn't really hear what is said. For this reason, marginal listening is the most dangerous of the three levels. There is enormous room for misunderstanding when a salesperson is not concentrating on what is being said. Moreover, the prospect cannot help but feel the lack of attention, which insults him and diminishes the trust bond. It may be funny in comedy when family members continually respond to each other with, "Yes, dear," regardless of what is said; in real life, however, it's not funny.

Marginal listening can occur in salespeople of all levels of experience. Salespeople who are unsure of themselves often concentrate so hard on what they will say next that they stop listening. On the other hand, the old pro who may have the attitude that he has heard it all before, wants the prospect to hurry up and finish so the "important" business can continue. The truly important information, however, lies in what the prospect is saying and the trust bond that is being developed.

Evaluative Listening

> PROSPECT: What I need, really, is a way to reduce the time lost due to equipment breakdowns.
>
> SALESPERSON: (defensively) We have tested our machines in the field, and they don't break down often.

Evaluative listening, the second level of listening, requires somewhat more concentration and attention to the speaker's words. At this level, you are actively trying to hear what the prospect is saying, but you aren't making an effort to understand his intent. Instead of accepting and trying to understand a prospect's message, the evaluative listener categorizes the overall argument (or statement) and concentrates on preparing a response. The speaker in our example obviously has had some experience with breakdowns. This indicates an area that the salesperson should pursue to discover the nature and type of breakdowns involved.

The evaluative listening phenomenon is a result of the tremendous speed at which a human can listen and think. While a person speaks at an average rate of 120 to 160 words in a minute, the mind is capable of listening and thinking up to four times that speed. It is then no wonder that evaluative listening is the level of listening that we employ the most in everyday conversations. It establishes a very difficult habit to break.

Of course, evaluative listening greatly speeds up sales conversations. The salesperson anticipates the prospect's words and is ready with a response almost as soon as the prospect finishes speaking. The concentration of the evaluative listener, however, is misplaced, and the results are potentially dangerous to the sales relationship (and, therefore, to the sale).

Most of the salesperson's attention is on a response, whether it is an agreement or a rebuttal. Therefore, an evaluative listener forms opinions about the prospect's words before the message is complete and risks inaccurately understanding the message being sent. Furthermore, the speed with which the mind works promotes distractions if attention is not fully channeled to listening. The opportunity then arises for highly emotional words to arouse emotion or distraction in the listener, who may then concentrate entirely on an examination and possible rebuttal of the prospect's emotional remarks. Stressful behavior often results, and the trust bond is lost.

Active Listening

> PROSPECT: What I need, really, is a way to reduce the time lost due to equipment breakdowns.
>
> SALESPERSON: Could you tell me what kind of breakdowns you have experienced and in what way you need to have them handled more effectively?

Active listening is the third and most effective level of listening. The active listener refrains from evaluating the prospect's message and tries to see the prospect's point of view. Attention is not only on words spoken, but also on the thoughts and feelings of the prospect. Listening in this way requires a suspension of personal thoughts and feelings in order to give attention solely to listening. It means figuratively "putting yourself into someone else's shoes." It also requires the listener to indicate to the prospect both verbally and nonverbally that what the prospect is saying is really being absorbed.

As mentioned, listening in this manner is tiring. It takes great concentration. However, if you really want to develop the skill of listening, you must expand this power of attention. Some exercises help to improve this concentration level.

One such exercise involves interpreting, in your own words, your understanding of the speaker's message before giving a reply. You might practice using clarifying questions here to check your understanding. Your interpretation of the speaker's message has to meet the intended meaning to the speaker's satisfaction before you are able to voice your own message. This exercise requires a patient, understanding friend. It will slow conversation to a snail's pace, but it will certainly point out the amount of misunderstanding that infiltrates conversations and how it breaks down communication.

For another exercise, find a tape recording of a speech or conversation. Then use a timer to mark (audibly) a three-minute interval (or five, if you're daring) during which you concentrate on the message as if the speaker were your prospect. When the timer goes off, stop the tape and note everything you can remember having been said—not just the main points. Play back the tape for any surprises, and practice until you eliminate these surprises.

GUIDELINES FOR ACTIVE LISTENING

Being a good listener involves applying rules of courtesy and common sense—and a bit more. Rudeness is rarely intended, but enthusiasm for a subject and personal desire to get things moving often override courtesy. Sometimes, too, salespeople are so content with their own point of view that they simply forget to listen to what the prospect is saying.

Good relations between you and your prospect develop over a period of time, and listening plays an important part in that successful development. By listening to a prospect's problems and needs, you will be taken into her confidence; and that confidence requires an understanding on the salesperson's part that translates into action. As you act to help the prospect solve dilemmas and to positively affect the prospect's goals, you solidify the relationship.

Listening is a skill that the following guidelines are designed to help develop. They are centered in four areas: A) listening to the prospect; B) reducing or eliminating noise; C) organizing the message you hear; D) checking your listening.

A. Listen to the Prospect

1. Let the Prospect Talk   When an important person speaks, you listen. In sales, the most important person is the prospect. Wait for the prospect to finish speaking, and then respond to what has been said. Interrupting a prospect's comments or rapid-firing statements during a pause in the prospect's statement is not only a possible irritation, it actually slows conversations, for the prospect must regain his train of thought after each interruption. The only interruption a person likes is applause. A prospect will accept this form of assent and approval with a smile. Even so, his train of thought may be lost. Nods and smiles of encouragement are accepted and helpful when not overdone.

Given the chance to speak uninterrupted, the prospect may reveal interesting facts and valuable clues to aid you in helping to solve problems or satisfy needs—facts and clues which an interruption may have cut short. As the prospect reveals interests, you can tailor your sales presentation to fit that prospect's unique needs. You can dispense with those aspects of the presentation which are inappropriate for *that* prospect at *that* point in time. This benefit is probably a great contributor to the success of salespeople who are careful listeners. They are better able to pick up and use clues to prospect needs that their evaluative listener counterparts miss.

By encouraging the prospect to talk and take an active part in the sales presentation, she may end up selling herself. She may solve her own problems by talking about them with you. She may even come up with some product benefits that you hadn't thought of before. In addition, being encouraged to talk allows the prospect personal autonomy and keeps her from feeling pressured into a sale. By building confidence and reducing tension, the trust bond between you and your prospect is strengthened. A prospect who sells herself is more likely to be fully committed and less likely to have buyer's remorse. She will likely become a staunch defender of your product, be open-minded with you in future dealings, and be an excellent source of referrals and a center of influence.

Besides helping you develop an effective trust bond with your prospect, allowing your prospect to talk can aid in keeping up the interest in the sales discussion. Outside distractions always threaten to draw attention away from a conversation. Thus, by encouraging the prospect to participate, you have a better chance of retaining a high level of attention. After all, the person doing the talking is always interested in what is being said. It isn't the lecturer who falls asleep!

2. *Listen for the Prospect's Psychological Needs* As you center your interest on the prospect, be aware not only of product needs but also of psychological needs. Product needs are often the only concern in a sales discussion, for both prospect and salesperson are ready to discuss them. Psychological needs, however, do exist, and the salesperson who can identify them will be better able to help the prospect in the way that he wishes to be helped. Psychological needs are subtle and more difficult to define, for they are *internal* with the prospect.

Through careful listening, you will hear reasons behind the selection of a product or service. Some prospects may react to the packaging; others to product prestige; others to efficiency capabilities or other performance features. The prospect buys not just a product or service, but a reflection and comment on the person behind the choice—the prospect. We all know the difference in the statements a Porsche and a Cadillac make about their drivers. Both products are in the same price range and both project wealth. One, however, also projects a casual, flamboyant personality and the other a conservative, steady personality.

Another kind of psychological need lies within the sales situation itself. It has to do with prospect–salesperson relationships. Some prospects thrive on reassurance; others have a strong need to be supported. All wish to feel understood. Prospects feel relieved when they find a salesperson who understands what they have to say about their problems. This is one of the reasons that they buy from a particular salesperson. Understanding the prospect is a cornerstone in the Non-Manipulative Selling philosophy.

Become sensitive to the prospect's use of personal pronouns ("I" and "we") because these signal certain areas and subjects which are of interest to that particular prospect. Make a conscious effort to focus on the prospect's needs by emphasizing pronouns like "you" and "your."

B. Reduce or Eliminate Noise

1. *Listen Attentively* Listen attentively and let your prospect *know* that you are. When possible, try to ensure an atmosphere or privacy that avoids external distractions. Face your prospect squarely with uncrossed arms and legs, and lean slightly forward in a relaxed posture. Establish good eye contact. Use affirmative head nods where appropriate, but not to the point of overdoing them. Let your entire body indicate that you are at ease and interested. Intermittently acknowledge your prospect's message with "uh-huh," "I see," "I understand," "yes," or other appropriate remarks.

Developmental and clarifying questions also indicate attention and invite your prospect to concur or correct and then to continue or elaborate. Phrases like, "Tell me more about that," "Can you give me an example?" or "Then what?" indicate strong interest in what your prospect is saying.

2. *Minimize the Impact of Distractions*   Train yourself to listen carefully to your prospect's words *despite* interruptions. Distractions may be external to the conversation, such as a ringing telephone or other office noise. Particularly insidious, however, is the effect of internal distractions on the sales environment. You cannot control the prospect's emotional thoughts, but you can do a lot to control your own. Most important, you need to be aware of your own internal noise. One kind of internal distraction is the effect that prospect idiosyncrasies have on you. If something about the prospect's speech or image or mannerisms is attracting your attention, deal with it by forcing yourself to concentrate still more on the message. Focus attention solely on the words, ideas, feelings, and cues to the underlying intent of your prospect.

Another kind of internal distraction is that caused by emotional deaf spots. Deaf spots are caused by words or actions that make your mind wander. Once you hear or see them, you no longer hear the speaker. Everyone is affected by this now and then. Try to discover your individual stumbling blocks and prepare to deal with them. When prospect idiosyncrasies bother you, plan ways to involve yourself more actively with getting the message whenever you feel your concentration slipping.

Finally, try to remain relaxed and removed from extreme emotions. Emotions of any kind hinder listening. Remember the last time you laughed so hard that you had to struggle to get back on the track? Anger is particularly detrimental to communication. When a word or idea triggers anger, logical thinking is lost. A good listener puts aside strong emotions as best he can in order to be open to the entire message.

C. Organize the Message You Hear

Organizing the message you hear involves true listening. (This does not imply evaluative listening, through which the listener selects the content.)

1. *Take Notes*   Do not trust memory when facts and data are important; take notes, but make sure that you ask your prospect's permission before doing so. Use phrases and key words to indicate the pros and cons of arguments rather than writing complete thoughts. All you need is reminder phrases to jog your memory. Read and review your notes as you have time to be sure that they make sense to you. Always be sure to review the notes again before subsequent contacts with your prospects.

2. *Listen to Everything*   Your role is that of a sounding board for your prospects. Try to understand your prospects without making value judgments. Understand *with* them, not about them. This means that you take a sincere interest in everything your prospect has to say. Do not listen only for what you want to hear. What the prospect is interested in saying gives you clues to his or her motivations, needs, and feelings. As you do this, *be selective* in terms of identifying specifically what your prospect is telling you that can assist you in meeting his or her needs and solving his or her problems.

3. Identify Main and Supportive Points in the Prospect's Message Listen for your prospect's main ideas. As you do this, also identify those points made in support of the ideas. Specific facts and examples are important only as they relate to the main themes, and they can cause misunderstandings if taken out of context. Take advantage of pauses to review portions of the discussion that have already been covered (using good questions). *Ask yourself,* "What is his point?" or "What is this getting at?" If you guess correctly, your understanding and retention increase. If you are incorrect, you will have time to correct your outline and be alert to judgments or assumptions that you may have subconsciously and incorrectly made.

4. Support and Reinforce Key Prospect Statements Anytime your prospect makes a statement that highlights a key need or is directly or indirectly supportive of your proposal, reinforce it with a clarifying question.

5. Listen Between the Words Unless listening is coupled with other skills, it can mislead you. What is said may not be what the prospect means. He may say he likes a product, but there is something wrong; you sense that he doesn't like it all that much. How do you know? Sixth sense? We prefer to call it "listening between the words." Learning to read those subtle (sometimes not-so-subtle) signals that speak more honestly than words saves many a salesperson from improper sales advice.

Each individual has a unique way of nonverbally expressing mood and attitude changes, and a good listener will strive to understand all of these cues. The communication of these unspoken thoughts and feelings can be recognized (when incongruent with the verbal) through eye contact where changes of mood are expressed. Watch, too, for changes in the sound of the voice, speaking pace, breathing, facial expressions, posture, body movement, and many more observable aspects of your prospects.

In trying to interpret nonverbal cues, listen for *total* meaning. In other words, the verbal meaning is not enough; visual and vocal cues provide powerful sources of information. Your ears allow you to hear the content, but both your ears and eyes aid you in interpreting and understanding the feelings and actions underlying the prospect's actual words. Use all of your senses. The chapters on vocal quality, image, and body language give additional ways for you to fully listen to the prospect.

D. Check Your Listening

Here's a chance to further reduce noise. The following questions and concerns, if applied to each sales situation, will help you check the accuracy and completeness of the communication.

- Do you understand the speaker's words in the speaker's way?
- Do you restate the ideas accurately? For this, use clarifying questions. As you do this, you will also demonstrate to your prospect that you are truly interested in understanding the message. Use phrases such as, "Do I hear you saying . . . ?" "I understand your major concern to be. . . . " or ". . . Is that correct?"
- Can you pinpoint the speaker's underlying assumptions and compare them with your own?
- Can you determine the speaker's information source? Is it data, experience, observation, or opinion?
- Does the message make sense when taken in context with the entire conversation? If not, can you explain the inconsistency?

Consistently check to see if your prospect wants to comment on, or respond to, anything you have said. This request for feedback allows the prospect a chance to clarify or expand ideas of which you may otherwise remain ignorant. It also reduces the tension that arises when a prospect feels his or her message is not truly understood, despite the apparent satisfaction of the salesperson.

IRRITATING LISTENING HABITS

The preceding listening strategies are meant to help you foster a free-flowing, open communication climate with your prospects. On the other hand, there are listening habits which irritate prospects and tend to erect barriers to effective information exchange. Before discussing the irritating listening habits, let's review the guidelines for good listening:

Review of Guidelines to Good Listening

A. Listen to the prospect.
  1. Let the prospect talk.
  2. Listen for the prospect's psychological needs.
B. Reduce or eliminate noise.
  1. Listen attentively.
  2. Minimize the impact of distractions.
C. Organize the message you hear.
  1. Take notes.
  2. Listen to everything.
  3. Identify main and supportive points in the prospect's message.
  4. Support and reinforce any of your prospect's statements that lead toward the solution of the identified problem.
  5. Listen between the words.
D. Check your listening.

The following list presents nearly two dozen of the most commonly irritating listening habits. As you review the list, you may wish to identify which of the guidelines for good listening is being betrayed. As you read the list, also try to honestly identify any habits that you may have. If you find any (and you probably will), work quickly on overcoming them in order to fully implement your active listening habits. For your benefit, for comparison, the letter and number of the good listening habit appears after the bad habit.

1. He does all the talking; I go in with a problem and never get a chance to open my mouth. (A.1, A.2)
2. He interrupts me when I talk. (A.1, A.2)
3. He never looks at me when I talk; I'm not sure that he's listening. (B.1)
4. He continually toys with a pencil, paper, or some other item while I'm talking; I wonder if he's listening. (B.1, B.2)
5. His poker face keeps me guessing whether he understands me or is even listening to me. (C.4, D)
6. He never smiles; I'm afraid to talk to him. (C.4)
7. He changes what I say by putting words into my mouth that I didn't mean. (C.1, C.3, C.4)
8. He puts me on the defensive when I ask a question. (C.2, D)
9. Occasionally he asks a question about what I have just told him that shows he wasn't listening. (B.1, B.2)
10. He argues with everything I say—even before I have a chance to finish my case. (A.1)
11. Everything I say reminds him of an experience he has either had or heard of. I get frustrated when he interrupts, saying, "That reminds me. . . ." (A.1, B.1, C.4)
12. When I am talking, he finishes sentences for me. (A.1)
13. He acts as if he is just waiting for me to finish so he can interject something of his own. (A.1, B.1)
14. All the time I'm talking, he's looking out the window. (B.1)
15. He looks at me as if he is trying to stare me down. (C.4)
16. He looks as if he's appraising me. I begin to wonder if I have a smudge on my face, or tear in my coat, or something. (B.2, C.4)
17. He looks as if he is constantly thinking "No" or questioning the truthfulness or value of what I'm saying. (B.1, C.4)
18. He overdoes showing he's following what I'm saying . . . too many nods of his head, or "mm-hms" and "uh-huhs." (C.3, C.5)
19. He sits too close to me. (B.2)
20. He frequently looks at his watch or the clock while I am talking. (B.1, B.2)
21. He is completely withdrawn and distant when I'm talking. (B.1, C.4)
22. He acts as if he is doing me a favor in seeing me. (B.2, C.1, C.4)
23. He acts as if he knows it all, frequently relating incidents in which he was the hero. (A.1, B.1)

SUMMARY

The results of a survey of purchasing agents across the United States conducted by the National Society of Sales Training Executives indicated that the number one shortcoming they perceived of salespeople in terms of selling skills was *listening.* Learning to listen effectively pays off in stronger trust bonds and increased sales. Prospects and customers feel relieved to find salespeople who actively listen and understand what they have to say about their problems and needs. Once that occurs, they generally reciprocate by listening to the salesperson and by trying to understand why a particular product or service will meet their needs. That leads to an open, honest information exchange between prospect and salesperson. Isn't that what selling is all about?

For the process of communication to be truly successful, an exchange of information must take place: prospects and customers provide information about problems that require solutions in exchange for salespeople providing information on potential solutions. In such a communication process, active listening is absolutely necessary. It tends to encourage understanding and cooperation in a sales relationship. Thus it is a master skill and an important part of tension management.

There are three levels of listening, each requiring a different depth of concentration from the listener. As you progress from one level to the next, understanding and clear communication increases.

The first level of listening is *marginal* listening, which involves the least concentration and attention of the three levels. The listener is easily distracted by his or her own thoughts and fleeting impressions, leading to a visible lack of attention given to the prospect and great potential for considerable misunderstanding of the prospect's message. Such visible lack of attention insults the prospect and diminishes any trust bond that may have been building up to that point.

The second level of listening is *evaluative* listening, which requires more concentration and attention to the speaker's words. The salesperson who is an evaluative listener, however, although trying to actively listen to the prospect's message, is not hearing the intent of the message. Instead, he is categorizing what he hears and anticipating what the prospect will say next. He then prepares his responses while the prospect is speaking and is ready to provide those responses the moment the prospect finishes speaking. A salesperson communicating in this way forms opinions about the prospect's words before the message is complete and runs a high risk of inaccurately understanding the prospect's intent.

Active listening is the third and most effective level of listening. The active listener refrains from evaluating the prospect's message and tries to see the prospect's point of view. Attention is not only on the words spoken, but also on the thoughts and feelings of the prospect. Listening in this way requires suspending personal thoughts and feelings in order to give one's entire attention to listening.

There are four guidelines designed to develop the skill of active listening. They are: 1) listen not only to what the speaker says but also to his psychological needs as well; 2) reduce or eliminate noise by listening attentively and minimizing the impact of distractions; 3) organize the message you hear by taking notes, listening to all that your prospect has to say, identifying main and supportive points in the prospect's message, supporting key prospect statements, and listening between the words; and 4) check your listening by requesting and giving feedback.

Learning to listen effectively pays off in open, honest information exchanges with prospects and customers, thus building long-lasting sales relationships and increasing sales.

DISCUSSION
QUESTIONS

1. Describe the three levels of listening.
2. The next time you talk to a friend, make a mental note of your level of listening.
3. Why does the most effective level of listening require the most effort?
4. What do you listen for besides a person's words when you are actively listening?
5. How can you reduce and eliminate noise?
6. How can you organize and remember what the other person is saying during a conversation?
7. What should you do to check your listening?
8. What should you do if your prospect is thinking about something else and not listening to you?

CHAPTER SIXTEEN

Feedback

CHAPTER OBJECTIVES	**1** Identify the feedback skills necessary for effective communication.
	2 Understand the use of feedback skills in clarifying communication.
	3 Understand the use of feedback in reading and responding to a customer's reactions to the salesperson and his message.

Have you ever completed a task or handed in a report, felt really pleased with it, and received nothing, no comments? Did you feel tension rise within you? Didn't you wish someone would say something—anything? A smile would have helped! Even some criticism would have been welcome. Those feelings stemmed from a desire for feedback.

Most of us use feedback automatically. When you lean forward to show interest, when you frown, when you say, "Let's see if I understand," whenever you audibly or physically signal a reaction to what someone says or does, you are using feedback. Good communication depends on it.

Feedback in the sales process is often misused and misunderstood. Salespeople have been known to frustrate customers by constant interruption to assure proper communication. Others have sounded as if they were criticizing the customer instead of reacting to the customer's statements. Others have forgotten the power of body language in the feedback process and have allowed unpleasant, communication-retarding signs of boredom or dislike to feed back to the customer. These problems can be overcome and proper feedback techniques learned. Properly used, feedback simply and effectively increases the accuracy of the communication between people and does a great deal to reduce tension and build trust.

This chapter explores the feedback skills that you can use to clarify the communication between you and your customers and explains how to read and respond to customers' reactions to you and your message.

TYPES OF FEEDBACK

There are two types of feedback: verbal and nonverbal. Each serves a specific purpose in the communication process.

Verbal Feedback

As the name implies, verbal feedback involves questions, statements, descriptions, and other spoken comments where the meanings of the words carry the feedback message. Through verbal feedback, you typically ask for clarification of feelings or thoughts. You may also feed back viewpoints or interpretations of your own to make sure that your customer's understanding of your key points is on target.

Verbal feedback is also useful for checking on the pace and priorities established. For example, this question might be helpful to check on how you are doing when with a prospect: "My manager tells me that I sometimes get carried away with my enthusiasm and move along too quickly. Would it be more helpful to you if I covered these topics more slowly?" This not only shows interest in the customer's desires and needs, but it also lets the customer understand you better and encourages him to ask you to slow down or speed up the presentation. You could ask, "Would you like me to get right into the details of the proposal, or do you have some other questions first?" This again gives the customer a feeling that his needs are important. It also lets you sense more about him and the priorities that he has. Through the resulting feedback from the customer, you can then adjust your pace and priorities to meet his needs, thus encouraging an atmosphere of trust.

Feedback lets you explain to someone else how you are interpreting not only what he is saying but also how it is coming across to you—how you are reading the nonverbal feedback you are getting. For some examples:

"Shall we explore that issue some more?" (This might be said on seeing increased customer interest.)

"How do you think that will work?" (This might be said on seeing either increased or decreased interest. It attempts to get issues into the open.)

"You look puzzled. Can I explain something a little better?"

Feedback helps prevent errors in understanding. The variety of meanings for even simple words may prompt a salesperson to assume that he understands the meaning of his customer's communication when, in fact, he may have misinterpreted it. Then misunderstandings are followed by breakdowns in the buyer–seller communication process, decreased trust, and lost sales.

The importance of feedback can be demonstrated with an example that commonly occurs in sales. There are many ways to interpret someone's words. Imagine a salesperson who has just given a good presentation. The customer turns to the salesperson and says, "Gee, I really like it, but it's just too expensive."

What does the customer mean by "it's too expensive"? The phrase "it's too expensive" can have several meanings: 1) "It's more money than I have; I have $10 and it costs $15." 2) "It costs $15. I have $15, but I don't think it is worth $15." 3) "I have $15. I agree it is worth $15, but not to me. It's more than I need. Have you got a less expensive one?"

Feedback eliminates the guesswork. If you encountered the problem above, you would ask your customer what he meant by "it's too expensive." Then you would be able to deal with his thoughts in a precise manner.

Using feedback during the entire process of communication ensures that both you and your customer are speaking the same language. For example:

1. During your presentation, describe to your customer the relevant aspects of the image in your mind just to make sure that both of you are talking about the same thing. ("I plan to show you just how this product can answer your need for _____, _____, and _____.")

2. If the customer does not feed back your message, it is wise for you to ask him or her to do so. ("What do you see or think of when I say that this service is 'people-oriented'?")

3. Feed back your *interpretation* of what your customer said rather than feeding back the customer's exact words or a simple paraphrase of his or her words. (For a customer who wants a continuous training and upgrading package: "If I hear you right, you would like to be kept informed of any changes in the system and have us train you whenever the change warrants it.")

Verbal feedback is informational in nature and typically begins with statements such as:

"Let me be sure I understand your major concerns."
"Let me see if I can summarize the key points we've discussed."
"I hear you saying. . . . "

It typically ends with questions such as:

"Did I understand you properly?"
"Was I on target with what you meant?"
"Were those your major concerns?"

This allows you to clarify understanding and meaning quickly and accurately.

Nonverbal Feedback

Remember when the word "vibes" was in vogue? "Good vibes" meant something made a person feel good. Well, both good and bad vibes are a result of nonverbal feedback. Without saying a word, people can communicate the full range of attitudes and feelings: openness, enthusiasm, confidence, nervousness, indifference, defensiveness.

The skilled salesperson uses nonverbal feedback for the same overriding goal as verbal feedback—to continue the customer–seller interaction in a positive atmosphere of trust and credibility. The sensitive, perceptive salesperson takes cues from the customer's nonverbal feedback to structure the content and direction of his own message. He also sends appropriate nonverbal messages to his customer to enhance and clarify his verbal statements.

Nonverbal communication skills such as your vocal quality and your image help convey your attitudes and ideas. Even the way in which you move, stand, and sit sends messages to observers. When these messages are reactions to something another person is saying and doing, and when the other person can read them, you have given nonverbal feedback. Some of your customers may have been trained in reading some of the more obvious of your nonverbal feedback statements. Very few will be trained to pick up the more subtle cues. Most will merely react to what you feed back without being aware of why they are picking up the signals you are giving them—and only if your signals are loud and clear. However, if your nonverbal feedback is under your conscious control, and if you choose to look interested and to both encourage positive and discourage negative directions, you will begin to see just how helpful nonverbal feedback can be in clearing away communication barriers.

EFFECTIVE USES OF FEEDBACK

If you took a few moments and really thought about it, you could probably recall numerous times that you could have smoothed over some problems in communication simply by using feedback. Effective communication between two people is not easy. You really have to practice to make it work. The proper use of questioning skills helps. Utilizing active listening helps. Sensitivity to nonverbal behavior helps. But without feedback, all of these skills are for naught. Through effective use of feedback skills, you can create a good communication environment for you and your prospect.

The following guidelines will help you use your feedback skills effectively:

1. Give and Get Definitions

Interpretation of words or phrases may vary from person to person, group to group, region to region, or society to society. The words we use in everyday conversations almost inevitably have multiple meanings. According to Dr. William V. Haney in his book *Communication and Organizational Behavior,* the 500 most commonly used words in our language have more than 14,000 dictionary definitions. He goes on to give an example using the word "fast":

> A person is considered "fast" when he can run rather quickly. However, when

one is tied down and cannot move at all, he is also considered "fast." "Fast" also relates to periods of noneating, a ship's mooring line, a racetrack in good running condition, and a person who hangs around with the "wrong" crowd of people. In addition, photographic film is "fast" when it is sensitive to light. On the other hand, bacteria are "fast" when they are insensitive to antiseptics.

Because of the variety of meanings of even simple words, salespeople who assume that they understand the true meaning of customers' communications, in fact, may not. This leads to subsequent misunderstandings, breakdowns in the communication process, and decreased trust. During the process of questioning and listening, use feedback. Give and get definitions.

2. Do Not Make Assumptions

Making assumptions invariably gets you into trouble. During interpersonal communication, it is highly dangerous to make the assumption that the other person either thinks or feels as you do at that moment. The other person may have a frame of reference that is totally different from your own. He reacts and perceives according to what he knows and believes to be true, and that may be very different from your reactions, perceptions, and beliefs. Do not assume anything in communication. If you do, you stand a very good chance of being incorrect. Do not assume that you and the other person are talking about the same thing or that the words and phrases you are both using are automatically being understood. People who make assumptions commonly use this classic phrase: "I know exactly what you mean." People usually use that statement without even using feedback skills to determine exactly what the other person does mean. By using more feedback and fewer assumptions, you will be happier and more accurate in your communication.

3. Ask Questions

Questions have many uses. We have discussed several of these in the chapter on questioning. Remember to use questions to test for feedback. A good rule of thumb is: "When in doubt, check it out." One of the best ways to check it out is to clarify meaning through the effective use of your questioning skills.

4. Speak the Same Language

Abstain from using words that can easily be misinterpreted or mistranslated, especially technical terms and company jargon. These terms, which are so familiar to you, may be totally foreign to the people with whom you talk. Simplify your language and your technical terms so that your prospects and customers can understand you, even though you might think that they do or should know what the terms mean.

5. Be Constantly Tuned In

Learn to constantly be on the lookout for and recognize those nonverbal signals that indicate that your line of approach is causing your customer to lose interest. If you are alert, your customer will give you this information through diminished interest and a lowered level of responding. With sensitivity and perception, you can react to this feedback by changing your pace or topic, by questioning, or by doing whatever is needed in order to recapture the customer's attention and interests.

On the other hand, also be sensitive to customer feedback that communicates that it is appropriate for you to move on in the sales process.

6. Use Feedback Constantly Throughout the Sales Process

Feedback is not a tool that is used sporadically during a meeting with a prospect or a customer. It is used throughout the sales process by the salesperson and his prospect or customer. Clarification is frequently needed in response to statements or other cues made by the prospect. For example: "I'm not sure that this is exactly what we are looking for, but it's close." Such a statement made by a prospect should not pass but should be clarified by the salesperson: "What is it that you are looking for exactly?"

7. Use Feedback to Bridge Phases of the Sales Process

Besides using feedback throughout each phase of the sales call, also use your feedback skills to connect one phase of the sales process with the next. For example, after gathering information from the prospect but before proposing possible solutions, a salesperson may say, "We have talked about a lot of things here in terms of what you are looking for. Let me make sure that I understand what is important to you and which things are more important than others." The salesperson then summarizes what he understood when he gathered information and, in so doing, he receives valuable clarification from the prospect that will help him be more accurate in the proposing phase.

Feedback bridges should also occur between the phases of proposing and confirming, and confirming and assuring. Between proposing and confirming, a salesperson would provide a benefit summary, thus clarifying what he has proposed and ensuring his prospect's complete understanding and acceptance. Between confirming and assuring, there is the clarification of the tasks and responsibilities of each party, both the buyer and the seller. There is also the clarification of success criteria as well. For example, a salesperson may say, "Mr. Adams, imagine in six months we are talking about this product that you purchased from me, about which you are very excited. What would have happened in those six months that would prompt you to be that excited? What are the evaluation criteria that you will use to determine the product's success?

The proper and effective use of feedback skills maintains and enhances our communication with prospects and customers. When properly used, feedback can improve your presentations, reduce tension, and create a sense of trust and credibility which leads to a higher probability for consummating sales.

SUMMARY

Good communication depends on feedback, the audible or physical signals or reactions to what someone says or does. Properly used, feedback simply and effectively increases the accuracy of the communication between people and does a great deal to reduce tension and build trust in the business relationship.

There are two types of feedback: verbal and nonverbal. Each serves a specific purpose in the communication process.

Verbal feedback, as its name implies, involves questions, statements, description, and other *spoken* comments where the meanings of the words carry the feedback message. Through verbal feedback, you may: 1) typically ask for clarification of feelings or thoughts; 2) respond with viewpoints or interpretations of your own to make sure that your customer's understanding of your key points is on target; and 3) check on the pace and priorities preferred by your customer.

Verbal feedback lets you explain to someone else how you are interpreting not only what she is saying but also how it is coming across to you—how you are reading the *non*verbal feedback that you are receiving from them. Verbal feedback thus helps to prevent errors in understanding and should be used throughout the entire communication process to ensure that both you and your customer are speaking the same language.

Nonverbal feedback is the communication of attitudes and feelings without saying a word. The skilled salesperson uses nonverbal feedback for the same overriding goal as verbal feedback—to continue the customer–seller interaction in a positive atmosphere of trust and credibility.

Effective communication between two people is difficult. Properly using your questioning skills, actively listening to your customer, and being sensitive to nonverbal behaviors help. But without feedback these skills will not make your communication completely effective.

There are several guidelines to help us use feedback skills effectively: 1) Give and get definitions to ensure that we and our prospects are truly understanding what we are communicating. 2) Do not assume anything in communication—clarify to ensure correct understanding. 3) Ask questions to clarify meaning if in doubt. 4) Speak the same language by not using words and jargon that can easily be misinterpreted or mistranslated. 5) Be constantly tuned in to nonverbal signals that your customers are giving. 6) Use feedback constantly throughout the sales process by using it *within* each phase of the sale as well as using it as a bridge *between* each phase of the sale.

The proper and effective use of feedback skills maintains and enhances our communication with prospects and customers. When properly used, feedback can improve your presentations, reduce tension, and create a sense of trust and credibility which leads to a higher probability for consummating sales.

DISCUSSION
QUESTIONS

1. Define verbal and nonverbal feedback.
2. What role do they play in communication?
3. What would happen if people did not give and receive feedback during a conversation?
4. What are some ways to ask for feedback from a customer?
5. What are some ways to clarify your understanding of what someone just said?
6. Listen to conversation at home and with your friends. Make a mental note every time you hear a misunderstanding that could have been avoided with the use of feedback.

CHAPTER SEVENTEEN

Body Language

CHAPTER OBJECTIVES	1 Introduce and discuss the concept of body language and the necessity of its mastery for successful professional sales.
	2 Understand how to interpret messages communicated through body language—through clusters of gestures.
	3 Recognize our body language's influence on our sales message and its reception by our prospects and customers.

> He that has eyes to see and ears to hear may convince himself that no mortal may keep a secret. If his lips are silent, he chatters with his fingertips; betrayal oozes out of him at every pore.
>
> SIGMUND FREUD

As Freud's remark emphasizes, people express much about what they think or feel even when they remain silent. This is their *body language,* those physical gestures and positionings which reveal thoughts and attitudes.

Body language is certainly not a new phenomenon. Before people developed language as a tool of communication, they used body language to make their needs and desires known to other people. Also known as *kinesics,* body language describes human interaction exclusive of written and spoken words. This broad definition encompasses everything from the most subtle raising of an eyebrow to the precise movements of the sophisticated sign language used by the deaf.

There are some nonverbal gestures that have universal symbolism. The position at the head of the table has long been reserved for the leader of the group. In recent times, this position of honor has also been extended to the host of a gathering. It is a custom that was honored even before the time of King

Arthur, when the Round Table was developed as an attempt to administer democracy by eliminating the appearance of having one leader. Another universal gesture is raising the hands above the head, which has long symbolized surrender and submission.

Some gestures are even more expressive than words. Conjure up the image of a person slapping his forehead, perhaps accompanied by an audible groan. Don't you already know that he has just remembered something he should have done? Implicit in his gesture is an apology to those around him for his oversight. Other well-known gestures are saluting, tipping one's hat, shaking hands, shrugging shoulders, waving good-bye, forming an "O" with the thumb and forefinger, and blowing a kiss. All are forms of body language; all communicate something to those present.

Body language communication is rapid. Research shows that even when exposure to a situation is reduced to $\frac{1}{24}$ of a second (the time it takes to show a single frame of film), people often grasp the meaning. At $\frac{1}{8}$ of a second, comprehension goes up dramatically and rises somewhat more up to a little beyond one second. Therefore, a body position or gesture that lasts just over one second will generally be understood by a person sensitive to body language.

Ability to understand body language is apparently not related to IQ, ability to take tests, or other signs of academic achievement. Practice is the only thing that tends to improve how well people understand its messages. People who were tested for body language comprehension generally scored higher on second and succeeding tests.

Reading body language gives you a powerful communication tool. Through body language, people express their conscious and subconscious emotions, desires, and attitudes. Since body language is stimulated by a subconscious need to express feelings, it is often more reliable than verbal communication. It may even contradict verbal expressions. Thus body language as an outlet for feelings can function as a lie detector to aid a watchful listener in interpreting words. If you are observant, you can read through body language a prospect's current level of sincerity and commitment and have an additional tool for testing the progress of the sales relationship and perhaps moving that relationship in a more positive, trust-building direction.

In addition to increasing your understanding of your prospect, the study of body language can also help improve the prospect's understanding of you. Body language is an important part of having your prospect perceive the sales message the way you wish it to be perceived. The better able you are to transmit your message so that your prospect receives it as you intended, the more effective your sales presentation will be.

This chapter explores the skill of dealing with and using body language. It is time-tested and presented to give you an overview of this extensively studied method of communication. We discuss the implications of individual, often-observed gestures. These are insufficient communication, however, unless considered as *clusters* of gestures which *together* state a message.

INTERPRETING BODY LANGUAGE GESTURES

Body language involves the interpretation of many kinds of body gestures. Major areas of the body which communicate messages are the face (especially the eyes and lips), hands, arms, and legs; in addition, body posture and walk are significant communicators. Following are some of the more simple gestures that, once learned, will aid you in interpreting the feelings and attitudes that your prospect or customer may not communicate to you verbally but will reveal through his body language.

The Face

The face is one of the most obvious and expressive manifestations of a person's attitudes and feelings. Facial expressions reveal the emotions behind words and serve as important feedback to the things you are saying. Often facial expressions can speak for themselves, independent of words. This happens, for example, when someone drops his mouth open in awe or when a person's eyes widen in fear. The face is so expressive, in fact, that we become uncomfortable when meeting with a person who remains expressionless. Just consider an individual with a poker face.

The Eyes   Think of the terms "shifty eyes," "beady eyes," "a look of steel," or "windows of the soul." All of these refer to the eyes and are just a sampling of the awareness that people have for the communication coming from the eyes.

What people do with their eyes is a powerful determinant of how comfortable they feel being with us. Someone who "looks you up and down" would make you feel physically threatened. Someone whose eyes dart around the room quickly would make you suspicious and tense. In the opposite extreme, eye contact that is held too long would also make you feel uncomfortable.

When people are comfortable with others, they tend to maintain good eye contact with them. The comfortable person has a tendency to look you straight in the eyes when speaking. Prospects and customers tend to avoid eye contact with you when an uncomfortable question is asked. Monitor eye contact during your conversations and pursue topics that increase it for that will build trust. If you can, steer clear of topics that decrease eye contact, for those topics increase tension and reduce trust.

We talk about an increase and a decrease of eye contact. Be sure to note what is habitual for the particular person with whom you are meeting. People have differing habitual tendencies and the cue lies in a movement away from the habitual eye contact, not in some predetermined amount of contact.

People also tend to have more eye contact when they listen than when they talk. A prospect's eye contact with you usually indicates interest in what you are saying or doing.

The Mouth   A person's mouth can be an excellent indicator of his attitude and feelings. Have you ever talked to someone who was so boring that you couldn't help but yawn?

Smiles are also good feedback, whether they are wide grins accompanied by laughter, usually indicating approval and enjoyment, or fixed and phony, indicating boredom or condescension. However, two kinds of smiles have been noted as danger signals to meaningful communication. The "simple smile" is a slight turning up of the corners of the lips without exposing any teeth. This indicates a probable lack of interest and a mind preoccupied with things other than the ongoing conversation. In the "oblong smile," the lips are drawn fully back from both the upper and lower teeth, forming an oblong shape. The smile appears to lack depth or real involvement in any of the ongoing feelings. The prospect is probably unappreciative of the remarks or activity. Generally, unlike the simple smile, some eye contact exists.

Frowns, which are frequently accompanied by a contorted mouth, indicate that someone disagrees or is unhappy with a situation.

The Body

The Hands and Arms   It is very difficult for most people to keep their hands still while talking or listening; thus a person's hand and arm movements communicate a great deal. Because there are so many hand and arm movements, the best approach is to list them:

HAND TO FACE OR HEAD

- Rubbing a portion of the face or head may signal doubt, disinterest, or frustration.
- Rubbing the eyes or ears with a hand or finger may indicate doubt or lack of interest.
- Rubbing the back of the neck may indicate frustration or tension.
- Rubbing or touching the nose usually indicates a strong feeling of dislike. (It is almost as much of a no signal as when the prospect uses the word. While a person may rub his nose because it itches, keep in mind that there is a difference in mannerism. The gesture in question here is a light rubbing, subtle and often accompanied with squirming in the chair, twisting the body into a silhouette position, physically withdrawing.)
- Stroking the chin with the fingers shows thoughtfulness, consideration, careful study, and analysis. This may also be accompanied by a slight squinting of the eyes, as if trying to see an answer to the problem in the distance.
- Pinching the bridge of the nose while closing the eyes usually means either great concern or a splitting headache, which is also worth your note and concern.
- Leaning back and supporting the head with both hands shows a feeling of superiority, authority, and being at ease.
- Bringing a hand to the mouth can mean shock or astonishment.
- Tugging at one ear may mean the customer wants to interrupt.
- Placing one's head in an open hand and dropping the chin and eyes often conveys boredom.

• Bringing the hand to the cheek with the fingers bent and the index finger at the temple usually indicates an interest and attentiveness, especially when your prospect leans forward in his chair (or leans forward from a standing position) toward you.

• Resting the chin in the palm of the hand with the forefinger placed near the nose and the other fingers bent across the chin and below the mouth may express a critical evaluation. When this is associated with the body drawn back and positioned away from you, the prospect's thoughts are usually critical, cynical, or in some other way negative toward what you are doing or saying.

HAND TO HAND

• Clenching the hands tightly usually indicates that the prospect is being over-powered and suspects you of trying to impose an attitude. It may also convey strong disagreement. The prospect will usually be tense and a difficult person with whom to relate.

• Tightly clasped hands with stares, a side-turned body, and crossed legs may indicate that you have gone too far.

• Wringing the hands usually indicates extreme anxiety.

• Rubbing the palms of the hands gently usually shows expectation and delight. (This is not to be confused with wringing the hands. Rather, this gesture is a soft rubbing of the hands by which the customer conveys interest and involved anticipation of what you are going to say or do.)

• Joining fingertips in an upward, prayer-like manner (steepling) indicates self-confidence.

• Joining the hands behind the back while standing indicates a superior or supervisory attitude.

CROSSED ARMS

• Crossed arms tend to indicate protection and defensiveness. They seemingly act as a protective guard against an anticipated attack or a fixed position from which the prospect would rather not move. As long as your prospect is in this position, it is unlikely that you will get full agreement to what you are saying or doing.

The Legs

• Crossed legs can mean disagreement. Customers who tightly cross their legs are not "open" to you and your presentation and may be telling you that they disagree with what you are saying or doing. Consistently interpreting crossed legs as meaning resistance, however, can sometimes be an error. Most people naturally sit with their legs crossed, so use caution in assuming that crossed legs always mean the person is listening with "deaf ears."

Posture (Sitting and Standing) A person's attitude is often reflected in how they hold themselves:

• Leaning forward usually indicates interest.
• Leaning back may mean a person is aloof, defensive, superior, or threatened.
• Standing erect may mean a person feels good about himself.

- Standing with a slouch—a drooping back—may reflect a drooping self-image.
- Sitting on the edge of the chair, leaning forward, shows interest and involvement.
- Sitting with a leg over the chair or a foot on the desk shows an irreverence toward the other person. This may include hostility or rebellious indifference.
- Sitting erect with a stiff back and with feet planted securely on the floor while staring straight ahead may mean that the prospect is not paying attention; his or her mind is far away. It is often an attempt to look interested without being involved.
- Sitting with legs crossed and the crossed leg bouncing may mean the customer is nervous or bored.

Handling Accessories   The way a customer handles objects such as pens, pads, watches, eyeglasses, and cigarettes also serves as body language. The scope and aims of this book curtail our going into the long list of meanings inherent in a full exploration of gestures with accessories. However, to give you a small idea of the enormous breadth involved in reading gestures involving accessories, we present only one, that of handling eyeglasses. Many (not all) of the gestures involved with eyeglasses extend to other accessories and things within reach, such as pens and pencils.

- Dropping the glasses onto the bridge of the nose shows that the customer is disbelieving, unless, of course, the glasses are bifocals. Bifocals are normally worn lower than regular glasses.
- Removing the glasses and slowly cleaning them is a way the customer either gains time or gives some thought to what is being said. When repeated, it may indicate a desire to pose a question, ask for clarification, or raise opposition. Be prepared to question for the reason.
- A gesture similar to cleaning glasses is putting the earpiece in the mouth. This may indicate that the customer is trying to keep from speaking in order to concentrate on listening. It may also mean the customer craves more information.
- Sometimes a customer will quickly take off his glasses and toss them onto a table or his lap. This gesture usually indicates that he was either insulted or offended in some way. By such a gesture he is communicating resistance to what is being said. A clarifying question may help here. ("Do you see how . . . ?")
- If the customer is sitting, holding his glasses in the same hand that is supporting his chin with his eyes cast downward, you can assume he is bored.

TRAIT OR STATE?

In your analysis of *all* nonverbal behavior, you must determine what the individual customer's normal behavior is. Is that which you are observing a trait which your customer *always* exhibits or is it a manifestation of the state he is in temporarily? A customer who always fidgets in his chair will require a different interpretation than someone who is normally relaxed.

You must also guard against making inferences from single gestures or behaviors. Yawning may be meaningless by itself. If, however, it is accompanied by supporting the head with one hand and drooping eyes, you can assume either boredom or fatigue has set in. The important thing to remember is to look for *clusters* of behaviors. Assume nothing from a single piece of evidence, otherwise your interpretation may be self-defeating.

Interpreting and Using Gesture Clusters

Gesture clusters are the series of gestures which together provide clues to how your customer is receiving you and your message. There are classic patterns or clusters of behavior which represent certain emotions or thoughts. Seeing the clusters and knowing what they mean will help you become more familiar with the body language you observe on a day-to-day basis.

Classic Clusters Certain combinations of gestures are especially reliable indications of people's feelings. They may be used to augment, emphasize, contradict, or be unrelated to verbal pronouncements. Therefore, reading body language messages through interpreting gesture clusters is a continuous process of analysis. Consider these classic clusters:

Openness. In this situation, your customer signals sincerity and a cooperative attitude, as he wants to work toward an agreeable solution with you. The characteristics of this attitude are: hands open; legs uncrossed; arms gently and loosely crossing lower body; coat unbuttoned or removed; getting together by moving closer; leaning forward.

Figure 17.1: Openness and Enthusiasm

Openness   **Enthusiasm**

Enthusiasm. Small upper or inward smile; erect body stance; hands open, arms extended; eyes wide and alert; lively and bouncy; voice lively and well-modulated.

Defensiveness. When your customer feels in psychological danger, he assumes a defensive position. The traits to look for are: body rigid; legs and/or arms tightly crossed in protective gestures; lips pursed; fists clenched; fingers clenching the crossed arms; head down with chin depressed toward the chest; little head movement/stiff neck; minimal eye contact with occasional sideways or darting glances; leaning back in chair.

Anger. Assuming that self-control is maintained, the anger body gestures are: body rigid; fists clenched; lips closed and held in a tight thin line; continued eye contact with dilation of the pupils; sometimes squinting of the eyes; shallow breathing.

Evaluation. When your customer is listening intently to your words in order to judge their merit, the body position shows evaluative gestures. These include: sitting in the front portion of the chair with the upper torso projected forward; head slightly tilted; hand to cheek gesture, where head is often supported by the hand; stroking of the chin or pulling the beard.

Readiness. This positive situation is characterized by: leaning forward in a chair in an open position; hand possibly placed mid-thigh; relaxed but alive facial expression; standing with hands on hips, feet slightly spread.

Critical Evaluation. In this situation, which is generally less desirable than the evaluation gesture cluster, your customer will: be more drawn back; have hand to cheek, or chin in palm, with all fingers under the mouth except the index finger, which follows the side of the nose.

Figure 17.2: Defensiveness and Anger

Defensiveness   **Anger**

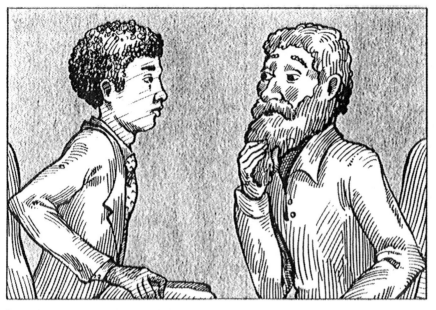

Readiness   **Evaluation**

Figure 17.3: Readiness and Evaluation

Nervousness. Common indicators of nervousness are: clearing throat; hand to mouth movements; covering mouth when speaking; tugging an ear; twitching lips or face; playing with objects and fidgeting; shifting weight while standing; tapping fingers; waving foot in circular motion; plucking at collar or ringing neck with finger inside shirt collar; incongruent laugh; pacing; deep sighs; whistling; cigarette smoking; biting/picking nails; poor eye contact; preoccupation with clothing; jingling money in pockets.

Suspicion and Secrecy. These attitudes can be recognized by such gestures as: failing to make eye contact or resisting glances from you; glancing sideways at you by slightly turning the body away; rubbing or touching the nose; squinting or peering over glasses. The first sign of suspicion and secrecy may be an unrelated and incongruent pattern of gestures. There may be a conflict between what your customer says and what his or her body projects, or there may be a series of incongruent body gestures. In these cases, expect suspicion.

Rejection and Doubt. Rejection and doubt are characterized by some of the same gestures as suspicion and secrecy, as they all are related feelings which indicate a negative reaction. These include: touching and rubbing nose; squinting or rubbing eyes; arms and legs crossed; body withdrawn; throat clearing; hand rubbing or ear tugging; glancing sideways; raising an eyebrow.

Reassurance. In order to reassure themselves, customers may: pinch the fleshy part of their hands; gently rub or caress some personal object such as a ring, watch, or necklace; bite fingernails or examine cuticles.

Confidence and Authority. Easily recognized gestures include: steepling of hands (fingers together, pointed up; the higher the hands held, the greater the confidence); resting feet on desk; leaning back with hands laced in back of head; continuous eye contact; proud, erect body stance with shoulders squared;

Nervousness   **Critical Evaluation**

Figure 17.4:   Nervousness and Critical Evaluation

Figure 17.5:   Suspicion/Secrecy and Rejection/Doubt

Suspicion and Secrecy   **Rejection and Doubt**

thumbs in coat pockets; hands on lapels; reduced hand to face gestures; smiling inwardly; tipping back in chair.

Boredom and Indifference. Relaxed posture; slouching; doodling; drooping eyelids; blank stares, little eye contact; yawning; slack lips; legs crossed, foot kicking; tapping of fingers; expressionless stare; little visual feedback; staring at hands or fingers; supporting head with hand; posture aimed at exit.

Acceptance. A customer shows acceptance by displaying honesty and sincerity. This includes: hands to chest; open arms and hands; touching; moving closer to the other person.

Self-control. Self-control gestures are manifested when your customer is holding something back. They include: wrists gripped behind the back; crossed and locked ankles; fists clenched; pupils contracted; lips closed or pursed.

Frustration. Customers exhibit frustration through the following gestures: hands tightly clenched or fists shaking; hand wringing; rubbing back of neck; controlled, short breathing; blind staring; running hands through hair; lips tightly closed; stamping a foot; pacing.

Remember, you must take care to look for *clusters* rather than for isolated gestures. Body language will imply *what* the person is feeling but not *why* it is being felt. You must, therefore, ask questions to determine the reason for the change in emotion. It is the *changes* that you want to note. A movement from one emotional state to another can serve as a *buying signal* for you. Buying signals show the prospect moving either toward or away from you or your product. For example, if at the beginning of an appointment, a prospect starts out being

Figure 17.6: Confidence/Authority and Reassurance

Confidence and Authority   Reassurance

Boredom and Indifference   Acceptance

Figure 17.7:   Boredom/Indifference and Acceptance

Figure 17.8:   Frustration and Self-Control

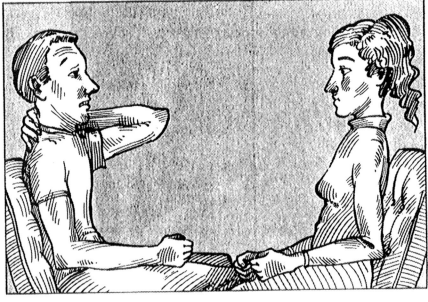

Frustration   Self-Control

defensive and suspicious but gradually moves to acceptance and openness, then you have a much better chance of consummating the sale than if the movement was in the opposite direction.

Another positive sign that a customer is moving toward a purchase is *an upward look with rapid blinking*. Chances are, whatever you have been discussing is being seriously considered. The customer may have already made a favorable decision on the big issue and may be meditating on the details. Patience is needed here. Refrain from further sales talk until the meditation is complete.

Look for changes in body postures and gestures. They often indicate a comparable change in mental attitudes. If a customer decides to buy, the most obvious signs are of *relaxation*—unlocking of the ankles, palms extended outwardly toward you, and movement toward the front of the chair generally accompanies this. All indicate the customer is listening, tuning in, ready to move ahead. The customer may start to *nod* in agreement and even *copy* your gestures. Recognize these signs and move to the next stage of the sales process. Otherwise, you may start to oversell and risk boring the customer. Even if you have a list of benefits yet to convey, resist. As long as your basic commitments to the customer in the sales process have been fulfilled, move on; move at the customer's speed.

Changes, of course, may be in a negative direction also. Be wary of the change in which the customer tightens up, closes his or her limbs, and leans back. Through these gestures, the customer is showing rejection, indicating that you are probably not being effective. Alter your approach when this happens.

YOUR USE OF BODY LANGUAGE

Be as aware of your own body positions as you are of those of your customer. As in verbal communication, you not only receive but also send nonverbal signals to your customer. Your customer may not have the awareness of body language that you have, but he will still be affected unconsciously by the body language you project. You certainly do not want to undermine your presentation or the strength of your product by projecting a negative image with your body. For example, if you greet your customer with a slap on the back (assuming this is strictly a business acquaintance), the customer may feel uneasy without being able to really express why.

As a matter of fact, your gesture clusters can directly affect the gestures of your customer. Studies have demonstrated that people who exhibit *expressionless stimuli*, such as blank expressions and a removed, disinterested air, produce lowered amounts of expression in others. A simple head nod in agreement encourages the same in your customer, while a combination of head nods and warm smiles when used with restraint seems to open the customer to expressing similar feelings. People who sit in open, relaxed positions are seen as more persuasive, active, and better liked than those who sit in a tight, closed manner. These more open people are also able to affect greater opinion change than those who are closed. On the other hand, defensiveness, anger, or frustration on the part of your customers may be a direct result of aggressiveness, dominance, or other negative body language on your part.

As a professional salesperson who is primarily concerned with the customer's needs, the mastery of body language is essential to the communication and sales processes. You should be aware, however, that body language is comprised of symbols, and the interpretation of those symbols is rather inexact. You should always validate your observations with questions in order to ensure the accuracy of your interpretations.

SUMMARY

Body language involves messages that are sent visually—those physical gestures and positionings that reveal the thoughts and attitudes of the sender. Body language describes human interaction exclusive of written and spoken words. This broad definition encompasses everything from the most subtle raising of an eyebrow to the precise movements of the sophisticated sign language used by the deaf.

Communication by body language is rapid. Research shows that even when exposure to a situation is reduced to ¼₄ of a second (the time it takes to show a single frame of film), people often grasp the meaning.

The ability to read body language is a powerful tool, for through body language people express their conscious and subconscious emotions, desires, and attitudes. As a form of communication, it can often be more reliable than verbal communication. It may even contradict verbal expressions.

In addition to increasing your understanding of your prospect, the study of body language can also help improve the prospect's understanding of you. Body language is an important part of having your prospect perceive you and your sales message the way you wish to be perceived.

Reading body language includes the interpretation of many kinds of body gestures. The face, hands, arms, and legs all communicate messages, as do a person's posture and walk. Messages of body language also extend to the handling of accessories such as pens, pads, watches, eyeglasses, and cigarettes.

In your analysis of all nonverbal behavior, you must determine what the individual customer's *normal* behavior is. A customer who always fidgets in his chair will require a different interpretation than someone who is normally relaxed.

You must also guard against making inferences from single gestures or behaviors. It is important to always look for *clusters* of behaviors. Assume nothing from a single piece of evidence, otherwise your interpretation may be self-defeating.

Gesture clusters are the series of gestures which together provide clues to how your customer is receiving you and your message. Certain combinations of gestures are especially reliable indications of people's attitudes and feelings.

They may be used to augment, emphasize, or contradict verbal pronouncements or they may be unrelated. Therefore, reading body language messages through interpreting gesture clusters is a continuous process of analysis.

Although gesture clusters may imply *what* a person is feeling, they will not tell you *why* he is feeling the way he is. Therefore, you must ask questions to determine the reason for the expressed emotion.

When reading body language, you will want to pay particular attention to the changes in a customer's body language—changes in his body postures and gestures. A movement from the indication of one emotional state to another can serve as a buying signal, which shows the prospect moving either toward or away from you or your product.

Be as aware of your own body positions as you are of those of your customer. As in verbal communication, you not only receive but also send non-verbal signals to your customer.

Research has proven that our gesture clusters can directly affect the gestures of our customers and prospects. People who sit in open, relaxed positions are seen as more persuasive, active, and better liked than those who sit in a tight, closed manner. More open people are also able to effect a greater opinion change than those who are closed.

The mastery of body language is essential to the communication and sales processes for professional salespeople who are primarily concerned with customers' needs. Body language is comprised of symbols, however, and their interpretation can be inexact. Therefore, you should always validate your observations with questions in order to ensure the accuracy of your interpretations.

DISCUSSION QUESTIONS

1. How does an understanding of body language improve your ability to communicate?
2. Why do "actions speak louder than words"?
3. Is it enough to observe a single nonverbal behavior and draw a conclusion from it?
4. What is meant by "trait or state"?
5. Which is more important, the nonverbal behavior you observe or the change in a person's behavior? Why?
6. When you make an assumption about someone's thoughts or feelings based on body language, how should you verify it?
7. What is the flip side of observing body language?
8. How do the messages you convey with your body language affect other people's attitudes, your credibility, and their willingness to change?
9. Observe other people's reactions when you are tense vs. relaxed; open vs. closed. What are the differences?
10. Is body language an exact science that is 100 percent accurate? If so, why? If not, what is its value?

CHAPTER EIGHTEEN

Proxemics

<table>
<tr><td>CHAPTER
OBJECTIVES</td><td>1 Introduce and discuss the concept of proxemics.
2 Understand the application of the guidelines of proxemics to building
successful sales relationships.</td></tr>
</table>

How do you feel when someone takes your favorite cup to drink from (or uses a favorite item—your special pen, perhaps)? That uncomfortable feeling results from a proxemic violation. *Proxemics,* the study of personal space and the movement of people within it, is another important influence on the communication process, and, in fact, is a specific, recognizable form of nonverbal communication. It involves how we move around within our space to ease and aid communication.

The "space" that we give to another person is determined partly by our culture. For example, Europeans and Latin Americans in general feel more comfortable than North Americans when it comes to standing close to others when talking with them. Therefore, the generalizations we make in this chapter apply primarily to North Americans.

PROXEMIC ZONES (PHYSICAL PERSONAL SPACE)

Can you imagine visiting friends and sitting in their living room where the chairs and sofa are separated by a distance of twenty feet? It would feel quite awkward for most of us. It would also be uncomfortable if the furniture were set only two feet apart. In the former case, the distance would be too great to promote a personal feeling. In the latter case, the distance would be too close for comfort. Unconsciously, we all have standards of how near or far other people should be from us when we are talking with them. When these zones are not respected, we feel uncomfortable and become distracted. The proxemic zones, or bubbles of space, around a person are actually extensions of that person's behavioral style and are greatly influenced by his culture.

For most North Americans, there are four basic zones of interaction:

Public Zone	12+ feet
Social Zone	4–12 feet
Personal Zone	2–4 feet
Intimate Zone	0–2 feet

Sales relationships most frequently begin in the social (consultative) zone of 4 to 12 feet. This is a comfortable distance at which to exchange greetings and talk about business. Naturally, one would move into the personal zone of 2 to 4 feet when shaking the prospect's hand, but remaining that close should only be done at the prospect's invitation after a professional relationship has been established.

A person's proxemic zones should never be violated. Some people become upset when someone stands too close to them. We must be aware of this and guard against becoming too chummy when it is not appropriate. A prospect or customer may not be able to pinpoint his reason for feeling uncomfortable and will probably attribute his discomfort to the salesperson's product or attitude. No matter what he thinks, the point remains the same: he is being distracted. When he becomes distracted, the communication process then breaks down, thus wasting the time of both the salesperson and the customer.

The sales implications of proxemic violations should be obvious. A violation of your customer's proxemic zones without verbal or nonverbal invitation most likely will lead to greater tension and decreased trust. The buyer–seller relationship then deteriorates and becomes nonproductive. The sales relationship can also deteriorate, however, if your customer verbally or nonverbally signals that it is all right for you to move from one proxemic zone to a closer one

Figure 18.1: The proxemic zones surrounding a person

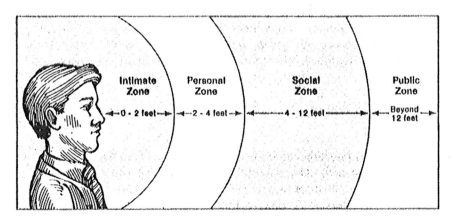

and you refuse the invitation. The customer may then perceive you as cold and aloof and only interested in the sale rather than him or her as a person. A proxemic violation can therefore be twofold: trespassing into zones without invitation, or refusing an invitation to move into a closer zone.

PSYCHOLOGICAL PROXEMICS

Up to this point, we have only discussed physical proxemics. There is another important dimension to the study of proxemics, however—the psychological dimension.

Every relationship a person has is defined within certain boundaries. It is these boundaries that make some behaviors proper and others improper. It is possible to insult someone simply by going beyond the proper boundaries of your relationship without consent. For example, you would make a business associate uncomfortable by calling her "dear" or "sweetheart." On the other hand, you would make people with whom you are intimate feel awkward by addressing them as Mr., Miss, Ms., or Mrs.

One of the authors once had an acquaintance who, for some unknown reason, never referred to him by name. It was always "Hi" and "Good-bye," instead of, "Hi, Tony," or "Good-bye, Tony." Although this may seem minor, it made Tony feel awkward. If the relationship had been important enough, he would have confronted this person. Instead, the relationship remained stagnant and slowly faded away. The same can happen in a business relationship. To avoid letting a business relationship fade away, acknowledge that your prospect is an individual by calling him or her by name. Of course, you do not want to overdo it or you will appear to be too eager. Also avoid violating psychological zones by calling your customer a friendly name which is too intimate for the relationship. An example of this is Buddy. If you approach every client with "Hi ya, Buddy!" they will begin to take you much less seriously than you would like.

In the chapter on questioning, we talked about questions being appropriate at some times and inappropriate at other times. Using a personal question or a very friendly term too soon, at the wrong time, or even using it at all may violate another person's psychological space. This verbal intrusion can be as destructive as a physical violation of space. That is why the interrogation of some some attorneys and police officers are so intimidating; they violate a person's mental space.

PROXEMIC TERRITORIALITY

Another facet of proxemic behavior is that of *territoriality*. We each develop our own "turf"—a space for our personal property. Have you ever become upset with someone who sat in your chair? Leaned on your desk? Picked up some object of yours without permission? That is territorial proxemics in action. In fact, studies have shown that customers fail to listen to what is being said if the salesperson is also handling some object that belongs to the customer.

When someone invades your territory, knowingly or unknowingly, you usually feel unsettled by the intrusion and feel a degree of tension. This tension could eventually lead to suspicion and distrust. With that in mind, imagine what goes through a customer's mind when you invade his or her territory. Be careful when you assume you can handle something that belongs to a customer; it is far better to ask permission.

Research into territorial proxemics has revealed two categories of territory, in addition to their zones, that people attempt to protect. These include:

1. *Fixed-feature territory.* The unmovable boundaries, such as doors to an office and the walls of a house, are fixed features.
2. *Semifixed-feature territory.* This includes movable objects and their arrangement, such as furniture, books, paintings, and knickknacks.

We all like to protect and control our own territory, but we are not always granted that desire. For instance, you seek, and often have, control over your fixed-feature territory. The walls of your office or house keep intruders out. There are times, however, when others intrude into your fixed-feature territory. When this happens, tension levels can skyrocket and trust levels plummet. Think of how you would feel if you had your door closed and someone walked into your office or your room without knocking and uninvited.

Now consider your customers. Have you ever stopped by without an appointment to visit a customer and stuck your head into his or her office without knocking? How do you think it makes that customer feel about you?

Respecting your customer's territory, both fixed and semifixed, is important. Avoid the temptation to move or play with small items of theirs no matter how insignificant they may appear to be. Doing so will only suspend communication, cause tension to go up in the relationship you are trying to build, and decrease the trust and concentration on the part of your customer. The irony is that it doesn't matter if the object is breakable, unbreakable, valuable, or inexpensive. All that matters to your customer is that it is part of his territory and you don't have the right to play with it.

PROXEMIC CATEGORIES

Some people are more sensitive than others about how close other people stand to them, how familiar they become, or how much others respect their privacy.

In general, people can be divided into two categories: contact and noncontact. Those of the contact category don't mind getting close to others physically or psychologically. Those who are in the noncontact category, on the other hand, tend to remain more at a distance both physically and psychologically, tending to be more formal and business-oriented. When these two major patterns of proxemic behavior meet, their interaction normally results in a clash. The contact people unknowingly get too close physically and/or psychologically to the noncontact people, whereas the noncontact people do not get close enough physically and/or psychologically to the contact people.

Contact and noncontact people frequently have unpleasant perceptions of each other, based on their proxemic behavior. The noncontact people are seen as cold, unfriendly, or impolite by the contact people. Noncontact people, on the other hand, perceive the contact people as overly friendly, clinging, and smothering. Interestingly enough, this concept of contact and noncontact behavior relates directly to the four behavioral styles. Thinkers and Directors tend to exhibit noncontact behavior, while Relaters and Socializers have a tendency to be contact people. This helps explain why some styles naturally cause tension for other styles—their proxemic behaviors are incompatible.

As a salesperson, you should be flexible in your behaviors so you can adapt to either category as each is encountered. Being stubborn only alienates people. Be more sensitive to the needs of your customers and you will build stronger business relationships.

SUMMARY

Proxemics, an area of nonverbal communication, is the study of personal space and the movement of people within that space. It is an important area to understand because our perception and use of personal space in relation to other people can greatly affect the communication process.

People tend to keep distances or zones between themselves and others. These bubbles of space are actually extensions of their behavioral style and are significantly influenced by their culture.

We all have standards of how near or far other people should be when we are talking with them. When these zones are not respected, we feel uncomfortable and become distracted from the communication process.

For most North Americans, there are four basic zones of interaction: the public zone (12+ feet); the social zone (4–12 feet); the personal zone (2–4 feet); and the intimate zone (0–2 feet). Sales relationships most frequently begin in the comfortable social zone of 4 to 12 feet. Such a distance is appropriate for exchanging greetings and discussing business. Although moving closer is appropriate for shaking hands, remaining that close should only be done at the customer's invitation after a professional relationship has been established.

A person's proxemic zones should never be violated. The sales implications of proxemic violations are obvious. A violation of your customer's proxemic zones without verbal or nonverbal invitation most likely will lead to greater tension and decreased trust, causing the buyer–seller relationship to deteriorate and become nonproductive. This buyer–seller relationship can deteriorate in two ways: by trespassing into zones without invitation, or by refusing an invitation to move into a closer zone.

Psychological proxemics involves the mental zones of a person's mind. For every relationship a person has, he has defined parameters. It is these parameters that make some behaviors of another person appropriate and other behaviors inappropriate. A verbal intrusion, such as using personal questions or a particularly friendly term too soon, at the wrong time, or even at all can be as destructive as a physical violation of space.

Proxemic territoriality is another facet of proxemic behavior which refers to one's "turf," or space for personal property. When such territory is invaded by someone knowingly or unknowingly, a person feels unsettled by the intrusion and feels a degree of tension. Such tension eventually leads to suspicion and distrust of the invader.

There are two categories of territory: fixed-feature territory, which refers to immovable boundaries, and semifixed-feature territory, which refers to movable objects and their arrangement. Both territories of customers should be respected. Not paying close attention to this may suspend communication with them, causing tension to increase in the relationship that is being built, and decreasing trust and concentration on the part of the customers.

There are two categories of proxemic behavior: contact and noncontact. People who are in the contact category do not mind getting close to others physically or psychologically. Those in the noncontact category tend to remain more distant, both physically and psychologically, tending to be more formal and business-oriented. When these two major proxemic behavior patterns meet, their interaction normally results in a clash. The contact people unknowingly get too close physically and/or psychologically to the noncontact people, whereas the noncontact people do not get close enough physically and/or psychologically to the contact people.

The concept of contact and noncontact behavior relates directly to the four behavioral styles. Thinkers and Directors tend to exhibit noncontact behavior, while Relaters and Socializers have a tendency to be contact people. This helps explain why some styles naturally cause tension for other styles—their proxemic behaviors are incompatible.

In attempting to establish a trust bond, salespeople must be careful not to offend their customers by violating their proxemic zones or territories. Salespeople can use this concept of proxemics to improve their trust bonds with their customers. Care should be exercised in not moving too fast (getting too close too soon, thus increasing tension) or too slow (refusing the customer's invitation).

By respecting, understanding, and effectively using the concepts of proxemics, you will help your customers to feel at ease, listen better, and feel better about you. It will also greatly ease your job of building the trust bonds necessary for good sales relationships.

DISCUSSION QUESTIONS

1. What is meant by proxemics and how can it affect your ability to communicate with people?
2. How do you feel when someone does not respect your proxemic zones? How can you avoid making others feel this way?

3. What is psychological proxemics and how do you know what is proper for different people?

4. What is the difference between contact and noncontact people? How should each be treated?

5. List the four behavioral styles. For each, describe how you would change your physical and psychological proxemics to make that type of person comfortable.

6. In the school cafeteria or another public place, observe people standing and talking. What can you assume about their relationships based on their proxemics?

CHAPTER NINETEEN

The Effective Use of Voice

CHAPTER OBJECTIVES	1 Introduce and discuss the concept of vocal qualities and their relationship to successful professional sales.
	2 Present guidelines to using the concept of vocal qualities in the professional sales environment.

Voice quality, like body language and proxemics, conveys a message independent of the words spoken. More often than not, the quality of your voice gives the listener important clues to the meaning of the words. Many jokes, especially sarcastic or facetious ones, work only because of changes in voice quality. A working knowledge of voice quality will help you be more effective at listening, speaking; *and* selling.

What do you think a person who is speaking loud and fast is feeling? You may think that the person is excited or enthused or angry or even frustrated. Just to know that someone is currently speaking loud and fast, however, does not mean anything on its own. The person may be from the Northeast and *naturally* speaks loud and fast. The person may come from a large family and has always had to speak loud and fast to be heard. So what does it mean when a person is speaking loud and fast? Nothing! However, if that person typically speaks softer and slower and, at a particular point during a conversation, begins speaking louder and faster, that probably *does* mean something. Generally, this is a positive sign, but it might also be negative.

Every sentence we speak is uttered with sounds that by their speed, relative stress, volume, and rhythms say as much as or more than the words themselves. Knowledge of how this works will help you listen to your customer better and indicate ways to say what you wish to say with greater impact. In this chapter, we will take a closer look at the many different emotions people can project simply through the tone of their voice.

INFORMATION FROM VOICE QUALITIES

You have always picked up some information from the sound of another's voice. High emotions (joy, anger, affection, and the like) come across as readily in the sound as in other visual and verbal (word-meaning) cues. Think about the difference in the voices of the angry mother and the lonely father when saying, "Susie, come here." Many of us have talked with someone on the phone and known that that person was really angry, even when the words were, in themselves, fairly matter-of-fact. The importance of understanding nonverbal communication is best described when looking at the word "oh." If you looked up "oh" in the dictionary, its definition is given as: an interjection. In reality, an interjection is not a definition; it's a part of speech. Basically, "oh" has no definition until you add nonverbal communications—the voice tone that goes with it, the body language, and any other nonverbal cues. For example, let's look at a few different "ohs." "Oh" can mean surprise; it can mean question; it can mean approval; it can mean disapproval. Not only can it mean different things, it can also mean diametrically opposed things, based on *how* you say the word. You already know how to recognize these cues. However, you can learn—or further develop an ability—to read cues in vocal qualities that are far more subtle. Then you can act to encourage or circumvent a change in attitude or thinking before the emotion gets high or the change in idea becomes entrenched.

The two steps for obtaining information from vocal qualities are deceptive in that they are simple; but as with so many skills, they may be awkward or unimportant to use at first and take on power as you apply them repeatedly.

1. Identify the Customer's Characteristic Vocal Qualities

What is characteristic for one person is not for another. If you think back on behavioral styles, you recall that Relaters and Thinkers tend to move more slowly than Socializers and Directors. That generally shows up also in their speed of speaking and in some of the other voice qualities (such as pitch and volume). To identify a person's personal and habitual vocal qualities, listen for individual characteristics in the following areas:

Resonance	How resonant is the person's voice?
Pitch	Is the person's voice high or low?
Speed	How quickly does he normally speak?
Volume	How loudly does he speak?
Clarity	Are words enunciated well? Is his speech crisp or slurred?
Inflection	What are the normal expressive changes in his voice?

2. Note Changes from the Characteristic Vocal Qualities

Once you know a person's characteristic vocal qualities, you can be alert for changes. When people change from their normal vocal habits, take note; they are communicating something extra. It may indicate a point of emphasis, of importance, of concern, or of a shift in thinking or attention. Catch these hints at an early stage, and you can often do something about the direction of the communication.

How do you tell by these rather subtle cues whether the trend is in a positive or negative direction? Remember that this is a *refinement* of skills; it takes time to learn. You can grow into skillful use of the techniques over time, and your selling world won't end before you gain a high level of skill. Now let's look at what some of the changes can mean to you.

Upward Changes in Volume and Speed Generally, this indicates a change in a positive direction. Joy, cheer, and enthusiasm all emerge from this kind of change. But so does anger. If the rhythm is clipped (from what is a normal flow), question very sensitively to clear up the communication and eliminate a potential growth in anger. If the rhythm is not clipped, you may still want to verify the implication of the change.

Downward Changes in Volume and Speed Generally, this tendency raises a warning. Some of the emotions to which this change is a prelude are boredom, sadness, and affection (misplaced in a sales environment). However, it could indicate satisfaction, especially if the pitch rises. So, note the change and check it out.

Greater Resonance and Lessened Clarity These changes generally go along with downward changes in volume and speed, and also raise a flag of warning. Once again, however, they could indicate a movement toward satisfaction. Picking this out is an important part of your decision to move on to another stage of the sale or in circumventing negative characteristics.

Changes in Rhythm In music, when something is about to happen, when there is to be a change in mood, the rhythm changes. So it is in vocal patterns. What these changes indicate varies greatly in individual situations. But be alert to any changes and check them out. Move more carefully when the rhythm becomes clipped, as this is characteristic of anger and defensiveness. Take care, also, with a more drawn out rhythm. The person may only be pondering a point, or he or she may be expressing disbelief.

Remember that ANY change may be the customer's application of conscious change in order to stress a point, to be sure that you understand something of importance. Your responsibility, then, is to fall back on your listening and questioning skills to get at the root of the change.

Once your listening and questioning skills have determined the positive or negative nature of the change, you can do something about the situation. Often, the very act of sensitive questioning will turn a negative situation around. Be sure to listen for changes back to the characteristic vocal qualities. You can encourage favorable trends by increased signs of interest and support or, where appropriate, by moving on in the sales process.

When you question, remember that although you may be hearing changes in vocal characteristics, what you are hearing said is the meaning of the words. Speak to the customer in terms of how the *message* is coming across to you, not in terms of the vocal qualities noted. For example, if you ask your customer, "Are you with me?" and she says, "Y . . . e . . . e . . . s . . . ," you might say, "I hear you saying 'yes,' but I get the impression that something else is on your mind. Would you mind sharing it with me?" Remember that you are trying to show your sensitivity skills, not your analytical skills.

The important thing to keep in mind with any of the foregoing changes is that when they are happening, *be aware of their occurrence.* Then use your clarification skills to determine specifically what those changes are indicating on the part of your customer. Your responsibility is to fall back on your listening, questioning, and feedback skills to understand the root of the change. Once the exact nature of the change has been determined, you are able to do something about it. If it is positive, you can capitalize on it. If it is negative, you can try to turn the negative situation around before it is too late.

VOICE QUALITIES AND EMOTIONS

There are many changes in voice quality which are germane to specific emotions for all of us. Like body language, you should recognize these states for effective communication:

Affection	Upward inflection, low volume, slow speed, good clarity
Anger	Loud volume, irregular inflection, high speed and pitch
Boredom	Low volume, slow speed, little clarity, little inflection
Cheerfulness	High volume, fast speed, irregular inflection
Impatience	Medium to high pitch, high speed
Surprise	High pitch and volume, ascending inflection
Defensiveness	Increased speed, medium to low clarity
Sadness	Low volume, crack in pitch, slow speed, little clarity or inflection

Your Use of Voice Quality for Better Communication

Even as you get information from your customer by listening to her vocal qualities, so your customer is getting information from you. The quality of our voices reflects the emotional content of our words and it is therefore a somewhat unconscious form of behavior. It is for this reason that we must be aware of what our vocal qualities are communicating lest we convey more messages than we intend. This is especially true over the telephone where the customer has no visual clues to observe such as body language. It is easy for doubt, fear, boredom, and fatigue to undermine what we are saying to the customer. If you are cognizant of your vocal quality, you can turn those emotions into enthusiasm, confidence, and interest.

Vocally, you should strive to convey those qualities that make up your professional image. Below is a list of some of the ways you can achieve this:

1. Project a strong, full voice. (Confidence)
2. Speak clearly and distinctly. (Intelligence)
3. Use pitch, volume, and inflection to convey your attitude toward your customer and your product. (Enthusiasm)
4. Use changes to emphasize points:
   a. Lower the speed at important points.
   b. Pause slightly after important points to let the message settle.
   c. Raise or lower the volume. Either will emphasize the point stated. Raised volume will tend to indicate optimism and enthusiasm. Lowered volume tends to sound confidential and concerned.
5. Avoid monotonous speech—vary your qualities. (Interest)
6. Speak naturally and relax. (Trust)
7. Finally, though this is not a vocal quality, watch your customer. Emphasize the points that appear of interest by using the techniques mentioned above. As you can see, timing in speaking and using vocal qualities is helpful to you and informative to your customer.

If you follow the suggestions above, not only will you make a positive impression on your customer, but he will also be assured of understanding you. A study at Yale University revealed that the poorer the use of vocal qualities while speaking with a customer, the greater the speaker's and the listener's discomfort and anxiety. Thus, a good use of vocal qualities ties in with the whole concept of trust and confidence: tension up, trust down; tension down, trust (and sales) up.

The suggestions in this chapter can be very effective *if* they are used appropriately. By using the proper vocal intonation, you can draw attention to those areas of your message that are of utmost importance and benefit to your customers. Overuse or overemphasis of these methods may annoy your customers, taking their attention away from the sales interview. Remember, your use of these vocal skills must be natural and spontaneous, or you will appear to be insincere.

SUMMARY

Voice quality, like body language and proxemics, conveys a message independent of the words spoken and gives the listener important clues to the meaning of what is spoken. Every sentence we speak is uttered with sounds that by their speed, relative stress, volume, and rhythms say as much or more than the words themselves.

There are two steps for obtaining information from vocal qualities: 1) identify the customer's characteristic vocal qualities; and 2) note the changes from the characteristic vocal qualities, both as to kind and direction of change.

It is important to note that what is characteristic for one person in terms of vocal qualities is not characteristic for another. When identifying a customer's characteristic vocal qualities, you should notice the following areas: resonance, pitch, speed, volume, clarity, and inflection.

Once you have noted what is characteristic and habitual in vocal qualities for a certain person, you should then notice the *changes* from those characteristic qualities. Changes from the norm communicate messages which may indicate points of emphasis, importance, concern, or a shift in thinking or attention. By noting these changes at an early stage in your meeting with a prospect or customer, you can often do something about the direction of the communication.

Changes that you are looking for in the customer's vocal qualities are upward or downward changes in volume and speed; greater resonance and lessened clarity; and changes in rhythm.

It is important to remember that what the changes mean varies greatly in individual situations. Therefore, it is important to determine what the changes truly indicate, and this is done by skillfully questioning and listening to understand the root of the change.

Once your listening and questioning skills have determined the positive or negative nature of the change, you can do something about the situation. Often, through sensitive questioning, you can turn a negative situation into one that is positive. Be sure to listen for changes back to the characteristic, normal vocal qualities for that person. You can then encourage favorable trends by increased signs of interest and support or, where appropriate, by moving on in the sales process.

There are many changes in voice quality which are germane to specific emotions for all of us. Like body language, you should recognize the vocal qualities of these emotions to ensure effective communication: affection, anger, boredom, cheerfulness, impatience, surprise, defensiveness, and sadness.

Even as you receive information from your customer by listening to his vocal qualities, so your customer is receiving information from you. The quality of your voice reflects the emotional content of your words and it is therefore a somewhat unconscious form of behavior. It is for this reason that you must to be aware of what your vocal qualities are communicating.

Vocally, you should strive to convey those qualities that make up your professional image. By so doing you will not only make a positive impression on your customer, but he will also be assured of understanding you.

DISCUSSION
QUESTIONS

1. What six characteristics comprise voice quality?
2. Why must you get to know someone before drawing conclusions from their vocal quality?
3. What is the appropriate thing to do when you sense something unusual in someone's voice?
4. What are some typical emotions carried in the voice and what changes do they make in pitch, inflection, and other vocal qualities?
5. What voice qualities make the best impression?
6. Enthusiasm can be conveyed in your voice. What effect does too much enthusiasm have?
7. Should you use different voice qualities with people with different behavioral styles? Explain your answer.

Part VI

SELF-MANAGEMENT SKILLS

Running your life successfully is not unlike running a company. Both require having a clear vision of what you want to accomplish; setting priorities and goals; managing your time for maximum efficiency; and striking a balance between various facets of your life and business.

Self-management skills will give you the insight and techniques for achieving all of the above. Chapter 20 discusses the many facets of life that must be balanced to remain cool, calm, and collected. To achieve this balance and accomplish those things to which you aspire, it is important to set goals. Goal-setting follows basic guidelines that increase the likelihood of attainment.

Chapter 21 will teach you how to manage your time. Time is a precious commodity that most people don't appreciate until they run out of it. To get ahead in the world, it is essential to learn how to use your time properly.

CHAPTER TWENTY

Your Sales Career
and Your Life

CHAPTER OBJECTIVES

1. Emphasize the importance of *balanced* goal-setting in all the key areas of a salesperson's life: mental, physical, family, social, spiritual, career, and financial.
2. Explain the brainstorming process.
3. Explain the goal-setting process.
4. Develop an understanding of how one's assumptions affect one's behavior.
5. Understand the process of visualization and the use of role models to aid one's personal and career growth.

For many years, people lived with the mistaken belief that their home life and their work could be totally separate. Many people gave their families and personal lives a back seat to their careers, chasing the carrot of success while other facets of their lives suffered.

In the 1960s the pendulum began to swing in the other direction. Young people in our country started questioning the traditional values of the establishment. They denounced the work ethic and advocated recognizing people as individuals with needs which extended beyond work alone. They had a good point, although perhaps they pushed the pendulum too far in the other direction. It is undeniable, however, that a person's needs and identity encompass more than what he or she does for a living.

BALANCE

We all need to keep our lives in balance. It is important to realize and accept the fact that many needs must be fulfilled if we are to be well, adjusted, and happy.

Our basic needs fall into seven categories:

Mental	The functions of the mind—memory, concentration, learning, creativity, reasoning, mathematical ability, etc.
Physical	The many functions of the body—overall fitness, percent of body fat, skills and abilities, agility, endurance, etc.
Family	Your relationships with your special friends and your family
Social	Your relationships with people outside the family and outside your business
Spiritual	Your religious, philosophical, and humanitarian beliefs.
Career	Your involvement in your professional field, both in and out of the office.
Financial	The management of your financial resources and obligations

In many ways we are like the fragile ecosystem of the environment in which we live. The different elements of our lives are interdependent. One need affects the others, especially when it is grossly neglected. For example, we all know that financial problems affect personal outlook, health, social life, and family life. It is for this reason that practitioners of holistic medicine examine all facets of a person's life when they search for the cause of a physical illness.

There is no escaping the fact that we are complex beings with complex needs. Our needs are dynamic rather than static—that is, they are constantly changing. At one point in our lives the development of a career may require more time than our spiritual or family needs. At some other time, physical needs may be emphasized more than social or financial needs. Just because one need is more urgent than others does not mean that the others disappear. They, too, must receive at least a minimal amount of attention. Rarely can a need be completely neglected without unpleasant consequences.

To begin your sales career *effectively,* you need to work at bringing your life into balance. This requires *goal-setting*—identifying the end results you would like to achieve for each facet of your life. Only then can you plan the concrete steps and intermediate goals which stand between your present situation and your ideal concept of yourself.

THE IMPORTANCE OF GOALS

> Most people aim at nothing in life . . . and hit it with amazing accuracy.
> ANONYMOUS

Such a statement is a sad commentary about people, but it is true. It is the striving for and the attainment of goals which makes life meaningful. Lewis Carroll stated this point beautifully in *Alice In Wonderland (Through the Looking Glass):*

> ALICE: Mr. Cat, which of these paths shall I take?
> CHESHIRE CAT: Well, my dear, where do you want to go?
> ALICE: I don't suppose it really matters.
> CHESHIRE CAT: Then, my dear, any path will do!

No matter what kind of traveling you do—whether it is through your life or across the country by car—if you do not know where you are going, you will never know if you have arrived. Taking any road will leave your fulfillment to chance and that is not good enough!

People who have no goals walk around feeling emotionally, socially, spiritually, physically, and professionally unbalanced. This can only cause anxiety. People who have goals are taken seriously and are respected by their peers. It is a sign of strength when you make decisions positively affecting the direction of your life.

History demonstrates innumerable examples of the importance of goal setting. Can you imagine the following exchange taking place after Sir Edmund Hillary returned from Mount Everest?

REPORTER: Congratulations, Sir Edmund! Tell me, why did you become the first man to conquer Mount Everest?
SIR EDMUND: I was just wandering around trying to become inspired when I ended up on the top of this mountain.
REPORTER: Really! Did it work?
SIR EDMUND: Yes, but by the time I got back I forgot what my brilliant idea was!

Of course, this scenario is absurd because such a monumental feat such as climbing Mount Everest would take some serious goal-setting and planning. Naturally, Sir Edmund had to work hard to gain the knowledge and physical skill necessary for the climb. He also had to acquire the help of a team of experts and procure all the equipment. The planning stages must have taken an enormous amount of time—longer, no doubt, than the climb itself.

The same principles apply to success in sales. You must identify your goal and map out the steps that will take you there. Goals, when earnestly pursued, give people reasons to do some things and to avoid other things. We know a young man who has never been involved with drugs or in trouble with the law. We marvel at his good fortune and strength of character. When he was ten years old, he set himself a goal, to be an astronaut. At last report he had graduated from the U.S. Air Force Academy with a degree in astronautical engineering. His goal was so important that he avoided doing anything to hurt his chances of success. Goals give us purpose and channel our energies.

It is easy to spot a person who has a clear set of goals. That person is the one who exudes a sense of purpose and determination. He or she has abundant energy and is willing to put more time and effort into any given task. Being goal-oriented helps one become more positive, optimistic, and assertive.

We can think of ourselves as bodies of water. Someone without goals is like a stagnant lake, spread out, lying motionless surrounded by a ring of mountains and unable to go anywhere else. A goal-oriented person is like a river forging its way through the obstacles in its way, the mountains. The river has movement. It is exciting and it carries things with it in its flow of enthusiasm.

In recent years many studies have focused on productivity. One finding repeatedly confirmed is that people who continuously set, pursue, and monitor their career goals are more productive than people who just work at a job. Pride in and ownership of one's choices are important ingredients in career satisfaction and success. In contrast, the uninspired worker goes home at the end of the day, having gained nothing more than a few dollars and a lot of aggravation.

Even on the factory-worker level, it has been shown that productivity will increase if a better incentive (goal) is provided for the worker. We all know that piece workers are more productive than salaried employees. This proves the WIIFM principle: **What's In It For Me?** The greater the rewards are, the higher the drive is to attain the goals set. The individual chooses the goals with the most desirable payoff.

Time magazine reported a national survey a few years ago which found that only 3 percent of those surveyed had *written* personal goals; 97 percent of the people had no goals at all or had only thought about them. They had not committed their goals to writing. Interestingly, the 3 percent who had written goals were found to have accomplished much more than any of the 97 percent. Almost every speaker, writer, and educator in the area of sales success agrees that committing your goals to paper is a necessary step in committing one's life to attaining those goals. If you take the time to do this you will stack the odds in your favor and be on your way to becoming one of those in the successful 3 percent.

The dividends reaped by investing in yourself are unlike any found in the financial world. When you clarify your values and set goals in all the major areas of your life, the right roads appear in front of you like mirages in the desert. Yet they are *real!* Choices become infinitely easier to make and you have taken a giant step toward living a balanced life.

FOUNDATION DEVELOPMENT

Unfortunately, our society is externally-oriented. We judge books by their covers, people by their wealth or beauty, and jeans by their designers. Our culture teaches us superficial values by which to live and judge others. These values are not conducive to the development of the qualities of inner strength, sensitivity, patience, thoughtfulness, compassion, or other virtues necessary for well-adjusted, happy individuals. Yet, to strive long and hard toward an important goal, one should possess a firm foundation of these inner qualities. This is true for any endeavor requiring inner fortitude.

The same principle applies to psychotherapy. Before a client can start on the path to being well-adjusted (balanced), his or her basic values must be explored and clarified.

Building a successful sales career is like building a house. If your foundation of inner qualities is strong, you can continue to rise on each completed accomplishment. If your foundation is weak, however, it could all crumble in a storm, such as a selling slump or weak economy.

ASSUMPTIONS AND THEIR EFFECT ON BEHAVIOR

When you stop operating under the assumption that things will go on as they are forever, you can then initiate some changes. More often than not, our assumptions are what limit our perceived options. Negative assumptions set up internal obstacles which automatically defeat us. One of the most common negative assumptions in sales is, "I'll never get that account, why should I waste my time?" If you assume that you will not get an account, then you won't! Either you will pass it by or you will predetermine the outcome by your attitude. Predetermining the outcome could be saying to the buyer, "You're not interested in this product, are you?" Ninety-nine times out of 100 she will prove you right by saying, "No."

Some of the negative assumptions in sales are:

- "The economy is bad so people aren't buying."
- "I'll never make as much money as I want."
- "I'll never find a product/service I can honestly be enthusiastic about."
- "They don't need my product/service."
- "They won't like me."
- "I'm not smart enough."
- "They won't be able to afford my product/service."
- "I'll never be able to call on X number of accounts per week."
- "A man will never buy from me." (for saleswomen)
- "A woman will never buy from me." (for salesmen)
- "People don't like salespeople."

Such negative assumptions usually become self-fulfilling prophecies. You assume you cannot do something and then you act in ways that guarantee your failure. You have then reinforced your original assumption. This could go on and on until you quit sales altogether.

Dr. Eden Ryl, in her film, "You Pack Your Own Chute," conceptualized the relationship between assumptions and behaviors in a different way. She said: $A_1 \rightarrow B_1$ where A stands for assumption, B stands for behavior, and the arrow is read as "leads to." When you assume that you are capable of a certain behavior and *only* that behavior, then your actions will be consistent with and limited by that assumption. If you want new behaviors and higher achievements, it is doubtful that you will ever achieve them until you expand your assumptions about what you can do. For example, let's say you want to set a goal of selling 60 units of a product or service within the next 60 days. B_2 is the new behavior you desire. A_2, however, does not yet exist because you have never sold 60 units in 60 days. So you need to expand your assumptions. Create an assumption (A_2) which says you *are* capable of selling that much. Then and only then can $A_2 \rightarrow B_2$. You will have allowed yourself to go beyond your old limitations.

POSITIVE THINKING

In recent years there has been much criticism levied at positive thinking, probably because it has been exploited and overcommercialized. The fact remains, however, that positive thinking works. If you are serious about succeeding in your chosen field, it will be necessary for you to cultivate positive thinking as a habit.

One way to become a positive thinker is to monitor your thoughts. In the late 1960s, Dr. Albert Ellis founded a psychological school of thought called Rational Emotive Therapy. His theory was that people feel what they think. It makes sense, therefore, to change your thinking if you want to change the way you feel.

Dr. Ellis prescribed a simple exercise in which you consciously make the effort to change your thoughts every time a negative thought arises. It takes practice, but it works wonders when you try. As you go about your day, every time a negative thought comes up, you simply stop what you are thinking, take that thought, and analyze it. The analysis comprises asking yourself questions that defuse the potency of the thought. They can be questions such as: Is this thought true or am I imagining the worst for myself? Would it be catastrophic if the worst thing did come true? (Ellis insists NOTHING is catastrophic.) If I am exaggerating my fear, how can I rewrite that thought to reflect the reality of the situation? What *is* the reality of the situation? It's ok to acknowledge fear without blowing it out of proportion and getting upset.

The thought process, obviously, will vary for different people in different situations. The common denominator, however, is the fact that negative thoughts do cause negative feelings. Negative feelings, in turn, limit your actions, effectiveness, and, ultimately, your success and happiness. By shedding your negative thoughts (most of which are fears), you make room for constructive and creative thoughts and the willingness to take risks. Most negative emotions are ways of taking up time so you won't have to take risks.

Negative thinking is a part of our language as well as our thought patterns. By analyzing your thoughts with an eye towards the words you use, you will make giant strides toward thinking positively. The objective of changing your language is to take responsibility for your thoughts and feelings.

Adjectives that end in "-ed" imply that an external source is creating the effect on you. That is not the case. You are the source of your thoughts and feelings. You are, therefore, able to turn around your thinking by rewriting the way you say and think certain things. For example:

SELF-INFLICTED CONDITION:	CHANGE TO:
I'm afraid	I'm scaring myself by imagining. . . .
I'm confused	How am I confusing myself?
I'm depressed	I am depressing myself by telling myself . . .
I'm trapped	I'm trapping myself by thinking . . .
I'm worried (related to fear)	I'm worried because I'm scaring myself by imagining that . . .

Positive thinking takes practice because we are socialized to be negative thinkers. When you add up all the years you've been thinking self-defeating thoughts, you'll realize it takes a commitment to undo all those years of habit. The outcome of the effort, however, is the ability to accomplish anything you want.

SELF-CONFIDENCE

Self-confidence is the food which feeds our personal growth. It is an absolutely indispensable part of achievement. Self-confidence stems from the self-awareness of our intrinsic worth as individuals. We are blessed with an incredible amount of potential, most of which is untapped. George Santayana once wrote, "Man is as full of potentiality as he is of importance." Santayana's thought also implies that the choice is ours, *which it is.*

Self-confidence works best when based on your own knowledge and self-respect, rather than on comparisons of yourself with others. A wise person once said, "Don't compare yourself to other people because you will feel either pompous or bitter . . . and neither one is desirable." So our self-confidence has to exist in a vacuum, which it can. It feeds on the knowledge gained from discovering one's inner potential.

MODEL FOR ACHIEVEMENT

After you have discovered your potential and taken responsibility for it, you can begin to become aware. Awareness starts with evaluating your strengths and weaknesses in the light of your current situation. You then expand your assumptions to accept more possible goals for yourself. This leads you to expand your actions and eventually to achieve your goals. The model for this process is:

Awareness ➤ Beliefs ➤ Goals ➤ Plans ➤ Actions ➤ Achievements

One step leads sequentially to another. After an achievement you re-evaluate yourself and find that each new feather in your cap makes you feel capable of accomplishing more and more. Your beliefs (assumptions) then expand, making more goals possible. The effect gains momentum and grows like a snowball rolling downhill. In this way, greatness is achieved through small stepping stones.

THE FILTER OF ONE'S SELF-CONCEPT

Ideally, all new ideas could start at the awareness stage and move on to the belief stage. However, something called a self-concept may get in the way. Our self-concept is the image we hold of ourselves. It is the evaluation we justly or unjustly make based on everything we have known about ourselves.

Most of us arrive at an inaccurate self-concept. We are negative thinkers by habit. This biased self-concept acts as a filter to limit the amount of new things that we feel we are capable of doing. What happens is this: A new thought or feeling comes into our awareness. It comes up against the filter, which compares it to our self-concept. If the idea is consistent with our self-concept, then the new idea is accepted and becomes a belief. If the idea is not consistent with our self-concept, however, it is rejected.

It is for this reason that developing a healthy self-concept is one of the most valuable things you can do for yourself. By practicing positive thinking, improving yourself as a person, and continuing to take risks, your self-concept will improve.

THE PROCESSES OF BRAINSTORMING, GOAL-SETTING, VISUALIZING, AND ROLE MODELING

Brainstorming

A valuable way of exploring your values and goals is through *brainstorming*. In brainstorming, you give free flight to your ideas on a specific problem to be solved. Opening your mind in this way can be valuable. By letting ideas flow without judging them, you will generate many times the ideas produced through the normal reasoning process. After abundant ideas have been generated, you can go back to evaluate their usefulness.

Brainstorming unleashes all the creative capacities in our minds. It does this by removing the restrictions and guidelines under which we have been taught to operate. The rules for brainstorming are as follows:

1. *Suspend all judgment.* This is a time to remove your internal censor. Nothing is unimportant or too silly to include when brainstorming.

2. *Think quantity, not quality.* The more ideas you generate, the better the chances are of hitting on something new and useful. Bad ideas can always be thrown out later.

3. *Extrapolate and crossfertilize.* No matter how nonsensical it may seem, take your ideas to the *n*th degree. Combine ideas in unusual ways to stimulate new ideas.

4. *The wilder the better.* This is a time to be "way out." Some of the best ideas are unconventional ones.

5. *Evaluate later.* Do not close your mind to any suggestions. Let the ideas percolate. An idea that seemed ridiculous yesterday may be ingenious tomorrow.

To brainstorm, find a time when you will not be distracted. Sit comfortably with a pencil and paper. The purpose of the brainstorming session should be stated in the form of a question or a problem to be dealt with. The question must be specific, such as, "How can I increase my inventory of prospective buyers?" Once the question has been posed, you should immediately begin jotting down ideas. It is important to record the first thing that comes to your mind. Do not judge, write! Make notes in brief phrases to save time. After a predetermined time limit, you can fill in the details of your notes.

Brainstorming can be done alone or in groups. If you are working alone, a tape recorder is faster than taking notes. Again, speak only key words and phrases. Do not worry about explanations now. You will know what you were talking about when you listen to the tape later.

After you have finished, review your notes. Examine all the possibilities as they come up. Discard unusable ideas only at the end. It is important and worth repeating that *you should suspend all judgment during this exercise.* Often wild and crazy ideas, when put together or altered slightly, turn out to be novel, effective solutions. So let yourself go. This is a time to have fun with a creative challenge. You will find that you have a broader range of choices after brainstorming than you thought possible before.

Now that you see how the process works, we would like you to try it. Pose a question to yourself. Write it at the top of a sheet of paper and then take three to five minutes to come up with as many ideas as possible. Be sure to put yourself on a time limit and aim for *quantity,* not quality. Take the time now to complete this exercise. Have fun with it!

Can you see how the ideas flow when you let down your defensive censor? Perhaps you even felt a little silly writing down some of the ideas. Would you feel self-conscious if someone read what you wrote? Fear not, we all have those feelings when we first try brainstorming.

When considering your life's goals, apply the brainstorming process to your goals in each of life's key areas. Brainstorm each category using the rules we have just discussed. When doing such an exercise, allow approximately two minutes per category, using one page per category. Again, shoot for *quantity* and let your imagination take over.

Once you have finished, review what you have written and add anything you might have forgotten. When you are satisfied with your responses, look them over and circle the one idea under each category that stands out as being most important. Do not worry about what others might think or what is socially acceptable. Such an exercise allows you to see your goals in black and white, on paper, where they should be.

After completing your review, you should have a total of seven circled semi-finalists, one from each of the seven groups. Whether or not there is repetition is unimportant. Examine the seven goals, disregarding which group they came from, and choose the three that are the most pressing to you. Write those three on a separate sheet of paper with the title, "My Three Most Important Goals." These three goals represent the most important goals in your life *at this time.* Naturally your circumstances change from day to day and from year to year. Rarely will a goal endure for your entire life. Whether your goals are short-term or long-range, you can see that such an exercise forces you to identify those things most important to you at this moment.

With all the insight you have at hand, create a hierarchy of goals from the lists compiled. As valuable as it is to isolate your most precious goals, it is equally important to set out some less substantial goals for which to strive. So take the seven categories and list all the secondary goals which you feel are worthy of action. You now have a better idea of where you are and where you would like to be in every facet of your life. As an example, here is a list which one of the authors compiled for himself a few years ago:

- *Career Goals.* Make three more sales per week; earn a Master's Degree in marketing.
- *Family Goals.* Call Mom and Dad once a week; spend ten minutes daily with my spouse and each child.
- *Spiritual Goals.* Go to church once every two weeks; be more helpful to people every day.
- *Social Goals.* Go to weekly Rotary Club meetings; socialize with more salespeople and exchange ideas.
- *Mental Goals.* Stop worrying so much about money and success; improve my memory of names; increase my vocabulary proficiency; broaden my knowledge.
- *Physical Goals.* Eat less junk food; do stress reduction exercises every night; floss teeth every night; maintain an ideal weight.
- *Financial Goals.* Own my own home; purchase a sports car; provide for an ample retirement fund by the time I'm 55 years old.

Goal-Setting

When most people are asked, "What are your goals in life?" they respond with something like, "To be happy, healthy, and have plenty of money." On the surface this may seem fine, but as goals which lead to actions, however, they are not sufficient. After you have determined some goals, it is important to put them in a workable form. For goals to be *effective and workable,* they must meet the following rules:

1. *A goal must be personal.* This means that your goal must be something you *want* to do rather than something that you think you *should* do. Know your reasons for having the goal. Whether you want to achieve something for status, money, or good health is secondary as long as you want it badly enough to work hard for it.

2. *Your goal must be positive.* It is an automatic response to think of the thing you are told *not* to think about. This is because the mind cannot *not* think of something when told to do so. We tend to focus on ideas and actions from a positive framework. When you think a negative thought such as, "I will not smoke today," your mind perceives it as "I *will* smoke today," and you end up thinking more about smoking than usual. Phrasing it in a positive way, such as "I will breathe only clean air today," serves the same purpose and is more effective.

3. *Your goal must be written.* Written goals take a jump in status from being nebulous thoughts to bona fide entities on paper. Their being written serves as a visual reminder and thus continually reconfirms their importance. They gain credibility just by being written; we have been trained from childhood to believe written statements. This can be seen in the statement from the movie, *The Ten Commandments:* "So let it be written, so let it be done." When things are put in writing they become official in our minds. A written goal strengthens our commitment to accomplish it.

4. *Your goal must be specific.* If you set your goal by saying, "I will increase my sales next year," the chances are that you will not do it. You must be specific in order to avoid the lack of commitment which comes with being vague. A more workable and motivating goal would be, "I will increase my sales next year by 10 to 15 percent." This revised statement has several advantages. It defines the increase for which you are striving as well as the range of the desired increase. Giving yourself some leeway is more realistic than expecting to hit your goal exactly on the mark. If you increase your sales 13 percent instead of 15 percent, you have still succeeded.

5. *Your goal must be a challenge.* A goal must motivate you to work harder than you have in the past. It must move you forward. Set your goals beyond your reach so that you will have to stretch a bit. The more you stretch, the more limber your goal-achieving abilities will become.

6. *Your goal must be realistic.* Everything is relative to time and space. What is unrealistic today may be totally within reason five years from now. For years it was believed that the fastest a man could run a mile was four minutes. It was unrealistic to aspire to run any faster until Dr. Roger Bannister broke the four-minute mile in 1954. Since then hundreds of runners have done the same. In any field we never really know what the upper limits are. How, then, do we define realistic? For our purposes, the best definition must come from you and your values. You must ask yourself, "What price am I willing to pay to accomplish this goal?" You should always weigh the payoffs and the sacrifices involved before coming to a conclusion. *Realistic* is ultimately your decision.

Now that you know the rules for setting goals, you can apply them to the goals you set for yourself. It would be a good idea to make some worksheets and use them for every primary and secondary goal you want to achieve. For each goal, do the following:

1. *Define your goal.* Your first task is to determine whether your goal meets all the requirements of the rules listed above. If it does, then write it as clearly as possible at the top of your worksheet.

2. *Examine obstacles that stand in your way.* This is a time to guard against negative assumptions and other self-defeating thoughts. Remember the definition of realistic. An obstacle blocks you only if you let it. You should also write down your innovative ways of overcoming obstacles.

3. *W.I.I.F.M.—What's in it for me?* Write down *why* you want to achieve the goal. What kind of payoff is motivating you?

4. *Plan your action.* You need to carefully list the steps that will bring you closer to your goal. The smaller the increments, the easier they will be to accomplish. There is a German proverb which says, "He who begins too much accomplishes little."

5. *Project a target date for your goal.* State your deadline in a range, such as, "between March 15th and April 1st." Think carefully about the amount of time you need. Too little time will increase the pressure and frustrate you. Too much time may reduce your drive.

6. *Know how you will measure your success.* Goals should be described in terms of the final outcome of an activity rather than as the activity itself. This is part of being specific. Instead of saying, "I will be running more in four to six months," you could say, "I'll be running three miles instead of two miles in four to six months."

When using these worksheets, fill them out completely and *keep them visible!* Put them in a place where you will see them every day. Check off items as you complete them. Use them to chart your progress and take pride in your accomplishments.

Visualizing

Visualization is an indispensable tool in helping people attain their goals. Musicians and athletes have proven that visualization is an effective substitute for real practice. In visualizing your goals, you will live your accomplishments in your mind's eye. The more of the five senses that you can involve in this exercise, the greater your chances are of accomplishment.

For example, you may want to be the Salesperson of the Year in your company. You know that each year an awards banquet is given during which a plaque is presented to the year's sales leader. You may choose to focus on this banquet for your visualization exercise. Here is what you do:

Make yourself comfortable. Close your eyes and relax. Slowly and systematically go through all of the five senses. Imagine what you would be experiencing at the banquet.

Sight. What would you see there? You would see other salespeople and their spouses. Imagine what they are wearing. You would see tables decorated and waiters scurrying about. You would see the bar and people standing around talking. Keep expanding what you "see" for several minutes.

Sound. What would you hear? You would hear the chatter of people. You would hear laughter, the tinkling of glasses, music from a band, and people talking. You would also continually hear people coming up to congratulate you. Imagine that!

Smell. Imagine all the smells you would experience: women's perfume, food, alcohol, men's cologne, the smell of floral decorations. What else?

Feel. What would your tactile sensations be? You would feel people rubbing up against you in the crowded room. You would feel others shaking your hand. What else?

Taste. Taste in your mind the champagne you will be drinking. Taste the food you will be eating. Experience the sweet taste of success—in advance!

Most importantly, imagine the exhilaration you will feel when you are called to receive the award! Take your time during this exercise and enjoy it. The more you can "visually" attend this banquet, the more motivated you will become.

To aid in your visualization exercise, you might want to start a visualization file. This is an envelope or folder into which you put pictures, clippings, letters, and other reminders of what it will be like to succeed. Your file should also contain letters or awards which you have received in the past. Anything that makes you feel good about yourself can be included in the file. It can then be used as a source of motivation and inspiration, especially if you begin to feel a little down or unmotivated. We all need to be reminded of our past accomplishments once in a while. Be your own best friend—remind yourself!

Role Modeling

Many people concentrate only on the goal they wish to attain but there is more to the picture. Successful people in every field have certain characteristics in common. These common characteristics do not occur by chance; they are an integral part of goal attainment. It is worth your time to analyze the constructive characteristics of people who are now where you would like to be.

One effective method is to choose role models. These are people to admire and emulate. Your choices can include people who are dead or living as long as you are familiar with their personalities and accomplishments.

Harry Truman knew the value of role models. When he was in the White House he reportedly went into the Lincoln bedroom, looked at the late president's picture, and asked, "What would Lincoln have done if he were in my situation?" The answers to this question gave Truman the insight and direction he was seeking. It worked because Truman felt Lincoln was a man worth emulating.

In choosing role models, several things must be kept in mind:

1. *Keep them off the pedestal.* There is no doubt that you will choose people whom you see as being above you because of what they have accomplished. That is good. What is not good is to put them on a pedestal, thereby making them larger than life. We are all human. We all have strengths and weaknesses. You must not lose this perspective. Putting role models on pedestals only further separates you from them.

2. *Isolate their strong points.* You need to look at the person you wish to emulate and analyze the precise qualities he or she possesses which you need to acquire. Sit down and write out the characteristics which seem to encourage their success. Use concrete examples of their behaviors which you can adapt to your own situation.

3. *Remain yourself.* Quite often the tendency when admiring someone is to try to become his or her clone. People who seem to have it all together have done all the work for you. It seems that all you have to do is imitate them. This is a dangerous way to think because you are not working on your own personality.

In the final analysis, you are you. It is impossible to become exactly like someone else. And why should you want to? Remain yourself while you acquire new traits to help you achieve your goals.

Sometimes it is helpful to have a symbol of another person's virtues. This symbol will actually remind you of that person and his or her qualities. It can take the form of a picture, a possession (e.g., your father's pocketwatch), or some abstract thing such as a rock. It will be useful as long as it makes the association in your mind.

Multiple Models   A workable system of role modeling is to examine the traits of several people whom you admire. This will help you avoid hero worship of a single person. Write down their virtues as you did before, without identifying to whom they belong. When you are with these people, look for more behaviors which reflect their success. The best models are successful people in your own field. Their behaviors are directly translatable to your life and will have more meaning to you.

QUESTIONS TO ASK.   Acquiring good habits from others will accelerate you towards your goal. Ask yourself these questions to get the most out of your role models:

1. What would they do in my situation?
2. What do they do every day to encourage growth and to move closer to a goal?
3. How do they think in general? In specific situations?
4. Do they have other facets of life in balance? What effect does that have on their well-being?
5. How do their traits apply to me?
6. Which traits are worth working on first? Later?

Mentors   A mentor is someone you admire and under whom you can study. Throughout history the mentor–protege relationship has proven quite fruitful. Plato and Aristotle studied under Socrates, one of the early mentors, and later emerged as great philosophers in their own right. Mentors are worth cultivating if you can find them.

However, the same cautions hold true here as for any role model. It is better to adapt the mentor's philosophies to your life than to adopt his or her entire personality. Be suspicious of any mentor who seeks to make you dependent on him. It is better to have him teach you how to fish than to have him catch the fish for you. That way you will remain in control. Under the right circumstances mentors make excellent role models. The one-to-one setting is highly conducive to learning as well as to friendship.

ROLE PLAYING

Role playing is like acting. You define a desirable behavior and then act it out for practice. Since practice makes permanent, role playing will help you master new behaviors. It can be done alone or with a partner and need not take more than a few minutes. Like anything else, the more you do it, the better you will become.

One form of role playing would be to get together with a friend and playact. Define a situation and the desired behaviors. Then run through it, trying your best to act as you would like to in real life. For example, let's say you want to learn to relax more as a salesperson. You and your friend would set up a situation in which you play the salesperson and your friend plays the buyer. You would then interact with the buyer in ways which allow you to relax more than you have in the past. You would practice using more eye contact, holding your body in a relaxed posture, listening more, joking with the buyer, and so on. Afterward, you and your friend would discuss how each of you felt during the exercise. You would repeat this over and over until you have made some progress. Role playing is an excellent way to introduce new behaviors in a relaxed, nonthreatening atmosphere.

It seems that we are forever returning to the fact that we need to change our thinking. Perhaps this is so because our obsession with negative thinking is so great (and so great an impediment to our progress). Role playing through visualization is an effective way to change our thoughts. Basically, you imagine a situation and how you previously felt in it. You then think of more positive thoughts and feelings and practice using them in the problematic situation.

For example, we knew someone who had a fear of asking people for appointments. His typical thoughts in that situation were, "Why should I ask? He's going to reject me," or, "If he rejects me, I will be devastated." He started role playing new thoughts in the old situation. Instead of negative assumptions and negative thinking, he substituted, "I'm going to ask because I have as much of a chance of being accepted as rejected. I'm going to expect acceptance and will get it. I'm not going to invite rejection through my attitude. And if I do get rejected, big deal! It's not the worst thing in the world!" Through visualization he practiced and in real life became able to relax and approach more people for appointments.

Role playing new behaviors can also be done through visualization. Instead of imagining what you would think and feel in a situation, you imagine what you would *do*. In your mind you can change the undesirable behaviors and have the new behaviors carry over into real life.

THE THOUGHT DIET CARD

The *thought diet* is a tool that you can use on a daily basis to help you achieve your goals. It breaks down those goals into daily actions that are bite-sized and easy to do. By showing you the steps along the way, the thought diet will keep you from being overwhelmed by your lofty goals.

There are three rules for using the thought diet:

1. Write a thought diet card and read it daily. A thought diet card can be a list or a paragraph stating affirmations of the way you would like your life to be. A thought diet card feeds your conscious and unconscious mind the positive thoughts and personal goals that you want to achieve. These wishes should be stated in the present, not in the future. For example, "I am calling on three more customers per week." "I am spending a half hour each night with my children." "I am running three miles every other day." "I am eating only nutritious food." Repetitive reading of your thought diet card will reinforce your desires and keep your actions on target. It will be especially effective if read before going to sleep.
2. Avoid associating with people who drag you down emotionally. Instead, associate with people who are positive and from whom your optimism can grow.
3. Make it meaningful. Read and fill out the card sincerely; do not just go through the motions. You will be kidding no one but yourself if you don't take it seriously.

Primary Goal

In the first section of the thought diet card, write your primary goal. Write out as explicitly as possible that goal which is strongest and affects your motivation the most at this point in time.

Daily Growth

The second section of the card is for writing in the characteristics that you are developing. Write out five key characteristics that you need to develop to achieve your goal. State these personal characteristics in ways which adhere to the rules of goal-setting.

Action Plan

The third section of the card is the action section. Here you will write out the minimum daily standards which you will perform every day to move you closer to your goal. Again, be specific. Following are some examples of minimum daily standards:

- *Mental.* I will spend 15 minutes every evening doing visualization exercises.
- *Physical.* I will do a minimum of five push-ups and ten sit-ups every morning.
- *Career.* I will read something related to my career for at least 15 minutes before going to bed.
- *Financial.* I will keep a complete record of every expense.
- *Spiritual.* Each day I will do one good deed to help someone less fortunate than I.
- *Family.* I will relax over dinner and enjoy a meaningful conversation with my family.
- *Social.* I will take time to call one of my new friends.

Read the thought diet card twice a day until everything becomes a habit. Once you have developed constructive habits you can move on to new behaviors. Fill out a new card and practice the new challenges every day until they become habits. In this way you will painlessly move closer and closer to your goals.

There is more to life than making a sale, although we all know many salespeople who would argue that point. The fact is that having a balanced life will not only make you happier, it will make you a better salesperson.

Ultimately it all comes down to something Benjamin Disraeli once wrote: "The secret of success is constancy of purpose."

SUMMARY

The emphasis of this chapter was the discussion of several influences on one's life which can be positive or negative, depending on the individual, and the introduction of several suggested processes to follow which can lead to both a more successful sales career and a happier life in general.

Creating balance among the seven need categories in our lives is particularly important, for each category can positively or negatively affect the others, depending on the attention or lack of attention it receives. These seven categories are: mental, physical, family, social, spiritual, career, and financial. To begin a sales career effectively, we must work at bringing our lives into balance. This requires goal-setting—the identification of the end results we want to achieve for every facet, every need category, of our lives. Only then can we plan the concrete steps and intermediate goals which stand between our present situation and our ideal concept of ourselves.

People who have a clear set of goals in life exude a sense of purpose and determination, are taken seriously by others, and are respected by their peers. In contrast, those who have no goals feel emotionally, socially, spiritually, physically, and professionally unbalanced, causing anxiety. To be successful in sales, we must identify our goals and map out the steps that will allow us to reach those goals. Choices become infinitely easier to make when we know the direction we are following in our lives and in our careers.

Our basic assumptions can have a positive or negative effect on our behavior, thus affecting both our careers and our lives in general. More often than not, it is our assumptions that limit our perceived options. Negative assumptions, which set up internal obstacles that can automatically defeat us, usually become self-fulfilling prophecies. We assume we cannot do something and then act in ways that guarantee our failure, which in turn reinforces our original assumption. Our negative assumptions, therefore, must be replaced by positive assumptions that can in turn receive positive results.

Brainstorming, goal-setting, visualizing, and role modeling are four processes that we can use to become more successful in our efforts.

Brainstorming is a valuable way of exploring our values and goals. It gives free flight to our ideas on specific problems to be solved. Ideas flow freely without being judged, thus many more ideas are generated than through the normal reasoning process. After a large number of ideas has been generated, we can review the list and evaluate each one's usefulness. The *initial* aim is for quantity, not quality.

Brainstorming can be used to determine our most important goals in the seven need categories. Through a process of review and elimination, the three most important goals for immediate attention can be determined, with others that also warrant action becoming our secondary goals. Such an exercise gives us a better idea of where we are and where we would like to be in every area of our lives.

When setting goals for action, we must remember the rules for goal-setting: goals must be personal; they must be positively stated; they must be written; they must be specific; they must be a challenge; and they must be realistic.

Visualizing is an indispensable tool in helping us attain our goals. It is a process through which we live our accomplishments in our mind's eye. The more of the five senses that we involve in the process, the greater our chances of actually accomplishing that which we visualize.

Role modeling is the process of selecting successful individuals of the present or of the past whom we admire and wish to emulate, analyzing the characteristics that we believe led to their success, and incorporating those characteristics through practice into our own lives. When selecting role models, it is important to keep in mind three things: keep the role models off pedestals; isolate their strong points; and remain ourselves.

In working toward achieving our goals and making positive changes through role modeling, it is especially helpful to create a thought diet card which should be reviewed a minimum of twice a day. On it is written our primary goal, five of the positive characteristics we are trying to develop, and a specific action plan we have created for each of the seven need categories. A new thought diet card is prepared when everything on the first card has been achieved.

A balanced life achieved through processes that help us identify and reach our goals will not only give us happier lives, but will make us more successful, more effective salespeople.

DISCUSSION QUESTIONS

1. Why is it important to set goals?
2. What are the six criteria goals should meet?
3. What are the five ground rules for brainstorming?
4. What is the relationship between your assumptions and your behavior?
5. Think of something you would like to do but stopped yourself from doing because of a negative assumption.
6. Break down and analyze the assumption in Question 5 until it no longer presents an obstacle to action.
7. What is the process of visualization and why does it work so well?
8. Review your answers to the questions at the end of Chapter 4. Did

negative thinking get in the way of your contacting a role model of working to improve yourself? If so, review the characterics of excellence and set short-term goals to improve three of them.

9. Brainstorm and fill in as many answers to the following phrase as you can: "If I thought I could, I would . . ."

10. Go over the answers to Question 9 and, for each one, answer the following question: "What's stopping me?"

CHAPTER TWENTY-ONE

Time Management

CHAPTER	**1**	Discuss the efficient and effective management of time.
OBJECTIVES	**2**	Introduce the purpose and use of a time log.
	3	Develop an awareness of time wasters, thus encouraging their control.
	4	Discuss procrastination and the ways to effectively handle it.

Time is nature's greatest force. Nothing can stop it; nothing can alter it. Unlike the wind, it cannot be felt. Unlike the sun, it cannot be seen. Yet, of all nature's forces, time has the most profound effect on us.

Time remains constant, but our *perception* of it changes. When we focus on it, it slows down. When we turn our backs on it, it speeds up. Our illusion makes us think it is something tangible. We arrange it, divide it up, give some to our friends. Sometimes we feel it is precious; at other times we waste it. We give it the power to heal when we say, "Time heals all wounds." It can also kill, as when we live stressful lives because we "never have enough time." On a day-to-day basis, nothing is defined and redefined in our minds as much as time. It's a wonder we can still recognize it!

Herein lies our power. Because things are as we perceive them, we can choose to see time as a manageable commodity and live our lives according to that assumption. It works, too! The first step is to take responsibility and *want* to control our time, one of the secrets of successful people—they work at shaping those things which others think are uncontrollable.

As a professional salesperson, you will have to manage your time effectively if you hope to be successful. Think of yourself as a business. Imagine having an employee who comes to work and does not get as much done as you would like. It would not be long before you started to manage his time for him, watching him carefully to make sure he continued to be productive. That employee in your business is you. *You* are your greatest boss and your most valuable asset is *time!* This chapter will show you how to get the most out of this elusive resource we call *time.*

EFFICIENCY VS. EFFECTIVENESS

In discussing time management, some people would argue, "What we need to be is more *efficient* with our time!" Other people would claim, "Let's not worry so much about efficiency, let's be more effective!"

For the purpose of this discussion, we will draw a distinction between the two. *Efficiency* means doing things right. *Effectiveness* means doing the right things. Working efficiently is doing things with the least amount of wasted effort. Efficiency gets you from point A to point B via a straight line. Inefficiency goes in circles, zig-zags, and gets fewer mpg. Effectiveness means doing the things that yield results. Effectiveness takes aim at the target and hits it, even if it's behind you. Effectiveness *works,* often to the chagrin of efficiency.

The relationship between efficiency (E_1) and effectiveness (E_2) is:

$$E_1 + E_2 = R \text{ (results)}$$

It takes a certain amount of both effectiveness and efficiency to obtain any result. As in math, however, the proportions are not always equal. Using numbers instead of letters, the equation can be:

$$4 + 6 = 10$$
$$3 + 7 = 10$$
$$5 + 5 = 10$$
$$9 + 1 = 10$$

In each case, the result is the same but the individual contributions are different. So too, the amounts of efficiency and effectiveness can vary for any given result.

Many new salespeople, when learning about time management, ask the question, "Which should I work on first, efficiency or effectiveness?" In theory and practice, the best answer is to improve your effectiveness first. Effective selling will produce sales and give you time to work on efficiency. It is much better to aim your sights at the result than to worry about the process. Too often we get bogged down in the means and lose sight of the end.

Like all of the other changes to which we aspire, before you can improve your use of time, you need to know where you are now. Taking the time to analyze your habits will lead the way to more effective time management in the future.

To analyze your habits, you should first review *circadian rhythm,* the high and the low points of your effectiveness during the day. Everyone has a prime time. Some of us are morning people; others are night people. Whether this involves a biological determinant or not is secondary. What is important is to note your patterns of effectiveness. Find your best time of the day. Do you sell more in the mornings or in the afternoons? Are you in a fog until noon? Once you know when you are at your best, you can organize your day to coincide with your prime time. This is just the beginning of your gaining control of your most valuable asset—time.

THE TIME LOG

In order to control your time, you have to know what you are doing with it now. We would like you to do an exercise which is going to take about half an hour each day for 15 days. You will not have to go on a crash diet or run three miles a

Figure 21.1:   A Sample Time Log for Keeping Track of Daily Activities

HOUR	TIME FRAME	ACTUAL TIME	DESCRIPTION OF ACTIVITIES	COMMENTS FOR BETTER TIME USE
7	0-30			
	30-60			
8	0-30			
	30-60			
9	0-30			
	30-60			
10	0-30			
	30-60			
3	0-30			
	30-60			
4	0-30			
	30-60			
5	0-30			
	30-60			

TIME LOG FOR _____ DATE _____ DAY _____   ANALYSIS

day, but we guarantee that by the end of the second week you will have grown. The insight you gain from keeping track of your activities is that on which you base your time management goals. How will you know which bad habits to change unless you monitor your present way of doing things? It would be like going to a doctor and telling him you think you need to lower your blood pressure. Would you be happy if he prescribed a drug without taking your blood pressure first? If you want to increase your sales through more efficient time management, you need to pinpoint exactly how. Otherwise you will be as uncommitted as if all of your goals were unwritten!

So take the time every day to complete your time logs. Use the suggested format given in Figure 21.1, beginning with 7:00 A.M. and expanding it to 11:00 P.M. Fill in your activities for 10-minute intervals throughout the day. Try not to allow more than an hour to pass without recording what you have done. It is really not as much work as it seems and it will soon become a habit.

At the end of each day, you should conduct a time analysis by asking these questions:

1. What went right today? Why?
2. What went wrong today? Why?
3. What time did I start on my top priority task? Why? Could I have started earlier?
4. What patterns do I see in my time logs?
5. What part of the day was most productive? Least productive?
6. What were my three biggest timewasters today?
7. What activities need more time? Which need less time?
8. Beginning tomorrow, what will I do to make better use of my time?

Try to be as exact as possible in determining what happened that day. Also be specific in stating the ways in which you will improve tomorrow.

At the end of 15 days, analyze the time logs to determine your six most important activities during that time and list them. Then determine the six least important things and compute the total amount of time spent on each of these activities.

TIME LOG ANALYSIS

My Six Most Productive Activities   Between (Dates)_____
   1.   Total Time:_____
   2.   Total Time:_____
   3.   Total Time:_____
   4.   Total Time:_____
   5.   Total Time:_____
   6.   Total Time:_____
My Six Least Productive Activities   Between (Dates)_____
   1.   Total Time:_____
   2.   Total Time:_____
   3.   Total Time:_____
   4.   Total Time:_____
   5.   Total Time:_____
   6.   Total Time:_____

After you have written your six most and your six least productive activities and the time spent on each, you will be equipped to set some time management objectives. Use the skills you learned in the chapter on goal-setting. Write out your objectives and develop an action plan for each. Then follow through!

Eliminating Time Wasters

A systematic evaluation of time wasters reveals that they come from the people around you as well as from within yourself. Some time wasters are unavoidable, but reducible nonetheless, and you need to identify the most frequent sources of those time wasters in your day. Use a worksheet like Figure 21.2a to develop a profile of your time-wasting activities. Be honest with yourself and base your answers on an average day. After you have completed Part One, choose the three biggest time wasters and enter them in the spaces in Part Two. Then think of ways in which you will overcome those time wasters.

As a means of comparison, a list of time wasters compiled by Leo Moore of MIT is below. Most researchers find the same handful at the top of their own lists, indicating that they are problems common to everyone:

Telephone	Procrastination
Meetings	"Fire fighting"
Reports	Special requests
Visitors	Delays
Delegation	Reading

In all positions and occupations, there are time wasters—that is, areas in which we tend to lose or waste time during our work day. How much of your time is spent in these areas?

SETTING PRIORITIES

When setting your time priorities, there are two famous laws to remember:

Parkinson's Law:
Work tends to expand to fill the time allotted for its completion. Setting priorities is therefore twice as important. If you do not know what your priorities are, your other work will expand to fill in the extra time. It will take longer for you to accomplish less.

Pareto's Principle:
Pareto's Principle, in this situation, states that 80 percent of your results comes from 20 percent of your efforts. Another way to to look at it is that 80 percent of your business comes from 20 percent of your customers. It's also called the "80-20 Rule."

Thus, if your time is worth x amount per hour to you, you need to spend

TIME WASTERS

	None	Some	A Lot
1. Overpreparing for calls.	——	——	——
2. Scheduling less important work before more important work.	——	——	——
3. Starting a job before thinking it through.	——	——	——
4. Leaving jobs before they are completed.	——	——	——
5. Doing things that can be delegated to another person (across or down; not upward).	——	——	——
6. Doing things that can be delegated to modern equipment (providing such exists in your work).	——	——	——
7. Doing things that actually aren't a part of your real job.	——	——	——
8. Keeping too many, too complicated, or overlapping records.	——	——	——
9. Pursuing prospects you probably can't sell.	——	——	——
10. Paying too much attention to low-yield prospects.	——	——	——
11. Handling too wide a variety of duties.	——	——	——
12. Failing to build barriers against interruptions.	——	——	——
13. Allowing conferences and discussions to wander.	——	——	——
14. Conducting unnecessary meetings, visits, and/or phone calls.	——	——	——
15. Chasing trivial data after the main facts are in.	——	——	——
16. Socializing at great length between tasks.	——	——	——

Figure 21.2a: Time Wasters Evaluation and Solutions (Part One)

your time doing things that pay you more than your time is worth. What is your time worth? To get an idea, look at Figure 21.3.

With your time being worth this much, you need to increase the use of your time in high priority activities which bring the greatest payoff. It does not make sense to wash your car during the day when your time is worth $25 per hour or more to you. Arrange your day to take advantage of your earning potential.

Identify your high priority (most important payoff) activities for each of the perspectives below as if you were an active salesperson today. Think about the most important things you would do from three different perspectives: your

Figure 21.2b: Time Wasters Evaluation and Solutions (Part Two)

OVERCOMING TIME WASTERS

1. Time waster _____
   Strategies for minimizing

2. Time waster _____
   Strategies for minimizing

3. Time waster _____
   Strategies for minimizing

YEARLY INCOME*	EVERY HOUR IS WORTH (40 HR. WEEK)	1 HR/WK OF SELLING TIME IS WORTH*
$ 5,000	$ 2.56	$ 128.00
$ 7,500	$ 3.84	$ 192.00
$ 10,000	$ 5.12	$ 256.00
$ 20,000	$10.25	$ 512.50
$ 30,000	$15.37	$ 768.50
$ 40,000	$20.50	$1,025.00
$ 50,000	$25.62	$1,281.00
$ 60,000	$30.74	$1,537.00
$ 70,000	$35.86	$1,793.00
$ 80,000	$40.94	$2,047.00
$ 90,000	$46.10	$2,305.00
$100,000	$51.23	$2,561.00

*Based on approximately 50 working weeks per year.

Figure 21.3: What Your Time Is Worth, Based on Yearly Income

sales manager's, your customers', and your own. After identifying those for each category, identify the six priorities that stand out regardless of perspective.

PERSPECTIVES

-My Sales Manager:
-My Customers and Prospects:
-My Own:
-Overall High Priority Activities:

Use a "To Do" List

A list of things to do for each day and week is a valuable aid to managing your time. A "to do" list organizes your thinking and planning onto one form in the least amount of time with the maximum amount of efficiency. Such a list is especially helpful if it coincides with the record keeping you already do for your company. After a short time you will find yourself handling a greater volume of work without increasing your stress. You will simply become more efficient.

Because we are creatures of habit, it is a good idea for you to fill out your "to do" list at the same time every day. In this way you will be committed to a routine and won't be tempted to procrastinate. Whether you fill it out in the evening or first thing in the morning is unimportant. You should keep in mind, however, that you are often in a hurry in the morning and may be tempted to skip it.

As we mentioned before, Parkinson's Law states that work expands to fill the time allotted for it. Your "to do" list should, therefore, define a specific amount of time (if possible) for each activity. This will keep work from expanding too much.

To Do List

Action	Priority	Time Needed	Date Due ✔

Scheduled Events

8:00	
8:15	
8:30	
8:45	
9:00	
9:15	
9:30	
9:45	
10:00	
10:15	
10:30	
10:45	
11:00	
11:15	
11:30	
11:45	
12:00	
12:15	
12:30	
12:45	
1:00	
1:15	
1:30	
1:45	
2:00	
2:15	
2:30	
2:45	
3:00	
3:15	
3:30	
3:45	
4:00	
4:15	
4:30	
4:45	
5:00	
5:15	
5:30	
5:45	
6:00	

Notes

Evening

Reprinted with permission from Merrill E. Douglass, Time Management Center, Grandville, Michigan.

Figure 21.4:   A "To Do" List to Help Set Priorities

Your activities should be listed in order of priority. Work on high priorities first and keep in mind what your time is worth. In listing the activities, it is helpful to spell out the result as well as the process. For example, you might list: "Between 12:00 noon and 1:00 P.M., go to manufacturer's rep luncheon and get at least three business cards from prospects." Stating when, where, and what you are going to do increases your chances of doing it successfully. In addition, use action verbs such as write, call, meet, and complete to describe your activities.

As the day goes by, check off completed activities and make any notes that seem relevant. In the evening, make out a new "to do" list for the next day and include any activities you could not complete that day. Always save your "to do" lists for future reference.

Records of Time Use

Some companies require their salespeople to keep accurate records, others do not. The experts in time management all agree that the more records you keep, the more you will be aware of the opportunities for sales, for prospecting, and for improving your use of time. Examples of valuable records to keep include the following:

- Number of sales calls
- Number of calls resulting in interviews
- Number of interviews resulting in attempts to confirm the sale
- Number of actual sales
- Number of sales that stay on the books

Through systematic record keeping you will learn, among other things, what phase of the sale gives you the most trouble. It is suggested that you graph or chart your performance to get a visual illustration of your strengths and weaknesses.

Another highly valuable record to keep is your daily time log. Not only will this depict your efficiency on a day-to-day basis, it will also speed your writing of monthly reports. In fact, you might be able to staple your daily time logs together to compose your monthly report. If you get in the habit of taking five minutes each day to answer the time analysis questions suggested earlier, you will quickly gain invaluable insight into your patterns of both productive activity and time wasting. Like written goals, daily written proof of your inefficiency will have more of an effect on your motivation than just thinking about it.

MENACES OF TIME

Procrastination

Don't put off for tomorrow what you can do today.

Procrastination is like a virus. It creeps up on you slowly, drains you of energy, and is difficult to eliminate if your resistance is low. Procrastination is a close relative of incompetence and a first cousin to inefficiency. We all procrastinate from time to time. What is important is to avoid procrastinating things that are important. You can overcome procrastination if you recognize it and take responsibility for it. Do not make yourself the "victim" by claiming to be lazy. Laziness means simply not caring enough to act.

The suggestions below will help you conquer procrastination:

1. *Choose one area* in which procrastination plagues you and conquer it. Set up a procrastination priority and action steps. For example, if you are putting off calling qualified prospects, simply set a goal of calling on X number every day or week.

2. *Give yourself deadlines.* Remember: In moderation, pressure motivates; however, *extreme* pressure debilitates. Set appointments, make commitments, write out your goals, and otherwise develop the determination to succeed.

3. *Do not duck the difficult problems.* Every day we are faced with both difficult and easy tasks. Tackle the difficult ones first so that you can look forward to the easy ones. If you work on the easy ones first, you might expand the time that they take in order to avoid the difficult ones waiting for you.

4. *Break all large or difficult tasks into their smaller subparts.* Many people put off difficult or large tasks because they appear too huge to tackle in a reasonable time frame. They feel that if they start and complete the large task in one time period, they will be unable to accomplish any of the other tasks that they have to do on that day. The answer is to break all large or difficult tasks into their smaller subparts. You can then do each of the subparts of the larger project over a series of days, if appropriate. Tony recalls:

   Several years ago, when I was writing my book, *Non-Manipulative Selling*, I procrastinated writing it (even *starting* to write it) past two deadlines from my publisher. Finally, the publisher informed me that my third and *final* deadline would be 90 days from that day. If I did not meet this deadline, they would ask me to return the advance money they had given me when we signed the book contract.

   As I approached my final deadline in a state of depression, a close friend gave me a very simple idea that helped me finish the book. He said that if I wrote only three pages of the book per day the first thing each morning, the book would be done well before the deadline. Three pages per day seemed like such an easy task (and it was) that I finished the 180-page book in less than 30 days (some days I wrote many more than three pages).

5. *Don't let perfectionism paralyze you.* This is a problem which many writers have. They sit at their typewriters waiting for the "right" words to come out. What they are doing is avoiding the process of writing. Be prolific in your activities. You can always go back later and polish those things that you feel can be better. Better yet, you can delegate the polishing to someone else.

Because humans are so susceptible to procrastination, you must work at building up your immunity to it. Effective action is the best medicine.

Paperwork

The first step in handling paperwork is to do yourself the favor of reducing it. Do so by delegating as much as you can to a secretary or other co-worker. After you have reduced the quantity, you can then handle the rest efficiently.

Have a secretary screen your mail, if possible. Have it put in order of priority so that you can act on the most important pieces first. Junk mail would be on the bottom. Important mail and information would go in the middle and letters requiring an immediate response would go on top. Set a time for opening your mail and keep it the same every day. Obviously, this should be scheduled during an otherwise nonproductive time.

Try to answer any correspondence immediately. After you have read the letter, write your reply on the back and give it to a secretary to type. An even more efficient method is to use a dictation machine or tape recorder. Record your correspondence and leave the rest to your secretary.

Some companies prefer to use form letters instead of replying personally. This is acceptable in some circumstances, but not when you are communicating with prospects or customers.

The other mail you receive should be dealt with in the same way. Act immediately on whatever you can. If you receive a magazine, flip through it and clip out articles you intend to read. Try categorizing your reading material into three groups: articles you must read soon, articles you should read, and articles that would be nice to read. Clipping the article makes it more accessible. Stacking ten articles about one subject is much more practical than stacking ten magazines. The magazines look like more work and discourage you from diving into them.

Naturally more than mail will accumulate on your desk. Adopt a policy of picking up paperwork only once. This means that you should not look at something and put it back down where you found it. It is much wiser to take some form of action on the item. Decide what to do with it and move it along to the next step toward completion.

Down Time

Down time normally refers to time when a machine is out of service. Your down time includes unstructured minutes and hours during the day when you cannot get anything significant accomplished. These periods arise during traffic jams, in waiting rooms, when people fail to show up for appointments, and so on. You can fill this time instead of wasting it.

There are ways of doing nothing creatively. You can sit and relax. You can look at your "to do" list and change it, if necessary. You can think about your goals or the obstacles that you face and how you are going to overcome them. This is a good time to do your visualization exercises. Imagine yourself calling on that account that you have been dreading. Imagine yourself as successful and you should improve your chances of becoming successful.

Remember those articles you clipped and saved? If you carry them with you, they can be read while you are waiting for someone. It is amazing how many little tasks can be done in 10-minute time slots. Down time is also useful for making phone calls, unless, of course, you are in traffic. Consider getting a phone for your automobile. You can call ahead to your next appointment, call the office, and so on. With this in mind, you might want to write phone numbers on your "to do" list so they will be readily accessible.

The important thing about down time is to avoid wasting it. Do not fight yourself and the world and become aggravated. Relax and see it for what it is: more of that valuable asset which you so desperately need—time.

Interruptions

Most people who phone or visit you at home or at work do so under a false yet unquestioned assumption that you are free and receiving company. Few ever call and say, "Hi, are you busy?" Or if they do it's, "Hi, are you busy? [Yes] Oh, good . . . I wanted to tell you about this delicious pastrami sandwich I just had. . . ." Just what you need to hear in the middle of a busy day! It is no wonder so many business people have high blood pressure!

Despite the selfishness of the intruders, we, too, operate on a false assumption. Ours is that we cannot be blunt and sound inhospitable or ungracious. We usually just grit our teeth and resent them, not a very healthy situation.

There is a place for courtesy, but courtesy does not have to extend *carte blanche* to callers who interrupt the flow of thoughts, destroy concentration, or impede the continuity of effort. As a professional salesperson with limited time and unlimited work, you need to cultivate a direct, diplomatic way of handling interruptions.

The Telephone There are two ways to control the intrusion of telephone calls: a skilled secretary or an answering machine. An answering machine simply postpones the call and puts it in your hands to be returned. Having a skilled secretary is even more efficient and should be used if possible. You will have to communicate effectively with your secretary to determine the procedures for the four different kinds of calls you will receive.

1. *Direct traffic.* Your secretary's first duty is to determine the urgency of the call and whether it can be referred; many calls can be handled by others or even by your secretary.
2. *Automatic call-back.* Some calls can be handled only by you but are not sufficiently urgent to warrant an interruption. Your secretary can ask the caller, "May he call you back when he is free?" Or better yet, "Can you call again later?" The automatic call-back is a highly effective way to avoid intrusions.
3. *Brief interruption.* Sometimes your secretary can be helpful to you and your caller. By putting the caller on hold and asking you for a brief response to a quick question, you are saved the trouble of calling back later and the caller is satisfied.
4. *Urgent! Interrupt immediately!* There will always be calls that you will predesignate as warranting an interruption. These you can handle on the spot. Hopefully, few of your daily calls fall into this category.

THE CALL-BACK SYSTEM. Now that your secretary has headed off the onslaught of calls, you have the burden of returning them. Create a system for returning calls which includes time-saving habits such as:

1. Determine the time of day to return calls. You may want to avoid calling in the late morning or late afternoon. At these times, chances are greater that you will catch the other party facing lunch engagements or leaving for the day. These time pressures will make him less likely to take calls or want to spend much time on the phone.

2. Returning calls gives the caller the chance to solve the problem on her own. Sometimes a caller will seek other sources for answering the question that she called about.

3. Information can be prepared in advance when you use the call-back system. Your secretary can pull files and gather any documents needed to answer the customer's questions. This is obviously a time saver for you.

OUTGOING CALLS. The telephone is, of course, one of life's greatest time savers. It saves time over writing letters, making trips, and meeting with people. It can also be a great time *waster*. To avoid spending more time than necessary in calling people back, add these suggestions to the ones covered previously.

1. *Curtail the length of your calls.* This may seem obvious, but how can you do it? One effective way is to choose your opening. Don't say, "Hi, Tom, how are you?" You may be opening a can of worms. You are better off saying, "Hi, Tom, I need to ask you a few quick questions if you have a minute." Then launch into the questions as soon as you get the OK. It is also important to be able to terminate your calls promptly. Be decisive and say, "I guess that covers it, Tom. Thanks for your time; speak to you soon. Goodbye." If you carry on business conversations succinctly, perhaps people will realize you are a busy person and will not waste your time when they call you.

2. *Be organized.* List the questions or topics you wish to discuss and have them in front of you. There is nothing worse than saying, "Uh, I forgot the other question I was going to ask you . . ." if you lose your train of thought.

3. *Group your calls by type.* If you are making sales calls, make them all at once. This will give you the advantage of the momentum of a mind set. You will be in a certain thinking mode and will not have to change gears for every other call.

Visitors Visitors have the same effect as telephone calls. Again, the ideal situation is to have a secretary run interference for you. This must be done in a professional, diplomatic way.

1. Authorize your secretary to handle appointments and give her or him the authority to screen visitors also. If in doubt, your secretary can set up tentative appointments subject to your approval.

2. Set fixed "visiting" hours. You cannot be receptive to visitors all day, just as a surgeon cannot have visitors in the operating room. Have your secretary tell people who drop by that you are busy with a customer.

3. During appointments, have your secretary monitor the visit. If it goes on for longer than normal, she can call or come in to tell you about an obligation you must attend to. You then have an easy way to terminate the meeting if necessary.

4. Block all interruptions when you have visitors. You can't talk to someone in your office and receive phone calls simultaneously.
5. Try not to socialize during business visits. Impress your visitor with how busy you are and hope he gets the hint.
6. Terminate your visits by standing up. This is an obvious sign that it's time to go. Walk your visitor to the door and say goodbye without standing by the door or elevator chatting, unless, of course, you want to.

RELAXATION AND STRESS REDUCTION

In our goal-oriented, hypermotivated, money-making workday we often deny ourselves much needed periods of relaxation. Like a high-powered sports car, we can be very impressive at high speeds but sacrifice distance, efficiency, and physical integrity in the process. Our bodies and minds are designed to work well if they are not overtaxed. Frequent periods of relaxation and stress reduction are important to the longevity of our bodies and minds.

All too often the sacred coffee break is abused rather than maximized. People become focused on the process rather than the desired result of the break. A coffee or lunch break should be used as a time to relax so that you are more effective when you return to work. The relaxation you seek during a break should achieve three things:

1. *It should provide distraction.* You should get your mind off the job, preferably into the wild blue yonder. You'll feel much more refreshed when you land again.
2. *It should alleviate tension.* Our jobs often produce stiffness in the neck, abdomen, and lower back. You could do some physical activity or relaxation exercise to relieve these tensions. Many people have changed their habits in recent years. They are no longer rushing through a big meal at the lunch counter or restaurant. Instead they run, swim, play basketball, walk, or simply relax in their offices.
3. *It should be short enough not to severely interfere with your workday.* But it should be long enough to provide you with some benefits.

There is no denying the importance of relaxation, despite its being unproductive. As John Wanamaker once said, "Those who do not take the time for relaxation are obliged sooner or later to find time for illness."

CHANGING BAD HABITS

> Habit, my friend, is practice long pursued, that at the last becomes the man himself.
>
> EVENUS, 5th century B.C.

Managing your time efficiently and effectively will require some changes in your behavior and thinking. Those changes require *practice*. As with your goals, in order to practice you must first become aware of your needs and define those you will attend to first. If you have already done this, you are now much closer to effecting change in yourself than you ever were.

Giant strides, when looked at closely, are made up of many small steps. In overhauling your management of time, you, too, need to take small steps. Choose one area that you would like to improve. It could be procrastination, delegation, or relaxation. It is your choice, but select one now.

Take the time to respond to the questions below. Answer all the questions thoroughly so that you can devise a solid goal and some action steps. Start today doing those things that will make you a better manager of your time. After you have improved in one area, choose another and use the same questions to define the steps. In this way, you will practice the necessary activities that will later be your good habits.

TIME MANAGEMENT ACTION PLAN

---

1. What is the idea I would like to implement?
2. What are the potential obstacles that stand in my way?
3. Why do I want to implement this idea? What's in it for me?
4. What is my action plan? How will I specifically implement the idea?
5. What is my target date/deadline for implementing the idea?
6. How and when will I measure my success?

Time is like money. Unless you have more than you know what to do with, you will want to control your assets yourself. If you think of time as money, you will find yourself wasting less of it.

SUMMARY

The focus of this chapter was effective time management, an important key to a successful career in sales. To be a successful salesperson, you must manage your career as a business and your time as its most valuable asset.

When discussing time management, there is an important distinction between two commonly used words in association with time management: efficiency and effectiveness. Efficiency means doing things right; effectiveness means doing the right things. The relationship between the two can be written $E_1 + E_2 = R$ (results). It takes a certain amount of effectiveness and efficiency to obtain any result. The amount of each can vary with each result. Of the two, improving effectiveness should receive first attention, for effective selling will produce sales and free up time to work on efficiency.

Managing time more effectively requires a careful analysis of what you are doing now with your time. The diligent use of a time log for 15 days will produce an excellent list of your activities for every 10-minute segment of those 15 days. At the end of each day you should conduct an analysis by answering several important questions that help guide you to better use of time the following day. Once the 15-day period has passed, the entire log is analyzed to determine both the six most productive and the six least productive activities. Such an exercise can help you to set some time management objectives.

Another helpful exercise in addition to conducting a time analysis is reviewing the extensive list of time wasters provided in Figure 21.2. Reviewing those and determining which consume considerable time can then lead to the development of strategies for minimizing or completely overcoming them.

Setting priorities is an important factor in using time effectively. High priority activities need to be accomplished first, taking advantage of your greatest earning potential. One of the best methods of setting priorities for a day's activities is to prepare a "to do" list such as the one illustrated in Figure 21.4, with each planned activity listed according to its priority. Preparing such a list organizes your thinking and planning onto one form in the least amount of time with the maximum amount of efficiency.

Systematic record keeping is another valuable method of getting and then maintaining control of time. Suggested records to be kept include: number of sales calls, number of calls resulting in interviews, number of interviews resulting in attempts to confirm the sale, number of actual sales, and number of sales that stay on the books. Such a system will help you identify the phase or phases of the sales process that give you difficulty, which in turn helps you focus your efforts for improvement.

There are several common menaces of time: procrastination, paperwork, down time, and interruptions. Procrastination is best handled by determining what areas it plagues the most; choosing one area to conquer at a time; setting reasonable deadlines; and tackling difficult problems first.

Paperwork is best handled by first delegating as much as possible to a secretary or a co-worker, then prioritizing that which remains. That which is most important (requiring immediate action or response) is placed at the top, less important mail and information are placed in the middle, and junk mail is placed on the bottom.

Down time is time during the day when nothing significant can be accomplished, such as those minutes spent in waiting rooms, during traffic jams, and when people fail to show for appointments. It can be handled creatively by using it for such activities as planning, writing "to do" lists, visualizing, and reading.

Another menace of time, the interruption, takes two forms: telephone interruptions and visitors. The ideal situation for handling both is to have a skilled secretary to run interference. To best handle outgoing calls, curtail the length of the calls, be organized, and group calls by type. As for visitors, have fixed "visiting hours" when possible, have visits monitored by a secretary when feasible, block all interruptions when a visitor is present, try not to socialize during business visits, and terminate your visits by standing.

Managing time efficiently and effectively requires some changes in behavior and thinking. Changes require *practice*. To practice effectively, you must first become aware of your needs and define those needs which require attention first. Attention should then be given to each need identified, one at a time, until all have been improved to your satisfaction.

By remembering that time is like money, you will find that you waste less of it and your business—your sales—will be more successful because of it.

DISCUSSION QUESTIONS

1. What is effective use of time? What is efficient use of time? If you could have only one to start, which should it be?
2. What will a time log show you about the way you spend your day?
3. List five of your time wasters.
4. What can you do to eliminate your time wasters?
5. What is Pareto's Principle (the 80-20 rule)? What does it imply about setting priorities?
6. What are the steps to stop procrastinating?
7. Think of five times during your day that are down time for you. What are five things you can do during those times to be more productive?
8. Take the time to answer the questions in the Time Management Action Plan for at least one reasonable goal.

Index

A

Acceptance
  boredom/indifference and, 283, 284
  product, 198
Accessories, handling, 278
Account profile, 97–106
Accounts
  analysis, 96–106
  call scheduling, 236–37
  classification, 97
  expanding services, 238–39
  servicing, 231–33
  volume and profit worksheet, 106
Achievement model, 311–12. *See also* Role
  models
Actions, observing, 44
Active listening, 256
  between the words, 260
  guidelines for, 256–61
  noise and distractions, 258–59
  organizing message heard, 259–60
  to prospects, 251–58
Adversary attitude, 220
Advertising, 140–42
  sources and methods, 142
Alda, Alan, 33
Ali, Muhammad, 33
Alice in Wonderland (Carroll), 306
Allen, Woody, 40
All in the Family, 69
Anger, defensiveness and, 280
Animated behavior, 33
Annual reviews, of account activities, 237–
  38
Appearance, dress and, 60–62
Are You Listening? (Nichols and Stevens),
  253
Arm movements, interpreting, 276–77

Arrogance, technological, 5–6
Association, learning by, 206
Assumptions
  and behavior, 309
  feedback and, 269
  making, 269
Assurance, customer, 10, 162, 231–40
Attention, getting and holding, 204–5
Audience, understanding, 208

B

Background noise, telephone, 172
Bad habits
  action plan, 338
  changing, 337–38
Balance sheet, "Ben Franklin," 219
Behavior
  assumptions and, 309
  impatient, 35
  indirect, 34–35, 44, 53
  informal, 33
  intuitive, 33
  open vs. self-contained, 32–34
  perception of, 23–24, 29
  relaxed, 33, 285
  reserved, 34
  rule-oriented, 35
Behavioral flexibility, 46–52, 56
  chart, 51
  guidelines for implementing, 48–52
  openness and directness, 47–48
  socializers and directors, 48–49
  thinkers and relaters, 50–52
Behavioral styles, 31–46
  actions and environment, 44–45
  four types, 36–42
  identification of, 44–46
  and interpersonal problems, 43

Behavioral styles (*continued*)
  openness and directness, 32–35
  pace and priority conflicts, 42–43
  socializers and directors, 36–39
  thinkers and relaters, 39–42
Benefits, product, 197, 210
Berrera, Rick, 73
Best solutions, agreeing on, 199
Blank expressions, 285
Blinking, and upward looking, 285
Body language, 62, 215, 242, 273–87
  changes in, 285
  facial expressions and, 32
  handling accessories, 278
  interpreting gestures, 275–78
  salesperson and customer, 285–86
  trait vs. state, 278–85
Bond, James, 35
Boomerang method of handling objections,
  221
Boredom/indifference, and acceptance,
  283, 284
Brainstorming, 312–14
Break-even volume (BEV), and account
  profile, 102
Budgetary constraints, and buying power,
  192
Bunker, Archie, 69
Buyer's remorse, 234
Buying
  decision-makers in process, 189–90
  emotional reasons for, 188–89
  time factors in, 190
Buzz words, questions free of, 244

C

Call
  hours, 101
  reluctance, 20, 179
  scheduling and account servicing, 236
  visualization, 227
  See also Sales calls
Call-back system, 335–36
Call-ins, 179
Call frequency planner, 109–11
  worksheet sample, 110
Canned presentations, 201–2
Canvassing, 125, 137
Career goals, 314. *See also* Sales career
Carroll, Lewis, 306
Cautious behavior, 34
Centers of influence, 137
Centers of interest, in qualifying prospects,
  125
Challenging goals, 315
Circadian rhythm, 325
Civic organizations, membership in, 123,
  137
Claims, proving, 157

Closeness, 33
Closing, confirming vs., 213–16
Cold calling, 20, 28
Colleagues, prospects as, 220
Comfort zone, in tension management, 22–
  23, 28
Commitment, 228, 229
Communication and Organizational Behavior
  (Haney), 268
Communication skills, 12–13, 241–301
  feedback and body language, 265–87
  and productivity, 23
  proxemics and voice skills, 288–301
  questioning and listening, 243–64
  verbal and nonverbal, 12–13, 241–42
Community relations, 144
Company, knowledge in sales planning, 86,
  87
Company leads, 122, 136
Competition, eliminating, 201
Competitive behavior, 35
Competitive edge, 157
Competition analysis
  in sales planning, 89–94
  worksheet, 91
Competitors, market share, 92
Complaints, handling, 235
Confidence, establishing, 195, 201
Confidence/authority, and reassurance,
  281, 283
Conflict, shying away from, 34
Confrontational behavior, 35
Contacting customers, 163–80
  letters, 165–71
  methods and results, 163–65
  synergistic approach, 165
  drawing up, 228
Conventions, 137
  and trade shows, 126
Cooper, Alice, 147
Cosby, Bill, 35
Cost per hour (CPH), method of time valu-
  ation, 101
Courtesy, and punctuality, 65
Creativity, and risk-taking, 75
Credibility, 196
  of publicity, 145
Critical evaluation, nervousness and, 281,
  282
Cross-fertilization, extrapolation and, 313
Curiosity, 188
Curtis, Steve, 124
Customers, 136
  assuring satisfaction, 10, 162, 231–40
  contacting, 163–80
  files of, 112
  handling complaints of, 235
  as prospect source, 121–22
  reference sources, 94–95
  replenishing of, 119

in sales planning, 94–96
upgrading, 239
voice qualities, 296
warning signals, 236–37
winning back, 237

D

Daily activities, sample time log of, 326
Dallas, 31
Data collection, in territory control, 112–13
Davis, Sammy, 70–71
Deadlines, 333
Decision-makers, 152, 153
  and buying process, 189–90
Decision-making, 33, 157
  confirming criteria, 196–97
Defensiveness, and anger, 280
Definitions, feedback used to give and get, 268–69
Demonstrations, 205–9
  delivery and length, 209
  materials and tools, 207–8
  power of, 205–6
  purpose and approach, 208
  understanding audience, 208
Developmental questions, 248
Dictation, 169–70
Digressive behavior, 33
Direct behaviors, 35, 55
  observing, 44
Direct mail, 128–32, 137
  campaign budget worksheet, 132
  follow-up and record keeping, 131–32
  techniques, 129–30
Directional questions, 249
Directness, 34–36, 53
  determining, 35
  increasing or decreasing, 47–48
  scale, 34
Directories
  mailing lists from, 129
  and tip clubs, 127
Directors, 38–39
  characteristics of, 38
  sales flexibility with, 49
Dishonest feelings, avoiding, 221–22
Distractions, 337
  minimizing impact of, 259
Douglass, Merrill E., 331
Down time, effective use of, 334–35
Dramatic behavior, 33
Drawings, mechanical or schematic, 207
Dress
  and appearance, 60–62
  checklist for, 64
  shirts/blouses, appropriate combinations, 63
  ties/scarves, appropriate combinations, 63

Dress for Success (Molloy), 58, 63
Drinking, smoking and, 64–65

E

Eastwood, Clint, 33
Easy objections, 218
Echo and listen method of handling objections, 220
Effectiveness, efficiency vs., 325
Einstein, Albert, 75
Ellis, Albert, 310
Emerson, Ralph Waldo, 71
Emotions
  as buying reasons, 188
  voice qualities and, 298–99
Enhancement skills, for successful non-manipulative selling, 11–13
Enthusiasm, 33
  excellence and, 70–72
  openness and, 279, 280
Environment, 44
  behavioral clues, 45
Ethics, honesty and, 75
Evaluation
  readiness and, 280, 281
  of rejection, 222–27
Exhibits, and showmanship, 205
Expanding services, 238–39
Expense reports, 112
Expressionless stimuli, 285
Expressive behavior, 35
Extended focus, excellence and, 73
Extrapolation, and cross-fertilization, 313
Eye contact, 62
  interpreting, 275
Eyeglasses, handling, 278

F

Face-to-face calls, 179–80
  opportunities and stumbling blocks, 180
Facial expressions
  and body language, 32
  interpreting, 275–76
Family goals, 314
Fear, 189
Feedback, 242, 265–72
  bridges in sales process, 270
  effective uses of, 268–70
  questions and jargon, 269
  types of, 266–68
  verbal and nonverbal, 266–68
Feel-felt-found method of handling objections, 220
Field, Marshall, 231
Financial goals, 314
First impression, 60–65
  courtesy and punctuality, 65
  dress and appearance, 60–62

First impression (*continued*)
eye contact, 62
posture and handshake, 62–64
silent messages, 62
smile and hygiene, 64–65
smoking and drinking, 64–65
Flexibility
behavioral, 46–52
excellence and, 69–70
Follow-up
and customer satisfaction, 231–40
and record keeping, 131–32
Foot-in-door image, 4–5
Forceful behavior, 35
Form letters, guidelines for evaluating,
170–71
Freud, Sigmund, 273
Friends, 136
and social contacts, 123
Friendship tree, worksheet, 124
Frowns, 276
Frustration, and self-control, 283, 284
Full-scale demonstrations, tests and, 207

G

Gary, Romain, 74
Gesture clusters
boredom/indifference and acceptance,
283, 284
classic types, 279–83
confidence/authority and reassurance,
281, 283
defensiveness and anger, 280
frustration and self-control, 283, 284
interpreting and using, 279–85
nervousness and critical evaluation, 281,
282
openness and enthusiasm, 279, 280
readiness and evaluation, 280, 281
suspicion/secrecy and rejection/doubt,
281, 282
Gestures
copying, 285
interpreting, 275–78
and symbolism, 273–74
Goal-setting, 314–16
action plan and target date, 316
balanced, 305–6
challenging and realistic, 315
personal and positive, 315
written and specific, 315
Goals
assessment of, 185–87
brainstorming for, 313
defining and examining, 315–16
importance of, 306–8
types of, 314
Golden Rule, in relationship strategies, 30
Good vibes, 267

Government publications, 95
Guarded behavior, 33

H

Hand movements, interpreting, 276–77
Handshake, 62–64
Haney, William V., 268
Hawn, Goldie, 33
High-pressure sales process, 7
Hillary, Edmund, 307
Hill Street Blues, 33
Honesty, and ethics, 75
Humor, sense of, 74
Hygiene, 64–65

I

Iacocca, Lee, 35, 39
Ideas, quantity vs. quality, 313
Image
post-call checklist, 223, 224
public relations, 144–45
Image of excellence, 12, 17, 57–78
creativity and risk-taking, 75
enthusiasm and self-esteem, 70–72
extended focus, 73
first impression, 60–65
flexibility and sensitivity, 69–70
honesty and ethics, 75
knowledge depth and breadth, 65–69
sense of humor, 74
Imitation, 188
Information-gathering, 8–11
Insight, learning by, 206
Interpersonal problems, behavioral styles
and, 43
Interruptions, handling, 335–37
Intervention concept, 26–27
Introductory calls, 20, 125, 179
Irritating listening habits, 261–62
Issue-oriented behavior, 33

J

Jargon, 244
feedback and, 269
Judgment, suspending, 312, 313

K

Key accounts, worksheet, 105
Kiam, Victor, 39
Kinesics. *See* Body language
Knowledge, depth and breadth of, 65–69

L

Lasting impression, of demonstration, 206
Learning

auditory and visual, 206
principles, 206
Leg movements, interpreting, 277
Letters, 165–71
personal and form, 166–71
Listening skills, 242, 253–64
attentive, 258
checking, 260–61
effective, 178
evaluative, 255
irritating habits, 261–62
levels of, 254–56
See also Active listening
Lists, using "to do," 330–32
Love, 188

M

Magazines, 145
newspapers and, 67
Mail, screening, 334
Mailing lists, 128–29
Mailings, effective, 130–31
Maltz, Maxwell, 68
Managing objections, 217–22
avoiding feeling dishonest, 221–22
methods for, 220–21
Marginal listening, 254–55
Market
potential, 89
share, 92
trends, 91
Market segments, 88
breakdown worksheet, 95
needs worksheet, 93
Marketing plan, 82
*M*A*S*H*, 33, 35
Mediocre salespersons, 58
Meeting a prospect, 8, 161, 163–83
Memorized presentation, 201–2
Mental goals, 314
Mentors, 318
Merrill, David, 69
Messages, identifying main and supportive
points, 260
Mock-ups, and models, 207
Molloy, John, 58, 63
Moonlighting, 37, 39
Moore, Leo, 328
Moore, Mary Tyler, 35
Mouth gestures, interpreting, 276
Multiple role models, 318

N

Name recognition, 139, 149
Need gap, 21–22
Negative thinking, language-related, 310
Neophyte salesperson, organizing for pre-
sentations, 200

Nervousness, and critical evaluation, 281,
282
Newsletters, prospects from, 133
Newspapers, and magazines, 67
Newsweek, 67
Nodding, 285
Noise, reducing or eliminating, 258–59
Non-manipulative selling (NMS)
assuring customer satisfaction, 231–40
confirming purchase, 213–30
defined, 6
enhancement skills, 11–13
information-gathering, 8–11
meeting prospects, 163–83
personal tension and, 20–21
philosophy of, 3–15
proposing solutions, 195–212
sales pipeline and, 7, 10, 11
skills, 161–240
studying needs, 184–94
Nonverbal feedback, 267–68
Nonverbal communication skills, 242
Note taking, 259

O

Objections
difficult, 219
converting to questions, 220
easy and difficult, 218–19
managing, 217–22
types of, 217–19
Oblong smile, 276
Occupations, of socializers, 37
Open behavior, 33, 53
observing, 44
Open-ended questions, 247
Openness, 32–34, 53
and enthusiasm, 279, 280
increasing or decreasing, 47
scale, 32
Opinion leaders, 125
Opportunities, territory, 107–11
Organizations, membership in, 123–24
Outgoing calls, managing, 336
Outlined presentation, 202–3

P

Paperwork, 112
handling, 333–34
Pareto's principle, 96, 328
Parkinson's law, 328, 330
Participation, learning by, 206
Past experiences, relevant, 191
Pauley, Jane, 31, 42
Peale, Norman Vincent, 72
Perfectionism, overcoming, 333
Performance standards, in territory control,
111

Personal calls, alternatives to, 111
Personal goals, 315
Personal letters, 166–70
    dictating, 169–70
    guidelines and samples, 166–69
    informative style, 166
Personal observation, prospects from, 135
Personal space. *See* Proxemics
Personal tension, 19–21, 28
"Personality bomb," 52
Phobia, telephone, 172–73
Photographs, publicity, 147
Physical goals, 314
Physical and mental distance, 32
Pictures, 207
Political considerations, within company,
    191
Positive goals, 315
Positive thinking, 310–11
Post-call checklist, 222–27
Posture, 62, 277
    changes, 285
Potential solutions, soliciting and suggest-
    ing, 197–98
Power of Positive Thinking (Peale), 72
Pre-call planning, 175–77, 187, 199
Presentations, 199–209
    "canned," 201–2
    effective, 200–201
    poor characteristics of, 200–201
    getting and holding attention, 204–5
    memorized and outlined, 201–3
    pre-call planning, 199–200
    types of, 201–4
    See also Demonstrations
Press releases, 145
    sample, 146
Prestige, 188
Priorities, setting, 96, 328–32
Problem solving
    in territory management, 113
    setting priorities, 192–93
Problems, difficult, 333
Procrastination, 332–33
Product
    benefits and acceptance, 197–98
    selling additional, 239
    knowledge, 5
    knowledge in sales planning, 86–88
    specifications, 191
Productivity
    studies, 307–8
    tension and, 22–23
Professional organizations, membership in,
    123–37
Program presentation, 203–4
Promotional strategies, 13, 79, 139–50
    objectives of, 140
    personal worksheet, 148
    types of, 140–41

Proposals
    post-call checklist, 225, 226
    preparing and presenting, 203
Proposing solutions, 9, 161, 195–212
    decision-making criteria, 196–97
    objectives of, 196–97
    preliminary planning, 198–99
    presentations, 199–209
Prospecting, 13, 79, 118–38
    action plan worksheet, 134, 135
    customer sources, 119
    scientific, 137
    successful systems, 135
Prospects, 136
    actions and environment, 44–45
    active listening to, 257–58
    canvassing for, 125–26
    current situation, 155
    feelings, 189
    files of, 112
    goals and problems, 156
    meeting, 8, 161, 163–83
    post-call checklist, 224, 226
    qualifying, 119–35
    questions from, 158, 215
    sources of, 120–36
Proxemics, 242, 288–94
    personal and intimate, 289
    physical and psychological, 288–90
    public and social, 289
    territoriality and categories, 290–92
    zones, 288–89
    See also Body language
Psychocybernetics (Maltz), 68
Psychology, 310
    of situation, 188–89
Psychological needs, listening for, 258
Psychotherapy, 308
Public relations, 141, 143–45
    image projected by, 144–45
    methods, 144
Public speaking, 144
    prospects from, 133–34
Publicity, 141, 145–47
    credibility and subtlety, 145
    different forms, 145–47
Publics, 144
Punctuality, courtesy and, 65
Purchase confirming, 9, 161, 213–30
    vs. closing, 213–16
    evaluating rejection, 222–27
    managing objections, 217–22
    post-call checklist, 225, 226
    recognizing opportunities, 214–16
    time factor, 216

Q

Qualifying prospects, 119–35
    centers of interest, 125

civic and professional organizations, 123–24
conventions and trade shows, 126
customers and company leads, 121–22
direct mail, 128–32
directories and tip clubs, 127
friends and social contacts, 123
newsletters and seminars, 133
personal observation, 135
public speaking, 133–34
study groups, 128
Qubein, Nido, 165
Questioning skills, 241, 243–52
and strategies, 244–46
Questions
broad to narrow, 244
clarifying and developmental, 248
converting objections to, 220
directional and testing, 249
feedback and, 269
focused and nonthreatening, 245
nonspecific and consultative, 246
open-ended and closed-ended, 247
permission to ask, 244
phrasing and pausing, 246
sensitive, 245
simple and effective, 244
strategic uses of, 248–50
structuring, 245
third-party opinion, 250
types of, 246–47

R

Rational emotive therapy, 310
Readiness, and evaluation, 280, 281
Reading, 67–68
people, 31
Realistic goals, 315
Reality, as selling tool, 186–87
Reassurance, confidence/authority and, 281, 283
Record keeping
follow-up and, 131–32
in territory control, 112–13
Records
of time use, 332
types and analysis, 112–13
Referrals, expanding services through, 238
Rejection, evaluating, 222–27
Rejection/doubt, suspicion/secrecy and, 281, 282
Relaters, 41–42
sales flexibility with, 50–52
Relationship skills, 12, 17–78
and strategies, 17, 30–56
tension and, 21, 28
Relaxation, and stress reduction, 337
Return on time invested (ROTI), and account profile, 101

Reynolds, Burt, 37
Risk-taking, creativity and, 75
Rivalry, 189
Role models, 311–12, 317–18
choosing, 317–18
multiple, 318
Role playing, 319
Ryl, Eden, 309

S

Sales
confirming, 222–28
making, 227–28
pipeline, 120
potential, 89
process, 7, 270
promotion, 141–43
volume, 200
Sales calls
cold vs. introductory, 20, 28
commitment asked for, 158
information needed before, 153–58
objectives, 156
planning guide, 153–58
preparing for, 13, 79, 151–60
questions to uncover needs, 156
success criteria, 158
Sales career, 305–23
achievement model and self-concept, 311–12
assumptions and behavior, 309
brainstorming and goal-setting, 312–16
foundation development, 308
and goal-setting, 305–8
positive thinking and self-confidence, 310–11
thought diet card, 319–21
visualization and role modeling, 316–19
Sales management skills, 13, 79–160
promotional strategies, 139–50
prospecting, 118–38
sales call preparation, 151–60
Salespersons
basic needs, 306
behavior perception, 23–24
body language, 285–86
excellent vs. mediocre, 57–59
image of, 3–5
life of, 305–23
training of, 4–6
Sales planning, 81, 85–96, 151–52
company and product knowledge, 86–88
competition analysis and customer information, 89–96
situation and market analyses, 85–89
strategies and controls, 85
two-stage model, 83–85
Samples, 207
Santayana, George, 311

Secretaries, dealing with, 177–78
Selective perception, and customer satisfaction, 234
Selectivity, in demonstration, 206
Self-concept, filtering of, 312
Self-confidence, 311
Self-contained behavior, 32, 53, 283
  observing, 44
Self-esteem, excellence and, 72
Self-management skills, 11–12, 303–40
  and sales career, 305–23
  time management, 324–40
Self-preservation, 189
Selling, bird's eye view, 79
Seminars, prospects from, 133
Sensitive words, 209
Sensitivity, excellence and, 70
Service report, sales and customer, 112
Showmanship, exhibits and, 205
Silent messages, 62. *See also* Body language
Simple smile, 276
Sitting. *See* Posture
Situation
  assessment of, 185–87
  psychology of, 188–89
Situation analysis, stage of sales plan, 83
Smile, 64, 276
Smoking, and drinking, 64–65
Social contacts, 136
  friends and, 123
Social goals, 314
Socializers, 36–38
  occupations of, 37
  sales flexibility with, 48–49
Socrates, 318
Solutions
  agreeing on, 199
  proposing, 9, 161, 195–212
Special events, sponsorship of, 144
Specific goals, 315
Specifications, product, 191
Spiritual goals, 314
Star Trek, 31, 39
Statements, supporting and reinforcing, 260
Steele, Richard, 74
St. Elsewhere, 39, 42
Stress
  management, 34
  reduction, 337
Study groups, 128
Studying needs, 161, 184–194
  organizing and problem-solving, 187–193
  post-call checklist, 223, 225
  prospects, 8–9, 223, 225
  situation and goals, 185–187
  topics, 187–192
Success, measuring, 316
Suits
  appropriate combinations, 63
  colors and styles, 60–62

Summary reports, 112–13
Surveys, conducting, 203
Suspicion/secrecy, and rejection/doubt, 281, 282

T

Technical products, 191
Technical terms, questions free of, 244
Technological arrogance, 5–6
Telephone prospecting, 171–79
  best times to call, 174
  brevity and pre-call planning, 174–77
  call-back system, 335–36
  choosing words carefully, 178
  correct information, 177
  cost effectiveness, 171
  dealing with secretaries, 177–78
  effective listening, 178
  hang-ups and call-ins, 178–79
  interruptions, 335–36
  organizing and monitoring, 173–74
  phobia, 172–73
  planning worksheet, 176
  sample log, 175
  vocal quality and background noise, 172
Television, 68
Tension
  alleviating, 337
  categories of, 19–22, 28
  personal and need, 19–22
Tension management, 17, 19–29
  as master skill, 27, 29
  productivity and behavior, 22–24
  and relationships, 22–27
  techniques, 24–27
Territoriality, proxemic, 290–91
Territory analysis, 81–96
  need for, 81–82
Territory management, 13, 79, 81–117
  account analysis, 96–106
  control measures, 111–14
  five commandments of, 114
  objectives and strategies, 107–14
  opportunities and problems, 107–11
  problem solving, 113
  time factor in, 96–106
Testimonials, 205, 250
Testing questions, 249
Thinkers, 39–41
  sales flexibility with, 50
Third-party opinion questions, 205, 250
Thought diet card, 319–21
Tickler file, 112
Time, 67, 308
Time log, 326–28
  analysis, 327
  sample, 326
Time management, 11, 69, 324–40
  action plan, 338
  in buying process, 190

changing bad habits, 337–38
down time and interruptions, 334–37
efficiency vs. effectiveness, 325
lists and records, 330–32
procrastination and paperwork, 332–34
relaxation and stress reduction, 337
setting priorities, 328–32
Time-oriented behavior, 33
Time wasters, 328
evaluation and solutions, 329, 330
worksheet, 329
Tip clubs, directories and, 127
Today Show, 31, 42
Topics, study, 187–92
Trade associations, 144
Trade directories, 89
Trade journals, 66
Trade shows, 137
conventions and, 126
Training, adequate and appropriate, 5–6
Transfer of learning, 206
Truman, Harry, 317
Trust, establishing, 185, 195

U

U.S. News and World Report, 67
Understated behavior, 34

V

Verbal feedback, 266–67
Verbal skills, 12–13, 241–42

Visitors, interruptions by, 336–37
Visualization, 227, 316
Voice qualities, 172
for better communication, 299
and emotions, 298–99
identifying characteristic, 296
information from, 296–98
noting changes in, 297
Voice skills, 242, 295–301
improving, 299
resonance and clarity, 297
rhythm changes, 297
volume and speed, 297

W

Warm behavior, 33
Warm prospects, 139
Williams, Robin, 31
Women's Dress for Success Book (Molloy), 64
Written goals, 315
Wrong information, 218

Y

Yale University, 299
Yawning, 278
Yerkes-Dodson productivity law, 22–23
"You Pack Your Own Chute," 309

Z

Ziglar, Zig, 71

Printed in the United States
123145LV00003B/1-32/A

9 780962 516122